T0273269

ARCHITECTURES AND MECHANISMS FOR LANGUAGE PROCESSING

The architectures and mechanisms underlying language processing form one important part of the general structure of cognition. This book, written by leading experts in the field of sentence processing, brings together linguistic, psychological, and computational perspectives on some of the fundamental issues concerning these architectures and mechanisms. Several general introductory chapters offer overviews on important psycholinguistic research frameworks and highlight both shared assumptions and controversial issues. Subsequent chapters explore in detail syntactic and lexical mechanisms, statistical and connectionist models of language understanding, the crucial importance of linguistic representations in explaining behavioral phenomena, evidence from a variety of studies and methodologies concerning the interaction of syntax and semantics, and the implications for cognitive architecture. The book concludes with a set of chapters presenting recent accounts of select issues of interpretation, including quantification, focus, and anaphora in language understanding. *Architectures and Mechanisms for Language Processing* will appeal to students and scholars alike as a comprehensive and timely survey of recent work in this interdisciplinary area.

Matthew W. Crocker is a research scientist in computational linguistics at the University of Saarbrücken.

Martin Pickering is a reader in psychology at the University of Glasgow.

Charles Clifton, Jr., is a professor of psychology at the University of Massachusetts, Amherst.

ARCHITECTURES AND MECHANISMS FOR LANGUAGE PROCESSING

Edited by

MATTHEW W. CROCKER
University of Saarbrücken

MARTIN PICKERING
University of Glasgow

CHARLES CLIFTON, JR.
University of Massachusetts, Amherst

CAMBRIDGE
UNIVERSITY PRESS

32 Avenue of the Americas, New York NY 10013-2473, USA

Cambridge University Press is part of the University of Cambridge.

It furthers the University's mission by disseminating knowledge in the pursuit of education, learning and research at the highest international levels of excellence.

www.cambridge.org
Information on this title: www.cambridge.org/9780521631211

First published 2000

A catalogue record for this publication is available from the British Library

Library of Congress Cataloguing in Publication data

Architectures and mechanisms for language processing / edited by Matthew W. Crocker, Martin Pickering, Charles Clifton, Jr.
p. cm.
ISBN 0-521-63121-1 (hardbound)
1. Natural language processing (Computer science) I. Crocker, Matthew W. II. Pickering, Martin, 1966– . III. Clifton, Charles, 1938– .

QA76.9.N38A76 1999
006.3′5 – dc21 99-11605
CIP

ISBN 978-0-521-63121-1 Hardback
ISBN 978-0-521-02750-2 Paperback

Contents

Contributors

Amit Almor
Hedco Neuroscience Building, University of Southern California, Los Angeles, CA 90089-2520 USA

Gerry T. M. Altmann
University of York, Heslington, York, YO1 5DD UK

Colin Brown
"Neurocognition of Language Processing" Research Group, Max Planck Institute for Psycholinguistics, Wundtlaan 1, NL-6525 XD Nijmegen, The Netherlands

Charles Clifton, Jr.
Department of Psychology, University of Massachusetts, Amherst, MA 01003 USA

Steffan Corley
Sharp Laboratories of Europe, Oxford Science Park, Oxford, OX4 4GA UK

Matthew W. Crocker
Department of Computational Linguistics, University of Saarbrücken, 66041 Saarbrücken, Germany

Marica De Vincenzi
Institute of Psychology of the National Research Council (CNR), viale Marx, 15, 00137 Roma, Italy

Lyn Frazier
University of Massachusetts, Amherst, MA 01003 USA

Peter Hagoort
"Neurocognition of Language Processing" Research Group, Max Planck Institute for Psycholinguistics, Wundtlaan 1, NL-6525 XD Nijmegen, The Netherlands

Joy E. Hanna
Department of Brain and Cognitive Sciences, Meliora Hall, River Campus, University of Rochester, Rochester, NY 14627 USA

Barbara Hemforth
Centre of Cognitive Science, Institute of Computer Science and Social Research, University of Freiburg, Friedrichstr. 50, 79098 Freiburg, Germany

James Henderson
Department of Computer Science, University of Exeter, Exeter, EX4 4PT UK

Lars Konieczny
Centre of Cognitive Science, Institute of Computer Science and Social Research, University of Freiburg, Friedrichstr. 50, 79098 Freiburg, Germany

Richard L. Lewis
Department of Computer and Information Science, The Ohio State University, 2015 Neil Avenue Mall, Columbus, OH 43210 USA

Paola Merlo
Département de Linguistique, Faculté des Lettres, Université de Genève, 2 rue de Candolle, CH-1204 Genève, Switzerland

Linda M. Moxey
Human Communication Research Centre, Department of Psychology, University of Glasgow, Glasgow, G12 8QF UK

Martin J. Pickering
Human Communication Research Centre, Department of Psychology, University of Glasgow, Florentine House, 53 Hillhead Street, Glasgow, G12 8QF UK

Anthony J. Sanford
Human Communication Research Centre, Department of Psychology, University of Glasgow, Glasgow, G12 8QF UK

Christoph Scheepers
Department of Psychology, University of Glasgow, Glasgow, G12 8QF UK

Michael J. Spivey-Knowlton
Department of Psychology, Cornell University, Ithaca, NY 14850 USA

Suzanne Stevenson
Department of Computer Science and Center for Cognitive Science, Rutgers University, New Brunswick, NJ 08903 USA

Michael K. Tanenhaus
Department of Brain and Cognitive Sciences, Meliora Hall, River Campus, University of Rochester, Rochester, NY 14627 USA

Matthew J. Traxler
Department of Psychology, Florida State University, Tallahassee, FL 32306-1270 USA

Preface

The chapters in the present volume constitute a selection from the papers presented at AMLaP-95, the first conference on "Architectures and Mechanisms for Language Processing." AMLaP-95 came about when members of the Human Communication Research Centre at the Universities of Edinburgh and Glasgow decided to have a small workshop in which a few psycholinguists from the United States could get together with a few European researchers and share research ideas. These organisers envisioned a meeting of researchers who are particularly interested in interdisciplinary approaches to psycholinguistics, researchers who could discuss their progress in bringing techniques of experimental psychology, linguistics, and computer science to bear on questions of how people understand and produce language.

An announcement of the workshop resulted in an unexpectedly large number of enthusiastic responses and requests to participate, and the small workshop grew into a two-day conference in Edinburgh, with invited and presented papers and two poster sessions. It quickly became clear that there was a demand in Europe for a meeting like AMLaP-95, a need similar to that met by the annual CUNY Conference on Human Sentence Processing in the United States.

The AMLaP meeting emphasises bringing computational, linguistic, and psychological perspectives to bear on questions of language processing. Its scope covers a broader range of topics, from word recognition to discourse comprehension, in addition to sentence processing. Further, to encourage contributors to emphasise the relevance of their work to key theoretical issues, the AMLaP meetings were designed to have a specific focus on architectural issues in psycholinguistic theory. The papers and posters presented at the conference were of gratifyingly high quality and indicated that there would be a continuing demand for an annual conference like AMLaP-95. This need has since resulted in AMLaP meetings in Torino, Italy; again in Edinburgh; and in Freiburg, Germany.

A few contributors to AMLaP-95 were asked to prepare written versions of their presentations for the present volume. A selection of presentations was chosen which would present a fair sampling of the approaches represented at the conference and constitute a useful high-level introduction to current psycholinguistic research. The authors were asked to present "position statements" which would be accessible to psycholinguistic newcomers and to highlight the relevance of their work to issues of the architecture of the human sentence processing system. The organisers of the conference, Matt Crocker and Martin Pickering, together with Chuck Clifton, wrote an introductory chapter intended to provide a guide to the psycholinguistically uninitiated. This guide surveys the field of psycholinguistics, discusses the concepts of architecture and mechanism in cognitive theories, and provides a brief preview of the chapters that follow.

The conference organisers were assisted in selecting papers and posters by a programme committee that consisted of Gerry Altmann, Holly Branigan, Charles Clifton, Jr., Simon Garrod, Simon Liversedge, Don Mitchell, and Matt Traxler. In addition to acknowledging the fine work done by the committee, the organisers would like to thank the people who made AMLaP-95 possible. Local staff and students, Dawn Griesbach, Hilary Leckridge, Dyane McGavin, Merce Prat, and Patrick Sturt, organised the details of the event and actually made it happen; they have our deepest thanks. The conference was sponsored and supported by the Human Communication Research Centre, the Centre for Cognitive Science of the University of Edinburgh, and the Department of Psychology of the University of Glasgow; the organisers are grateful for the generous support these groups provided. The editors of the present volume would also like to express their thanks to the contributors, and finally to the people at Cambridge University Press who encouraged and facilitated its preparation, including Lisa Albers, Natalie Davies, Beatrice Santorini, Helen Wheeler, and especially Christine Bartels.

Matthew W. Crocker
Martin J. Pickering
Charles Clifton, Jr.

February 1999

1

Architectures and Mechanisms in Sentence Comprehension

MARTIN J. PICKERING, CHARLES CLIFTON, JR., AND MATTHEW W. CROCKER

The architectures and mechanisms underlying language processing form one important part of the general architectures and mechanisms underlying cognition. In this book, the contributors largely focus on the question of what architectures and mechanisms underlie sentence comprehension, but it is our belief that their contributions illuminate the general nature of human language processing in the context of cognition as a whole. Because of the scope of these contributions, this introduction primarily concentrates on sentence comprehension. However, our perspective is to try to use evidence from sentence comprehension to understand the overall nature of language processing.

Let us first try to explain what we mean by architectures and mechanisms, and why these are important. We assume that the human language processor is a particular kind of computational device, and as such needs an organisation that we call its architecture. For instance, the processor might have two components, one dealing with word recognition, and one dealing with putting different words together into sentences. These processes might be completely distinct, in that the second processor could employ the output of the first processor, but have no impact on its internal workings. If so, we would know something about the architecture of the language processor. Architecture, therefore, refers to the static arrangement of components.

In contrast, the mechanisms are the dynamic workings of the language processor. A description of mechanisms is, in effect, a claim about the events in which the architectural components participate and about the causal structure of these events. If word recognition, say, works by decomposing words into component morphemes, processing each morpheme, and then putting the interpretations of the morphemes together, then this process would need a mechanism to describe it. A detailed understanding of the processes involved brings us closer to a description of the mechanisms that are used. Clearly, an understanding of the mechanisms relies on an understanding of the architecture, and vice versa.

The mechanism underlying some process, such as word recognition, can be described as being causally independent of other mechanisms only if a distinct component of the architecture deals uniquely with word recognition. If different architectural components are involved in the process of word recognition, then their causal interactions must be taken into account in describing the mechanisms underlying word recognition.

This description may give the impression that architecture is purely concerned with isolating components and fitting each component into the whole by showing which components impact on which other components. This is too simple. As Lewis (this volume) argues, a full description of cognitive architecture goes beyond "module geography" (J. D. Fodor, 1990, cited in Lewis). Lewis proposes that a specification of a functionally complete architecture must include (at least) a specification of the memories and the primitive processes the modules use, a specification of how the modules pass information among themselves, and a specification of how processes are initiated and terminated. This should include answers to questions such as what processes can go on in parallel and how processes must be arranged so that one must complete before the next can begin.

Why should understanding architecture and mechanisms be important? We might believe that the interesting things to understand about language concern the question of why we say what we say, why conversations work as they do, and so on. Of course these are interesting questions, but they are different from the issue at hand here. The question of understanding architectures and mechanisms is no different from the question of understanding the architectures and mechanisms that underlie other aspects of cognitive psychology, such as, for example, visual perception, skilled performance, or reasoning. Ultimately, we are concerned with a particular cognitive process, that of language processing, and with how it relates to the rest of cognition.

Let us now concentrate on the specific question of sentence comprehension. This is concerned with the way in which people determine the meaning of a sentence. Sentence comprehension lacks a simple definition, yet its general boundaries can be identified. Most obviously, it is concerned with the process of going from sound or written text to meaning. It assumes that words have been recognised. What it is principally concerned with is the way that the processor combines the meaning of words to produce a meaning for a sentence as a whole. A large part of this process involves parsing: determining how people obtain a particular syntactic analysis for a sentence or sentence fragment. This has been the traditional focus of sentence processing research and describes the majority of the contributions to this book. However, sentence comprehension goes beyond syntactic analysis. It includes aspects of semantic interpretation, as found in the processing of quantifiers like *every* and *a*. For example, *Every boy climbs a tree* is ambiguous between two interpretations, depending on whether each boy climbs the same tree or not. A theory of sentence comprehension needs to explain how the processor constructs and selects a particular interpretation. Likewise, pronouns like *he* or *she* are often ambiguous, but the processor normally makes a decision about which entity they refer to. In general, we can say that theories of sentence comprehension draw upon the assumptions and distinctions employed in theoretical linguistics, primarily in syntax and formal semantics (see Almor, this volume; Frazier, this volume; Moxey & Sanford, this volume).

General knowledge plays an extremely important role in sentence comprehension. Consider (1) and (2):

(1) The boy saw the girl with the flowers.

(2) John gave Bill some food because he was hungry.

Both of these sentences are formally ambiguous, but in both cases general knowledge disambiguates them. In (1), the prepositional phrase *with the flowers* can attach high, to the verb phrase *saw the girl*. But this produces the implausible meaning that the boy used the flowers to see the girl. Therefore, the prepositional phrase has to attach low, to the noun phrase *the girl*. This produces the plausible meaning that the boy saw the girl who had the flowers. In (2), the antecedent of *he* could be *John*. But this leads to the implausible interpretation that John gave away food because he was hungry, so the antecedent of *he* has to be *Bill* instead. In both cases, general knowledge is used to determine the appropriate analysis. Sentence comprehension is concerned with the impact of general knowledge on language comprehension.

However, the study of general knowledge itself is not part of psycholinguistics, and sentence comprehension is not interested in all processes that employ general knowledge. For instance, it is not primarily concerned with the issue of what inferences are drawn on the basis of the final interpretation assigned to a sentence. Resolving this question is presumably a goal of an account of general cognition, rather than of sentence comprehension in particular. In order to be able to make this distinction, we need to assume that sentence comprehension produces a kind of output that can be employed by other cognitive systems (cf. J. A. Fodor, 1983). This is a common, if not universal, assumption.

In this introductory chapter, we discuss the mechanisms that may be employed in sentence comprehension and discuss hypotheses about the architecture of the processor. The field of sentence comprehension is extremely controversial in many respects. Here, we attempt to identify points of agreement and to circumscribe the areas of debate. Researchers certainly disagree about the actual architectures and mechanisms, but they appear to agree about the questions that need to be addressed, about the range of reasonable positions, and about the types of methodologies that are appropriate.

Moreover, we believe that researchers may actually agree about actual architectures and mechanisms to a greater extent than at first appears. For example, all theories assume that sentence comprehension is highly incremental: once a word is recognised, it is rapidly integrated with preceding context. In addition, there is little dispute about the sources of information that are relevant to sentence comprehension. In areas of considerable controversy, there is often agreement about the kinds of evidence that could be used to distinguish theories. Most of the arguments concern broad issues of architecture and mechanism, such as whether the processor works in serial or in parallel, whether it always has to construct a fully-specified interpretation, when it is able to draw upon different sources of information, and whether it employs statistical information in choosing an analysis. Our introduction considers these issues, amongst others. In most cases, we employ examples from parsing, but many of these issues also apply to other aspects of sentence comprehension. First, we highlight the highly incremental nature of most aspects of sentence comprehension.

1.1 Incrementality

In the comprehension of both spoken and written language, words are encountered sequentially. Experimental evidence indicates that a great deal of processing occurs immediately, before the next word is encountered (e.g., Just & Carpenter, 1980; Tyler & Marslen-Wilson, 1977). A very important effect of this is that decisions are often made when a sentence fragment is ambiguous in some way. Word recognition is not normally delayed (e.g., Marslen-Wilson, 1987; Rayner & Duffy, 1986), even if disambiguation occurs after the ambiguous word (e.g., Rayner & Frazier, 1989). More relevantly, there is normally no measurable delay before syntactic analysis and some aspects of semantic interpretation begin (though it is impossible to be sure that there are no circumstances under which delay occurs). However, some higher level aspects of processing may be delayed – it is an open question how far incrementality goes.

Evidence for incremental parsing comes from the vast literature showing garden-path effects. Briefly, the sentence *The horse raced past the barn fell* (Bever, 1970) is hard (in part, at least) because people initially assume that *raced* is an active past-tense verb, and hence that *the horse raced past the barn* is a complete sentence. When they encounter *fell*, they realise this is impossible and reinterpret *raced* as a past participle in a reduced-relative construction (cf. *The horse that was raced past the barn fell*), or fail to understand the sentence entirely. In other words, they are "led up the garden path" by such a sentence. From this, we can tell that they have performed incremental syntactic analysis and committed to it, before reaching *fell*. Experimental evidence strongly supports this conclusion for many different sentence types and suggests that syntactic analysis begins very rapidly (e.g., Frazier & Rayner, 1982).

Evidence also supports the intuition that people start to understand sentences as they hear or read them. Most famously, Marslen-Wilson (1973, 1975) showed that subjects' errors in shadowing a text at a lag of only 300 milliseconds were constrained by semantic context. This demonstrates that the meaning of what is heard can be rapidly integrated with general knowledge (though it is conceivable that integration occurs during production rather than comprehension). Data from eye-tracking gives more direct evidence for incremental interpretation. For instance, Traxler and Pickering (1996b) found that readers were disrupted as soon as they read the word *shot* in (3):

(3) That is the very small pistol in which the heartless killer shot the hapless man yesterday afternoon.

Hence, they must have semantically processed the sentence fragment up to *shot* when they first encounter the word. Many other experiments using various methods also provide good evidence for incremental semantic processing (e.g., Boland, Tanenhaus, Garnsey, & Carlson, 1995; Clifton, 1993; Garrod, Freudenthal, & Boyle, 1994; Holmes, Stowe, & Cupples, 1989; Swinney, 1979; Trueswell, Tanenhaus, & Garnsey, 1994; Tyler & Marslen-Wilson, 1977). Hence, the language processing system must very rapidly construct a syntactic analysis for a sentence fragment, assign it a semantic interpretation, and make at least some attempt to relate this interpretation to general knowledge.

There may, however, be some limits to incrementality. For instance, Frazier and Rayner (1987) claimed that syntactic category ambiguities may not be resolved immediately (e.g., in *the desert trains* the word *trains* is not immediately categorised as a noun or a verb); see Corley and Crocker (this volume) for discussion. In a similar vein, Frazier and Rayner (1990) suggested that readers may not resolve the distinct senses of words like *newspaper* (the concrete object vs. the abstract institution sense). However, incrementality does seem to be the norm, even when it might not be expected. For example, a case where syntactic analysis might reasonably be delayed occurs in verb-final languages, such as Dutch and Japanese, where the parser often encounters more than one noun phrase before a verb. Evidence suggests that the parser does attach and interpret these noun phrases as co-arguments, before the subcategorising verb is reached (e.g., Bader & Lasser, 1994; Crocker, 1994; Frazier, 1987b; Sturt & Crocker, 1996). This rules out, or at least entails substantial revision of, head-driven and delay models of parsing such as Marcus (1980), Abney (1989) and Pritchett (1992). Another possible case of delay relates to "non-primary" phrases (Frazier & Clifton, 1996).

In anaphoric resolution, the evidence for incrementality is more controversial, and it is possible that only some anaphoric resolution is immediate. Good evidence for incrementality comes from Marslen-Wilson, Tyler, and Koster (1993) in listening and from Garrod et al. (1994) in reading. However, Garrod et al.'s study suggested that pronouns are only resolved immediately if they refer to a well-focused and unambiguous antecedent. In addition, Greene, McKoon, and Ratcliff (1992) presented data from a priming task that suggests that readers may not, under some conditions, bother to resolve the antecedent of an unambiguous pronoun immediately. Another interesting area concerns the resolution of quantifier-scope ambiguities, but here there is little evidence about incremental processing (e.g., Kurtzman & MacDonald, 1993 investigated preferred interpretations, but only by monitoring reading time on the next sentence).

Finally, it is possible that incrementality might be clause-bound, and that the processor links the interpretation of different clauses at clause boundaries. For instance, Millis and Just (1994) argued that readers process two clauses linked by a connective like *because* by interpreting each clause separately and only combining them at the end of the second clause. However, Traxler, Bybee, and Pickering (1997) found evidence that the processor detected implausible connections between clauses before the end of the second clause, so there is at least some evidence that incrementality extends to higher levels of semantic interpretation.

We conclude that a major constraint on the architectures and mechanisms underlying language processing is that they must support extremely incremental processing during comprehension. One important consequence is that the processor must be able to employ a great deal of information very rapidly. For instance, in syntactic processing it must be able to determine the syntactic category of a word when it is encountered. To do this, it needs to have access to the relevant syntactic information and to be able to apply this knowledge to the specific task that it faces. We now need to consider what these knowledge sources might be, and how the processor employs this information.

1.2 Knowledge Sources

In the 1980s, discussions of language processing often focused on the general question of whether the language processor was a module (e.g., J. A. Fodor, 1983; Forster, 1979; Rayner, Carlson, & Frazier, 1983; Taraban & McClelland, 1988; Tyler & Marslen-Wilson, 1987; see Garfield, 1987). But more recently, many researchers have started to focus on when and how specific sources of information are employed.

Most researchers assume representational modularity (Trueswell et al., 1994): sources of information like syntactic and semantic knowledge are represented separately. This assumption is standard to most generative grammar (e.g., Chomsky, 1965, 1981; Pollard & Sag, 1993; but see, e.g., Lakoff, 1986), and is assumed in the great majority of psycholinguistic research (though see McClelland, St. John, & Taraban, 1989). Some experimental evidence provides support for the standard position. For example, it is possible to prime syntactic structure in a manner probably independent of semantic factors, both in production (Bock, 1986) and comprehension (see Branigan, Pickering, Liversedge, Stewart, & Urbach, 1995). Also, evidence from event-related brain potentials (where electrical activity from the brain is measured as subjects perform a task) suggests that syntactic and semantic processing are distinct. Semantically anomalous words elicit a negative-going brain wave about 400 ms after the stimulus (Kutas & Hillyard, 1980; see also Garnsey, Tanenhaus, & Chapman, 1989). For instance, after *I drink my coffee with cream and*, the wave for the anomalous word *dog* is negative compared with the wave for *sugar*. In contrast, syntactically anomalous words produce a positive-going wave around 600 ms after the stimulus, whether the anomaly is due to ungrammaticality or to a garden-path construction (Hagoort, Brown, & Groothusen, 1993; Osterhout & Holcomb, 1992; Osterhout, Holcomb, & Swinney, 1994; Osterhout & Mobley, 1995; see Brown & Hagoort, this volume).

Assuming representational modularity, relevant sources of information include:

I. Syntactic Category Information

The lexical entry for each word indicates its syntactic properties. For example, the entry for *vanishes* states that it is an verb and that it is intransitive (taking a subject but no object). Psycholinguistically, this might count as one source of information or as two, if major-category information (being a verb) is separated from subcategorisation information (being intransitive). If the latter is the case, then the processor might base initial processing decisions on major-category information alone (e.g., Ferreira & Henderson, 1990; Mitchell, 1987). Also, the lexicon presumably stores some information about how frequently a word is used in a particular construction. This could affect initial parsing decisions (e.g., Trueswell, Tanenhaus, & Kello, 1993).

II. Grammatical Features

English pronouns, for instance, have to be in the accusative case (e.g., *him*) when they are the object of a verb. In English, grammatical feature information is very limited, but case, number, and gender are all important in other languages.

III. Grammatical Rules

In traditional phrase-structure grammar, grammatical information is separate from lexical-category information (e.g., Chomsky, 1965). So, a syntactic rule stating that a sentence can consist of a noun phrase followed by a verb phrase is distinct from lexical rules indicating the categories of particular words like *vanishes*. More recent linguistic theories have reduced the syntactic component of the grammar and included more information in lexical entries (e.g., Chomsky, 1981; Pollard & Sag, 1993). However, some theories assume that the grammar consists of a number of separate modules (Chomsky, 1981). In psycholinguistics, attempts to reduce the distinction between syntax and lexicon are found in constraint-based theories (e.g., MacDonald et al., 1994). An important conclusion is that, at a representational level, it is unclear how many sources of syntactic information can be distinguished.

IV. "Sense-Semantic" Information

Some analyses are plausible, some implausible. This kind of semantic information may be useful to the process of syntactic ambiguity resolution. For example, *When the ball rolled the man jumped* is locally ambiguous: *rolled* could be intransitive (as it turns out to be), or transitive. However, the transitive analysis is implausible: a ball is unlikely to be the agent of an act of rolling. The parser might use this plausibilty information to determine that *rolled* is probably intransitive. One type of sense-semantic information is due to selection restrictions (Katz & J. A. Fodor, 1963): certain verbs normally require arguments of a particular semantic type (e.g., animate subjects) to be felicitous.

V. Discourse Context Information

Sometimes a particular analysis is only likely in a particular context. Altmann and Steedman (1988) argued that *I saw the man with the binoculars* is most likely to mean that I used the binoculars if only one man has been mentioned, but that the man had the binoculars if more than one man has been mentioned, since the additional information is only necessary if we need to distinguish between different men.

VI. Prosody and Punctuation

Some patterns of accent, intonation, and timing can convey information about syntactic structure and about the relation of an utterance to a discourse. Newly introduced information, for instance, is likely to receive a pitch accent, and a phonological break can sometimes signal the boundary between two syntactic constituents. In written language, punctuation plays something of the same role. In *When the ball rolled the man jumped*, a comma can be placed before *rolled*. No comma would be used if *the man* were the object of *rolled*.

VII. Information about Discourse Focus

In a text like *John was going to meet his friend. He was in a good mood*, John is the focused character (or thematic subject), not the friend, and the pronoun preferentially refers to John. It may be that the processor makes use of this information to direct processes in parsing (e.g., Britt, Perfetti, Garrod, & Rayner, 1992) or anaphoric resolution (e.g., Garrod et al., 1994; Marslen-Wilson et al., 1994).

1.3 Restricted or Unrestricted?

We can distinguish two basic positions, which we call restricted and unrestricted accounts (following Traxler & Pickering, 1996a). Restricted accounts propose that there is some stage during which the parser ignores some of these sources of information, even though they are potentially relevant (e.g., Ferreira & Henderson, 1990; Frazier, 1987a; Mitchell, 1987, 1989). Such models in practice always assume serial processing. Parsing is a two-stage process, with different principles accounting for initial decisions and ultimate decisions.

Unrestricted accounts propose that all sources of information can be employed in initial parsing decisions. This position is adopted by so-called constraint-based models of parsing, as well as by other closely related accounts (e.g., MacDonald, 1994; MacDonald, Pearlmutter, & Seidenberg, 1994; Taraban & McClelland, 1988; Trueswell et al., 1993; Trueswell et al., 1994; Tyler & Marslen-Wilson, 1977). Current models assume ranked-parallel processing. Parsing is a one-stage process, with no principled distinction between initial parsing decisions and later decisions.

For instance, consider the processing of (4) (Trueswell et al., 1994, following Ferreira & Clifton, 1986):

(4) The evidence examined by the lawyer turned out to be unreliable.

After *the evidence examined*, the sentence fragment is compatible with two syntactically different continuations: a reduced relative continuation, as in (4), and a main clause continuation, as in *The evidence examined the witness*. The processor has to decide which analysis to favour (i.e., adopt or foreground). On an unrestricted account, the parser draws upon (at least) two knowledge sources relevant to this decision: information about syntactic analyses, and information about semantic plausibility. Let us assume that the processor also seeks to favour the most likely analysis (roughly as in constraint-based accounts). It will note that *examined* is much more commonly used as a verb in a main clause analysis than as a participle in a reduced relative analysis; but it will also note that the main clause analysis is bound to be highly implausible, because evidence cannot examine anything, whereas the reduced relative analysis may well be plausible, because evidence can be examined. These two "constraints" push the processor in opposite directions. They might be roughly equal in strength, which would imply that the processor would not exhibit a clear or uniform preference for either analysis.

In contrast, a restricted account might prohibit one knowledge source from affecting initial processing. In the garden-path theory (Frazier, 1979, 1987a), the processor initially pays attention to some syntactic information, but not to information about plausibility. This theory predicts that the main clause analysis is adopted as it is the syntactically simplest analysis (according to Minimal Attachment), but other restricted theories predict that this analysis is adopted because it is the more frequent (e.g., Ford, Bresnan, & Kaplan, 1982), or for other reasons. The implausibility of the analysis does not prevent it from being initially favoured, though it may well be dropped later.

This distinction between restricted and unrestricted accounts is very general and can be divorced from the question of how the information that is available is actually used. So it is not necessary for unrestricted accounts to seek to favour the most likely analysis, as constraint-satisfaction models do. Neither is it necessary for restricted accounts to be driven by syntactic strategies like Minimal Attachment, as in the garden-path account. However, the distinction remains an important architectural issue that separates different classes of accounts of parsing, and it can also apply to other aspects of language comprehension like anaphor resolution. For related discussion, see Altmann (this volume).

1.4 Parallel or Serial?

A parallel account considers multiple analyses at the same time. Consider first what we can call *pure unrestricted parallelism*, where the processor initially constructs all possible syntactic analyses in parallel, and regards all analyses as being of equal importance (e.g., Forster, 1979). For instance, after *The horse raced* in Bever's sentence, the processor would represent both the main clause and the reduced relative analyses. After *The horse raced past the barn fell*, the processor would drop the main clause analysis and continue with the reduced relative analysis without experiencing any difficulty. However, we know that this account cannot be correct, because the reduced relative analysis causes a garden-path effect. It therefore could not have been as available as the main clause analysis.

However, there are still two possible kinds of accounts. In a serial parsing model, one analysis is selected. In Bever's sentence, the parser may adopt the main clause analysis. If this analysis becomes impossible, then the parser must abandon this analysis and start again. In a ranked-parallel model, one analysis is foregrounded, and any others are backgrounded. In Bever's sentence, the main clause analysis may be foregrounded, and the reduced relative analysis backgrounded. If the main clause analysis becomes impossible, then the parser must change its ranking of analyses.

Obviously, parallel models can differ in many respects, depending on how many analyses are maintained, what kind of ranking is employed, for how long the different analyses are considered, or whether parallelism is only employed under certain conditions or with certain constructions. Currently, however, by far the most influential kind of parallel model is the constraint-based account. On these accounts, different analyses are weighted according to how compatible they are with a range of constraints, roughly corresponding to the knowledge sources discussed earlier. For instance, an analysis will be foregrounded if it is highly frequent, highly plausible, highly compatible with the prosody employed, and so on. As the sentence progresses, different analyses may become more or less activated on the basis of new information (see Merlo & Stevenson, this volume; Tanenhaus, Spivey-Knowlton, & Hanna, this volume).

Alternatives to this kind of continuous competition of alternative analyses are possible. For instance, Gibson (1991) proposed a beam-search mechanism in which analyses which are close enough in complexity to the simplest analysis are retained. Analyses are then dropped if their complexity, measured in a way proposed by Gibson, exceeds the complexity of the simplest analysis by some threshold value.

There is a great deal of overlap between parallel and unrestricted accounts on the one hand and between serial and restricted accounts on the other. It is unclear to what extent this is necessary. Formally, it is certainly possible to have a parallel restricted account, where different analyses, for example, are weighted on the basis of construction frequency alone. A serial unrestricted account is harder to envisage. Partly this is because some influences such as plausibility cannot have their effect until the analysis has been constructed. In order to conclude that *The man read the air* is implausible, the processor must have decided that *the air* is the object of *read*, not the subject of a subordinate clause (e.g., *was of poor quality*). To do this the processor must have computed the object analysis. But since plausibility information is not available while computing the analysis, the processor could not be unrestricted. It is impossible to get round this without computing analyses in parallel.

However, there is an important difference between two different kinds of parallel account: the extended-parallel account, like the constraint-based model (cf. Gorrell, 1989); and the momentary-parallel model, where different analyses are proposed in parallel, but evaluation between alternatives is effectively immediate. The referential or incremental-interactive account of Altmann and Steedman (1988) (cf. Crain & Steedman, 1985) is of this latter kind. Here, alternative analyses are proposed in parallel, and contextual information chooses between them immediately, on the basis of how felicitous the analyses are with respect to discourse context (see the section on Referential Theory for more detailed discussion). This account involves momentary parallelism, but is otherwise serial. It is similar in spirit to many models of lexical ambiguity resolution (e.g., Swinney, 1979), where all alternative meanings of a word are proposed, but all but the most contextually appropriate (or frequent) meaning is rapidly abandoned. We discuss these different accounts of ambiguity resolution in relation to data in the following section.

1.5 Proposals for Selecting Analyses

To this point, we have emphasised questions of cognitive architecture, considered broadly to include matters of how the operation of the cognitive components is controlled. We have considered what knowledge sources are available to the parser, and what restrictions there are on its use of information. We have also considered the related question of whether the parser concentrates on developing a single analysis, or distributes its computation over multiple analyses in parallel. We now turn to questions of mechanism: precisely how does the parser use the information that is made available to it to construct and make decisions about the analysis or analyses it is computing?

1.5.1 Serial, Restricted, Strategy-Based Theories

All restricted accounts assume that some syntactic information has priority in the initial structuring of the sentence, and they also assume that sense-semantic information and discourse context are not employed during this initial process. However, these accounts vary in other ways, often relating to the syntactic framework that they assume. A large number of accounts are what we can call strategy-based, in that they assume that the processor follows a particular strategy or rule in initial processing. By far the best known account is the garden-path model proposed by Frazier (1979) and discussed in many other places (e.g., Clifton, Speer, & Abney, 1991; Ferreira & Clifton, 1986; Ferreira & Henderson, 1990; Frazier, 1987a, 1990; Frazier & Rayner, 1982; Rayner et al., 1983; cf. Frazier & J. D. Fodor, 1978; Gorrell, 1995; Kimball, 1973).

This model assumes that initial parsing is directed by two fundamental principles, defined by Frazier (1979) as follows:

I. Minimal Attachment

Attach incoming material into the phrase marker being constructed using the fewest nodes consistent with the well-formedness rules of the language.

II. Late Closure

When possible, attach incoming material into the clause or phrase currently being parsed.

If these two principles are in conflict, then Minimal Attachment takes precedence. For example, Minimal Attachment predicts how people process (5a,b):

(5) a. The spy saw the cop with binoculars but the cop didn't see him.
(5) b. The spy saw the cop with a revolver but the cop didn't see him.

Both sentences are syntactically ambiguous, but (5b) is pragmatically disambiguated. The phrase *with binoculars* in (5a) can attach high to *saw*, so that the spy saw with the binoculars, or low to *cop*, so that the cop had the binoculars. The phrase *with a revolver* in (5b) can attach high or low as well, but this time only low attachment is plausible (as seeing with a revolver is not possible). According to Frazier's assumptions about phrase structure, high attachment is "minimal" because it involves one fewer node than low attachment. Hence the processor initially attaches the prepositional phrase high, to *saw*. In (5a), this analysis is plausible, so the parser encounters no problems. But in (5b), this analysis is implausible, and so the parser has to change its analysis to low attachment. (Note that Late Closure would make the opposite prediction, but Minimal Attachment takes precedence.)

In accordance with this prediction, Rayner et al. (1983) found that (5b) became harder to process than (5a) after readers encountered the disambiguating prepositional phrase (see also Clifton et al., 1991; Frazier, 1979; Rayner, Garrod, & Perfetti, 1992). However, Taraban and McClelland (1988) and Spivey-Knowlton and Sedivy (1995) found that preferences can vary and therefore argued that Frazier's theory cannot be correct (see also Altmann & Steedman,

1988). A similar pattern of evidence for and against these principles is found for many other types of sentences. Overall, there is a great deal of controversy arising from a very large amount of often contradictory experimental data. To review this thoroughly would go far beyond the scope of this introductory chapter (see Mitchell, 1994; Pickering, in press; Trueswell & Tanenhaus, 1995, for detailed reviews).

Recently, there have been other serial restricted accounts that differ from Frazier's theory in detail, but that agree on the principle that initial decisions ignore semantic information. Some theories assume that initial decisions are determined by differences in terms of thematic relations (Abney, 1989; Crocker, 1996; Gibson, 1991; Pritchett, 1988, 1992). Pritchett proposed that the processor initially resolves syntactic ambiguities in favour of an analysis under which a thematic relation can be assigned, and the other accounts are similar in this respect. On most accounts, thematic-role assignors like verbs assign roles to arguments but not to adjuncts, so the models also assume a preference for argument over adjunct attachment. This can lead to different predictions from Minimal Attachment, in cases where Minimal Attachment involves adjunct attachment, whereas the other analysis involves argument attachment. At least some experimental evidence supports the account based on Minimal Attachment (Clifton et al., 1991).

1.5.2 Referential Theory

Discourse context affects the interpretation assigned to an ambiguous anaphoric noun phrase. Following Crain and Steedman (1985), Altmann and Steedman (1988) measured reading times on sentences like (6a,b):

(6) a. The burglar blew open the safe with the dynamite and made off with the loot.

(6) b. The burglar blew open the safe with the new lock and made off with the loot.

These sentences are formally ambiguous, in that the prepositional phrase *with the dynamite/new lock* can modify either the noun phrase *the safe* or the verb phrase *blew open the safe*, but Altmann and Steedman used prior context to pragmatically disambiguate them. A context sentence referred to either one or two safes. If only one safe had been mentioned, then the complex noun phrase *the safe with the new lock* is redundant, and hence the prepositional phrase in (6b) took comparatively long to read. If two safes had been mentioned, then the simple noun phrase *the safe* fails to pick out a particular safe, and hence the prepositional phrase *with the dynamite* in (6a) took comparatively long to read.

Altmann and Steedman's (1988) Referential Theory claims that the parser constructs different analyses in parallel and uses discourse context rather than syntactic structure to provide immediate disambiguation. Hence it employs momentary parallelism. One prediction of this account is that discourse context will affect the earliest stages of processing. Evidence for this claim does exist. Using self-paced reading, Altmann and Steedman found effects of discourse context as the prepositional phrase was read. Other studies have shown similar effects, on a range of constructions, using self-paced reading and eye-tracking (Altmann, Garnham, & Dennis, 1992; Altmann, Garnham, & Henstra, 1994; Britt, 1994; Britt et al., 1992; Spivey-Knowlton, Trueswell, & Tanenhaus, 1993; Trueswell & Tanenhaus, 1991). However, other studies have not shown immediate effects (Clifton & Ferreira, 1989; Ferreira & Clifton, 1986; Mitchell, Corley, & Garnham, 1992; Rayner, Garrod, & Perfetti, 1992). The latter studies may have used contextual manipulations that were too weak, making them inadequate tests of Referential Theory. Alternatively, the studies in the former group may have mistakenly identified effects of a fast, meaning-based revision as effects of initial analysis.

Another prediction of Referential Theory is that disambiguation cannot be affected by a syntax-driven strategy, since success in referring is the basis of choice among the parallel analyses. This seems to be incorrect. Context appears to make a larger contribution in cases where other constraints produce a fairly weak preference for one analysis over another, such as attachment ambiguities like (6), than in cases where there may be a strong initial preference, such as reduced relatives like (4). Britt (1994) provides particularly convincing evidence about this. Her subjects read sentences like (7), with optional prepositional-phrase arguments, together with sentences with verbs like *put* that take an obligatory prepositional-phrase argument:

(7) a. He put the book on the chair before leaving.
(7) b. He put the book on the battle onto the chair.

She found that discourse context could remove the preference for high attachment in cases like (6), but not in ones like (7). The verb's desire to fill its obligatory arguments took precedence over contextual influences, for the contexts used by Britt. Note that one need not conclude that obligatory argument structure will always dominate contextual information. Tanenhaus, Spivey-Knowlton, Eberhard and Sedivy (1995) provided a particularly strong context by having subjects follow auditory instructions to manipulate actual objects (e.g., *Put the pencil in the box on the towel.*). The subjects' eye movements to the various objects suggested that aspects of this context (e.g., the existence of two pencils, only one of which was in a box) may have overridden the demands of obligatory arguments.

Referential Theory also has a more general limitation. It only applies to sentences that involve ambiguity between a simple and a complex noun phrase. Hence it cannot serve as a complete account of initial parsing decisions. However, the fundamental insight about the felicity of noun phrases has been incorporated into constraint-based accounts (e.g., Spivey-Knowlton et al., 1993): the weighting assigned to a referentially felicitous analysis is greater than the weighting assigned to a referentially infelicitous analysis. Constraint-based theories are able to provide an account of the simultaneous effects of referentiality and syntactic structure preferences.

Still, at least one puzzle remains. Most studies of referential effects do not find an absolute preference for the successfully referring analysis over the syntactic analysis preferred in isolation. They merely show neutralisation of the preferences observed when sentences are presented in isolation (e.g., Altmann et al., 1992; Altmann et al., 1994; Britt, 1994; Britt et al., 1992; Liversedge et al., 1998), though Altmann and Steedman (1988) found some evidence for override during initial processing. This result is inconsistent with the predictions of Referential Theory and is at least puzzling for constraint-based accounts. For a recent perspective on the status of the Referential Theory, see Altmann (this volume).

1.5.3 Parallel, Unrestricted Accounts

To this point we have considered two basic parsing mechanisms, one in which the parser pursues a single analysis, to the exclusion of all others, backtracking to alternatives as required, and a second which compares multiple analyses simultaneously. An additional possibility is a model which not only pursues multiple analyses in parallel, but crucially allows these structures to dynamically compete with each other in the ranking process. Thus, if we associate each competing analysis with an activation level and rank the alternatives according to the strength of their activation, the increase in activation for one analysis will correspondingly result in a decrease in activation for the others. In this way, the order of preferences may vary as additional words are encountered. Parallelism can be bounded by simply dropping analyses whose activation falls below some specified threshold. Such a proposal is a kind of extended-parallel account.

There are numerous ways in which competitive activation might be realised in the language processor. Stevenson (1994) and Merlo and Stevenson (this volume) propose a hybrid parser which permits alternative syntactic attachments to compete with each other. Crucially, only a limited space of alternatives is supported by the parser, and competition is based on syntactic information alone, resulting in a restricted model. In contrast, MacDonald et al. (1994) present a model in which syntactic representations and constraints interact freely with other levels of representation. The model is therefore relatively unconstrained with regard to the space of competing structures, and also with regard to the kinds of information brought to bear on the competition. So semantic and discourse constraints can directly influence competition between syntactic alternatives.

Interactive competitive-activation theories invite implementation as connectionist models. Relatively few explicit implementations exist, however. Tanenhaus, Spivey-Knowlton and Hanna (this volume) provide an overview of one attempt to construct connectionist models for the integration of frequency, thematic bias, context, and other sources of information. Their models focus on how the processor might select between two competing analyses, but do not address the question of how these analyses are constructed in the first place. Nonetheless, the models successfully capture the major experimental phenomena that have been observed in the garden-path situations to which they have been applied.

A further issue raised by unrestricted accounts concerns the distinction between lexical and syntactic ambiguity. MacDonald et al. (1994) argue that, as many of the syntactic constraints are determined by the properties of individual lexical items, parsing should simply be seen as an extension of the processes for lexical ambiguity resolution. In particular, they suggest that words emerge from the lexicon complete with their projected syntactic structure. Where words are syntactically ambiguous (e.g., verbs with several argument structures), all these structures are activated. Parsing proceeds by simply connecting these lexically projected structures and allowing competition between structures. The result is a uniform, parallel competitive-activation mechanism in which there is no principled distinction between lexical and syntactic ambiguity resolution. Corley and Crocker (this volume) consider this view in some detail, but argue for an alternative, restricted characterisation of lexical category disambiguation.

1.6 How Does Reanalysis Occur?

Research has traditionally concentrated on the question of how the processor decides upon an initial analysis, but it would be a mistake to consider such models of initial decision making to be complete models of processing. We know that processing does not always irrevocably break down after an initial misanalysis. If we consider examples such as (6), it is straightforward to recover from the preferred Minimal Attachment reading. Indeed, examination of large corpora suggests that the non–Minimal Attachment structure accounts for more than half of all occurrences of such examples (Hindle & Rooth, 1993). Hence people must reanalyse most of the time if they initially adopt the Minimal Attachment analysis.

In recent years, there has been increased interest in the issue of what happens after initial misanalysis. In the context of this discussion, reanalysis entails the recovery of an alternative syntactic structure to the "foregrounded" one. This might be achieved by naively reparsing the sentence fragment, by repairing the current analysis, or simply by selecting an alternative, if multiple parses are constructed in parallel. In addition to this underlying issue of the reanalysis mechanism, we identify two important questions: why is reanalysis sometimes easy and sometimes hard (or even impossible), and how does the processor choose a reanalysis if more than one is available? Not surprisingly, the architectures and mechanisms employed in initial analysis have implications for the possible mechanisms of reanalysis.

Intuitively, there are considerable differences in the difficulty of reanalysis:

(8) John recognised Bill would be leaving.

(9) The woman sent the letter was pleased.

In (8), readers may initially interpret *Bill* as the object of *recognised*, but they have little difficulty reanalysing it as the subject of an embedded sentence. But in (9), readers have considerable difficulty when they realise that *sent the letter* is not a verb phrase but a reduced relative. There are now many theories that attempt to determine which constructions are easy and which are hard to reanalyse (e.g., Gorrell, 1995; Pritchett, 1992; Stevenson & Merlo, this volume; Sturt & Crocker, 1996). A serious problem with this enterprise has been the difficulty of translating easy versus hard reanalysis, or conscious versus unconscious garden path, into measurable quantities.

Within a particular sentence type, it might be expected that reanalysis would be harder if people were misled for longer. We might expect that it would be harder to recover and start again if people were led further up the garden path, and so were unable to remember much of the alternative analysis. In fact, the real situation is considerably more complex than this. On the one hand, very short garden-path sentences like *The horse raced fell* can be extremely hard to recover from. On the other hand, Ferreira and Henderson (1991) (cf. Frazier & Rayner, 1982; Warner & Glass, 1987) found that syntactic characteristics of the ambiguous region were important determinants of processing difficulty. For instance, reanalysis was easier if the head noun was near the end of the ambiguous region than if it was near the beginning. Following Pickering and Traxler (1998), Pickering and Traxler (this volume) note further that semantic characteristics of the misanalysis affect difficulty of reanalysis, with plausible misanalyses being more compelling and thus harder to recover from than implausible misanalyses.

Sometimes, more than one reanalysis may be available after the processor realises it has misanalysed. For instance:

(10) The judge accepted the witness who recognised the suspect was deceiving himself all along.

Let us assume that the processor initially treats *the suspect* as the object of *recognised.* After *was*, this analysis becomes impossible, and reanalysis is necessary. But two possibilities exist: either the witness or the suspect might be deceiving himself. It is unclear what strategies are used to determine choice of reanalysis, and whether reanalysis is a restricted or an unrestricted process (see J. D. Fodor & Ferreira, 1998; Lewis, this volume).

1.7 Are the Mechanisms Universal?

Most of our discussion has assumed that there is a single, unified problem of how sentence comprehension occurs. This may be correct, or it may be too simplistic. For instance, sentence comprehension in healthy adults may differ from sentence comprehension in children or dysphasics. Even among healthy adults, there may be important individual differences. It may be that different people simply emphasise different processes, for instance by assigning different weights to different constraints, or it might be that people actually differ in their architectures and mechanisms. We leave aside these difficult and largely unresolved questions (see Just & Carpenter, 1992; but cf. Waters & Caplan, 1996).

Here we briefly address two other points: whether there are differences in the way that different languages are processed, and whether there are differences within languages for different syntactic constructions. In both cases, very little is known for certain, and we focus on issues that have been explored to some extent. Between languages, we consider the resolution of ambiguities involving complex noun phrases. Within languages, we consider the possible distinction between primary and non-primary relations, and the processing of unbounded dependencies.

1.7.1 Differences Between Languages

Parsing strategies might be universal, or they might be determined separately for individual languages. If they are universal, they must of course be sufficiently general to hold across languages with radically different syntactic properties. Some evidence supports this claim. For instance, Frazier (1987b) found support for predictions about the processing of verb-final constructions in Dutch on the basis of Minimal Attachment, even though the strategy was originally proposed for verb-medial constructions in English.

However, a considerable amount of evidence now suggests that Late Closure, at least, cannot hold for all languages, and it is hard to see how any other syntactically defined strategy could either. Cuetos and Mitchell (1988) had subjects read the Spanish equivalent of sentences like (11):

(11) Someone shot the (male) servant of the actress who was standing on the balcony with her husband.

This is eventually disambiguated low, so that the relative clause modifies *actress* rather than *servant*. Cuetos and Mitchell found that (11) caused processing difficulty, suggesting that readers had initially attached the relative clause high, to *servant*. There seems to be a substantial preference in Spanish and in several other languages (including French and Dutch) to interpret a relative clause as modifying the first noun in "NP of NP" constructions like those used by Cuetos and Mitchell. In English, though, and perhaps in Italian, there is much less evidence for a clear preference either way (Carreiras & Clifton, 1993; DeVincenzi & Job, 1995). This suggests a cross-language difference, perhaps because different languages use different parsing strategies or because different languages weight constraints differently. However, Gilboy, Sopena, Clifton and Frazier (1995) argued that the preference for high versus low attachment of relative clauses differs much more between different forms of complex noun phrases within one language than it differs between languages.

A great deal of this work has been on the complex noun phrase construction, because it is found in a very large number of languages. There is now a considerable amount of work on parsing in languages other than English (though far less than one might like), and it may eventually be possible to determine whether the process of sentence comprehension varies in interesting ways between languages or not.

1.7.2 Primary and Non-Primary Relations

Most parsing accounts have assumed that different kinds of modifiers are processed similarly. One exception is thematically driven accounts like Abney

(1989), which argue that arguments and adjuncts are processed differently, with the parser initially preferring to attach a noun phrase as an argument (see also Liversedge et al., 1998). Evidence is mounting for some kind of distinction between the way in which looser syntactic relations are constructed, compared with stricter relations such as those between verbs and core arguments like subjects and objects (see Hemforth et al., this volume).

A particular account of this difference is proposed by Frazier and Clifton (1996), who separated two parsing operations: Attachment and Construal. Attachment occurs with primary relations between verbs and their core arguments and follows the principles of Minimal Attachment and Late Closure. In contrast, non-primary relations are not initially attached, but instead are construed in relation to the current thematic-processing domain, which is defined in terms of the last constituent that introduced a thematic role. For instance, in (11), *the servant of the actress* is a single domain, essentially because the preposition *of* does not introduce a thematic role. The relative clause is then construed in relation to this thematic domain instead of being attached to the one or the other noun. The parser subsequently decides whether to attach high or low using many different knowledge sources. It might thus be correct to characterise Frazier and Clifton as proposing that primary relations are processed in a restricted manner, but non-primary relations in an unrestricted manner. This suggests an interesting difference between types of construction.

1.7.3 Unbounded Dependencies

An unbounded dependency occurs in the question in (12):

(12) Which man do you believe Mary loves a lot?

Such dependencies also occur in other constructions like relative clauses, topicalizations and *it*-clefts. Sentences like (12) are of great linguistic interest, because they present a serious challenge to simple accounts of the syntax of language. The problem is that the phrase *which man* is a long way from the verb *loves*, even though they stand in a close linguistic relationship. In particular, *which man* must be taken as the direct object of *loves*, even though it is not adjacent to the verb. In most constructions, verbs are very close to their arguments, but in unbounded dependencies there is no limit to the number of words or clauses that can separate them (see Henderson, this volume).

Unbounded dependencies present interesting problems for psycholinguistics as well. The processor has to determine that verb and argument are related, even though they are separated. Some linguistic theories (e.g., Chomsky, 1981) assume that the filler phrase *which man* moves from its canonical location after *loves* to its surface position, leaving a gap after *loves*. The filler and gap are related in a manner somewhat similar to the way that a pronoun and its antecedent are related. Psycholinguistic accounts based on this assume a process known as gap filling, in which the filler is stored in memory when it is encountered, the gap is found, and the filler is associated with the gap before interpretation proceeds (Clifton & Frazier, 1989; J. D. Fodor, 1978, 1989; see De Vincenzi, this volume). It may then be that processing unbounded dependencies has something in common with the processing of anaphoric relations, though there is little direct evidence about this.

Alternatively, the processing of unbounded dependencies might not involve any routines separate from other aspects of parsing. On such accounts, the filler associates with the verb directly, just like any other argument of a verb (Pickering & Barry, 1991; Traxler & Pickering, 1996b). J. D. Fodor (1978) and Clifton and Frazier (1989) propose specific accounts about the processing of unbounded dependencies. But it may be possible to make such predictions fall out of general parsing strategies that cover a wide variety of constructions (e.g., Pickering, 1994). Other questions concern the strategy that the parser uses to decide whether to form an unbounded dependency in cases of local ambiguity (e.g., Boland et al., 1995; J. D. Fodor, 1978; Stowe, 1986; Traxler & Pickering, 1996b).

1.8 The Architecture of This Book

Each contribution to this volume addresses a number of the issues considered in this introduction, while at the same time relating to the general theme of architectures and mechanisms. Hence, any imposed grouping of the chapters is bound to be somewhat arbitrary. We have decided to divide the book into four parts: Frameworks, Syntactic and Lexical Mechanisms, Syntax and Semantics, and Interpretation.

The Frameworks part includes those chapters that we feel provide broad perspectives on the architectures and mechanisms theme. Clifton focuses on the empirical debate within sentence-processing research concerning initial mechanisms of syntactic analysis, and he consolidates a number of recent findings. Lewis, on the other hand, takes a more computational view, applying principles of computation to cognitive models of language comprehension, and focusing on both initial structure building and reanalysis. Tanenhaus, Spivey-Knowlton and Hanna raise the issue of making empirical predictions within constraint-based models and illustrate how such models can be made to yield precise predictions about processing complexity. Altmann re-evaluates the Referential Theory in light of recent constraint-based accounts.

The three chapters in the Syntactic and Lexical Mechanisms part concentrate on specific subsystems involved in language processing. Corley and Crocker present new arguments for an encapsulated processor concerned with the determination of lexical category. Merlo and Stevenson provide linguistic and mechanistic explanations for differences in processing complexity of reduced relative clauses. Henderson addresses the problem of representing constituency within a connectionist parsing model and applies this approach to unbounded dependency constructions.

The Syntax and Semantics part includes those chapters that are primarily concerned with the role of these information sources during incremental processing. Brown and Hagoort present findings from event-related potential research which suggests that syntactic and semantic processing are neurologically distinct. Pickering and Traxler provide an overview of a number of eye-tracking experiments which consider the time course of both syntactic and semantic processing. Hemforth, Konieczny and Scheepers investigate how binding processes may be involved in selecting among syntactic alternatives. De Vincenzi provides an account of the processing of unbounded dependencies that considers both syntactic and referential factors.

The final part on Interpretation is concerned with processes that have traditionally been regarded as postsyntactic and that involve contributions from previous discourse. Frazier, however, demonstrates that some phenomena concerned with aspects of semantic interpretation can be accounted for by a single principle within the context of recent syntactic theory. Moxey and Sanford discuss the nature of focus effects and their interaction with quantification and negation. Finally, Almor considers the factors that underlie the processing of anaphoric expressions.

References

Abney, S.P. (1989). A computational model of human parsing. *Journal of Psycholinguistic Research* 18, 129–144.

Altmann, G.T.M., Garnham, A., & Dennis, Y.I.L. (1992). Avoiding the garden path: Eye-movements in context. *Journal of Memory and Language* 31, 685–712.

Altmann, G.T.M., Garnham, A., & Henstra, J.A. (1994). Effects of syntax in human sentence parsing: Evidence against a structure-based parsing mechanism. *Journal of Experimental Psychology: Learning, Memory, and Cognition* 20, 209–216.

Altmann, G.T.M., & Steedman, M.J. (1988). Interaction with context during human sentence processing. *Cognition* 30, 191–238.

Bader, M., & Lasser, I. (1994). German verb-final clauses and sentence processing: Evidence for immediate attachment. In C. Clifton, Jr., L. Frazier, & K. Rayner (Eds.), *Advances in sentence processing*. Hillsdale, NJ: Erlbaum. 225–242.

Bever, T.G. (1970). The cognitive basis for linguistic structures. In J. R. Hayes (Ed.), *Cognition and the development of language*. New York: Wiley. 279–362.

Bock, J.K. (1986). Syntactic persistence in language production. *Cognitive Psychology* 18, 355–387.
Boland, J.E., Tanenhaus, M.K., Garnsey, S.M., & Carlson, G.N. (1995). Verb argument structure in parsing and interpretation: Evidence from wh-questions. *Journal of Memory and Language* 34, 774–806.
Branigan, H.P., Pickering, M.J., Liversedge, S.P., Stewart, A.J., & Urbach, T.P. (1995). Syntactic priming: Investigating the mental representation of language. *Journal of Psycholinguistic Research* 24, 489–506.
Britt, M.A. (1994). The interaction of referential ambiguity and argument structure in the parsing of prepositional phrases. *Journal of Memory and Language* 33, 251–283.
Britt, M.A., Perfetti, C.A., Garrod, S.C., & Rayner, K. (1992). Parsing in context: Context effects and their limits. *Journal of Memory and Language* 31, 293–314.
Carreiras, M., & Clifton, C., Jr. (1993). Relative clause interpretation preferences in Spanish and English. *Language and Speech* 36, 353–372.
Chomsky, N. (1965). *Aspects of the theory of syntax*. Cambridge, MA: MIT Press.
Chomsky, N. (1981). *Lectures on government and binding*. Dordrecht: Foris.
Clifton, C., Jr. (1993). Thematic roles in sentence parsing. *Canadian Journal of Experimental Psychology* 47, 222–246.
Clifton, C., Jr., & Ferreira, F. (1989). Ambiguity in context. *Language and Cognitive Processes* 4, 77–103.
Clifton, C., Jr., & Frazier, L. (1989). Comprehending sentences with long distance dependencies. In G. Carlson & M. Tanenhaus (Eds.), *Linguistic structure in language processing*. Dordrecht: Kluwer. 273–317.
Clifton, C., Jr., Speer, S., & Abney, S.P. (1991). Parsing arguments: Phrase structure and argument structure as determinants of initial parsing decisions. *Journal of Memory and Language* 30, 251–271.
Crain, S., & Steedman, M.J. (1985). On not being led up the garden-path: The use of context by the psychological processor. In D. Dowty, L. Karttunen, & A. Zwicky (Eds.) *Natural language parsing*. Cambridge: Cambridge University Press. 320–358.
Crocker, M.W. (1994). On the nature of the principle-based sentence processor. In C. Clifton, Jr., L. Frazier, & K. Rayner (Eds.), *Advances in sentence processing*. Hillsdale, NJ: Erlbaum. 245–266.
Crocker, M.W. (1996). *Computational psycholinguistics: An interdisciplinary approach to the study of language*. Dordrecht: Kluwer.
Cuetos, F., & Mitchell, D.C. (1988). Cross-linguistic differences in parsing: Restrictions on the use of the late closure strategy in Spanish. *Cognition* 30, 73–105.
DeVincenzi, M., & Job, R. (1995). A cross-linguistic investigation of late closure: The role of syntax, thematic structure, and pragmatics in initial and final interpretation. *Journal of Experimental Psychology: Learning, Memory, and Cognition* 21, 1303–1321.
Ferreira, F., & Clifton, C., Jr. (1986). The independence of syntactic processing. *Journal of Memory and Language* 25, 348–368.
Ferreira, F., & Henderson, J. (1990). Use of verb information in syntactic parsing: Evidence from eye movements and word-by-word self-paced reading. *Journal of Experimental Psychology: Learning, Memory, and Cognition* 16, 555–568.
Ferreira, F., & Henderson, J. (1991). Recovery from misanalyses of garden-path sentences. *Journal of Memory and Language* 30, 725–745.
Fodor, J.A. (1983). *The modularity of mind*. Cambridge, MA: MIT Press.

Fodor, J.D. (1978). Parsing strategies and constraints on transformations. *Linguistic Inquiry* 9, 427–473.
Fodor, J.D. (1989). Empty categories in sentence processing. *Language and Cognitive Processes* 4, 155–209.
Fodor, J.D. (1990). Thematic roles and modularity: Comments on the chapters by Frazier and Tanenhaus et al. In G.T.M. Altmann (Ed.), *Cognitive models of speech processing: Psycholinguistic and computational perspectives*. Cambridge, MA: MIT Press. 434–456.
Fodor, J.D., & Ferreira, F. (Eds.). (1998). *Sentence reanalysis*. Dordrecht: Kluwer.
Ford, M., Bresnan, J.W., & Kaplan, R.M. (1982). A competence based theory of syntactic closure. In J.W. Bresnan (Ed.), *The mental representation of grammatical relations*. Cambridge, MA: MIT Press. 727–796.
Forster, K. (1979). Levels of processing and the structure of the language processor. In W.E. Cooper & E. Walker (Eds.), *Sentence processing: Psycholinguistic studies presented to Merrill Garrett*. Hillsdale, NJ: Erlbaum. 27–86.
Frazier, L. (1979). *On comprehending sentences: Syntactic parsing strategies*. West Bend, IN: Indiana University Linguistics Club.
Frazier, L. (1987a). Sentence processing: A tutorial review. In Coltheart, M. (Ed.), *Attention and performance XII*. Hillsdale, NJ: Erlbaum. 559–586.
Frazier, L. (1987b). Syntactic processing: Evidence from Dutch. *Natural language and linguistic theory* 5, 519–559.
Frazier, L. (1990). Exploring the architecture of the language processing system. In G.T.M. Altmann (Ed.), *Cognitive models of speech processing*. Cambridge, MA: MIT Press. 409–433.
Frazier, L., & Clifton, C. Jr. (1996). *Construal*. Cambridge, MA: MIT Press.
Frazier, L., & Fodor, J.D. (1978). The sausage machine: A new two-stage parsing model. *Cognition* 6, 291–326.
Frazier, L., & Rayner, K. (1982). Making and correcting errors during sentence comprehension: Eye movements in the analysis of structurally ambiguous sentences. *Cognitive Psychology* 14, 178–210.
Frazier, L., & Rayner, K. (1987). Resolution of syntactic category ambiguities: Eye-movements in parsing lexically ambiguous sentences. *Journal of Memory and Language* 26, 505–526.
Frazier, L., & Rayner, K. (1990). Taking on semantic commitments: Processing multiple meanings vs. multiple senses. *Journal of Memory and Language* 29, 181–200.
Garfield, J. (Ed.) (1987). *Modularity in knowledge representation and natural language processing*. Cambridge, MA: MIT Press.
Garnsey, S.M., Tanenhaus, M.K., & Chapman, R. (1989). Evoked potentials and the study of sentence comprehension. *Journal of Psycholinguistic Research* 18, 51–60.
Garrod, S.C., Freudenthal, D., & Boyle, E. (1994). The role of different types of anaphor in the on-line resolution of sentences in a discourse. *Journal of Memory and Language* 33, 39–68.
Gibson, E. (1991). *A computational theory of human linguistic processing: Memory limitations and processing breakdown*. Unpublished doctoral dissertation, Carnegie-Mellon University, Pittsburgh, PA.
Gilboy, E., Sopena, J., Clifton, C., Jr., & Frazier, L. (1995). Argument, structure and association preferences in Spanish and English compound NPs. *Cognition* 54, 131–167.
Gorrell, P. (1989). Establishing the loci of serial and parallel effects in syntactic processing. *Journal of Psycholinguistic Research* 18, 61–73.

Gorrell, P. (1995). *Syntax and perception.* Cambridge: Cambridge University Press.
Greene, S.B., McKoon, G., & Ratcliff, R. (1992). Pronoun resolution and discourse models. *Journal of Experimental Psychology: Learning, Memory, and Cognition* 18, 266–283.
Hagoort, P., Brown, C.M., & Groothusen, J. (1993). The Syntactic Positive Shift as an ERP-measure of syntactic processing. *Language and Cognitive Processes* 8, 439–483.
Hindle, D., & Rooth, M. (1993). Structural ambiguity and lexical relations. *Computational Linguistics* 19, 103–120.
Holmes, V.M., Stowe, L., & Cupples, L. (1989). Lexical expectations in parsing complement-verb sentences. *Journal of Memory and Language* 28, 668–689.
Just, M.A., & Carpenter, P.A. (1980). A theory of reading: From eye fixations to comprehension. *Psychological Review* 87, 329–354.
Katz, J., & Fodor, J.A. (1963). The structure of a semantic theory. *Language* 39, 170–210.
Kimball, J. (1973). Seven principles of surface structure parsing in natural language. *Cognition* 2, 15–47.
Kurtzman, H.S., & MacDonald, M.C. (1993). Resolution of quantifier scope ambiguities. *Cognition* 48, 243–279.
Kutas, M., & Hillyard, S.A. (1980). Reading senseless sentences: Brain potentials reflect semantic incongruity. *Science* 207, 203–205.
Lakoff, G. (1987). *Women, fire, and dangerous things: What categories reveal about the mind.* Chicago: University of Chicago Press.
Liversedge, S.P., Pickering, M.J., Branigan, H.P, & van Gompel, R.P.G. (1998). Processing arguments and adjuncts in isolation and context: The case of *by*-phrase ambiguities in passives. *Journal of Experimental Psychology: Learning, Memory, and Cognition* 24, 461–475.
MacDonald, M.C. (1994). Probabilistic constraints and syntactic ambiguity resolution. *Language and Cognitive Processes* 9, 157–201.
MacDonald, M.C., Pearlmutter, N.J., & Seidenberg, M.S. (1994). Lexical nature of syntactic ambiguity resolution. *Psychological Review* 101, 676–703.
Marcus, M.P. (1980). *A theory of syntactic recognition for natural language.* Cambridge, MA: MIT Press.
Marslen-Wilson, W.D. (1973). Linguistic structure and speech shadowing at very short latencies. *Nature* 244, 522–523.
Marslen-Wilson, W.D. (1975). Sentence perception as an interactive parallel process. *Science* 189, 226–228.
Marslen-Wilson, W.D. (1987). Functional parallelism in spoken word recognition. *Cognition* 25, 71–102.
Marslen-Wilson, W.D., Tyler, L.K., & Koster, C. (1993). Integrative processes in utterance resolution. *Journal of Memory and Language* 32, 647–666.
McClelland, J.L., St. John, M., & Taraban, R. (1989). Sentence comprehension: A parallel distributed processing approach. *Language and Cognitive Processes* 4, 287–335.
Millis, K.K., & Just, M.A. (1994). The influence of connectives on sentence comprehension. *Journal of Memory and Language* 33, 128–147.
Mitchell, D.C. (1987). Lexical guidance in human parsing: Locus and processing characteristics. In M. Coltheart (Ed.), *Attention and performance XII.* Hillsdale, NJ: Erlbaum. 601–618.
Mitchell, D.C. (1989). Verb guidance and lexical effects in ambiguity resolution. *Language and Cognitive Processes* 4, 123–154.

Mitchell, D.C. (1994). Sentence parsing. In M.A. Gernsbacher (Ed.), *Handbook of psycholinguistics*. San Diego, CA: Academic. 375–410.

Mitchell, D.C., Corley, M.M.B., & Garnham, A. (1992). Effects of context in human sentence parsing: Evidence against a discourse-based proposal mechanism. *Journal of Experimental Psychology: Learning, Memory, and Cognition* 18, 69–88.

Osterhout, L., & Holcomb, P.J. (1992). Event-related brain potentials elicited by syntactic anomaly. *Journal of Memory and Language* 31, 785–806.

Osterhout, L., & Holcomb, P.J., & Swinney, D.A. (1994). Brain potentials elicited by garden-path sentences: Evidence of the application of verb information during parsing. *Journal of Experimental Psychology: Learning, Memory, and Cognition* 20, 786–803.

Osterhout, L., & Mobley, L.A. (1995). Event-related brain potentials elicited by failure to agree. *Journal of Memory and Language* 34, 739–773.

Pickering, M.J. (1994). Processing local and unbounded dependencies: A unified account. *Journal of Psycholinguistic Research* 23, 323–352.

Pickering, M.J. (in press). Sentence comprehension as an adaptive process. To appear in S.C. Garrod & M.J. Pickering (Eds.), *Language processing*. London & Cambridge, MA: UCL Press & MIT Press.

Pickering, M.J., & Barry, G. (1991). Sentence processing without empty categories. *Language and Cognitive Processes* 6, 229–259.

Pickering, M.J., & Traxler, M.J. (1998). Plausibility and recovery from garden paths: An eye-tracking study. *Journal of Experimental Psychology: Learning, Memory, and Cognition* 24, 940–961.

Pollard, C., & Sag, I.A. (1993). *Head-driven phrase structure grammar*. Stanford, CA and Chicago, IL: CSLI and University of Chicago Press.

Pritchett, B. (1992). *Grammatical competence and parsing performance*. Chicago: University of Chicago Press.

Pritchett, B.L. (1988). Garden path phenomena and the grammatical basis of language processing. *Language* 64, 539–576.

Rayner, K., Carlson, M., & Frazier, L. (1983). The interaction of syntax and semantics during sentence processing: Eye movements in the analysis of semantically biased sentences. *Journal of Verbal Learning and Verbal Behavior* 22, 358–374.

Rayner, K., & Duffy, S.A. (1986). Lexical complexity and fixation times in reading: effects of word frequency, verb complexity, and lexical ambiguity. *Memory & Cognition* 14, 191–201.

Rayner, K., & Frazier, L. (1989). Selection mechanisms in reading lexically ambiguous words. *Journal of Experimental Psychology: Learning, Memory, and Cognition* 15, 779–790.

Rayner, K., Garrod, S.C., & Perfetti, C.A. (1992). Discourse influences in parsing are delayed. *Cognition* 45, 109–139.

Spivey-Knowlton, M., & Sedivy, J. (1995). Resolving attachment ambiguities with multiple constraints. *Cognition* 55, 227–267.

Spivey-Knowlton, M., Trueswell, J., & Tanenhaus, M.K. (1993). Context and syntactic ambiguity resolution. *Canadian Journal of Experimental Psychology* 47, 276–309.

Stevenson, S. (1994). Competition and recency in a hybrid model of syntactic disambiguation. *Journal of Psycholinguistic Research* 23, 295–322.

Stowe, L. (1986). Parsing WH-constructions: Evidence for on-line gap location. *Language and Cognitive Processes* 1, 227–245.

Sturt, P., & Crocker, M. (1996). Monotonic syntactic processing: A cross-linguistic study of attachment and reanalysis. *Language and Cognitive Processes* 11, 449–494.

Swinney, D.A. (1979). Lexical access during sentence comprehension: (Re)consideration of context effects. *Journal of Verbal Learning and Verbal Behavior* 15, 681–689.

Tanenhaus, M.K., Spivey-Knowlton, M.J., Eberhard, K.M., & Sedivy, J.C. (1995). Integration of visual and linguistic information in spoken language comprehension. *Science* 268, 1632–1634.

Tanenhaus, M.K., & Trueswell, J.C. (1995). Sentence comprehension. In J. Miller & P. Eimas (Eds.), *Handbook of perception and cognition: Speech, language, and communication, second edition.* Vol. 11, 217–262. San Diego: Academic.

Taraban, R., & McClelland, J.R. (1988). Constituent attachment and thematic role assignment in sentence processing: Influence of content-based expectations. *Journal of Memory and Language* 27, 597–632.

Traxler, M.J., Bybee, M.D., & Pickering, M.J. (1997). Influence of connectives on language comprehension: evidence for incremental interpretation. *Quarterly Journal of Experimental Psychology* 50A, 481–497.

Traxler, M.J., & Pickering, M.J. (1996a). Case marking in the parsing of complement sentences: Evidence from eye movements. *Quarterly Journal of Experimental Psychology* 49A, 991–1004.

Traxler, M.J., & Pickering, M.J. (1996b). Plausibility and the processing of unbounded dependencies: An eye-tracking study. *Journal of Memory and Language* 35, 454–475.

Trueswell, J., & Tanenhaus, M.K. (1991). Tense, temporal context, and syntactic ambiguity resolution. *Language and cognitive processes* 6, 303–338.

Trueswell, J., & Tanenhaus, M.K. (1995). *Handbook of cognition & perception.*

Trueswell, J., Tanenhaus, M.K., & Garnsey, S. (1994). Semantic influences on parsing: Use of thematic role information in syntactic disambiguation. *Journal of Memory and Language* 33, 285–318.

Trueswell, J., Tanenhaus, M.K., & Kello, C. (1993). Verb-specific constraints in sentence processing: Separating effects of lexical preference from garden-paths. *Journal of Experimental Psychology: Learning, Memory, and Cognition* 19, 528–553.

Tyler, L.K., & Marslen-Wilson, W.D. (1977). The on-line effects of semantic context on syntactic processing. *Journal of Verbal Learning and Verbal Behavior* 16, 683–692.

Warner, J., & Glass, A.L. (1987). Context and distance-to-disambiguation effects in ambiguity resolution: Evidence from grammaticality judgments of garden path sentences. *Journal of Memory and Language* 26, 714–738.

Waters, Gloria S, & Caplan, David. (1996). The capacity theory of sentence comprehension: Critique of Just and Carpenter (1992). *Psychological Review* 103, 761–772.

Part I

Frameworks

2

Evaluating Models of Human Sentence Processing

CHARLES CLIFTON, JR.

The field of sentence parsing is currently blessed with intriguing theories of human sentence processing and with theorists who defend their theories with enthusiasm and dedication. This is far better than it was at the beginning of serious research into sentence parsing. The theory of derivational complexity was the best thing going, but it was a constantly moving target, whipping from one position to another as linguistic theory changed, and it always seemed possible to shoot it down wherever it went (see Gough & Diehl, 1978).

Things didn't get much better in the early 1970s, with the development of detective models of human sentence parsing (Fodor, Bever, & Garrett, 1974). Parsing theory was reduced to a list of "clues" that the parser might search for, and from which it might, in an associationistic fashion, project what kind of sentence it might be processing. Experimental research was dull, little more than the demonstration that this or that surface feature of sentences had something to do with comprehension (see Clark & Clark, 1977).

A turn for the better came in the mid-1970's with Kimball's principles (Kimball, 1973). Here were some explicit, economical statements of parsing preferences and decision rules that might have some broad applicability – something better than "look for a noun phrase after a transitive verb." Frazier (1979) brought this approach to a new maturity with her proposal that a pair of strategies could account for a wide range of the phenomena that had previously been accounted for in only an ad hoc fashion. These strategies, it turns out, could be empirically tested in new ways, and much of the work in the field of parsing for the next decade was devoted to testing them.

The research reported here was supported in part by Grant HD–18709 from the National Institutes of Health to the University of Massachusetts. The author would like to acknowledge and thank the HCRC, University of Edinburgh, for providing a stimulating environment in which to work while preparing the present report. He would also like to thank Lyn Frazier for her comments on an earlier version of this paper.

Table 2.1. *Structural parsing principles*

Minimal attachment: Do not postulate any potentially unnecessary nodes (Frazier, 1987).
Late closure: If grammatically permissible, attach new items into the clause or phrase currently being processed (Frazier, 1987).
Minimal chain principle: Postulate required chain members at the earliest point grammatically possible but postulate no potentially unnecessary chain members. (DeVincenzi, 1991)
The underlying metaprinciple: Take the first available analysis.

A statement of the familiar principles of minimal attachment and late closure (Frazier, 1979; Frazier, 1987) together with DeVincenzi's (1991) minimal chain principle and Frazier's (1987) generalization of the strategies appears in Table 2.1. In order to interpret a sentence, one must interpret a structured string of words. Thus, if one interprets a sentence quickly, one must analyze it structurally even faster. Frazier's principles simply said, take the first available analysis, the first analysis you can compute, which will typically be the one with the least amount of structure added at each choice point.[1]

This simple and elegant idea has stimulated many tests, and gathered a great deal of support (Frazier & Rayner, 1982; Frazier, 1987; Frazier & Clifton, 1996). But as with any powerful idea, the garden-path theory has stimulated many competitors. There are modular models in many flavors – principle-based models that posit direct use of grammatical principles, models that posit limitations of memory and of processing capacity, models that claim the parser builds underspecified analyses, models that claim referential properties guide syntactic decisions, and so on (e.g., Crocker, 1994, 1996; Gibson, 1991; Gorrell, 1995; Pritchett, 1988, 1992). There are equally salient interactive models – constraint-satisfaction models, models that posit broad-scale competition

[1] The parsing strategies are often presented as responses to memory limitations or even as arbitrary strategies. However, the general conception of the parsing strategies in terms of accepting the first available analysis was present in Frazier's earliest statements. Frazier (1979:115) made this clear for minimal attachment: "If the Minimal Attachment analysis of incoming material requires fewer rules to be accessed than competing analyses require, then on the reasonable assumption that accessing more rules takes more time, the Minimal Attachment analysis . . . may be assumed to be available to the parser before any of the alternative analyses. Assuming that the parser is under considerable time pressure . . . it would be reasonable for it to pursue the first legitimate analysis of incoming material which is available to it."

Further, Frazier (1979:114) made it clear that late closure was not an independent strategy: "The Late Closure strategy is not a decision principle which the parser relies on when it is unsure about the correct attachment of incoming materials; rather, late closure of phrases and clauses is the result of the fact that the first stage parser functions most efficiently by (minimally) attaching incoming material with material on its left which has already been analyzed."

among analyses projected from specific lexical items, models that claim that the frequency of various constructions determines the degree of activation of each construction, and so on (e.g., MacDonald, Pearlmutter, & Seidenberg, 1994a, 1994b; McClelland, St. John, & Taraban, 1989; Tanenhaus, Boland, Mauner, & Carlson, 1993; Tanenhaus, Spivey-Knowlton, Eberhard, & Sedivy, 1995; Tanenhaus & Trueswell, 1995; Trueswell & Tanenhaus, 1994).

How does one evaluate these models? Different people have different bases for choosing among them (see Frazier, 1995). Some people argue that it is not worth considering a model that is not, in principle, able to deal with the gross phenomena of the world's various languages. It's not enough just to be able to give an account of data; you as theorist want to give an account of the underlying mental processes. Theorists who assume that these underlying processes are common to all people, speaking all languages, will summarily reject models that obviously fail to deal with well-attested forms of language. They will reject models that claim, for instance, that structure is projected only from heads of phrases. These models predict that users of head-final languages will have to wait for the end of each phrase, when the head arrives, to build any structure for that phrase, which human readers and listeners simply do not do. Further, models that only project structure from lexical items will never be able to deal with structures, such as adjuncts, that are not lexically dependent (see Frazier, 1995, for further discussion).

Other theorists emphasize experimental tests of the predictions of parsing models. But it is not easy to devise telling theoretical tests. Most parsing models concentrate their predictions on how temporary ambiguities are to be resolved and are pretty well tuned to handle at least the ambiguity resolution effects that are claimed to be relevant to them. Further, all the current parsing models have easily opened escape hatches. Garden-path theory, when confronted with data showing that some lexical or contextual factor cancels its predictions, can claim that the experimental data actually reflect the process of revising an initial analysis, and that any difficulty caused by having to reject the initial analysis was so slight in the face of reanalysis processes that it would not appear in the observable data. Theories that claim that construction frequency matters, when faced with apparent contradictions, can claim that the wrong level of construction was being counted. Theories that claim that referential context or world knowledge guides parsing can claim that manipulations of context or knowledge were simply inadequate. Theories that point to the operation of multiple sources of information can always add some new source. And so on.

Further, the actual predictions of any current theory in a specific complex situation can be less than obvious. The theories are complex, and the process of comprehending sentences is even more so. It is often unclear how the various processes involved in sentence comprehension will interact. Some theorists (especially Tanenhaus; cf. Tanenhaus, Spivey-Knowlton, & Hanna, this volume) have taken on the challenge of specifying the interaction of various processes and of determining whether the interactions permitted by a theory of interest in fact cover the empirical data. This is unquestionably a valuable enterprise, but certainly not the only valuable enterprise. Its value is compromised by the requirement that theorists pursuing it make quantitative commitments to matters that they know and care little about, commitments that can substantially affect the predictions they make (e.g., Tanenhaus's commitment to a "dynamic" reduction in criterion as time goes on, to prevent the parser from getting stuck without making a decision). It is also a difficult enterprise, since a theorist cannot know without a great deal of systematic exploration whether one set of claims about interactions will account for data from a wide range of experiments, or whether different claims must be tailored for each new set of data.

2.1 Crucial Dimensions

An alternative approach is to attempt to identify and test simple predictions of competing theories, ones that hold across wide ranges of sentence structures, and that do not depend on the interaction of multiple sources of information. In following this approach, it seems useful to try to identify some important dimensions on which theories differ. I will propose two.

The first is the dimension of whether there is a single uniform process of parsing or multiple distinct processes, perhaps acting in stages, perhaps simultaneous and interacting. Connectionist constraint-satisfaction models exemplify the former uniform-process model. Frazier's (1990) development of garden-path theories as multiple modules, operating in parallel and independently except insofar as they could communicate with one another through shared vocabularies, is an example of the latter kind of model, as is our current proposal, which we call Construal (Frazier & Clifton, 1996).

The second dimension is whether a single analysis is considered in detail at one time or whether a competitive process of evaluating multiple analyses at once characterizes parsing. Garden-path theory, of course, is the prototypical example of a depth-first, single-analysis model. Constraint-satisfaction theories are pure examples of theories that assume multiple simultaneous breadth-first analyses.

Other dimensions are possible, to be sure, including whether the parser first creates a complete, determinate analysis or an underspecified one that does not lay out all the details of a syntactic tree structure (e.g., Abney, 1991, 1995; Gorrell, 1995; Marcus, Hindle, & Fleck, 1983; Perfetti, 1990; Sturt & Crocker,

1996), and the dimension of how much detailed lexical information is used in creating analyses. At the moment, these other dimensions do not seem likely to afford the kinds of transparent tests permitted by the first two, so I will not discuss them further.

2.2 First-Pass Effects in Sentence Processing

The two dimensions of current interest – single versus multiple parsing processes, and depth-first versus breadth-first processing – have already received substantial attention. Much of this attention has focused on so-called early effects in sentence processing. This seems reasonable enough. Depth-first/multiple-process theories, such as garden-path theories, which claimed that a single analysis was initially created, evaluated, and kept or rejected, make predictions about the early stages of parsing. These early stages could be very different than later stages, when all relevant information eventually can be brought to bear.

Some of the most persuasive early evidence for garden-path models used eyetracking data to show that some disruptions of reading appear very quickly, even on the first fixation in a region of text (Frazier & Rayner, 1982; Rayner, Carlson, & Frazier, 1983). While the researchers who used eyetracking data to support depth-first parsing models acknowledged that various measures (including regressions and long first- and second-pass reading times) could indicate disruption, they claimed that quicker measures (including first-fixation duration) were more diagnostic of the initial garden path (see Rayner & Sereno, 1994). They suggested that data other than first fixations or gaze duration (including data from self-paced reading) are not maximally diagnostic about just when and where a sentence misanalysis is noted, since they can aggregate effects that arise during the reading of several different words (Rayner, Sereno, Morris, Schmauder, & Clifton, 1989).

Some researchers took this methodological suggestion a step further, and proposed that "any effect which manifests itself only in the pattern of *second* pass reading times cannot be said to be a first-pass parsing effect, while differences occurring in the first-pass reading times may be due to first-pass parsing effects" (Altmann, Garnham, & Dennis, 1992:686, italics in original). While Altmann et al. were careful to distinguish conceptually between first-pass parsing effects and first-pass reading times, not all psycholinguists take such care. If it were possible to promulgate a methodological principle such as "first-pass time effects = initial-analysis effects," then one could just look at the eyetracking record to settle the questions of whether initial analyses are constructed following the same principles as final analyses, and of whether multiple or single analyses are constructed initially. But no such simple solution is possible.

Eyetracking data do have some very real advantages over most commonly used alternatives. One is that eye movements can be measured during something very much like normal reading for comprehension. It is not necessary to devise an eyetracking task that requires processing outside the normal range of purposes for reading,[2] and in fact, it is almost never done. Outside the realm of eyetracking, such tasks are commonly used, perhaps with the goal of getting a small effect to show its head through the substantial noise of a self-paced reading task. Tasks that require memorization or detection of anomaly or ungrammaticality can be avoided in eyetracking, and that's a good thing because such tasks probably distort the normal reading process.

A second real advantage of eyetracking data was noted earlier. The eyetracking record contains some data (especially first-fixation duration) that seem to be primarily under local control, allowing strong inferences to be made about just when and where a sentence misanalysis is noted.

However, even with such advantages, eyetracking data do not provide a completely transparent window on the parsing process. Their value depends on what questions are being asked and on what experimental designs are being used. One heuristic for sorting out the specific value of eyetracking measures categorizes experimental materials in terms of whether the information that disambiguates a temporary ambiguity of interest (a) comes before that ambiguity, (b) is contained in the ambiguous word, or (c) follows the ambiguity. In case (c), any measure that indicates disruption can provide evidence about whether the ambiguity eventually received a single interpretation that needs revision. However, an eyetracking record can contain useful information about when and where the disruption appears (see Frazier & Rayner, 1982), and this information could in principle be used to help decide whether the disruption reflects a process of revision of a single analysis or, say, global plausibility effects.

Case (b) covers items like *He said he will come yesterday.* Such items clearly raise the question of whether the ambiguous word *yesterday* receives a single structurally based analysis which must be revised on the basis of its content or whether the alternative late-closure and early-closure analyses are both activated and allowed to compete. If it were the case that first-fixation (or first-pass) times directly reflect initial analysis and second-pass (or total) times reflect revision processes, then the eyetracking record could settle the question. But it

[2] I do not deny that this range is of interest. One may read quite differently when one is reading for pleasure, or to follow instructions, or to answer easy versus hard questions, or to find flaws in an argument, etc. See Carroll & Slowiaczek (1987).

appears that the content of the ambiguous word or phrase is processed while it is still being fixated, and that interpretation and revision processes can begin on that fixation (see Pickering & Traxler, 1998; Speer & Clifton, in press), and it also appears that the effects of the initial analysis can persist through later fixations (see Rayner et al., 1989). In some cases which approximate case (b) – for instance, *The man expressed his interest in the car* (Clifton, Speer, & Abney, 1991) – the details of the eye-movement record seem to contain useful information. Clifton et al. found that the status of the ambiguous prepositional phrase (*in the car*) as verb versus noun modifier affected first-pass reading time on the prepositional phrase itself, while its status as argument versus adjunct affected total reading time and first-pass time on the next region, supporting a distinction between the use of phrase-structure versus argument-structure information. The existence of such cases, however, does not support a slavish identification of certain eyetracking measures with certain underlying processes.

Case (a) is where the information of interest comes before the ambiguous region. Examples include studies of the effects of referential context (e.g., Altmann & Steedman, 1988; Ferreira & Clifton, 1986), studies of verb bias (Ferreira & Henderson, 1990; Kennison, 1995; Trueswell, Tanenhaus, & Kello, 1993), and effects of agenthood and thematic-role preferences (Stowe, 1989). Here, there is a good case for using eyetracking measures. A common purpose of such research is to determine whether the early information affects the initial analysis and not just reanalysis, or from a different perspective, whether the early information was integrated with or treated separately from other information that might be present at the locus of ambiguity. It has proved worthwhile to examine the eye-movement record for evidence about whether the early information eliminates the initial disruption that normally comes with disambiguation, or whether it simply speeds the eventual revision and reanalysis. Clifton (1992, 1993), for instance, showed that the effects Stowe (1989) observed in her self-paced incremental grammaticality-judgment task appeared clearly in his eyetracking data, but only in sentence regions that followed the ambiguity and in measures of total reading time. First-pass time in the region of the ambiguity showed different effects, apparently reflecting the plausibility of structurally determined analyses and not the thematic preferences observed by Stowe.

Even in this case, however, looking at the eyetracking record does not provide a definitive answer to the theoretical questions. Fully understanding the eyetracking record requires a better understanding of the processes of eye-movement control than we have now (see Reichle, Pollatsek, Fisher, & Rayner, 1998, for some recent advances), and understanding its relation to underlying processes involved in integrating different sources of information probably requires detailed modeling of the type that Tanenhaus (this volume) advocates. Progress in answering the questions advanced in this chapter will require conceptual and methodological tools beyond the sheer availability of an eyetracker.

2.3 Uniform Process versus Multiple Modules

I will return to the attempt to find interaction-free reflections of the two dimensions proposed earlier. First consider the dimension of uniform process versus multiple distinct processes. The primary kind of evidence that has been taken to support uniform-process parsing theories such as connectionist constraint-satisfaction theories has been demonstrations that corpus frequency or normative preferences predict parsing decisions. Frequency of experience has been taken to be the underlying, common causal factor; effects of experience are expressed in all activity, including both off-line activity of evaluating or completing sentences and on-line parsing activity.

There are some reasons to view this rush from correlational data to underlying process with a bit of skepticism. First, one must worry about the direction of causation. Why are the structures that are dispreferred less frequent than the ones that are preferred? And why do corresponding structures in different languages seem to have corresponding preferences (see Frazier, 1995)? If main clauses are preferred over relative clauses, and direct objects over sentence complements, in language after language, doesn't that have to be explained? The explanation may be in terms of communicative needs, or it may be in terms of processing ease. At our current level of knowledge, all we can say for certain is that it is unwise to take frequency as the causal factor.

Second, there is the problem of what to count when counting frequency. Merlo's (1994) work seemed to show that simple frequency counts did not predict parsing as well as production norms did. Does that mean that the wrong things were being counted, and that the right ones would predict well? Or does it mean that production norms reflect factors other than frequency of experience, perhaps even an element of parsing itself? In any event, it does seem that a theorist who says "frequency of experience determines parsing choices" doesn't really have a theoretical claim until he or she makes a commitment to what should be counted and justifies why that is what should be counted (see Gibson, Schütze, & Salomon, 1996; Mitchell, 1994).

Let me abstract beyond frequency as the potential common factor in uniform-process models. Such models, I think, generally predict that performance in one task should predict performance in another, as long as both tasks reflect the same choice among alternatives. That's perhaps too strong. It is possible to imagine that extraneous factors will influence one task but not the other. Still, the default assumption underlying the use of sentence completion data or choice data to predict ease of parsing must be that the tasks will both reflect the operation of the common factors that underlie sentence comprehension.

This means that one way of asking whether a uniform process underlies all sentence comprehension tasks is to probe for cases where the simple relationship between different tasks breaks down. Finding one dissociation between tasks doesn't bring the uniform-process enterprise crashing down, but it does say that there may be something to explain, perhaps in terms of distinct parsing processes. Similarly, finding close relations between performance in two distinct comprehension tasks doesn't prove the uniformity case, but it does constitute something to explain as well.

2.3.1 Adjunct Predication

Let me present two cases of dissociation between normative and on-line data and argue that they can best be understood in terms of distinct processes. The first one will examine the relation between off-line interpretation preferences and the occurrence of garden paths in parsing. Consider first adverb-interpretation sentences like those shown at the top of Table 2.2, which have been referred to as late closure sentences. They show a substantial preference for the final adverb, here *last week*, to modify the most recent verb. Actually, our current theory, Construal, does not claim that late closure applies here. Rather, the adverb is a non-primary phrase that is associated with and interpreted within the most recent thematic processing domain, which turns out to be the last clause, *that her friends arrived*.... Its preferred interpretation is within this clause, and forcing it to the higher clause requires a costly revision of association with the domain of the first clause. For ease of reference, though, I'll refer to these sentences as late-closure and early-closure sentences.

Consider now the second set of sentences in Table 2.2, the adjunct predication sentences. These have a very similar ambiguity. The adjunct predicate, *cold*, could in principle modify either the first or the second NP in the sentence, the subject or the object. In fact, there is a substantial tendency for adjunct predicates to prefer the object as host. These adjunct-predicate sentences, like the adverb-interpretation sentences just discussed involve a non-primary phrase associated with the entire domain of a sentence. According to Construal theory, the parser should have no trouble interpreting an adjunct predicate as taking either the subject or the object as its host since both are available within the current thematic processing domain. On the other hand, given the strong bias in favor of object predication in the final interpretations of these sentences, it seems

Table 2.2. *Garden-path and non-garden-path sentences*

Adverb interpretation
Ambiguous: *Marcie announced that her friends arrived last week.*
(She announced something last week: early closure, domain violation)
(Her friends arrived last week: late closure, appropriate domain choice)
Early closure: *Marcie announced that her friends will arrive last week.*
Late closure: *Marcie will announce that her friends arrived last week.*

Adjunct predication
Ambiguous: *The hungry boy ate the broccoli cold.*
(The boy was cold: subject predication)
(The broccoli was cold: object predication)
Subject predication: *The hungry boy ate the broccoli naked.*
Object prediction: *The hungry boy ate the broccoli raw.*

that a uniform-process model would be hard-pressed not to predict disruption in reading when the content of a sentence requires subject predication.

We (Clifton, Frazier, Rapoport, & Radó, under revision) performed the requisite experiment. We first normed a large number of ambiguous adjunct-predication and adverb-interpretation sentences by having subjects indicate which of the two available interpretations they made upon first reading each sentence. We then selected 24 tokens of each sentence type with a bias of about 80% in favor of the (late-closure, object-predication) reading. We then ran a self-paced reading study, using sentences like the disambiguated forms in Table 2.2. We measured the time to read the disambiguating final word of sentences whose content forced either an unpreferred or a preferred reading. We expected to find the usual garden-path effect for the early-closure adverb sentences, but we expected a different result for the subject-predication sentences.

The normative ambiguity-resolution data came out clearly. The two kinds of items had about the same off-line bias, over 80% preference for the form we expected to be preferred (83.0% preference for low-attached adverbs, 82.3% for object-host adjunct predicates). The self-paced reading data came out very clearly too, as shown in Figure 2.1. There was a highly significant garden-path effect for the adverb sentences, as expected, with over 150 ms reading time for what was generally a single disambiguating word. However, there was a trivial difference in reading time for subject versus object predication sentences. At the very least, there is something about these adjunct predication sentences that makes the dynamics of their processing very different than run-of-the-mill garden-path sentences. More than this, it means that saying something like "parsing preferences and parsing difficulty are determined by the

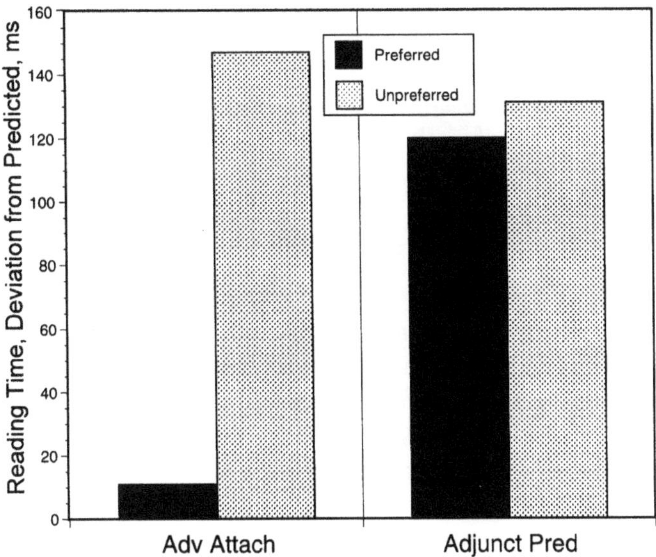

Figure 2.1. Reading time (deviation from time predicted as a linear function of region length, ms), disambiguating region of disambiguated adverb interpretation and adjunct predication sentences.

strength with which different structures are represented in memory" just won't do as a complete theory of parsing. Something more interesting than that is going on.

2.3.2 Her *Disambiguation*

Consider another example of a dissociation between offline preferences and online parsing difficulty, coming from processing of the personal pronoun *her*. *Her* is ambiguous between use as an object (*I saw her yesterday*) and as a possessive (*I saw her grant proposal*). Its preferred interpretation can be affected by the verb it follows. We (Clifton, Kennison, & Albrecht, 1997) first gathered norms on how often different verbs were followed by human direct objects, using a sentence completion task (*They* verbed *the* ______). The verbs that were frequently used with human direct objects included *convince, help*, and *amuse*, and the verbs that were frequently used with inanimate direct objects included *burn, prepare*, and *ruin*. We then took verbs that ranged widely in their bias toward human direct objects and determined how they biased the interpretation of *her* in another sentence completion task (this time one in which our subjects completed sentences of the form *They verbed her* ______). We found that verbs

Table 2.3. *Sample items for experiment on ambiguity of* her

Disambiguated in favor of *her* as object
The produceers harassed/hurried/prepared her frequently during rehearsals of the play about World War II.
Disambiguated in favor of *her* as possessive
The producers harassed/hurried/prepared her secretary during rehearsals of the play about World War II.

that were often used with human direct objects biased our subjects toward the object interpretation of *her*, while verbs that were seldom used with human direct objects biased them toward the possessive interpretation of *her*. The correlation between the two biases exceeded +.68.

This off-line preference might reflect some sort of strength of memory representations including either resolution of the lexical category of *her* (as possessive vs. personal pronoun) or resolution of the syntactic configurations in which *her* occurs. If so, then a uniform-process model using such representations would seem to predict that comprehension difficulty would be affected by the verb and the bias it induces. We tested this in a self-paced reading study, using materials like those in Table 2.3. The correlation between verb bias and the difference in time to read a region disambiguating the sentence in favor of an object or possessive interpretation of *her* was a negligibly small + .029. From one perspective, this absence of a bias is surprising, regardless of whether you accept a uniform process parsing model, since *her* is an instance of category ambiguity. Contextual bias does generally seem to affect the resolution of lexical ambiguities, but it didn't here. What we think happened is simply that whenever *her* was followed by a noun, late closure resulted in taking *her* as a possessive. But when *her* was followed by an adverb, it was taken without question as an object.

There's more to say about just how this worked, but the basic point is clear. A structural parsing factor – late closure – determined how *her* was interpreted in the on-line task. The factor of verb bias, how much a verb wanted a human object, that played such a big role in the normative task, just didn't play a role here. This seems to carry the same implication as the previous experiment: Strength of representations in memory, as tapped by off-line judgment tasks, does not exhaust the list of factors that affect parsing. An adequate theory of on-line parsing will have to appeal to processes other than the activation of pre-existing structures in memory and competition among these structures.

2.4 Single versus Multiple Analyses

Consider the second of my crucial dimensions distinguishing classes of models, namely, the dimension of single versus multiple analyses. Is the parser a device that imposes a single structure on an input string and uses it to guide interpretation, revising when problems are encountered? Or is it a device that recovers or creates several analyses simultaneously, allowing them to compete with one another for dominance?

2.4.1 Full Ambiguity

Given the inability to observe initial analyses directly (recall the discussion of first-pass effects), one must devise alternative methods. One method is predicated on a competitive, multiple-analysis model in which decisions are hardest and reading is slowest when there is maximum competition among the alternatives. Rayner's work with various colleagues on eyetracking during the reading of lexically ambiguous words is a paradigm example of research based on this notion (Duffy, Morris, & Rayner, 1988; Rayner & Duffy, 1986; Rayner & Frazier, 1989; see Rayner & Sereno, 1994). Words that are used about equally often in their two meanings are read more slowly than words that are more frequent with one meaning than another. Prior context can change this relation, speeding the reading of equibiased words and slowing the reading of a word whose context forces a normally dispreferred meaning. These data do not absolutely force a competitive evaluation model, but they certainly suggest one.

It would seem straightforward to use the same logic in parsing research and to determine whether reading is maximally disrupted when there are two (or more) equally attractive alternatives. I suspect things won't work this way. Instead, I suspect that disruption will be maximal when there is one overwhelmingly preferred alternative that has one piece of grammatical information cast against it. Single-analysis models are easily seen to be consistent with such an effect; multiple-analysis models may, at the very least, have to be tinkered with to accommodate it, and may not provide much in the way of an explanation of the effect.

The small amount of relevant research that exists does little to support competitive, multiple-analysis models. Traxler, Pickering, and Clifton (1998) measured eye movements while people read fully ambiguous relative clause sentences, like *The chapter of the thesis that had the misspellings was rubbish.* Reading times were actually faster in this case than in cases where the relative-clause attachment was disambiguated. That is, sentences with greater uncertainty (and presumably greater competition) were less disruptive than sentences with lesser uncertainty. It did not matter whether disambiguation favored modification of the first noun (*The thesis of the editors that had the misspellings . . .*) or the second one (*The editors of the thesis that had the misspellings . . .*) in examples like the one presented here, although it did in cases of a structurally based preference for one analysis over the other. The structurally preferred analysis resulted in reading times that were as fast as the fully ambiguous case, and faster than the structurally dispreferred analysis.

2.4.2 Crossover Experiments

A second method for investigating the single/multiple-analysis question is also basically simple. Most research on the limits of "garden pathing" demonstrates that some factor of content or context reduces or eliminates disruption for the normally dispreferred sentence form. Little research has explored the effects of the same factor on the form that is normally preferred. A demonstration that some factor reduces disruption in a normally dispreferred sentence constrains the depth-first/breadth-first contrast very little. A depth-first theorist could claim that the factor speeded reanalysis, while a breadth-first theorist could claim that the factor affected the weights of competing analyses. However, the effect on the normally preferred form could be theoretically much more informative (see Frazier, 1995). From the perspective of a competitive breadth-first model, whatever adds evidence for one form will generally take evidence away from another distinct form. Thus, the factor that makes the dispreferred form easier should make the preferred form harder. On the other hand, a single-analysis model would most naturally predict an asymmetry in effects. The preferred analysis is computed anyway. Factors that make it easy to give up need not make it any harder to keep. Evidence that makes the dispreferred analysis easier to compute, therefore, will not necessarily affect the processing of the preferred analysis.

These predictions have to be made with some caution. For instance, the prediction for single-analysis models, according to which factors that affect recovery from a garden path will not affect processing in the absence of a garden path, may have to be qualified by the recognition that the factors that make it easy to recover from a garden path may make the preferred analysis less felicitous, thereby slowing some aspect of reading. Conversely, the parallel-competition model's prediction of opposite effects on preferred and dispreferred analyses may have to be qualified by recognizing that adding information that supports and facilitates the normally dispreferred analysis may increase the total competition in the decision (especially when the eventual decision has to

Table 2.4. *Sample sentences from Ni, Crain, and Shankweiler, 1996*

A: Temporarily ambiguous, *the*
The students furnished answers before the exam received high marks.
B: Temporarily ambiguous, *only*
Only students furnished answers before the exam received high marks.
C: Unambiguous, *the*
The hunters bitten by the ticks worried about getting Lyme disease.
D: Unambiguous, *only*
Only hunters bitten by the ticks worried about getting Lyme disease.

be in favor of the normally preferred analysis), which would slow processing of all sentence forms.

There is, to my knowledge, only one published experiment in the constraint-satisfaction tradition that examines the effects of factors on processing of preferred sentence forms. This is Pearlmutter and MacDonald (1995). What they showed was that the top one-third of their subjects in terms of reading span may have been considering the normally dispreferred analysis on some occasions, creating an ambiguity effect so that the ambiguous preferred form was slower than an unambiguous one. The primary evidence concerning this effect came from correlational analyses involving only ten experimental items, items with predictor variables that very seriously violated the distributional assumptions of the correlation technique. From Pearlmutter and MacDonald's published item-by-item data, it is clear that there were one or two outlier items for some of their predictor variables. One cannot conclude anything at all from such correlations. A slightly unusual reading time for a single one of these outlier items could give a numerically large correlation coefficient, which would be taken to be significant by the normal tests – whose assumptions were violated. In fact, one might well attribute the effects Pearlmutter and MacDonald observed to a few highly motivated and perhaps bright subjects trying to second-guess what kind of trick the experimenter might be trying to pull on them.

One additional experiment has been reported that seems to give clear evidence that a factor that facilitates the dispreferred form hurts the preferred one. Crain, Ni, Shankweiler, Conway, and Braze (1996) followed up earlier research (Ni, Crain, & Shankweiler, 1996), which found that using *only* rather than *the* to begin an NP eliminated the disruption caused by a reduced relative clause continuation. Ni et al. (1996) had subjects read sentences like those in Table 2.4, using eye movement and incremental grammaticality-judgment tasks. They found the usual disruption in sentences like A, compared to morphologically disambiguated sentences like C. But the disruption disappeared in sentences like B, where *only* presumably demands a referential contrast set and thus licenses the relative clause. Crain et al. conducted an experiment in which they examined the effect of *only* on the preferred main clause–resolution sentences as well as on the dispreferred relative clause sentences, noting that Frazier (1995) had claimed that such an experiment would be crucial. They found that the presence of *only* did eliminate any garden pathing from the reduced relative clause sentences. They also found that the presence of *only* made temporarily ambiguous main clause sentences substantially harder to process (i.e., it seemed to induce garden pathing in the preferred-form sentences). That is, Crain et al. reported just the results predicted by a parallel constraint-satisfaction model (although they interpreted them in terms of the referential model of Crain & Steedman, 1985).

The Crain et al. (1996) results may not be the final word. Some of their main clause sentences with *only* seem to be quite implausible or at least infelicitous, perhaps because *only* sometimes requires a modifier to subdivide a referential set (as in *Only agents issued free tickets but were banned from the show yesterday*). Implausibility has clear and immediate effects on eyetracking (Clifton, 1993; Pickering & Traxler, 1998, Speer & Clifton, 1998). Further, several unsuccessful attempts have been made in the University of Massachusetts laboratories to replicate the Ni et al. (1996) and Crain et al. (1996) results. Two of these attempts used the exact materials from Ni et al. (1996), including both experimental and filler items (kindly provided by W. Ni). Neither an incremental grammaticality-judgment experiment (like Experiment 1 from Ni et al.) nor a self-paced reading experiment (using the design of their eyetracking Experiment 2) succeeded in replicating their effect of *only* on relative clause sentences. Figure 2.2 shows the self-paced reading results (lower panel), together with the results from the Ni. et al. paper (top panel). In our data, there was significant disruption in the temporarily ambiguous relative clause sentences with and without *only*, compared to sentences that were unambiguous by virtue of verb morphology. If *only* had any effect, it was as large on the unambiguous as on the ambiguous forms, suggesting that its effect was actually mediated by felicity or plausibility (see Liversedge, Patterson, & Underwood, 1997, for very similar results using different materials).

Although we did not examine effects on the normally preferred main clause sentences in the experiments that used the Ni et al. materials, we did so in experiments using materials we constructed ourselves. Our sentences were continued equally often as reduced relative and as main clause sentences, as shown in Table 2.5. We used eyetracking procedures to see whether *only* would facilitate the reading of reduced relative sentences but impede that of main clause sentences, as predicted by a competitive depth-first theory. We analyzed the

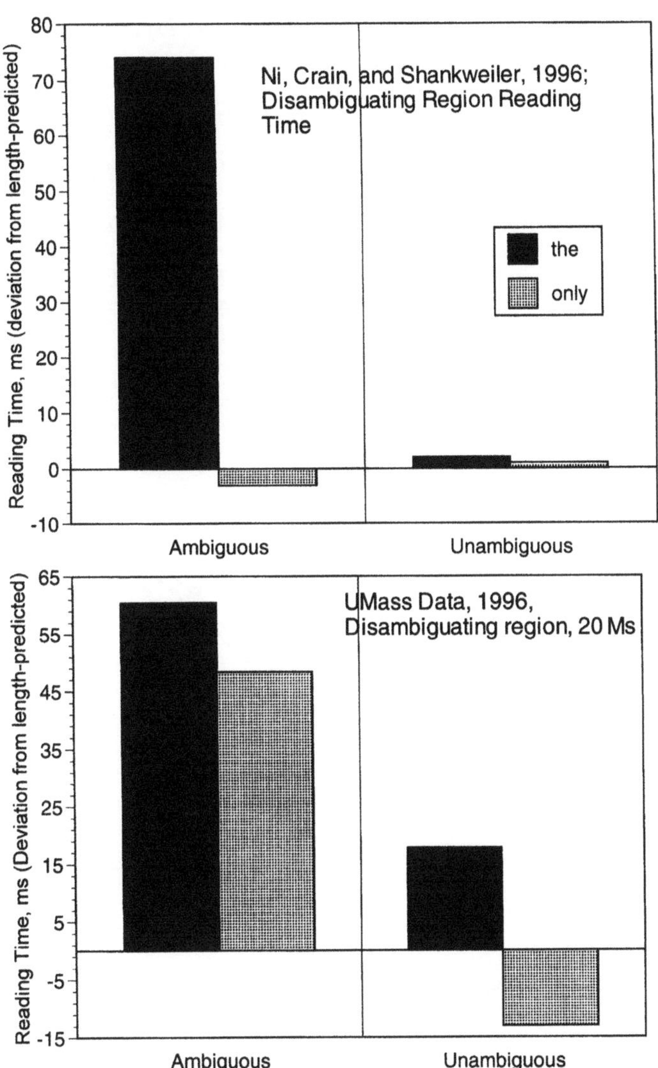

Figure 2.2. Top panel: First-pass reading time (deviation in ms from time predicted on the basis of analysis region length) reported by Ni, Crain, and Shankweiler, 1996. Bottom panel: Self-paced reading time (deviation in ms from predicted) collected at the University of Massachusetts, using materials of Crain et al., 1996.

data in a variety of ways, looking at measures of reading in each of the regions indicated by the slashes in Table 2.5.

The first- and second-pass reading times (see Figure 2.3) are representative of all our data. There was substantial garden pathing at the point where a sentence was disambiguated toward the relative clause structure. Most of our

Table 2.5. *Sample item used in crossover experiment*

A. Reduced relative clause, *the*
The student lent / money / paid it back. / The rich kid didn't. /
B. Reduced relative clause, *only*
Only students lent / money / paid it back. / The rich kid didn't. /
C. Main clause, *the*
The student lent / money / all the time. / The rich kid didn't. /
D. Main clause, *only*
Only students lent / money / all the time. / The rich kid didn't. /

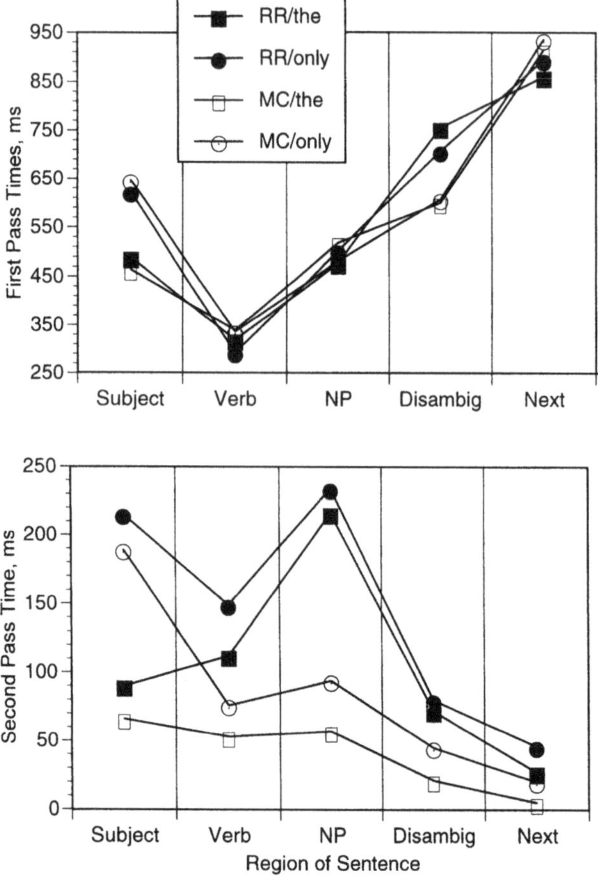

Figure 2.3. First- and second-pass reading times (ms), crossover experiment, using reduced relative clause vs. main clause ambiguity.

Table 2.6. *Materials used by Binder, Duffy, & Rayner, 1996 (Experiments 2 and 3)*

Sample biasing context, favoring reduced-relative construction:
The two daughters sat in their parents' home. . . . The younger sister outraged her family when she married a man of a different religion. . . .

1. Ambiguous, main verb
   The daughter disowned her unsupportive family and . . .
2. Unambiguous, main verb
   The daughter had disowned her unsupportive family . . .
3. Ambiguous, relative clause
   The daughter disowned her unsupportive family moved . . .
4. Unambiguous, relative clause
   The daughter who was disowned by her unsupportive family . . .

measures indicated faster reading for reduced relative clauses following *only* compared to those following *the*, with a suggestion of slower second-pass times following *only* for main clause sentences. However, the interaction between type of specifier and sentence form was never significant, and our findings using the Ni et al. (1996) materials suggest that we might have seen the same tendencies involving *only* in unambiguous as well as in ambiguous items, had unambiguous sentences been included in the present experiment.

This crossover experiment thus did not replicate Ni, Crain, and Shankweiler's (1996) basic finding that *only* eliminated garden pathing for reduced relative clauses. Therefore it cannot qualify as the test of multiple versus single analyses that we hoped it would be. We can't ask whether the facilitating effect of *only* on reduced relative clauses would be reflected as a disruption on main clauses if *only* does not in fact facilitate relative clauses. We have made two other attempts to test the prediction of symmetrical versus asymmetrical effects of some variable on preferred versus dispreferred constructions. One involved the effect of *only* on relative clauses versus sentence complements, and the other (Kennison, 1995) involved the effect of normed verb biases on sentence complements versus direct objects. Neither was fully successful, because neither showed robust effects of the variable on the normally dispreferred form.

However, our colleagues Binder, Duffy, & Rayner (1996) were more successful in this enterprise. They conducted an experiment comparing relative-clause and main-clause readings of temporarily ambiguous and unambiguous sentences, much as we did in the study described earlier. They manipulated the context in which the sentence appeared, contrasting contexts in which a nominal modifier was required to distinguish between two possible referents of a noun phrase from contexts that did not require such modification. A schematic example appears in Table 2.6, which also shows relevant portions of the ambiguous and unambiguous relative-clause and main-clause sentences being examined.

The difficulty of relative clause compared to main clause analyses is not always eliminated, or even affected, by theoretically relevant manipulations of context (Ferreira & Clifton, 1986; Britt, Perfetti, Garrod, & Rayner, 1992). However, it is infelicitous to use an unmodified definite noun phrase in a context containing two possible referents. This could disrupt reading of both ambiguous and unambiguous main clause sentences and facilitate reanalysis of temporarily ambiguous reduced-relative sentences, resulting in an apparent reduction of garden-path effects on relative clause sentences (Clifton & Ferreira, 1989; cf. Steedman & Altmann, 1989, for discussion of contrasting interpretations of this effect). In fact, Binder et al. did find that presenting main clause sentences in a two-referent context slowed reading for both ambiguous and unambiguous sentences. Further, Binder et al. concluded from a comparison of their Experiments 2 and 3 that presenting relative clause sentences in a two-referent context reduced garden pathing (see Figure 2.4). That is, the inferiority of temporarily ambiguous clauses compared to unambiguous relative clauses was reduced by presenting them in a context that had two potential referents. This effect could be interpreted either as a speedup in reanalysis or as a shift of initial preferences

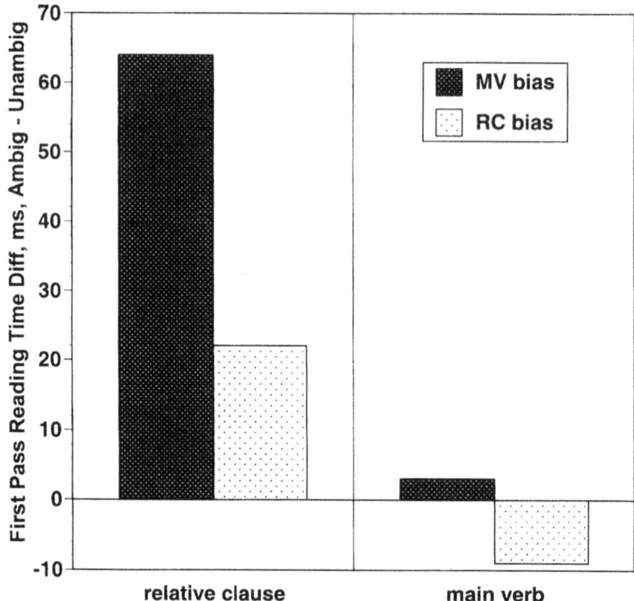

Figure 2.4. First-pass reading time differences (ambiguous–unambiguous), reported in Binder, Duffy, and Rayner, 1996.

from main-clause to relative-clause interpretations. In contrast, the difference between temporarily ambiguous and unambiguous main clause sentences was not affected by the contextual manipulation. The failure to find any increase in the relative difficulty of temporarily ambiguous main clause sentences indicates that context did not affect parsing preferences for main-clause versus relative-clause constructions. This is precisely the result predicted by depth-first theories of parsing.

2.5 Summary and Prospects

I have proposed that one profitable attitude to take in evaluating models of sentence parsing is to identify broad dimensions that cut across models of interest and to attempt to gather evidence about these dimensions. I focused on two dimensions along which current sentence-processing models differ, which I termed multiple versus uniform parsing processes and breadth-first versus depth-first parsing. I presented some evidence that saying something like "parsing preferences are determined by the strengths of structural representations" is far less than an adequate theory of parsing. Rather, distinct types of parsing processes must be postulated for different types of constructions and for different processing tasks.

I then presented several attempts to resolve the depth-first/breadth-first issue by investigating the effects that variables have on normally preferred as well as on normally dispreferred constructions (as suggested by Frazier, 1995). One attempt by Crain et al. (1996) seemed to show that a variable had symmetrical effects on preferred and dispreferred constructions. Their experiment, however, was methodologically flawed, and we have been unable to replicate the effect they reported on relative clause sentences. Our own attempts were inconclusive, because of our persistent inability to reduce the disruption caused when a temporary ambiguity is resolved in favor of the dispreferred form. However, Binder, Duffy, and Rayner (1996) were more successful, reporting that context affected processing of the dispreferred but not of the preferred form, in agreement with depth-first analyses of parsing.

I do not propose that the experiments presented here will settle the core issues of human sentence parsing. I do think, though, that the specific ways discussed here of addressing these core issues are promising enough to warrant additional experimental effort. I think, too, that the results to date show that depth-first modular theories are not yet quite ready to be put out to pasture.

References

Abney, S. (1991). Parsing by chunks. In R. Berwick, S. Abney, & C. Tenny (Eds.), *Principle-based parsing* (pp. 257–278). Dordrecht: Kluwer.

Abney, S. (1995). Chunks and dependencies: Bringing evidence to bear on syntax. *Computational linguistics and linguistic theory*. Stanford, CA: CSLI.

Altmann, G. T. M., Garnham, A., & Dennis, Y. (1992). Avoiding the garden path: Eye movements in context. *Journal of Memory and Language* 31, 685–712.

Altmann, G. T. M., & Steedman, M. (1988). Interaction with context during human sentence processing. *Cognition* 30, 191–238.

Binder, K. S., Duffy, S. A., & Rayner, K. (1996). *The effects of context on syntactic ambiguity resolution*. Paper presented at the 37th Annual Meeting of the Psychonomic Society.

Britt, M. A., Perfetti, C. A., Garrod, S., & Rayner, K. (1992). Parsing in discourse: Context effects and their limits. *Journal of Memory and Language* 31, 293–314.

Carroll, P. J., & Slowiaczek, M. L. (1987). Modes and modules: Multiple pathways to the language processor. In J. L. Garfield (Ed.), *Modularity in sentence comprehension: Knowledge representation and natural language understanding* (pp. 221–248). Cambridge, MA: MIT Press.

Clark, H. H., & Clark, E. V. (1977). *Psychology and language*. New York: Harcourt Brace Jovanovich.

Clifton, C., Jr. (1992). Tracing the course of sentence comprehension: How lexical information is used. In K. Rayner (Ed.), *Eye movements in visual cognition: Scene perception and reading* (pp. 397–414). New York: Springer-Verlag.

Clifton, C., Jr. (1993). Thematic roles in sentence parsing. *Canadian Journal of Psychology* 47, 222–246.

Clifton, C., Jr., & Ferreira, F. (1989). Ambiguity in context. *Language and Cognitive Processes* 4, 77–104.

Clifton, C., Jr., Frazier, L., Rapoport, T., & Radó, J. (under revision). Adjunct predication: Attachment or construal?

Clifton, C., Jr., Kennison, S., & Albrecht, J. (1997). Reading the words Her, His, Him: Implications for parsing principles based on frequency and structure. *Journal of Memory and Language* 36, 276–292.

Clifton, C., Jr., Speer, S., & Abney, S. (1991). Parsing arguments: Phrase structure and argument structure as determinants of initial parsing decisions. *Journal of Memory and Language* 30, 251–271.

Crain, S., Ni, W., Shankweiler, D., Conway, L., & Braze, D. (1996). Meaning, memory and modularity. Proceedings of the NELS 26 Sentence Processing Workshop. *MIT Working Papers in Linguistics* 9, 27–44. Cambridge, MA: MIT, Department of Linguistics and Philosophy.

Crain, S., & Steedman, M. (1985). On not being led up the garden path: The use of context by the psychological parser. In D. Dowty, L. Karttunen, & A. Zwicky (Eds.), *Natural language parsing* (pp. 320–358). Cambridge: Cambridge University Press.

Crocker, M. (1994). On the nature of the principle-based sentence processor. In J. C. Clifton, L. Frazier, & K. Rayner (Eds.), *Perspectives on sentence processing* (pp. 245–266). Hillsdale, NJ: Erlbaum.

Crocker, M. (1996). *Computational psycholinguistics: An interdisciplinary approach to the study of language*. Dordrecht: Kluwer.

DeVincenzi, M. (1991). *Syntactic parsing strategies in Italian*. Dordrecht: Kluwer.

Duffy, S. A. Morris, R. K., & Rayner, K. (1988). Lexical ambiguity and fixation times in reading. *Journal of Memory and Language* 27, 429–446.

Ferreira, F., & Clifton, C., Jr. (1986). The independence of syntactic processing. *Journal of Memory and Language* 25, 348–368.

Ferreira, F., & Henderson, J. (1990). The use of verb information in syntactic parsing: Evidence from eye movements and word-by-word self-paced reading. *Journal of Experimental Psychology: Learning, Memory, and Cognition* 16, 555–568.

Fodor, J. A., Bever, T. G., & Garrett, M. F. (1974). *The psychology of language: An introduction to psycholinguistics and generative grammar.* New York: McGraw-Hill.

Frazier, L. (1979). On comprehending sentences: Syntactic parsing strategies. *Bloomington, IN: Indiana University Linguistics Club.*

Frazier, L. (1987). Sentence processing: A tutorial review. In M. Coltheart (Ed.), *Attention and performance* (pp. 559–586). Hillsdale, NJ: Erlbaum.

Frazier, L. (1990). Exploring the architecture of the language system. In G. Altmann (Ed.), *Cognitive models of speech processing: Psycholinguistic and computational perspectives* (pp. 409–433). Cambridge, MA: MIT Press.

Frazier, L. (1995). Constraint satisfaction as a theory of sentence processing. *Journal of Psycholinguistic Research* 24, 437–468.

Frazier, L., & Clifton, C., Jr. (1996). *Construal.* Cambridge, MA: MIT Press.

Frazier, L., & Rayner, K. (1982). Making and correcting errors during sentence comprehension: Eye movements in the analysis of structurally ambiguous sentences. *Cognitive Psychology* 14, 178–210.

Gibson, E. A. F. (1991). A computational theory of human linguistic processing: Memory limitations and processing breakdown. Unpublished doctoral dissertation, Carnegie Mellon University.

Gibson, E., Schütze, C. T., & Salomon, A. (1996). The relationship between the frequency and the processing complexity of linguistic structure. *Journal of Psycholinguistic Research* 25, 59–92.

Gorrell, P. (1995). *Syntax and parsing.* Cambridge: Cambridge University Press.

Gough, P. B., & Diehl, R. L. (1978). Experimental psycholinguistics. In W. O. Dingwall (Ed.), *A Survey of Linguistic Science, Second Edition* (pp. 247–266). Stamford, CT: Greylock.

Kennison, S. M. (1995). *The role of verb-specific lexical information in syntactic ambiguity resolution.* Unpublished doctoral dissertation, University of Massachusetts, Amherst, MA.

Kimball, J. (1973). Seven principles of surface structure parsing in natural language. *Cognition* 2, 15–47.

Liversedge, S., Paterson, K. B., & Underwood, G. (1997). *Exploring the effects of quantifiers on parsing.* Poster presented at the Tenth Annual CUNY Conference on Human Sentence Processing.

MacDonald, M. C., Pearlmutter, N. J., & Seidenberg, M. S. (1994a). The lexical nature of syntactic ambiguity resolution. *Psychological Review* 101, 676–703.

MacDonald, M. C., Pearlmutter, N. J., & Seidenberg, M. S. (1994b). Syntactic ambiguity resolution as lexical ambiguity resolution. In C. Clifton, Jr., L. Frazier, & K. Rayner (Eds.), *Perspectives on sentence processing* (pp. 123–153). Hillsdale, NJ: Erlbaum.

Marcus, M., Hindle, D., & Fleck, M. (1983). D-theory: Talking about talking about trees. *Proceedings of the Twenty-first Annual Conference of the Association for Computational Linguistics* (pp. 129–136). Somerset, NJ: ACL.

McClelland, J. L., St. John, M., & Taraban, R. (1989). Sentence comprehension: A parallel distributed processing approach. *Language and Cognitive Processes* 4, 287–336.

Merlo, P. (1994). A corpus-based analysis of verb continuation frequencies for syntactic processing. *Journal of Psycholinguistic Research* 23, 435–457.

Mitchell, D. C. (1994). Sentence parsing. In M. A. Gernsbacher (Ed.), *Handbook of psycholinguistics* (pp. 375–410). New York: Academic.

Ni, W., Crain, S., & Shankweiler, D. (1996). Sidestepping garden paths: Assessing the contributions of syntax, semantics and plausibility in resolving ambiguities. *Language and Cognitive Processes* 11, 283–334.

Pearlmutter, N. J., & MacDonald, M. C. (1995). Individual differences and probabilistic constraints in syntactic ambiguity resolution. *Journal of Memory and Language* 34, 521–542.

Perfetti, C. (1990). The cooperative language processors: Semantic influences in an autonomous syntax. In D. A. Balota, G. B. Flores d'Arcais, & K. Rayner (Eds.), *Comprehension processes in reading* (pp. 205–230). Hillsdale, NJ: Erlbaum.

Pickering, M., & Traxler, M. (1998). Plausibility and the recovery from garden paths: An eyetracking study. *Journal of Experimental Psychology: Learning, Memory, and Cognition* 24, 940–961.

Pritchett, B. L. (1988). Garden path phenomena and the grammatical basis of language processing. *Language* 64, 539–576.

Pritchett, B. L. (1992). *Grammatical competence and parsing performance.* Chicago: University of Chicago Press.

Rayner, K., Carlson, M., & Frazier, L. (1983). The interaction of syntax and semantics during sentence processing: Eye movements in the analysis of semantically biased sentences. *Journal of Verbal Learning and verbal Behavior* 22, 358–374.

Rayner, K. and Duffy, S. (1986). Lexical complexity and fixation times in reading: Effects of word frequency, verb complexity, and lexical ambiguity. *Memory & Cognition* 14, 191–201.

Rayner, K., & Frazier, L. (1989). Selection mechanisms in reading lexically ambiguous words. *Journal of Experimental Psychology: Learning, Memory, and Cognition* 15, 779–790.

Rayner, K., & Sereno, S. C. (1994). Eye movements in reading: Psycholinguistic studies. In M. A. Gernsbacher (Ed.), *Handbook of psycholinguistics* (pp. 57–81). San Diego: Academic.

Rayner, K., Sereno, S., Morris, R., Schmauder, R., & Clifton, C., Jr. (1989). Eye movements and on-line language comprehension processes. *Language and Cognitive Processes* 4, 21–50.

Reichle, E. D., Pollatsek, A., & Rayner, K. (1998). Toward a model of eye movement control in reading. *Psychological Review* 105, 125–156.

Speer, S., & Clifton, C., Jr. (1998). Plausibility and argument structure in sentence comprehension. *Memory and Cognition* 26, 965–979.

Steedman, M., J., & Altmann, G. T. M. (1989). Ambiguity in context: A reply. *Language and Cognitive Processes* 4, 77–105.

Stowe, L. (1989). Thematic structures and sentence comprehension. In G. N. Carlson & M. K. Tanenhaus (Eds.), Linguistic structure in language processing (pp. 319–358). Dordrecht: Kluwer.

Sturt, P., & Crocker, M. (1996). Monotonic syntactic processing: A cross-linguistic study of attachment and reanalysis. *Language and Cognitive Processes* 11, 449–494.

Tanenhaus, M. K., Boland, J. E., Mauner, G., & Carlson, G. N. (1993). More on combinatory lexical information: Thematic structure in parsing and interpretation. In G. Altmann & R. Shillcock (Eds.), *Cognitive models of speech processing: The second Sperlonga meeting* (pp. 297–319). Hillsdale, NJ: Erlbaum.

Tanenhaus, M. K., Spivey-Knowlton, M. J., Eberhard, K. M., & Sedivy, J. C. (1995). Integration of visual and linguistic information in spoken language comprehension. *Science* 268, 1632–1634.

Tanenhaus, M. K., & Trueswell, J. C. (1995). Sentence comprehension. In J. Miller & P. Eimas (Eds.), *Handbook of perception and cognition: Speech, language, and communication, Second Edition* (Vol. 11, pp. 217–262). San Diego: Academic.

Traxler, M., Pickering, M., & Clifton, C., Jr. (1998). Adjunct attachment is not a form of lexical ambiguity resolution. *Journal of Memory and Language* 39, 558–592.

Trueswell, J. C., & Tanenhaus, M. K. (1994). Toward a lexicalist framework of constraint-based syntactic ambiguity resolution. In C. Clifton, K. Rayner, & L. Frazier (Eds.), *Perspectives on sentence processing* (pp. 155–179). Hillsdale, NJ: Erlbaum.

Trueswell, J. C., Tanenhaus, M. K., & Kello, C. (1993). Verb-specific constraints in sentence processing: Separating effects of lexical preference from garden-paths. *Journal of Experimental Psychology: Learning, Memory, and Cognition* 19, 528–553.

3
Specifying Architectures for Language Processing: Process, Control, and Memory in Parsing and Interpretation

RICHARD L. LEWIS

3.1 Introduction

An important goal in psycholinguistics is uncovering the architecture of human sentence comprehension. Most of the important issues in the field of sentence processing are questions about some aspect of the underlying architecture – for example, the relation of grammar and parser (Chomsky, 1965, 1980; Miller, 1962; Stabler, 1991), the modularity of syntactic processing (Ferreira & Clifton, 1986; Fodor, 1983; Forster, 1979; Frazier & Clifton, 1996; Just & Carpenter, 1992; Mitchell et al., 1992; Rayner et al., 1992), the number of interpretations pursued in parallel (Clark & Clark, 1977; Gibson, 1991; Gorrell, 1987; Kurtzman, 1985; MacKay, 1966), or the relation of linguistic processing to central cognition (Forster, 1979). The first goal of this chapter is to define precisely what it means to have a functionally complete sentence-processing architecture. The view of architecture developed here draws on general work on architecture in cognitive science (Anderson, 1983; Newell, 1973, 1980a, 1990; Newell & Simon, 1972; Pylyshyn, 1984), rather than focusing exclusively on the issue of modularity that has dominated discussions in sentence processing. This architectural analysis defines a set of functional constraints on theories, sharpens the set of questions that need to be answered, and reveals that some common theoretical approaches, including modularity, are incomplete in significant ways. The claim is that theories of human sentence processing should take the form of complete computational architectures.

A useful approach for discerning the shape of the human architecture is to look for extreme behavioral data points – phenomena that help sharply define both the impressive functional capacities of human comprehension as well as its limits. Taken together, these capacities and limitations comprise a bundle of behavioral oppositions; some of the major ones are summarized in Figure 3.1.

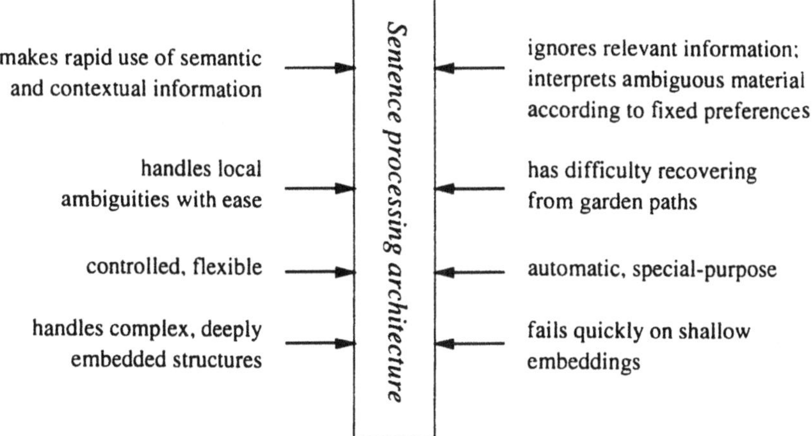

Figure 3.1. Human sentence comprehension can be characterized as a set of behavioral oppositions. These oppositions serve as useful empirical constraints by pushing on architectural models from opposite poles of capabilities and limitations. Section 3.2 describes the phenomena underlying these oppositions.

The second goal of this chapter is to bring to bear these functional and empirical constraints in proposing an architectural theory that embodies a simple set of claims about the processes, memories, and control structure underlying parsing and interpretation. The theory, NL-Soar, posits that human sentence processing is single-path with a limited repair capability, has an automatic but flexible control structure that is open to effects of learning, and depends on a minimal short-term memory that gives rise to syntactic interference effects. The theory explains the behavioral puzzles in Figure 3.1. It explains why sentence processing can appear to ignore relevant information as it pushes down the garden path, yet at times be sensitive to semantic and pragmatic context. It explains why some misinterpretations are difficult to recover from, yet others are imperceptibly easy to correct. It further explains how automatic processes can be redeployed in a controlled manner to recover from these difficult misinterpretations. Finally, it explains why human comprehension easily handles complex syntactic structures most of the time, yet fails miserably when pushed beyond certain very modest limits. Many of the novel aspects of the theory derive in part from the model's grounding in an independent theory of human cognitive architecture, Soar (Lehman et al., 1998; Newell, 1990, 1992).

The remainder of the chapter is organized as follows: Section 3.2 provides a brief overview of the empirical constraints outlined in Figure 3.1. Section 3.3 describes a set of functional constraints by answering the question: What constitutes a theory of sentence-processing architecture? Section 3.4 presents a specific architectural theory that responds to the functional and empirical constraints. Section 3.5 describes some of the empirical implications, and Section 3.6 concludes with a summary discussion and some remarks on the general approach.

3.2 Opposing Behavioral Constraints on Architecture

The first behavioral opposition in Figure 3.1 concerns the nature of ambiguity resolution: What guides the online interpretation of ambiguous material? A single example will serve to illustrate the major issues:

(1) The car *examined* by the mechanic was damaged.

Examined may be initially taken as the main verb, or as a reduced relative clause modifying *car*. The inanimacy of *car* makes it more likely that someone was examining the car (relative clause reading) than that the car was examining something (main verb reading). The question is whether such semantic information can be used online to guide the human parser down the right path. Ferreira and Clifton (1986) presented reading-time data that suggests that people ignore such nonsyntactic information. On the other hand, Trueswell et al. (1994) and Just and Carpenter (1992) present online studies suggesting that subjects can make rapid use of such semantic information in resolving the local ambiguity – they prefer the relative clause reading over the main verb reading, at least when the semantic constraints are sufficiently biased against the main verb interpretation.

There is by now a large body of empirical work on both sides of the issue, some work showing that semantic or contextual information is ignored in first-pass reading, and some showing clear effects. The studies cover a range of information types and ambiguity types. Many theoretical approaches now acknowledge the need to accommodate, at some level, both kinds of effects – attributing the difference to differences in lexical/syntactic frequency, for example (MacDonald et al., 1994; Trueswell et al., 1994). But the data is perhaps more insidious than is often acknowledged. Just and Carpenter (1992) provided evidence for individual differences in use of semantic information. In other words, some subjects appeared modular, and some did not (on material adapted from the Ferreira & Clifton, 1986, study). The implication for an architectural theory should be clear. Any architectural model must embody this opposition: it must be capable in principle of demonstrating both kinds of effects, and furthermore should identify the locus of variation that accounts for the individual differences (Just and Carpenter attribute them to working memory differences).

The remaining three oppositions in Figure 3.1 have received considerably less attention than the first. The second opposition concerns the other half of the ambiguity resolution story: How do people revise their interpretations of ambiguous material based on later disambiguating information? An important source of data that can be used to reveal the nature of revision processes concerns the contrast between ambiguous structures that can give rise to noticeable garden-path effects, such as the subject/object ambiguity in (2) (Frazier & Rayner, 1982), and those ambiguous structures that cause little or no perceptible difficulty, such as the subject/object ambiguity in (3) (Juliano & Tanenhaus, 1994; Mitchell, 1987; Pritchett, 1988):

(2) Although Mary forgot her husband didn't seem very upset yesterday.

(3) a. Mary forgot her husband at the airport yesterday.
    b. Mary forgot her husband needed a ride yesterday.

The structure in (2) can give rise to an impression of ungrammaticality, indicating a failure of reanalysis. The structure in (3) may produce longer reading times in the disambiguating region (e.g., an extra 50 ms on *needed* compared to unambiguous structures with overt complementizers (Ferreira & Henderson, 1990)), but does not usually cause noticeable difficulty, regardless of which interpretation is required. Why does reanalysis fail in structures such as (2) and succeed in structures such as (3)? A theory of reanalysis is required to explain the contrasts (Frazier & Rayner, 1982) – ambiguity resolution principles alone are insufficient.

The third opposition pits the apparent automaticity of parsing and interpretation against the capacity for more controlled, flexible comprehension. As Fodor et al. (1975) noted, the "overwhelmingly puzzling aspect of sentence comprehension is how people manage to do it so quickly." This impressive rapidity combined with the complexity of the task, the modular effects cited earlier, and certain other theoretical considerations have led many to posit automatic, informationally encapsulated processes underlying parsing and interpretation (Laberge & Samuels, 1974; Fodor, 1983; Frazier, 1978; Forster, 1979).

But the fact is that people do recover from garden-path effects, such as those just discussed, by some strategy of rereading, or more careful comprehension. Eye-tracking studies also reveal frequent and highly selective regressions during reading, to reparse or reconsider some part of the passage (Frazier & Rayner, 1982). Somehow, the automatic processes that initially delivered the wrong output must be overridden or redirected in some way. Furthermore, subjects are able to adopt quite different strategies for comprehension, ranging from extremely rapid surface skimming to directed comprehension in the service of specific problem-solving goals (Just & Carpenter, 1987). How can we reconcile this flexibility in comprehension with automaticity? Frazier (1990) discussed a form of this problem with respect to reanalysis and pointed out that simply assuming that post–first pass reanalysis is something accomplished by the "central processor" leads to some undesirable consequences, including the duplication of processes and knowledge in the modular linguistic processor and the central processor. In short, we cannot leave unexplicated the relation between automatic linguistic processes and more controlled central processes (Forster, 1979).

The fourth opposition concerns the contrast between easily parsed, complex embedded structures and relatively simple embeddings that cause complete breakdown. Consider the structure in (4), which contains four embedded clauses:

(4) The bird chased the mouse that scared the cat that saw the dog that ate the pumpkin that grew in the garden.

Such right-branching structures can be embedded essentially without limit. But one of the first clearly identified psycholinguistic phenomena was difficulty on center-embedded structures, which can cause severe problems at just two embeddings (Miller & Chomsky, 1963; Miller & Isard, 1964).

(5) The salmon that the man that the dog chased smoked fell.

The story is considerably more complex than this (Cowper, 1976; Gibson, 1991; Lewis, 1997). For example, double center-embeddings are not always unacceptable (which rules out a simple appeal to ungrammaticality). Consider the following subject sentence construction (Cowper, 1976):

(6) That the food that John ordered tasted good pleased him.

In (6), two sentences (*the food tasted good, John ordered*) are center-embedded within the matrix clause (*That . . . pleased him*) These effects are not due to ambiguity – they appear to be problems with a limited short-term memory (Miller & Isard, 1964). Thus, an architectural theory must specify the memory structure underlying parsing that accounts for acceptable embeddings, including acceptable center-embeddings, as well as unacceptably difficult structures.

3.3 What Is a Sentence Processing Architecture?

Before considering issues in specifying architectures for sentence processing, it is important to understand what a computational architecture is generally. The idea of an architecture was imported into cognitive psychology from computer science (Bell & Newell, 1971; Newell, 1973, 1990; Pylyshyn, 1984), and computer architectures provide a useful starting point for our purposes.

3.3.1 Functional Invariants: Process, Memory, and Control

In computer systems, the architecture of a computer refers to the fixed hardware structure that supports computation. The fixed structure of any digital computer – whether PC, mainframe, parallel or single-processor – can be described in terms of functional units that store and process bit vectors. The description is cast in a register-transfer language (e.g., Bell & Newell, 1971). Expressions in such a language are composed of registers (bit vectors), operations on registers, and control signals for triggering operations. For example, the expression in Figure 3.2 says that when bit P is set, then the result of adding register A and B is transferred to register A. The lefthand part of the expression is like a conditional statement that indicates when the operation should take place. A set of such expressions can provide a complete functional specification of the architecture of a computer, which can then be implemented as a collection of logic circuits.

There are three important functional invariants that hold across all computational architectures and implementations. The hypothesis is that these invariants hold not only of digital computers, but of any natural, artificial, or theoretical

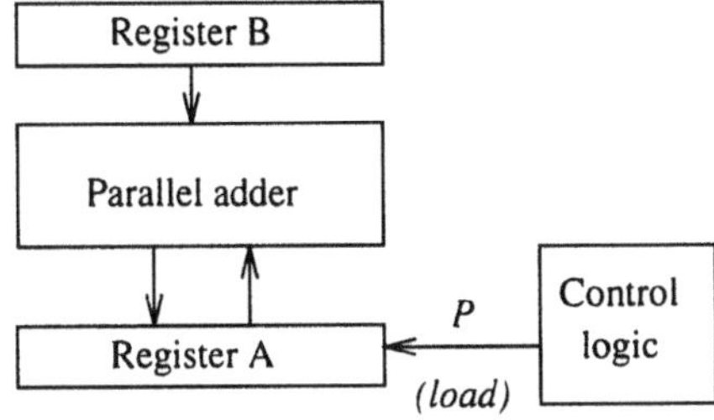

$$P : A \leftarrow A + B$$

Figure 3.2. Part of a register transfer description of a digital computer. Expressions in the register transfer language consist of primitive processes on some registers (memories), preceded by a control prefix indicating what triggers the given processes. The block diagram indicates the functional logic units for implementing the given expression, which adds registers A and B and transfers the result to A whenever control bit P is set.

device that performs computations, including classic symbolic architectures, connectionist networks, and brains.

> All computational architectures must support, minimally, the following functions: (1) a set of processing primitives; (2) a memory; and (3) a control structure, which specifies how the computational processes unfold over time.

Support for these functional invariants comes both from empirical practice in computer science and from theoretical analysis. All physically constructed computational devices embody these minimal functions, as do all theoretical models (e.g., Turing machines, Post productions, RAMs; Minsky, 1967) developed for investigating computability. Newell (1980a) also emphasized this tripartite functional division in his description of physical symbol systems, which are general computational architectures.

Each of these functions can be seen clearly in the register-transfer description of computer architectures. The processing primitives consist of the loads, adds, shifts, and so on that provide the building blocks for composing more complex operations. The memory at the register-transfer level consists of registers which store bit vectors, or banks of registers operating together as larger units addressed by position (i.e., RAMs). The control structure is specified by the set of control prefixes for each expression, which dictate exactly when each primitive process occurs. Any number of such processes may occur simultaneously; at the register-transfer level, parallelism is the norm for digital computers.

Another important property of the register-transfer functional description is that it abstracts away from the particular set of logical circuits chosen to implement the architecture (e.g., how the AND/OR gates are arranged), which in turn abstracts away from properties of the electrical circuits (e.g., their voltage and resistance properties). In general, physical computational systems can be described as a hierarchy of systems levels. Each level is a functional description that abstracts away from implementation details of the lower levels.

Computers also illustrate another important principle: All computational architectures distinguish fixed structure from variable content, and system behavior depends on both. We can capture this in the following slogan equation:

$$\text{Architecture (fixed structure)} + \text{content (variable)} \Longrightarrow \text{behavior}^{1}$$

[1] In a programmable architecture, the variable content includes the program, which is the primary determinant of behavior. Not all architectures are programmable, but all architectures process variable content.

Newell (1990) points out that for many systems, including natural cognitive architectures, we should speak of relatively fixed structure to allow for architectures that change or develop (perhaps slowly) over time.

What is the relevance of all this for psycholinguistics? If we take sentence processing to be an information-processing task, that is, one requiring computation, then we can assume that underlying this computation is some kind of fixed architecture that realizes the three basic functions enumerated earlier. Furthermore, we can assume that this architecture can and should be described at multiple levels, each involving a different technology. This in no way asserts that the architecture of human sentence comprehension will be anything like a digital computer or a Turing machine. Discerning the right shape of the functional architecture is the task of empirical psycholinguistics:

> An architecture for sentence processing is the fixed computational structure that supports comprehension – the control structures, memories, and primitive processes for parsing and interpretation.

Such a definition may seem to be too general to have any import for theory development, but this is not the case. The following sections describe in detail the implications of this definition for models of human sentence processing.

3.3.2 "Module Geography": Why Modules Are Not Enough

It is worthwhile to compare the view of sentence processing architecture just described with the view that has dominated psycholinguistics since the late 1970s. The dominant view holds that uncovering the architecture of sentence processing means identifying the independent processing modules that comprise comprehension. But the definition of architecture above gives no special mention of modules. The reason is simple: there is no a priori functional requirement for separate processing modules, as there is for the functions of memory, process, and control. The decomposition of architecture into modules is perfectly compatible with this view of architecture, but not required by it. Modularity is certainly an important empirical issue (see, for example, the references cited earlier) but it is not the only one.

In fact, just laying out a set of processing modules and their connections – what J. D. Fodor (1990) dubbed module geography – does not specify a functionally complete computational architecture. Perhaps most significantly, it does not specify any structure at all for the memories used in processing. For example, it specifies neither the short-term memory for partial structures nor the long-term memory of syntactic or lexical knowledge. It also does not specify the primitive processes that the modules use. It does not specify control of processing within the modules. Finally, it does not specify the relation of the control of central processing to the control of the modular processes. To be clear: the theoretical claims that modular theories make are important ones which often yield testable predictions. But they are a necessary, not sufficient, part of the characterization of sentence processing architecture.

Abstracting away from irrelevant details is a theoretical virtue, but the kinds of abstractions that module geography makes can lead to incorrect inferences from data. That such a possibility exists is clearly demonstrated by the working-memory research of Just and Carpenter (1992). Briefly, Just and Carpenter have argued that some garden-path effects that were previously interpreted in terms of a syntactically encapsulated module can instead be explained by individual differences in working-memory capacity. Such an explanation is not considered in a theoretical framework that systematically ignores the role of memory structures in parsing. This point should be taken regardless of whether one is convinced by the current body of empirical support for this particular model – the fact remains that such an explanation could in principle account for the data, and that these alternative explanations are only discovered by developing functionally complete architectures. The next few sections describe what it means to specify such an architecture.

3.3.3 Specifying Processes

We can characterize processes in two important ways. First, processes can be described by the way they change the content of memory; for example, by making syntactically legal attachments in a parse tree held in short-term memory. Second, the chronometric properties of process can be specified: how much time they require, and how their duration varies as a function of other variables. All of these specifications can be made at varying degrees of abstraction and approximation.

Many of the most fundamental distinctions about parsing made in psycholinguistics can be interpreted as theories about the available syntactic processes. These include bottom-up and top-down parsing (Chomsky & Miller, 1963; Kimball, 1973), head-driven (Pritchett, 1988), left-corner (Aho & Ullman, 1972; Johnson-Laird, 1983), licensing (Abney, 1989), and other mixed strategies. For example, a strong commitment to head-driven parsing implies an architectural set of processes that includes projection from lexical heads and attachment to existing nodes, but excludes predictive processes that create new syntactic nodes whose lexical heads have not yet arrived.

Single-path versus multi-path parsing is another important distinction in parsing processes and representations. However, it should not be confused with parallel versus serial processing. Whether processes occur in serial or in parallel is a control issue, not a distinction for processes per se. On the other hand, whether a parser pursues a single interpretation or multiple interpretations in parallel is a process and representation issue, not a control issue. The reason is that multi-path parsing requires a different set of processes and representations – it's not just single-path parsing run in parallel. At each local ambiguity or choice point, multi-path parsing requires one of two things to happen. Either a new copy (or copies) is made of the current structure, so that the two (or more) paths can proceed in parallel, or else the parser updates some sophisticated representation, like a chart (Earley, 1970), which permits existing structure to be used in multiple ways without copying. Both cases require additional processes and representations beyond that required by single-path parsing.

A complete architecture for sentence comprehension must support not only syntactic structuring, but also semantic interpretation, referential processing, and reanalysis as well. For example, it is a brute fact about natural language that any sentence processor must sometimes revise its interpretation of ambiguous material in the face of incoming disambiguating information. Lewis (1998) distinguishes four ways of realizing reanalysis functions: (1) backtracking (overt and covert) to prior decision points, (2) selection (and disposal) from parallel alternatives, (3) monotonic refinement of abstract commitments, and (4) repair of existing structures. The choice of reanalysis process depends on the processes assumed for initial structure building. For example, a single-path parser requires either a backtracking or repair solution.

Finally, specifying the time course of processes is important for relating the architectural theory to data on human sentence processing. Despite the widespread use of sophisticated chronometric techniques, most psycholinguistic theories say nothing quantitative about the time course of processing, seldom venturing beyond qualitative claims such as "revision takes time". The READER model of Thibadeau, Just, and Carpenter (1982) was an exception, though the model was only used to parametrically fit existing reading-time data, not generate new predictions.

3.3.4 Specifying Memories

Sentence comprehension requires a short-term working memory (STM) to hold the partial products of comprehension, and a longer-term memory (LTM) to hold lexical and grammatical knowledge or skill. We can characterize the architecture of memory in three important ways: (1) identifying different kinds of memory systems and their unique coding schemes or memory units, (2) specifying the nature of the acquisition and retrieval processes, and (3) specifying how memory is limited in its capacity to carry out its required functions.

Perhaps the most fundamental architectural question about memory in sentence processing is: How many kinds are there, and what does "kind" mean? Different memories may have different characteristic decay rates, coding schemes, refresh processes, and acquisition and retrieval processes. We have already assumed at least a functional division between STM and LTM, but many other divisions have been proposed as well. For example, within working memory, there is evidence for independent phonological (Baddeley, 1990), visual (Logie et al., 1990), and semantic (Potter, 1993) short-term stores. There are also behavioral and neuropsychological double dissociations between phonological (classic verbal) working memory and syntactic working memory, providing strong evidence for some kind of architectural independence (Larkin & Burns, 1977; Lewis, 1996; Martin, 1993; Potter, 1982). In a complex task such as language comprehension, all of these memories will interact to carry out the task.

Content-specific memories can be posited for LTM as well, but other distinctions are possible. In particular, the cognitive and neuropsychological memory literature has identified a set of distinct classes of LTM that include declarative versus procedural (Anderson, 1993), implicit versus explicit (Graf & Schacter, 1985), and semantic versus episodic memory (Tulving, 1983). It is not clear if all of these memory types will be relevant to explaining sentence processing, but their consideration at least raises some interesting issues, such as the relative contributions of procedural and declarative memory in parsing, and the extent to which parsing may be viewed as a cognitive skill governed by such general principles as the power law of learning (Newell & Rosenbloom, 1981), encoding specificity (Tulving, 1983), or statistical rule tuning (Anderson, 1993; Mitchell et al., 1995).

3.3.5 Specifying Control Structure

Specifying an architecture for comprehension requires specifying how the computational processes unfold over time – identifying the control structure. The control structure has implications for many important issues in sentence processing, including ambiguity resolution, automaticity, serial versus parallel processing, and the relation of parsing and interpretation to central cognition. Indeed, one could argue that it is the control structure that gives an architecture its distinctive shape.

There are five key issues in specifying control structure: (1) specifying how processes are initiated, (2) specifying how processes communicate information to other processes, (3) specifying what parts of the control are fixed and what parts depend on variable content, (4) identifying multiple streams of control, and (5) specifying the relation of the control of comprehension processes to the control structure of central cognition.

The latter issue is particularly relevant to sentence processing and concerns of modularity. The control of central processes is typically characterized as serial, not automatic, and open to any kind of variable content (Newell & Simon, 1972; Fodor, 1983), in sharp contrast to comprehension processes which are often characterized as automatic, parallel, depending on fixed and limited information pathways, and with a control flow independent of central cognition – that is, modular.

If one accepts this characterization of sentence processing control structure, at least to some degree, there are still a number of important questions remaining, such as: How can these automatic processes be deployed under the deliberate control of central cognition, and at what grain size? The answer to these questions must be architectural, in particular, a specification of the connections between the control structure of sentence processing and the control structure of cognition.

3.3.6 Summary: Some Overlooked Issues in Architecture

Architectural theories must specify processes, memories, and control structure to be functionally complete. This view of architecture has led us to identify some issues that are often overlooked in sentence processing theories:

- Many theories, in particular modular theories, are incomplete because they do not specify the nature of the memories used in parsing and interpretation.
- Most theories do not specify explicit processes for reanalysis in the face of disambiguating information.
- Most theories make little contact with general principles of human memory and skill (with statistical rule-tuning and frequency-based accounts being notable exceptions).
- Most theories of the control of parsing and interpretation processes do not specify how automatic and controlled processes interact, or how automatic processes can be deployed under deliberate control (e.g., in service of deliberate reanalysis).

3.4 NL-Soar: An Architectural Theory Based on Soar

This section describes an architecture for sentence processing that makes a set of specific claims about processes, memories, and control structure. The following section explores a few of the empirical implications of this architecture. In many ways, the model focuses on traditional concerns in parsing: ambiguity resolution and garden-path effects. But in other ways, it is an attempt to push in new directions to address the concerns of theoretical incompleteness raised in the last section.

The approach is to reduce the degrees of freedom in building the model by adopting as a starting point the assumptions of an existing theory of human cognitive architecture, Soar (Newell, 1990). Soar is not merely an implementation language for the computational model, but plays a fundamental theoretical role and accounts for many of the model's novel features and predictions. To the extent that we can derive principles of language processing from more general principles of cognition, we can increase the explanatory power of the theory.

3.4.1 Brief Overview of Soar

What does it mean for NL-Soar to be based on Soar? It means that NL-Soar specifies how the functional requirements of comprehension are computationally realized within the architectural mechanisms of Soar. The NL-Soar theory takes these mechanisms as given – theoretical hypotheses independently motivated by other functional and empirical considerations.

The key features of Soar can be summarized as follows. All cognitive activity occurs in problem spaces (Newell, 1980b; Newell & Simon, 1972), where operators are applied to states to make progress toward a goal. The current problem space context is represented in a short-term working memory. All knowledge that guides behavior (e.g., search control) is held in a long-term recognition memory. This memory consists of a set of condition-action associations (productions), which continually match in parallel against the working memory.

Soar's control structure is open and flexible. The flow of control is not fixed in advance, but is a function of whatever knowledge can be assembled at the time of the decision. The control structure is realized by an elaborate-decide cycle. In the elaboration phase, all associations whose condition patterns match the current working memory fire, retrieving knowledge about the current situation. These associations may propose new operators or problem spaces, apply operators (changing the state), or declare preferences about the relative desirability of operators and spaces. Associations fire automatically in parallel, or in sequence if there are inherent data dependencies. Next, a fixed decision phase interprets the retrieved preferences to determine the next step in the problem space – for example, deciding to apply one operator rather than another, or to change problem spaces.

Sometimes the immediate knowledge retrieved from the recognition memory is incomplete or inconsistent in some way, and no more progress can be made. Then Soar has reached an impasse. For example, Soar might reach an impasse if three operators are proposed but no immediate knowledge is available to select which one to apply next. Soar responds to an impasse by automatically generating a subgoal to acquire the missing knowledge in other problem spaces. The behavior in the subproblem spaces is guided in exactly the same manner as all behavior – by associations in long-term memory.

As knowledge is acquired from impasse-triggered problem solving, Soar's experiential learning mechanism, chunking, builds new associations in long-term memory which capture the results of the subgoal. The next time Soar encounters a similar situation, the new associations should allow it to recognize immediately what to do, avoiding the impasse. Soar is therefore an experience-based learner, continually making the shift from deliberation to recognition.

In terms of our previous account of architecture, Soar is clearly a complete functional architecture: it specifies processes (production firings to change working memory, the learning mechanism to add to long-term memory), memories (the declarative working memory, the associational production memory), and control structure (the automatic, parallel production match, and the serial, controlled decision cycle).

3.4.2 Primitive and Composed Processes for Parsing and Interpretation

Table 3.1 summarizes the NL-Soar theory. Since all cognitive activity in Soar takes place by applying operators in problem spaces, comprehension in NL-Soar is accomplished by a set of comprehension operators that apply to the

Table 3.1. *Basic characteristics of the NL-Soar theory.*

1. Comprehension is realized by rapid cognitive operators (~50 ms) that incrementally build representations in working memory of syntax, meaning, and reference. (Process)
2. Comprehension is single path, with a cue-driven repair process that corrects (some) misinterpretations. (Process)
3. Working memory for syntax is a functionally minimal and efficient structure for discriminating syntactic nodes. (Memory)
4. Control of comprehension is a mix of controlled serial and automatic parallel processes. The serial control is potentially a function of any knowledge, and open to modulation by learning. (Control)

Note: NL-Soar is the result of applying the Soar architecture to the task of efficiently comprehending language in real time, with a minimal set of functional mechanisms.

incoming linguistic input. The operators incrementally build two representations in working memory: a parse tree representing the syntactic structure of the input, and a situation model (Johnson-Laird, 1983; Kintsch et al., 1990), representing the semantic and referential content of the utterance. There are three major classes of comprehension operators, corresponding to the major functions of parsing, semantic interpretation, and reference resolution.

A single comprehension operator may be composed of several primitive construction processes realized by individual association firings. For example, there might be a specific operator for creating an NP and attaching it as an object of a preposition. This operator would be realized by a ripple of association firings, each corresponding to some primitive process of projection of syntactic nodes from lexical heads, or linking two nodes via an X-bar (Chomsky, 1981) structural relation. The set of comprehension operators is not fixed in advance, nor is it specified explicitly by the NL-Soar theory. Rather, the theory posits that the set of operators is acquired as a function of linguistic experience. Other comprehension operators are composed in a similar way. For example, semantic interpretation operators are composed from a primitive set of situation model constructors (see Lewis, 1993, for details).

3.4.3 Reanalysis by Limited Cue-Driven Repair

Soar adopts the single-state assumption: only one state per problem space is accessible in working memory at any given time. There is no architectural support for maintaining prior states in service of backtracking (Newell, 1990). Since each state in NL-Soar contains a representation corresponding to a particular interpretation, NL-Soar is a single-path comprehender. The critical functional question that this gives rise to is: What happens when the incoming input is inconsistent with the structure chosen for some locally ambiguous material?

Because previous states are not readily available, the correct interpretation must be recovered by either deliberately recomprehending the input, or by repairing the existing structures in working memory. NL-Soar posits that there exists such an online repair process which is constrained to ensure both limited match expense and limited problem space search. (Later we will also consider deliberate reprocessing of the input as a method of recovery.)

The minimal amount of new mechanism required to effect an on-line repair of syntactic structure is an operator that breaks an existing structural relation. We call this operator snip (Lewis, 1992; Lehman et al., 1991). In fact, snip does not complete the repair, it just destroys a bit of structure and then lets other link operators take over to finish the job. As an example of how snip works, consider what happens with the subject/object ambiguity in (7).

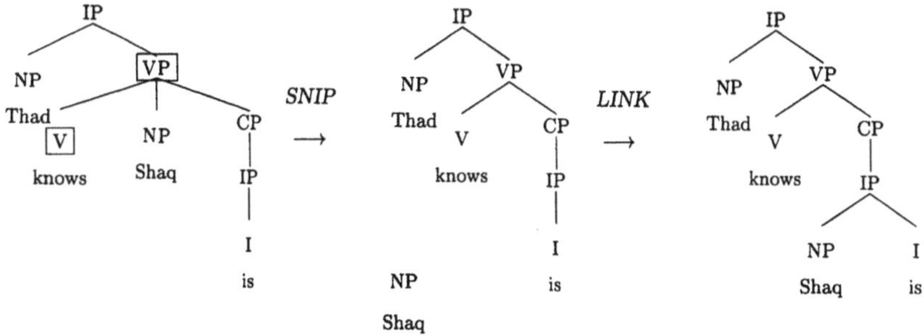

Figure 3.3. An example of simple cue-driven, destructive repair with the snip operator. The incoming CP competes for the same complement position as *Shaq*, triggering a snip to detach *Shaq*. Next, *Shaq* is attached as the subject of the incoming clause. The boxed nodes identify the locality of the inconsistency, which delimits the generation of snip operators.

(7) Thad knows Shaq is tall.

Shaq is initially attached in the complement position of *knows*. When *is* arrives, it is projected to the sentential complement node CP.[2] Next, a link is proposed to attach the CP in the complement position of *knows*. This proposal is made because *knows* can take sentential complements as well as nominals.

Figure 3.3 shows what happens next. The result is a momentary superposition of two separate interpretations, with two nodes competing for the same structural position (COMP-V′ of *knows*). This inconsistency triggers a local snip operator, which breaks the link between [$_{V'}$ knows] and [$_{NP}$ Shaq]. Next, [$_{NP}$ Shaq] is attached in subject position (SPEC-IP), and the repair is complete.

The initial attachment of the sentential complement was attempted despite the fact that another constituent was already occupying the complement position. This is the only way in which the attachment operators are nonstandard: they relax the constraint on uniqueness of complements and specifiers. Fodor and Inoue (1994) adopted a similar strategy, which they dubbed "attach anyway." The critical thing to note is that the constraints on the final output have not been relaxed. Only the set of processes and intermediate states that finally lead to the well-formed representation have changed.

The generation of snip is highly constrained. Snip is proposed only for structural relations that are local to a detected inconsistency (where 'local' is defined precisely as the maximal projection). The boxed nodes in Figure 3.3 identify the locality of the inconsistency. This is a cue-driven theory of repair, because the mechanism relies on simple, local structural cues that something has gone

[2] CPs are projected even in the absence of overt complementizers, following Pritchett (1992).

wrong with the parse. There are good computational reasons for such a tightly constrained repair. A free generation of snip for every link in the parse tree has two undesirable consequences. First, it leads directly to a potentially large, undiscriminated set of operators in working memory. Such sets are a source of exponential match cost in the recognition memory (Tambe et al., 1990). Second, even for moderately-sized syntactic structures, the introduction of freely generated snips increases the problem search space significantly. We can summarize the snip theory as follows:

> Automatic reanalysis is realized by a limited, cue-driven repair process. Repair works by locally and destructively modifying the given syntactic structure in working memory when an inconsistency arises, and then reassembling the pieces with the normal constructive parsing operators.

Section 3.5.1 explores the implications of limited repair for strong and weak garden-path effects.

3.4.4 Interference in Short-Term Memory

NL-Soar's working memory is shaped by two concerns: meeting the minimal functional requirements of parsing natural language, and keeping the processing efficient. These concerns lead naturally to a simple interference theory of short-term memory.

Partial constituents are indexed in working memory by the structural relations that they may enter into with other constituents. The relations correspond to X-bar structural positions (complement of preposition, specifier of NP, etc; though another ontology of relations could be adopted). Consider the prepositional phrase *with the dog*. We say that [$_{P'}$ with] assigns the COMP-P′ (complement of preposition) relation, and [$_{NP}$ the dog] receives or fills the COMP-P′ relation.

The representation in working memory is called the H/D set, for Heads and Dependents. The Heads part of the H/D set indexes nodes by the structural relations they may assign. The Dependents part of the H/D set indexes nodes by the structural relations they may receive. The H/D set in (8) corresponds to the situation in parsing *with the dog* after the [$_{NP}$ the dog] has been formed, but before creating the complete PP:

(8)	Heads	COMP-P′:	[$_{P'}$ with]
	Dependents	ADJOIN-N′:	[$_{PP}$ with]
		COMP-P′:	[$_{NP}$ the dog]
		COMP-V′:	[$_{NP}$ the dog]

Parsing is a bottom-up process of matching potential heads with potential dependents. For example, in (8), [$_{P'}$ with] and [$_{NP}$ the dog] may be joined by the structural relation COMP-P′, since [$_{NP}$ the dog] is indexed under COMP-P′ in the Dependents set, and [$_{P'}$ with] is indexed under COMP-P′ in the Heads set.

How should the representation be limited to ensure efficient processing? As mentioned earlier, independent theoretical and empirical work on the computational complexity of the recognition match (Tambe et al., 1990) has identified open, undiscriminated sets in working memory as the most significant source of match expense. An undiscriminated set is simply a set of elements in working memory indexed by a single relation or attribute. With such open sets, the recognition match becomes exponentially expensive and therefore psychologically and computationally implausible as the basis for efficient memory retrieval.

Large, undiscriminated sets may be created when multiple constituents are indexed by a single syntactic relation. For example, consider the right-branching structure in (9):

(9) Amparo thinks that Seth believes that John knows . . .

Such right-branching can lead to a unbounded set of nodes indexed by a single relation (in this case the complement of verb relation on the Heads set):

(10)

Heads	COMP-V′: [$_{V'}$ thinks], [$_{V'}$ believes], [$_{V'}$ knows] . . .

We can eliminate such open sets by limiting each relation to a small fixed number of nodes. But how many? To be able to at least parse basic sentential complements such as *I think that John likes Mary*, two nodes per relation are required. This is the minimum capacity required to realize the fundamental capability of natural language to compose new propositions from existing ones (Lewis, 1997). The NL-Soar theory makes the strong assumption that this minimal functionality characterizes the capacity of human syntactic short-term memory:

> Each syntactic relation in working memory indexes at most two nodes, the minimum required to achieve propositional composition. This limitation yields a similarity-based interference theory of syntactic STM.

Later, we will see precisely how the interference effects arise as a function of the structural similarity of working memory contents.

3.4.5 Control: Automatic but Flexible

What is the control structure of comprehension? As we saw in the earlier architectural analysis, this question is at the heart of many debates in sentence processing. NL-Soar provides a well-defined answer: the control structure of comprehension is the flexible control structure of Soar. This has several immediate implications. There is a mix of parallel and serial processes. The parallel firing of productions is automatic, and the control of the serial operators is open to modulation by multiple knowledge sources. There are no fixed architectural barriers to the kind of knowledge that may be brought to bear in selecting what path to pursue. Furthermore, the control knowledge is open to continuous modification by chunking. Any linguistic decision point can potentially be modified if new associations are learned and brought to bear at the appropriate time.

Because chunking is a general learning mechanism that operates over multiple impasse types, each aspect of comprehension is open to learning and improvement. New comprehension operators are learned by acquiring new associations that generate (propose) and apply (implement) the operators. The model can also learn new search control associations to guide parsing or semantic interpretation. The process of reference resolution results in associations that constitute a recognition memory of the content of a discourse (Lewis, 1993). Together, this growing collection of proposal, application, and control associations for syntactic, semantic, and referential operators constitutes the automatized comprehension skill. To summarize the control theory:

> Control of comprehension is two-layered, with a mix of serial and parallel processes. The parallel firing of primitive associations is automatic and uncontrolled; the serial selection of composed operators is controlled and a function of potentially any knowledge source. The control of operators is open to modulation by learning.

3.5 Testing the Theory Empirically

The theory has now been described in sufficient detail that we can explore a few of its empirical implications. Each of the following sections shows how some aspect of the architecture (e.g., the repair process, or control structure) makes predictions concerning some psycholinguistic phenomenon (e.g., strong garden-path effects), in particular, those phenomena that underlie the set of behavioral contrasts set up in Figure 3.1. There is space here to present only a few examples of the application of the theory; for fuller treatments, see Lewis (1993, 1996) and Lewis & Lehman (1997).

3.5.1 Limited Repair: Easy versus Difficult Garden-Path Effects

We claimed earlier that a theory of human parsing must answer two related questions: (1) How do people interpret locally ambiguous material, and (2) How do people revise their interpretations of ambiguous material based on later disambiguating information? Limited repair is an answer to the second question, and explains how the human sentence processor can sometimes rapidly leap off the garden path and find its way back onto the path to a successful parse. This section explores predictions that the snip-based repair mechanism makes concerning structural ambiguities, including some that derive from lexical categorial ambiguities. The structures presented here are a subset of the roughly seventy structures analyzed in Lewis (1993) and Lewis and Lehman (1997).

Subject/Object Ambiguities

We have already seen how the theory handles an easy subject/object ambiguity like (7). As an example of how the theory predicts a difficult garden path, consider the following from Frazier and Rayner (1982):

(11) Since Jay always jogs a mile seems like a short distance to him.

Here, *a mile* is taken initially as the complement of *jogs*, just as in (7). Because *jogs* does not take sentential complements, the initial phrase *Since Jay jogs* is adjoined to the incoming *seems*. In fact, this is its correct final position. However, $[_{IP}$ seems$]$ is still missing its subject. But in this case a snip operator is not generated for the complement relation between $[_{V'}$ jogs$]$ and $[_{NP}$ a mile$]$, because the relation is not local to the detected inconsistency (the missing obligatory subject). This situation is shown in Figure 3.4, with the boxed nodes again representing the locality of the inconsistency. As a result, $[_{NP}$ a mile$]$ is not reanalyzed as the subject of $[_{IP}$ seems$]$, and the necessary repair fails.

Difficult subject/object garden paths such as (11) show up cross-linguistically as well; for example, in Mandarin (Gorrell, 1991) and Hebrew (Pritchett, 1992).

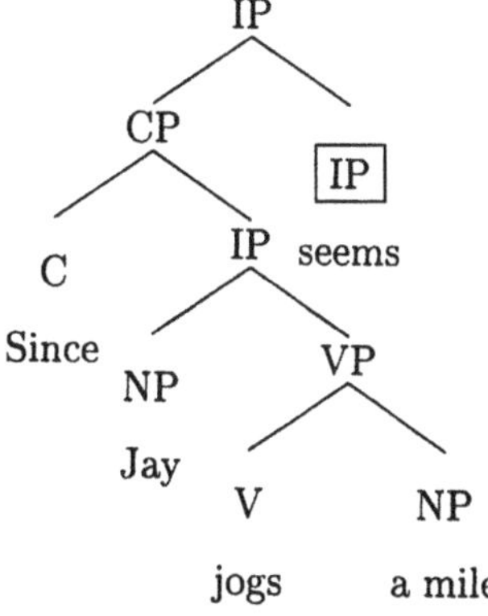

Figure 3.4. Failure to repair a subject/object ambiguity.

The explanation is the same as in the English example: the local snip is not generated to remove the object NP from complement position.

Main Verb/Relative Ambiguities

We now explore variations on the classic relative clause garden path. Consider the canonical example (Bever, 1970):

(12) The horse raced past the barn fell.

In the structure for the main verb interpretation of (12), the inflectional features that head the IP phrase adjoin to the verb, leaving a trace in the head of IP. (This joining of inflectional features to the verb is assumed in some form by many syntactic theories; e.g., McCawley (1988a) calls it Tense-hopping and assumes an adjunction structure like the one presented here.) On the other hand, passive forms like *driven* and *raced* are untensed. In the reduced relative reading of *the horse raced past the barn*, which uses the passive interpretation of *raced*, the inflection is not present.

Consider now the repair required to successfully parse (12). The main verb structure must be repaired into the reduced relative structure. This involves snipping the adjoined inflectional features. When *fell* arrives and is projected to VP, the only place it may attach is in complement position of I′. This produces an inconsistency local to the IP, as shown in Figure 3.5. However, this fails to

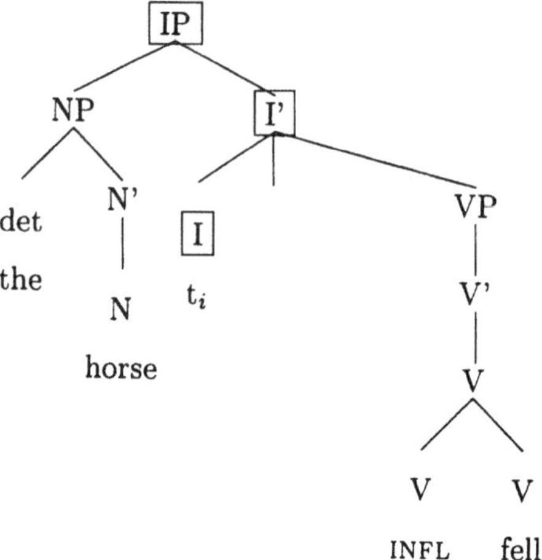

Figure 3.5. The main verb/reduced relative garden-path effect. When *fell* arrives and is projected to VP, the only place it may attach is in complement position of I′. This produces an inconsistency local to the IP (denoted by the boxed nodes). However, this fails to trigger all the required snips, in particular, the crucial inflection adjunction is left undisturbed, so the required passive reading cannot be recovered.

trigger all the required snips; in particular, the crucial inflection adjunction is left undisturbed, so the passive reading cannot be recovered.

The intervening modifier [$_{PP}$ past the barn] is irrelevant to this explanation. Thus, the theory correctly predicts the existence of very short reduced relative garden paths (Kurtzman, 1985; Abney, 1989):

(13) The boat floated sank.

Such examples are one demonstration of the independence of garden-path effects from length effects (Pritchett, 1992; Lewis, 1993).

Surprisingly, not all main verb/relative clause ambiguities produce garden-path effects. Mazuka et al. (1989) present an interesting unproblematic Japanese construction involving a main verb/relative clause ambiguity:

(14) a. Roozin-ga kodomo-o yonda.
old man NOM child ACC called
(The old man called the child.)
b. Roozin-ga kodomo-o yonda zyosee to hanasi-o sita.
old man NOM child ACC called woman with talk ACC did.
(The old man talked with the woman who called the child.)

In (14a), the NP NP V sequence *roozin ga kodomo o yonda* is interpreted as the main clause *The old man called the child.* In (14b), the relative clause reading is required, disambiguated by the appearance of *zyosee.* Unlike the familiar English main verb/reduced relative ambiguity, NL-Soar can repair the structure in (14b). The main clause interpretation is pursued initially, with [$_{NP}$ roozin] in subject (SPEC-IP) position and [$_{NP}$ kodomo o] in complement position of [$_{VP}$ yonda]. Next, [$_{NP}$ zyosee] arrives and the CP adjoins to [$_{N'}$ zyosee] as a modifying clause (unlike the English version, the relative clause is active, not passive, and therefore the clause remains tensed). The appropriate traces are generated in SPEC-CP and SPEC-IP position, in the same manner as English relative clauses. The SPEC-IP trace creates a local inconsistency at the IP node, triggering a snip of [$_{NP}$ roozin]. [$_{NP}$ roozin] is now available to attach as the subject of the incoming [$_{IP}$ to hanasi o sita], and the repair succeeds.

Lexical Categorial Ambiguities

Lexical ambiguity often gives rise to structural ambiguity. Consider the basic noun/adjective ambiguity in (15):

(15) a. The square is red.
b. The square table is red.

When *square* arrives, both categories are retrieved in parallel from the lexicon, and NP and AP nodes are projected. Next, the determiner *the* is attached in SPEC-NP position, forming [$_{NP}$ the square]. Then *table* arrives and is projected to NP. Next, the adjective phrase [$_{AP}$ square] is adjoined to [$_{N'}$ table]. Each syntactic link is well-formed, but two mutually incompatible bits of structure have been produced, since the single token *square* cannot simultaneously be an adjective and a noun.

A snip operator is immediately triggered by the inconsistency of syntactic structure attached to competing senses of the same lexical token. A locally generated snip breaks the SPEC-NP link between the determiner and [$_{NP}$ square]. Next, a link operator attaches the determiner in specifier position of [$_{NP}$ table], forming [$_{NP}$ the square table]. This completes the repair. In this way, the snip operator extends naturally to handle repairs involving lexical ambiguity.

We have now seen all three kinds of structural cues that trigger the snip operator:

1. Multiple phrases competing for the same structural position
2. Missing obligatory phrases (e.g., missing subjects)
3. Attachments to competing categorial interpretations of the same lexical item

NL-Soar also handles multiple lexical ambiguities. For example, noun/verb ambiguities may be preceded by adjective/noun ambiguities without causing difficulty (Milne, 1982; Pritchett, 1992):

(16) a. The square blocks the triangle.
  b. The square blocks are red.

NL-Soar effects the repairs in (16) in the same manner as in (15); see Lewis (1993) for details. Yet some noun/verb ambiguities do cause difficulty. If the unproblematic ambiguity in (16) is followed by a reduced relative, the result is a strong garden path (Milne, 1982; Pritchett, 1992):

(17) The building blocks the sun faded are red.

Suppose that *blocks* is initially taken as the main verb, and *sun* as the complement. When *faded* arrives, it can be attached as a reduced relative modifying *sun*. Once *are* is projected to an IP, no additional attachments are possible. Furthermore, there are no local inconsistencies to generate a snip, so the repair is never initiated.

Summary

As a theory of reanalysis, snip-based limited repair has a number of important features:

1. The theory is formulated independently of what guides the initial choice at the ambiguity point. Thus, the theory classifies structure types as potential garden paths, not definite garden paths. The repair theory determines whether or not a given inconsistent structure can be repaired. Whether a local ambiguity gives rise to a strong garden-path effect in any particular context is a function both of the ambiguity resolution process itself and the efficacy of the repair.
2. The theory is a cue-driven theory of repair, because it depends on a few simple local cues to trigger the repair process.
3. The theory is a functional theory in that it posits mechanisms to efficiently carry out the functions of reanalysis. NL-Soar is not a linguistic metric that distinguishes easy and difficult ambiguities. It is an implemented computational theory that classifies certain sentences as potential strong garden paths because it may fail to parse those sentences.
4. The theory posits that on-line repair is not costly; in fact, the prediction is that these small local repairs are a frequently occurring part of normal sentence comprehension.
5. The theory posits a minimal amount of additional new mechanisms and control to carry out the repair. The only new operator is snip; repair is carried out by snip and a sequence of the existing parsing operators. The only important new piece of control knowledge is a rule that says roughly: Don't relink what you just snipped.

3.5.2 Interference in STM: Easy versus Difficult Embeddings

This section explores some interesting predictions that the limited STM makes in the area of cross-linguistic embeddings. The goal is to provide just a glimpse of the empirical richness of the domain; for a comprehensive empirical exploration, see the over fifty constructions analyzed in Lewis (1993, 1996).

Consider again the classic double-embedded relative clause (Miller & Chomsky, 1963):

(18) The boy that the man that the woman hired hated cried.

The Dependents set must index the three initial NPs under SPEC-IP, since all three NPs will eventually occupy subject position:

(19) Dependents	SPEC-IP:	[$_{NP}$ the boy], [$_{NP}$ the man], [$_{NP}$ the woman]

This exceeds the posited capacity of two nodes per relation (Section 4.4). Failure will occur at one of the final verbs (which verb depends on which NP is dropped from the H/D set). It is important to note that failure does not occur just because nodes are removed from the set. Just as in standard short-term memory tasks, interference is only a problem if the item that is interfered with must be accessed later.

The uniform limit of two nodes per relation in the H/D set theory does not entail a prohibition against all double center-embedding. If that was the case, it would essentially be equivalent to Kimball's (1973) Principle of Two Sentences and fall prey to the same empirical problems (Gibson, 1991). Consider the pseudocleft construction, which has something like a Wh-clause in subject position:

(20) a. What the man saw was a dog.
b. [$_{IP}$ [$_{NP}$ [$_{CP}$ What the man saw]] was a dog]

The initial Wh-clause in pseudoclefts is an indirect question (Baker, 1989; McCawley, 1988b). The interaction of this structure with the H/D set leads to some interesting predictions. Because the initial Wh-word does not occupy SPEC-IP, it should be possible to embed an additional relative clause within the indirect question without causing difficulty. This prediction turns out to be true (Gibson, 1991):

(21) a. What the woman that John married likes is smoked salmon.
[$_{IP}$ What [$_{IP}$ the woman that [$_{IP}$ John married] likes] is smoked salmon.]

b. Dependents	SPEC-IP:	[$_{NP}$ woman], [$_{NP}$ John]
	SPEC-CP:	[$_{NP}$ what]

A final example from Japanese will illustrate the theory's application to a typologically distinct language. Though the English (18) causes difficulty with three stacked NPs, Japanese sentences that stack up to five initial NPs are acceptable to native speakers:

(22) John-wa Bill-ni Mary-ga Sue-ni Bob-o syookai sita-to it-ta.
John TOP Bill DAT Mary NOM Sue DAT Bob ACC introduced COMP say PERF
(John said to Bill that Mary introduced Bob to Sue.)

Although such sentences are surely complex, they do not cause the failure associated with (18). The H/D set can handle structures such as (22) because no single structural relation must buffer more than two NPs:

(23) Dependents	SPEC-IP:	[$_{NP}$ John], [$_{NP}$ Mary]
	COMP-V′:	[$_{NP}$ Bob]
	COMP2-V′:	[$_{NP}$ Bill], [$_{NP}$ Sue]

Apart from the cross-linguistic empirical coverage, the theory of syntactic short-term memory presented here has a number of important features:

1. The theory is a functional architectural theory of memory; it is not a linguistic metric that distinguishes easy and difficult embeddings (e.g., Gibson, 1991). It classifies certain sentences as difficult because the posited structure of memory fails to support a successful parse of those sentences.
2. The theory embodies a general principle of short-term memory limitation, similarity-based interference, which has been demonstrated in a number of different tasks and modalities, ranging from visual stimuli to sign language (Baddeley, 1966; Conrad, 1963; Magnussen et al., 1991; Poizner et al., 1981; Shulman, 1970; Waugh & Norman, 1965; Wickelgren, 1965).
3. It correctly predicts that difficulty can arise independently of ambiguity (Blauberg & Braine, 1974; Blumenthal, 1966; Foss & Cairns, 1970; Hamilton & Deese, 1971; Larkin & Burns, 1977; Marks, 1968; Miller & Isard, 1964).
4. It correctly predicts that deep embedding alone (even center-embedding) is insufficient to cause difficulty (see, e.g., (9) and (21)).

NL-Soar's model of working memory also captures two important theoretical convergences in recent accounts of syntactic short-term memory. First, the source of memory load is open or unsatisfied syntactic relations (Abney & Johnson, 1991; Gibson, 1991; Stabler, 1994). This leads naturally to a focus on stacking, rather than embedding per se, as the source of difficulty (Gibson, 1991; Hakuta, 1981; Mazuka et al., 1989). Second, increasing similarity makes things more difficult. This shows up clearly in the "broad but shallow" memory models of Reich (1969) and Stabler (1994), and the self-embedding metric of Miller & Chomsky (1963).

3.5.3 Some Implications of Control Structure

Recall from Section 3.4 that all processing in Soar and NL-Soar consists of a sequence of decision cycles proposing, selecting, and applying cognitive operators. Local ambiguity manifests itself by the simultaneous proposal of a set of operators corresponding to the different interpretations at the ambiguous point. For example, in (1) (repeated here as (24)), at the verb *examined*, two operators are proposed: one corresponding to the main verb structure, and one corresponding to the relative clause structure.

(24) The car examined by the mechanic was damaged.

Ambiguity resolution then takes place in the same way that all operator selection is realized in Soar: by drawing on available search control productions. In the case of the ambiguity in (24), a search control production can test the proposed operators and the semantic content of the subject (e.g., *evidence* or *car*), and prefer the relative-clause operator (or disprefer the main-verb operator) in the appropriate contexts. In this way, NL-Soar can model the rapid, on-line effects of semantic or referential context.

However, nothing guarantees that such search control productions will be available. If the knowledge is present only through deliberate processing, there may not be enough time to perform all the inferences necessary to make the right selection. Under press of time, there may be no alternative but to select one interpretation by some default preference. In such a case, NL-Soar is behaving in a modular fashion since the required knowledge sources are not applied on-line.

These and similar kinds of limitations that arise in NL-Soar are a kind of forgetting due to retrieval failure. In other words, the required knowledge may be present, but because the correct set of cues are not assembled in working memory, the knowledge is not evoked. The limitations emerge from the fact that Soar embodies Tulving's (1983) encoding specificity principle: the cues required for retrieval are a subset of specific aspects of the environment at learning time.

Lewis (1993) describes in detail further implications of NL-Soar's control structure, including the ability to deliberately recomprehend problematic ambiguities. This kind of flexible interplay between automatic and deliberate processing is a hallmark of Soar's control structure, but the fact that this structure nevertheless yields processing limitations, and that these limitations have modularlike properties, is somewhat surprising giving Soar's origins in purely functional concerns.

3.6 Conclusions

This chapter began by developing a set of empirical and functional constraints on information processing theories of sentence processing. The empirical constraints took the form of a set of behavioral oppositions that outline the impressive capabilities and severe limitations of human comprehension. The primary functional constraint was that sentence processing theories should take the form of complete computational architectures which specify the processes, memories, and control structures underlying human parsing and interpretation. This functional, architectural approach revealed several overlooked issues in sentence-processing architecture.

The empirical and explanatory power of the approach was demonstrated by presenting NL-Soar, a computational architecture for sentence comprehension. The theory covers a broad range of sentence-processing phenomena: strong garden-path effects and easy ambiguities, difficult and acceptable embeddings, modular and interactive ambiguity resolution effects, and aspects of the time course of comprehension. In the areas of garden-path effects and difficult/easy embeddings, the accounts are deep: the theory makes successful predictions on a collection of over a hundred cross-linguistic structures (Lewis, 1993).

The model has a number of important features that help push sentence processing theory in new directions (cf. Section 3.3.6). Among the most prominent of these is reducing theoretical degrees of freedom by adopting the assumptions of an independently motivated theory of cognitive architecture. One of the yields of such an approach was an explanation of how certain limitations in sentence processing embody some general principles of human memory and skill, in particular, similarity-based interference in STM, encoding specificity (Tulving, 1983), and *Einstellung* (Luchins, 1942). The model also simultaneously accounts for on-line effects of context and semantics and for subtle effects of syntactic structure that distinguish easy and difficult garden paths and embeddings. All of these implications and predictions flow from the interactions of some fairly simple core architectural assumptions: the two-layered parallel/serial control structure, the limited interference-based working memory, and the limited repair process.

Two objections might be raised to the theoretical approach advocated here. One might be called the problem of irrelevant specification, a problem with building computational models in general. The objection goes as follows. Computational models, because they force functional completeness, also inevitably lead to specification of irrelevant detail without empirical support. There are two responses to this. One response is to simply be careful about abstracting out the essential theoretical claims and identifying their empirical support. That has been the intention here; the underlying computational simulation undoubtedly contains many details that are not relevant to the core theoretical claims. The second response is inherent in the architectural approach itself: an architectural theory makes principled distinctions between the fixed structure that carries the theory, the variable content that is posited for some particular task, and the irrelevant implementation technology. Thus, the theoretical status of an architectural simulation is much clearer than is the case for information-processing simulations in general (Newell, 1990; Pylyshyn, 1984).

The second objection might be called the problem of "anything goes" cognizers. Many theorists have warned against abandoning highly constrained modular theories in favor of anything that approaches more general problem-solving machinery (Fodor, 1983; J. D. Fodor, 1990; Forster, 1979). Under this view, building a sentence-processing architecture within a general cognitive engine like Soar is exactly the wrong thing to do because it opens the door to unconstrained theorizing. But the general injunction should be against theories with too many degrees of freedom, not against general architectures per se. In fact, the approach taken here, to adopt Soar as a starting point, is precisely a way of eliminating theoretical degrees of freedom since the control structures and memories are independently motivated givens. Furthermore, this approach also seeks to find contact with other principles of cognitive processing (e.g., the memory principles outlined in Section 3.3.4), and thereby increase explanatory power. In the specific case of NL-Soar, the underlying general architecture (Soar) was the vehicle for making most of those connections and has actually led to a new theory that fits well with both the theoretical and empirical concerns of modularity (Lewis, 1996).

The work presented here is just a part of a larger ongoing movement toward more precise computational theories of sentence processing (e.g., Crocker, 1996; Gibson, 1991; Jurafsky, 1996; Just & Carpenter, 1992; Konieczny, 1996; Stevenson, 1994). What the current work adds to the theoretical mix is a concern for functional completeness and grounding in independent cognitive theory. In short, this kind of architectural approach begins to address the concerns of both Bever (1970), who wanted psycholinguistic theory to be motivated by general cognitive principles, and Forster (1979), who wanted psycholinguistic theory to be tightly constrained yet integrated with central processes. The general analysis and theory presented here are clearly just a first step down this path, but the initial results seem promising.

References

Abney, S. P. (1989). A computational model of human parsing. *Journal of Psycholingusitic Research*, 18:129–144.

Abney, S. P. & Johnson, M. (1991). Memory requirements and local ambiguities of parsing strategies. *Journal of Psycholinguistic Research*, 20:233–250.

Aho, A. & Ullman, J. (1972). *The theory of parsing, translation, and compiling. Volume 1: Parsing*. Prentice-Hall, Englewood Cliffs, NJ.

Anderson, J. R. (1983). *The architecture of cognition.* Harvard University Press, Cambridge, MA.

Anderson, J. R. (1993). *Rules of the mind.* Erlbaum, Hillsdale, NJ.

Baddeley, A. D. (1966). Short-term memory for word sequences as a function of acoustic, semantic, and formal similarity. *Quarterly Journal of Experimental Psychology*, 18:362–365.

Baddeley, A. D. (1990). *Human memory: Theory and practice.* Allyn and Bacon, Boston.

Baker, C. L. (1989). *English syntax.* MIT Press, Cambridge, MA.

Bell, C. G. & Newell, A. (1971). *Computer structures: Readings and examples.* McGraw Hill, New York.

Bever, T. G. (1970). The cognitive basis for linguistic structures. In Hayes, J. R., editor, *Cognition and the development of language*, pages 279–362. Wiley, New York.

Blauberg, M. S. & Braine, M. D. S. (1974). Short-term memory limitations on decoding self-embedded sentences. *Journal of Experimental Psychology*, 102:745–748.

Blumenthal, A. L. (1966). Observations with self-embedded sentences. *Psychonomic Science*, 6:453–454.

Chomsky, N. (1965). *Aspects of the theory of syntax*. MIT Press, Cambridge, MA.

Chomsky, N. (1980). Rules and representations. *The Behavioral and Brain Sciences*, 3:1–15.

Chomsky, N. (1981). *Lectures on Government and Binding.* Foris, Dordrecht.

Chomsky, N. & Miller, G. A. (1963). Introduction to the formal analysis of natural languages. In Luce, D. R., Bush, R. R., & Galanter, E., editors, *Handbook of Mathematical Psychology, Volume II.* John Wiley, New York.

Clark, H. & Clark, E. (1977). *The psychology of language: An introduction to psycholinguistics.* Harcourt Brace Jovanovich, New York.

Conrad, R. (1963). Acoustic confusions and memory span for words. *Nature*, 197:1029–1030.

Cowper, E. A. (1976). *Constraints on sentence complexity: A model for syntactic processing.* Ph.D. thesis, Brown University.

Crocker, M. W. (1996). *Computational psycholinguistics: An interdisciplinary approach to the study of language.* Kluwer, Dordrecht.

Earley, J. (1970). An efficient context-free parsing algorithm. *Communications of the ACM*, 13:94–102.

Ferreira, F. & Clifton, C., Jr. (1986). The independence of syntactic processing. *Journal of Memory and Language*, 25:348–368.

Ferreira, F. & Henderson, J. M. (1990). Use of verb information in syntactic parsing: Evidence from eye movements and word-by-word self-paced reading. *Journal of Experimental Psychology: Learning, Memory, and Cognition*, 16:555–568.

Fodor, J. A. (1983). *Modularity of mind: An essay on faculty psychology.* MIT Press, Cambridge, MA.

Fodor, J. D. (1990). Thematic roles and modularity: Comments on the chapters by Frazier and Tanenhaus et al. In Altmann, G. T. M., editor, *Cognitive models of speech processing: Psycholinguistic and computational perspectives.* MIT Press, Cambridge, MA.

Fodor, J. D., Fodor, J. A., & Garrett, M. F. (1975). The psychological unreality of semantic representations. *Linguistic Inquiry*, 6:515–531.

Fodor, J. D. & Inoue, A. (1994). The diagnosis and cure of garden paths. *Journal of Psycholinguistic Research*, 23:407–434.

Forster, K. (1979). Levels of processing and the structure of the language processor. In Cooper, W. E. & Walker, E. C., editors, *Sentence processing: Psycholinguistic studies presented to Merrill Garrett.* Erlbaum, Hillsdale, NJ.

Foss, D. J. & Cairns, H. S. (1970). Some effects of memory limitation upon sentence comprehension and recall. *Journal of Verbal Learning and Verbal Behavior*, 9:541–547.

Frazier, L. (1978). *On comprehending sentences: Syntactic parsing strategies.* Ph.D. thesis, University of Connecticut.

Frazier, L. (1990). Parsing modifiers: Special purpose routines in the human sentence processing mechanism? In Balota, D. A., Flores d'Arcais, G. B., & Rayner, K., editors, *Comprehension processes in reading.* Erlbaum, Hillsdale, NJ.

Frazier, L. & Clifton, C., Jr. (1996). *Construal.* MIT Press, Cambridge, MA.

Frazier, L. & Rayner, K. (1982). Making and correcting errors during sentence comprehension: Eye movements in the analysis of structurally ambiguous sentences. *Cognitive Psychology*, 14:178–210.

Gibson, E. A. (1991). *A computational theory of human linguistic processing: Memory limitations and processing breakdown.* Ph.D. thesis, Carnegie Mellon. Available as Center for Machine Translation technical report CMU-CMT-91-125.

Gorrell, P. (1987). *Studies of human syntactic processing: Ranked-parallel versus serial models.* Ph.D. thesis, The University of Connecticut.

Gorrell, P. (1991). Subcategorization and sentence processing. In Berwick, R. C., Abney, S. P., & Tenny, C., editors, *Principle-based parsing: Computation and psycholinguistics.* Kluwer, Dordrecht.

Graf, P. & Schacter, D. (1985). Implicit and explicit memory for new associations in normal and amnesic subjects. *Journal of Experimental Psychology: Learning, Memory, and Cognition*, 11:501–518.

Hakuta, K. (1981). Grammatical description versus configurational arrangement in language acquisition: The case of relative clauses in Japanese. *Cognition*, 9:197–236.

Hamilton, H. W. & Deese, J. (1971). Comprehensibility and subject-verb relations in complex sentences. *Journal of Verbal Learning and Verbal Behavior*, 10:163–170.

Johnson-Laird, P. N. (1983). *Mental models.* Harvard University Press, Cambridge, MA.

Juliano, C. & Tanenhaus, M. K. (1994). A constraint-based lexicalist account of the subject/object attachment preference. *Journal of Psycholinguistic Research*, 23:459–471.

Jurafsky, D. (1996). A probabilistic model of lexical and syntactic access and disambiguation. *Cognitive Science*, 20:137–194.

Just, M. A. & Carpenter, P. A. (1987). *The psychology of reading and language comprehension.* Allyn and Bacon, Boston.

Just, M. A. & Carpenter, P. A. (1992). A capacity theory of comprehension: Individual differences in working memory. *Psychological Review*, 99:122–149.

Kimball, J. (1973). Seven principles of surface structure parsing in natural language. *Cognition*, 2:15–47.

Kintsch, W., Welsch, D., Schmalhofer, F., & Zimny, S. (1990). Sentence memory: A theoretical analysis. *Journal of Memory and Language*, 29:133–159.

Konieczny, L. (1996). *Human sentence processing: A semantics-oriented parsing approach.* Ph.D. thesis, University of Freiburg.

Kurtzman, H. S. (1985). *Studies in syntactic ambiguity resolution.* Ph.D. thesis, Massachusetts Institute of Technology.

Laberge, D. & Samuels, S. J. (1974). Toward a theory of automatic information processing in reading. *Cognitive Psychology*, 6:293–323.

Larkin, W. & Burns, D. (1977). Sentence comprehension and memory for embedded structure. *Memory and Cognition*, 5:17–22.

Lehman, J. F., Laird, J. E., & Rosenbloom, P. S. (1998). A gentle introduction to Soar, an architecture for human cognition. In Scarborough, D., & Sternberg, S., editors, *Invitation to cognitive science*, Volume 4. Cambridge, MA: MIT Press.

Lehman, J. F., Lewis, R. L., & Newell, A. (1991). Integrating knowledge sources in language comprehension. In *Proceedings of the Thirteenth Annual Conference of the Cognitive Science Society*, pages 461–466. Also in P. S. Rosenbloom, J. E. Laird, and A. Newell, editors, *The Soar Papers: Research on Integrated Intelligence*, MIT Press, Cambridge, MA, 1993.

Lewis, R. L. (1992). Recent development in the NL-Soar garden path theory. Technical Report CMU-CS-92-141, School of Computer Science, Carnegie Mellon University.

Lewis, R. L. (1993). *An architecturally-based theory of human sentence comprehension.* Ph.D. thesis, Carnegie Mellon University. Available as technical report CMU-CS-93-226.

Lewis, R. L. (1996). Interference in short-term memory: The magical number two (or three) in sentence processing. *Journal of Psycholinguistic Research*, 25:93–115.

Lewis, R. L. (1997b). A theory of grammatical but unacceptable embeddings. In revision.

Lewis, R. L. (1998). Reanalysis and limited repair parsing: Leaping off the garden path. In Fodor, J. D. & Ferreira, F., editors, *Reanalysis in sentence processing* pages 247–285. Dordrecht: Kluwer.

Lewis, R. L. & Lehman, J. F. (1997). A theory of the computational architecture of sentence comprehension. Manuscript, Ohio State University.

Logie, R. H., Zucco, G. M., & Baddeley, A. D. (1990). Interference with visual short-term memory. *Acta Psychologica*, 75:55–74.

Luchins, A. S. (1942). Mechanization in problem solving. *Psychological Monographs*, 54(6).

MacDonald, M. C., Pearlmutter, N. J., & Seidenberg, M. S. (1994). The lexical nature of syntactic ambiguity resolution. *Psychological Review*, 101:676–703.

MacKay, D. G. (1966). To end ambiguous sentences. *Perception & Psychophysics*, 1:426–436.

Magnussen, S., Greenlee, M. W., Asplund, R., & Dyrnes, S. (1991). Stimulus-specific mechanisms of visual short-term memory. *Vision Research*, 31:1213–1219.

Marks, L. E. (1968). Scaling of grammaticalness of self-embedded English sentences. *Journal of Verbal Learning and Verbal Behavior*, 7:965–967.

Martin, R. C. (1993). Short-term memory and sentence processing: Evidence from neuropsychology. *Memory & Cognition*, 21:176–183.

Mazuka, R., Itoh, K., Kiritani, S., Niwa, S., Ikejiru, K., & Naitoh, K. (1989). Processing of Japanese garden path, center-embedded, and multiply left-embedded sentences. In *Annual Bulletin of the Research Institute of Logopedics and Phoniatrics*, volume 23, pages 187–212, University of Tokyo.

McCawley, J. D. (1988a). *The syntactic phenomena of English, Volume 1.* University of Chicago Press, Chicago.

McCawley, J. D. (1988b). *The syntactic phenomena of English, Volume 2.* University of Chicago Press, Chicago.

Miller, G. A. (1962). Some psychological studies of grammar. *American Psychologist*, 17:748–762.

Miller, G. A. & Chomsky, N. (1963). Finitary models of language users. In Luce, D. R., Bush, R. R., & Galanter, E., editors, *Handbook of mathematical psychology, Volume II.* Wiley, New York.

Miller, G. A. & Isard, S. (1964). Free recall of self-embedded English sentences. *Information and Control*, 7:292–303.

Milne, R. W. (1982). Predicting garden path sentences. *Cognitive Science*, 6:349–373.

Minsky, M., editor (1967). *Computation: Finite and infinite machines.* Prentice-Hall, Englewood Cliffs, NJ.

Mitchell, D. (1987). Lexical guidance in human parsing: Locus and processing characteristics. In Coltheart, M., editor, *Attention and performance XII* pages 601–681. Erlbaum, Hillsdale, NJ.

Mitchell, D. C., Corley, M. M. B., & Garnham, A. (1992). Effects of context in human sentence parsing: Evidence against a discourse-based proposal mechanism. *Journal of Experimental Psychology: Learning, Memory and Cognition*, 18:69–88.

Mitchell, D. C., Cuetos, F., Corley, M. M. B., & Brysbaert, M. (1995). Exposure-based models of human parsing: Evidence for the use of coarse-grained (non-lexical) statistical records. *Journal of Psycholinguistic Research*, 24:469–488.

Newell, A. (1973). Production systems: Models of control structures. In Chase, W. G., editor, *Visual information processing*. Academic, New York.

Newell, A. (1980a). Physical symbol systems. *Cognitive Science*, 4:135–183. Also available as CMU CSD Technical Report, Mar 1980; and in Norman, D., editor, Perspectives in Cognitive Science, Ablex, Norwood, NJ, 1981.

Newell, A. (1980b). Reasoning, problem solving and decision processes: The problem space as a fundamental category. In Nickerson, R., editor, *Attention and performance VIII.* Erlbaum, Hillsdale, NJ.

Newell, A. (1990). *Unified theories of cognition.* Harvard University Press, Cambridge, MA.

Newell, A. (1992). Precis of *Unified theories of cognition. Behavioral and Brain Sciences*, 15:425–492.

Newell, A. & Rosenbloom, P. (1981). Mechanisms of skill acquisition and the law of practice. In Anderson, J. R., editor, *Cognitive skills and their acquisition.* Erlbaum, Hillsdale, NJ.

Newell, A. & Simon, H. A. (1972). *Human problem solving.* Prentice-Hall, Englewood Cliffs, NJ.

Poizner, H., Bellugi, U., & Tweney, R. D. (1981). Processing of formational, semantic, and iconic information in American Sign Language. *Journal of Experimental Psychology: Human Perception and Performance*, 7:1146–1159.

Potter, M. C. (1982). *Very short-term memory: In one eye and out the other.* Paper presented at the 23rd Annual Meeting of the Psychonomic Society, Minneapolis.

Potter, M. C. (1993). Very short-term conceptual memory. *Memory & Cognition*, 21:156–161.

Pritchett, B. L. (1988). Garden path phenomena and the grammatical basis of language processing. *Language*, 64:539–576.

Pritchett, B. L. (1992). *Grammatical competence and parsing performance.* University of Chicago Press, Chicago.

Pylyshyn, Z. W. (1984). *Computation and cognition.* MIT Press, Cambridge, MA.

Rayner, K., Garrod, S., & Perfetti, C. A. (1992). Discourse influences during parsing are delayed. *Cognition*, 45:109–139.

Reich, P. (1969). The finiteness of natural language. *Language*, 45(4):831–843.

Shulman, H. G. (1970). Similarity effects in short-term memory. *Psychological Bulletin*, 75:399–414.

Stabler, E. P. (1991). Avoiding the pedestrian's paradox. In Berwick, R. C., Abney, S. P., & Tenny, C., editors, *Principle-based parsing: Computation and psycholinguistics.* Kluwer, Dordrecht.

Stabler, E. P. (1994). The finite connectivity of linguistic structure. In Clifton, C., Frazier, L., & Rayner, K., editors, *Perspectives in sentence processing.* Erlbaum, Hillsdale, NJ.

Stevenson, S. (1994). Competition and recency in a hybrid network model of syntactic disambiguation. *Journal of Psycholinguistic Research*, 23:295–322.

Tambe, M., Newell, A., & Rosenbloom, P. S. (1990). The problem of expensive chunks and its solution by restricting expressiveness. *Machine Learning*, 5:299–348.

Thibadeau, R., Just M. A., & Carpenter, P. A. (1982). A model of the time course and content of reading. *Cognitive Science*, 6:157–203.

Trueswell, J. C., Tanenhaus, M. K., & Garnsey, S. M. (1994). Semantic influences on parsing: Use of thematic role information in syntactic disambiguation. *Journal of Memory and Language*, 33:285–318.

Tulving, E. (1983). *Elements of episodic memory.* New York: Oxford University Press.

Waugh, N. C., & Norman, D. A. (1965). Primary memory. *Psychological Review*, 72:89–104.

Wickelgren, W. A. (1965). Acoustic similarity and retroactive interference in short-term memory. *Journal of Verbal Learning and Verbal Behavior*, 4:53–61.

4

Modeling Thematic and Discourse Context Effects with a Multiple Constraints Approach: Implications for the Architecture of the Language Comprehension System

MICHAEL K. TANENHAUS,
MICHAEL J. SPIVEY-KNOWLTON, AND
JOY E. HANNA

...And dicing Time for gladness casts a moan
These purblind Doomsters had as readily strown...
Thomas Hardy, *Hap*, 1866

4.1 Introduction

The ambiguity problem takes center stage in models of sentence processing because, to a first approximation, linguistic input is presented sequentially to the processing system in both spoken language and in reading. Thus, even unambiguous sequences of speech or text are briefly ambiguous. A rich empirical database now demonstrates that the processing system makes partial commitments that are closely time-locked to the input as it unfolds over time (for recent reviews see Tanenhaus & Trueswell, 1995, Pickering, Clifton, & Crocker, this volume). Because the syntactic information available to the system at any point in the sentence often underdetermines its structure, other constraints that are correlated with the syntactic alternatives could, in principle, provide information that is useful for syntactic ambiguity resolution.

For more than a decade, researchers in the sentence processing community have been relying on data from increasingly fine-grained measures of processing difficulty, especially eye-movement data, in an attempt to adjudicate among competing models of how correlated constraints are used in ambiguity resolution. But despite a rapidly growing experimental literature, an increasingly rich

This work was supported by NIH grant #HD27206.

empirical base, and a plethora of explicit parsing models, the basic architectural issues remain unresolved. We argue that this state of affairs is likely to continue until researchers in the sentence processing community begin to develop explicit quantitative models that (a) identify and quantify the relevant sources of constraint and (b) specify mechanisms that link information integration to processing time. In the absence of such models, we argue, it will be difficult, if not impossible, to discriminate among competing models. We claim that this is true, regardless of how fine-grained a response measure one uses, and regardless of how detailed one's assumptions are about the representational components of the system. We develop this argument by contrasting two different classes of models: serial two-stage models in which an initial structure is built using only a restricted set of grammatical information, and constraint-based models in which multiple constraints provide probabilistic support for partially activated alternatives. Some simple simulations show that there is no "signature" data pattern that can be used to distinguish between these models. However, clear predictions can be generated and tested once the relevant constraints are identified and quantified and an explicit integration algorithm is implemented that can be mapped onto processing time.

4.2 Two-Stage Models versus Constraint-Based Models

Bever's pioneering work (e.g., Bever, 1970), established that readers and listeners have strong preferences for certain syntactic sequences. For example, a noun phrase–verb–noun phrase sequence at the beginning of a sentence is typically taken to be a main clause. These preferences are revealed in garden-path effects for sentences with temporary syntactic ambiguities that do not conform to the preferred syntactic configurations, as is illustrated in the examples in (1).

(1) a. The horse raced past the barn fell.
    b. Sally warned the lawyer was greedy.

An important article by Kimball (1973) inspired a family of serial parsing models in which phrase-structure parsing principles guide the initial syntactic structuring of the linguistic input (e.g., Frazier & Fodor, 1977; Ford, Bresnan, & Kaplan, 1982). These modular two-stage models consist of a first stage of processing in which grammatical information is used to structure the linguistic input, and a second stage in which nongrammatical information is used to evaluate, and if necessary revise, the initial parse. For example, Ferreira and Clifton (1986) argued that "if the syntactic processor (or parser) is modular, it should initially construct a syntactic representation without consulting nonsyntactic information sources, such as semantic or pragmatic information or discourse structure ... Notice, however, that the modular view does not imply that this higher-level information is never consulted by the language processor. It is important to distinguish between *initial* and *eventual* [original emphasis] use of nonsyntactic information."

In the most influential proposal of this class, the garden-path model developed by Frazier and colleagues (Frazier & Rayner, 1982; Frazier, 1987), a provisional structure is assigned using only syntactic category information and a small set of structurally defined parsing principles such as Minimal Attachment or Late Closure. These principles are motivated by the assumption that memory limitations force a rapid structuring of the input. Information incorporated into the secondary evaluation and revision stage includes lexically specific syntactic and semantic information (e.g., information about the types of complements licensed by a verb and the semantic properties or thematic roles associated with these complements), and pragmatic information provided by real-world knowledge and/or discourse context. Processing difficulty reflects syntactic misanalysis and the time it takes the processing system to recover from the misanalysis.

In contrast, constraint-based theorists have argued against architectural restrictions on the use of particular classes of information in sentence processing. Rather, they have assumed that syntactic alternatives are evaluated in parallel with multiple sources of information providing probabilistic evidence in support of the alternatives (Marslen-Wilson, 1973), which compete with one another (Bates & McWhinney, 1989; Jurafsky, 1996; Taraban & McClelland, 1988; Spivey-Knowlton, Trueswell, & Tanenhaus, 1993; MacDonald, Pearlmutter, & Seidenberg, 1994; Tanenhaus & Trueswell, 1995). Processing difficulty occurs when the evidence supporting incompatible alternatives is uncertain or when subsequent evidence is inconsistent with the dominant alternative.

Empirical evidence throughout the 1980s seemed to provide strong support for the parsing principles advocated by two-stage theorists. Studies using reading-time measures demonstrated increased processing difficulty in the form of elevated reading times when a temporarily ambiguous sentence is disambiguated in favor of the structure that is inconsistent with category-based parsing principles (see Frazier, 1987 for a review). Moreover, the results seemed to hold when the structure inconsistent with the parsing preferences was supported by other sources of constraint. (For reviews, see Frazier, 1987; Mitchell, 1989; and Mitchell, Cuetos, Corley, & Brysbeart, 1995.) While there were several important empirical demonstrations that nonsyntactic constraints had clear effects on syntactic ambiguity resolution, reducing processing difficulty for the normally less preferred structure, or even inducing garden paths for the normally preferred structure (e.g., Altmann & Steedman, 1988; Taraban & McClelland, 1988), most of these studies used response measures such as self-paced reading that were often claimed to be less sensitive than finer-grained measures such as eye movements (cf. Rayner et al., 1989; Rayner & Morris, 1991). Thus the context effects could be attributed to the revision stage of the garden-path model. This type of argument has led researchers to focus more and more on response measures that are sensitive to the earliest moments of processing (cf. Altmann, Garnham, & Dennis, 1992, Mitchell, Corley, & Garnham, 1992).

More recent evidence indicates that lexically specific syntactic and semantic information, including the frequencies with which lexical items occur in different environments, and discourse-based constraints can reduce, and sometimes eliminate, many strong structural preferences (Altmann & Steedman, 1988, Britt, 1994, MacDonald, Pearlmutter, & Seidenberg, 1994; Spivey-Knowlton & Sedivy, 1995; Tanenhaus & Trueswell, 1995; Tanenhaus, Spivey-Knowlton, Eberhard, & Sedivy, 1995). For example, the sentences in (2) illustrate that for both of the types of ambiguities in (1), there are sentences with the same structure, but with different lexical items, that are read with little or no processing difficulty (Garnsey, Pearlmutter, Meyers, & Lotocky 1997; Trueswell, 1996; Trueswell, Tanenhaus, & Garnsey, 1994; Trueswell, Tanenhaus, & Kello, 1993).

(2) a. The land mine buried in the sand exploded.
    b. Sally said the lawyer was greedy.

Constraint-based theorists have taken these results as strong support for the principles underlying constraint-based models, arguing that differences across experiments can be attributed to the strength and availability of the constraints used in the materials (e.g., MacDonald et al., 1994; Pearlmutter & MacDonald, 1995; Spivey-Knowlton et al., 1993; Trueswell et al., 1994; Trueswell, 1996). These arguments have been bolstered by experimental studies demonstrating that the effectiveness of one kind of correlated constraint (e.g., semantic fit to potential argument positions) interacts with the strength of other local constraints (e.g., lexical frequencies). The same data patterns used by two-stage theorists to argue for an initial structurally defined stage in processing are claimed by constraint-based theorists to arise because multiple constraints conspired to support the analysis predicted by the parsing principles. When these constraints are accounted for, the parsing principles become redundant. Moreover, the same mechanism that accounts for biases in initial processing is claimed to account for revision effects.

The response of proponents of two-stage models has been to retain a two-stage architecture in order to capture clear cases of structural influences, at least for structures involving primary grammatical relations (e.g., Frazier & Clifton, 1996; Frazier, 1995). Four types of arguments are given in defense of maintaining a two-stage parser. First, constraint-based models do not offer a serious theoretical alternative to two-stage models because they are underspecified and too unconstrained (e.g., Frazier, 1995). Second, it is claimed that the experimental literature is equivocal, with some studies of the effects of correlated constraints supporting two-stage models, and others supporting constraint-based models. Third, it is argued that many of the experimental results that support constraint-based models use tasks that might not be sensitive enough to the earliest moments of language processing. The fourth argument is that the empirical testing ground should be shifted away from examining whether context eliminates processing load for less preferred interpretations towards examining whether support for the less preferred analysis can interfere with processing the normally preferred analysis. The rationale for this move is that whereas some revision effects might be so rapid as to be undetectable, effects of a less preferred structure on a normally preferred reading are strongly predicted by constraint-based models, but should never be observed according to two-stage models.

We agree that constraint-based models need to be more explicit about the nature of the constraints and how they combine, and about how constraint integration maps onto processing difficulty. Clearly articulated constraint-based models make strong claims and falsifiable empirical predictions, whereas underspecified constraint-based models are difficult to evaluate. However, it is essential that two-stage theorists accept the same challenge. The interpretation of time-course data depends crucially on assumptions about how the mechanisms for information integration map onto processing difficulty. Unfortunately, these assumptions are rarely made explicit enough to generate quantitative predictions that could, in principle, be used to evaluate alternative models (but see Stevenson, 1994, for an exception). In the absence of explicit assumptions and quantitative models, it is difficult, if not impossible, to map the kinds of data that sentence processing researchers collect onto the kinds of processing architectures and mechanisms they want to evaluate.

The remainder of this chapter develops this argument using a generic constraint-based model in which multiple constraints provide evidence for competing syntactic alternatives. Simulations illustrate that subtle changes in the strength of constraints can account for the range of data patterns that have been found in studies examining the role of thematic fit on ambiguity resolution for the main clause/reduced relative ambiguity, including those data patterns that have been used to argue for a purely syntactic stage in parsing. We then describe some of our recent research investigating how discourse context affects ambiguity resolution. We show that the same parameters used to simulate a recent study by Spivey-Knowlton and Tanenhaus (1998) in which discourse context completely eliminated processing difficulty for the reduced relative ambiguity also simulate the data obtained in other studies in which context effects were delayed. We then show that the same parameters used to simulate offline "gated" completions for agent/location ambiguities in *by*-phrases predict the pattern of results in an eye-tracking reading study. Different patterns in first-pass reading times and total reading times, which might be used to argue for time-course differences, are also predicted by the simulations.

4.3 Modeling Thematic Fit

We begin by examining the effects of thematic fit in ambiguity resolution using the reduced relative/main clause ambiguity illustrated by the sentences in (3):

(3) a. The witness examined by the lawyer turned out to be unreliable.
    b. The evidence examined by the lawyer turned out to be unreliable.

As in many other syntactic ambiguities, the reduced relative ambiguity hinges on a lexical/morphological ambiguity: the *-ed* form for most verbs is used for both the simple past and the passive participle. Figure 4.1 illustrates the five constraints we will focus on. The first is the goodness of fit of the entity introduced by the first NP as the Agent or Theme for the ambiguous verb. The second is a structural frequency-based bias toward a main clause interpretation.

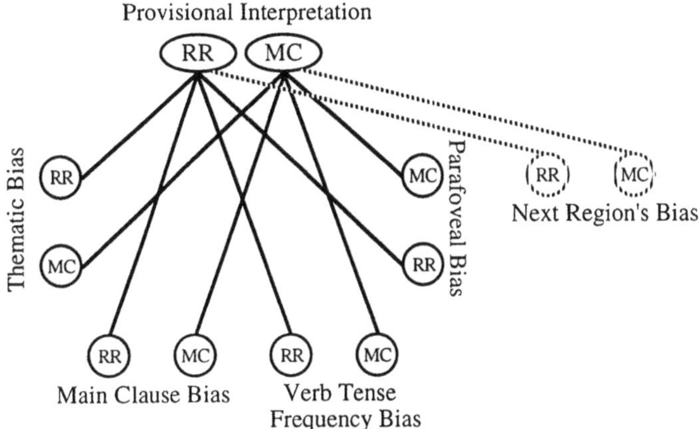

Figure 4.1. Schematic diagram of the generic constraint-based model and the constraints we modeled for the reduced relative/main clause ambiguity.

MacDonald et al. (1994) present a detailed description of the interaction of constraints that underlie this bias, arguing that it arises from an intersection of local lexical constraints, including tense, voice, and argument structure. Tabor, Juliano, & Tanenhaus (1997) show how category-based syntactic preferences can emerge in a lexically based system as a result of learning and processing dynamics. While we agree with these approaches, here, for the sake of simplicity, we will treat the main clause bias as a structural bias.

The third constraint is the relative frequency with which the *-ed* form of the ambiguous verb occurs as either a past tense or a passive participle. The fourth is the evidence provided by either a preposition or an article after the first verb, e.g., *by* in the sentences in (3). We assume that these four constraints are available as the verb is read, because the first NP has already been processed and the postverbal preposition or article, at least when it is short, will be available parafoveally.

The final constraint is the information provided by the NP in the next region of the sentence. Since this constraint typically becomes available during a subsequent fixation after the verb, we assume it is integrated after some competition has already taken place between the first four constraints.

We implemented a generic constraint-based integration mechanism using an architecture developed by Spivey-Knowlton (e.g., Hanna, Spivey-Knowlton, & Tanenhaus, 1996; McRae, Spivey-Knowlton, & Tanenhaus, in 1998; Spivey-Knowlton, 1994). The model does not generate syntactic alternatives; rather it is aimed at simulating the process of resolving a syntactic ambiguity once it is encountered by evaluating relevant constraints. Thus, the model can only be used to simulate ambiguity effects when ambiguous and unambiguous sentences with the same structure are compared. The syntactic alternatives for a locally ambiguous sentence become available in parallel with relevant nonsyntactic constraints providing evidence that is used as soon as it becomes available from the input. The alternative interpretations are resolved using recurrent feedback and normalization. Constraints are defined in terms of their support for the alternative interpretations of an ambiguous segment. Activations of the node pairs for each constraint (C_n) are first normalized: $Cn(norm) = C_n/\Sigma C_n$. Activations for the provisional interpretations (I) are then calculated as weighted sums of their corresponding constraint nodes (where the weights, w, must sum to 1): $I = \Sigma w_n C_n$. For the final operation within a cycle, the activation of an interpretation node is multiplied by the input that traveled up a particular pathway and is added to that corresponding constraint node's current activation: $C_n = C_n(norm) + Iw_n C_n$. The model cycles through these operations allowing converging biases among the constraints to cause the interpretation nodes to gradually settle toward one provisional (probabilistic) interpretation. The number of cycles until a criterion is reached is mapped onto magnitude of processing difficulty. To simulate data across successive fixations during reading we use a dynamic criterion (McRae et al., in press) in which the criterion is lowered by a constant (.01, in this case) after each cycle. After competition is finished in one region of a sentence, the probabilistic activation values are kept as they are (not rectified) when new input constraints are added from a new region of the sentence. To estimate offline preferences, we examine the activations (probabilities) of the interpretation nodes after a fixed number of cycles.

Consider what happens as the thematic fit of the first noun phrase as an Agent or Patient/Theme is varied in conjunction with other constraints in reduced relatives of the form NP V PP VP. We assumed a constant set of equal weights for the constraints. When new input constraints were encountered (four at the verb, and one more at the next region; see Figure 4.1) they were each given a weight of 1, which was then normalized by the sum of all weights. Thus, at the verb, each of the four constraints had a weight of .25. At the next region, the new input constraint was given a weight of 1, but then normalization by the sum of all weights put it at .5, and put the other four weights at .125 (thus insuring that the weights sum to 1). Thus, the constraints provided by most recent input are weighted more heavily than earlier constraints.

In the first simulation, we assumed a moderately strong thematic manipulation (.8 support for the relative clause/.2 support for the main clause (Good Themes), or vice versa (Good Agents)), a strong main-clause structural-frequency bias (.1/.9), verbs that were equibiased (.5/.5) toward a past tense or a passive participle, and parafoveal input that was equibiased (.5/.5) toward a main clause or a relative clause (i.e., not a postverbal *by*.). When competition at the verb was finished, and the next region was encountered, it provided strong evidence (.85/.15) in favor of a relative clause. Under these conditions, the model predicts more competition at the verb for Good Themes than for Good Agents. At the next region, the amount of competition is approximately equal, continuing at the same level for Good Themes, and increasing for Good Agents.

As Figure 4.2a illustrates, this is the data pattern reported in Ferreira and Clifton (1986, Experiment 1). Ferreira and Clifton used materials with characteristics similar to those that we assumed in this simulation (see Spivey-Knowlton et al., 1993; Trueswell et al., 1994; Burgess, Tanenhaus, & Hoffman, 1994). However, they interpreted the elevated reading times at the verb and next region for Good Patients (Poor Agents) as evidence that readers were aware of the poor thematic fit between the NP at the Agent Role, but were unable to use thematic constraints to avoid the garden path associated with

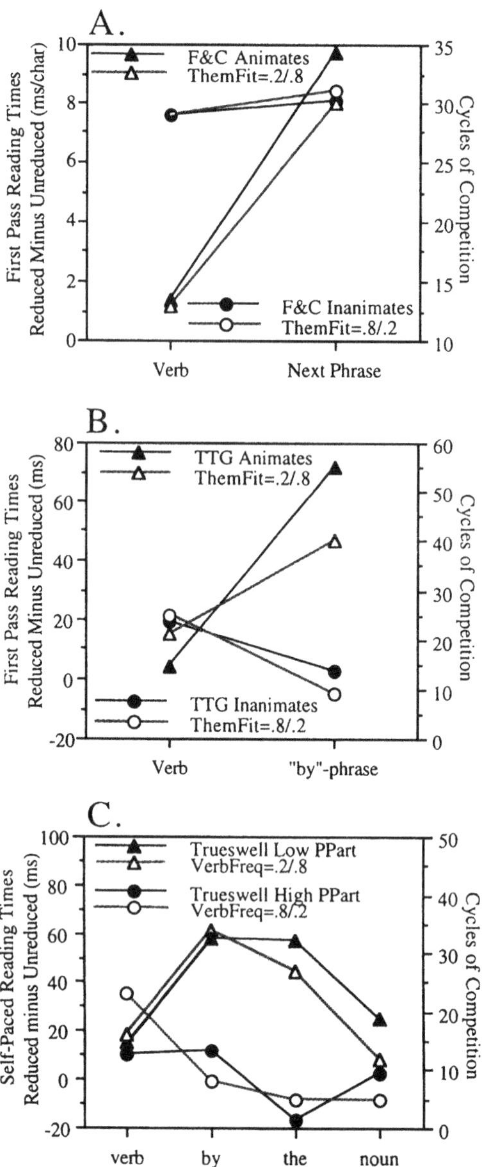

Figure 4.2. Processing difficulty as a function of cycles of competition for different constraint weights plotted against results from experiments in the literature using stimuli with similar characteristics. Scales for the simulations differ because different response measures were used in each experiment. Panel A shows a moderately strong thematic constraint, strong main-clause bias, verbs that used equally often with *-ed* as a simple past and a passive participle, and neutral parafoveal information along with first-pass reading times in ms/character from Ferreira and Clifton (1986). Panel B shows a moderately

initially interpreting the NP V sequence as a main clause, because initial attachment decisions considered only syntactic category information. Our example simulation shows that just this data pattern is predicted from a constraint-based model as a function of the strength of the competing constraints.

As the biases associated with the constraints change, the amount of competition will change, resulting in different data patterns. Next, we increased parafoveal support for the reduced relative by assuming that the PP was always introduced with *by*, as in (3). *By* will be available parafoveally at the verb, and it provides strong support for the reduced relative. Thus, we changed the bias of the input values for the parafoveal constraint from an equibias to .85/.15. Figure 4.2b shows that this simulation reproduces the data pattern found by Trueswell et al. (1994), who manipulated thematic fit in much the same way as Ferreira & Clifton (1986), but always used a *by* to introduce the disambiguating prepositional phrase. Trueswell et al. (1994) found a small, nonsignificant, increase in reading times at the verb for reduced relatives with Good Themes compared to unambiguous controls, and no significant difference at the *by*-phrase. Good Agents showed a large reduction effect at the *by*-phrase. Note that Burgess et al. (1994) systematically manipulated thematic constraint and parafoveal and reproduced both the Ferreira and Clifton and Trueswell et al. data patterns in the same experiment.

In the third simulation, we held thematic fit constant and manipulated the constraints provided by the verbs by varying the biases associated with the Tense/Voice constraint. In this case, even without parafoveal input (as would be the case in word-by-word self-paced reading), the thematic fit bias in favor of the relative clause (.8/.2) is sufficient to eliminate processing difficulty at the *by*-phrase when the verb is typically used as a passive participle rather than a past tense (.8/.2), but not when the verb is typically used as a past tense (.2/.8). This is the result Trueswell (1996) reported using good Themes and manipulating verb tense frequency. Trueswell presented sentences with word-by-word self-paced reading in a moving-window format, thus eliminating parafoveal effects at the verb. Figure 4.2c presents results from this simulation overlaid with Trueswell's results. In order to simulate these conditions, we eliminated the parafoveal constraint shown in Figure 4.1, readjusting the weights on the other

Caption to Figure 4.2 *(cont.)* strong thematic constraint, strong main-clause bias, verbs that used equally often with *-ed* as a simple past and a passive participle, and parafoveal information provided by *by* along with first-pass reading times from Trueswell, Tanenhaus, & Garnsey (1994). Panel C shows a moderately strong thematic constraint, strong main-clause bias, verbs that are typically used with *-ed* as a passive participle, and no parafoveal information along with self-paced reading times from Trueswell (1996).

constraints so that they would sum to 1, and adding a new input constraint (at .85/.15 in favor of the relative clause) for each new critical word in the sentence following the verb.

Thus far, we have seen that by making small, well-motivated modifications in the input a constraint-based model with fixed weights can simulate a wide range of data patterns that have been observed in studies examining the effects of thematic fit on the processing difficulty for sentences with reduced relative clauses. Our point is not that a constraint-based model can simulate different data patterns. That is a trivial claim. Rather, our point is that different data patterns naturally arise out of an intersection of constraints even when all of the constraints are being used immediately upon becoming available. Moreover, the simulations demonstrate that there is no signature data pattern associated with delayed use of a constraint. It is not surprising, then, that different experimenters have found different results and arrived at different conclusions.

Note, however, that just because a constraint-based model can predict a range of different data patterns does not mean it is difficult to find evidence against constraint-based models and in favor of two-stage models. For example, one could simulate a two-stage model using the integration competition model by assuming that only a subset of constraints is used in initial processing, with other constraints coming into play after a delay. If such a model provided better fits than one that applied all constraints simultaneously, one would then have compelling evidence for a two-stage architecture. McRae et al. (in press) explored this approach manipulating thematic fit with the reduced relative ambiguity and concluded that thematic fit is not delayed relative to structural constraints.

Recently some two-stage theorists have argued that revision processes may be so rapid and effortless that the fact that processing difficulty can be eliminated for normally less preferred structures cannot be interpreted as definitive evidence against two-stage models (Frazier, 1995; Clifton & Frazier, 1996). Instead, they propose comparing predictions of constraint-based and two-stage models for the processing of preferred structures. The claim is that constraint-based models predict that competition from the less preferred reading should always interfere with the preferred reading, whereas two-stage models predict that such competition should never be observed. Although this argument might seem plausible, whether or not a constraint-based model actually predicts competition will depend upon the strength of the other relevant constraints. In fact, the simulations reported earlier all show negligible effects of the reduced relative clause (the less preferred reading) competing with the main clause at the verb, when the NP was a Good Agent. The following simulations illustrate how competition effects with the preferred structure (the main clause, in this case) are predicted to change with the strength and availability of constraints.

Table 4.1. *Constraint biases used in simulating processing difficulty at the verb in the preferred structure (main clause)*

	PTense-biased verbs	Equibiased verbs	PParticiple-biased
Verbs			
Parafoveal *the* (free reading)	Main clause = .1/.9 Thematic = .8/.2(.2/.8) Verb frequency = .2/.8 Parafoveal = .15/.85	Main clause = .1/.9 Thematic = .8/.2(.2/.8) Verb frequency = .5/.5 Parafoveal = .15/.85	Main clause = .1/.9 Thematic = .8/.2(.2/.8) Verb frequency = .8/.2 Parafoveal = .15/.85
No parafoveal *the* (self-paced reading)	Main clause = .1/.9 Thematic = .8/.2(.2/.8) Verb frequency = .2/.8	Main clause = .1/.9 Thematic = .8/.2(.2/.8) Verb frequency = .5/.5	Main clause = .1/.9 Thematic = .8/.2(.2/.8) Verb frequency = .8/.2

Consider an experiment in which thematic fit is manipulated as before, but with animate nouns that are either Good Patients (.8/.2) or Good Agents (.2/.8) of the ambiguous verb. However, now the ambiguity is resolved as a main clause. For example, compare materials such as those in (4) to unambiguous sentences such as those in (5):

(4) a. The doctor examined the sick child carefully.
    b. The patient examined the sick child carefully.

(5) a. The doctor had examined the sick child carefully.
    b. The patient had examined the sick child carefully.

We simulated this situation six ways, using the same model as in the previous simulations, with the same weights, and with the input biases shown in Table 4.1. For the next phrase region, we simply added one new input constraint with a strong bias, this time toward the main clause (.15/.85).

As shown in panel A of Figure 4.3, there is little effect of thematic fit at the verb when the sentences use verbs and parafoveal input (i.e., *the*) that support the main clause alternative. In fact, if we assume that a cycle of competition corresponds to roughly 1.5–2.0 ms, as suggested in the overlays of Figures 4.2, then we might expect (based on panel A) to see about 10–14 ms of processing difficulty at the verb for Good Agents and about 22–30 ms for Good Patients, an interaction that is not likely to reach significance. And at the disambiguating noun phrase, almost no differences would arise. If, by contrast, sentences in which the verbs have a frequency bias toward the passive participle (and therefore toward the relative clause) are used, and parafoveal input is excluded (as in word-by-word self-paced reading), then the model predicts a substantial difference in the amount of processing difficulty exhibited by sentences with Good Patients compared to sentences with Good Agent sentences (Figure 4.3, Panel F).

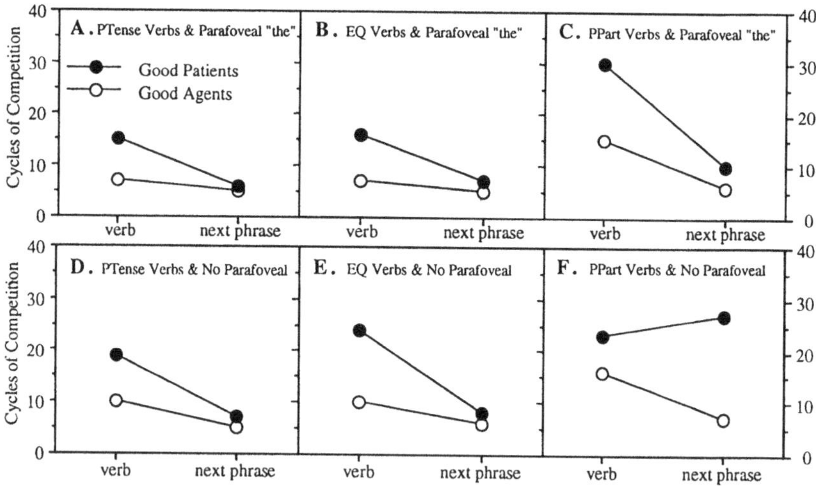

Figure 4.3. Competition at the ambiguous verb and at the following noun phrase for *-ed* verbs in which the first NP is either a Good Agent or a Good Theme of the verb for the three sets of weights shown in Table 4.1.

In conclusion, then, a range of temporal patterns, including those that have been argued to provide evidence for the delayed use of thematic constraints on syntactic ambiguity resolution, are naturally simulated by a constraint-based model simply by taking into account differences in the strength and availability of relevant constraints. Of course, merely demonstrating that there is a plausible combination of input biases and weights that will generate these data patterns is not in itself conclusive. Rather, one needs to independently quantify the biases on the constraints and then show that the same weights account for the observed data patterns as the strength of the constraints vary.

4.4 Modeling Discourse Constraints

We now focus on the interaction between constraints introduced by discourse context and intrasentential constraints in ambiguity resolution. Our goal is to evaluate the claim made by Spivey-Knowlton et al. (1993) and MacDonald et al. (1994) that a constraint-based framework can unify the conflicts in the literature on discourse context effects. We begin by applying the model presented in Figure 4.1 to some of our recent experiments in which sentences containing reduced relative clauses were preceded by biasing discourse contexts. These contexts manipulated referential support along the lines suggested by Crain and Steedman (1985) and Altmann and Steedman (1988).

Spivey-Knowlton et al. (1993) developed materials in which a sentence such as (6) with a reduced relative clause modifying the subject NP (*the actress*) was preceded by a context that introduced a single possible referent or two possible referents for the subject ((7a) and (7b), respectively).

(6) The actress selected by the director believed that her performance was perfect.

(7) a. An actress and the producer's niece were auditioning for a play. The director selected the actress but not the niece. The actress selected by the director believed that her performance was perfect.
b. Two actresses were auditioning for a play. The director selected one of the actresses but not the other. The actress selected by the director believed that her performance was perfect.

Completion studies established that the two-referent contexts resulted in more relative-clause completions for NP V fragments (e.g., *The actress selected* . . .) than one-referent contexts. We conducted self-paced reading and eye-tracking studies comparing reduced relatives to either full relatives (e.g., *The actress who was selected* . . .) or reduced relatives with morphologically unambiguous verbs (The actress chosen . . .). Full descriptions of the self-paced reading experiments are presented in Spivey-Knowlton et al. (1993) and a preliminary report of the eye-tracking results appears in Spivey-Knowlton and Tanenhaus (1994). A full description of the eye-tracking experiments and a complete description of the modeling presented here appears in Spivey-Knowlton and Tanenhaus (1998).

In order to model reading times with these materials, we eliminated the thematic bias constraint because all of the NPs were both good Agents and Good Patients for the ambiguous verb. We also added a discourse bias constraint. Thus the model has six constraints in all: (1) discourse bias, (2) clause bias, (3) voice/tense frequency for the ambiguous verbs, (4) *by* bias, (5) the bias from the noun in the *by*-phrase, and (6) the bias provided by the main verb. For simulating reading times in the eye-tracking study, we assumed that three regions would be sampled successively: (a) the ambiguous verb, (b) the noun in the *by*-phrase, and (c) the main verb. We assumed that the first four constraints would be available at the verb, with the bias from the noun coming into play on the next fixation and the bias from the main verb on the fixation after that. In order to simulate fixations across regions, we used the dynamic criterion that we described in the mini-simulations presented in the previous section, adjusting weights for new and old inputs using the same procedure described earlier.

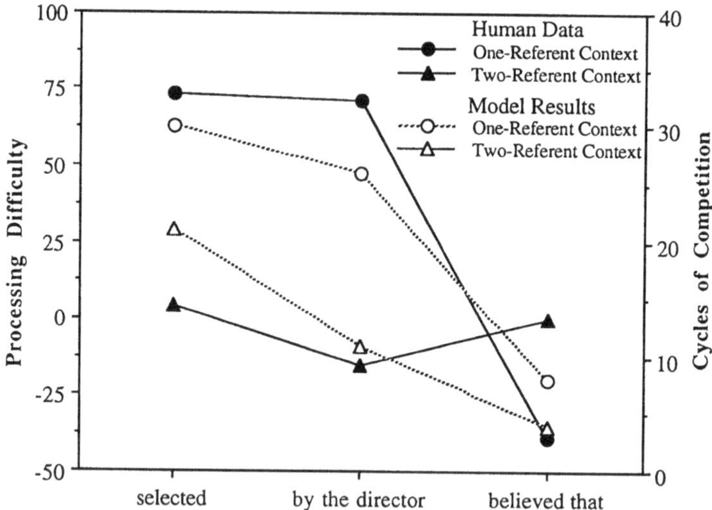

Figure 4.4. The integration-competition model approximates processing difficulty across all three critical regions for the two contexts in Spivey-Knowlton and Tanenhaus (1996, Experiment 2). Processing difficulty is computed as first-pass reading time in the reduced relative minus that in the full relative, for each region. Model results are overlaid on the data to show general correspondence of the patterns.

The first experiment we simulated was an eye-tracking experiment that used materials like those described in (6) and (7) with the reduced relative clauses compared to an unambiguous baseline with full relatives (e.g., *The actress who was selected by the director believed that her performance was perfect*). Unlike previous studies using discourse context and reduced relative clauses, we found an interaction between discourse context and type of relative clause (ambiguous or unambiguous) at the *by*-phrase in both first-pass and total reading times. We also found a suggestion of increased processing difficulty at the ambiguous verb for reduced relatives in one-referent contexts (see Figure 4.4).

In order to simulate the data we needed to choose input strengths and weights. We made the simplifying assumption that the weights on all of the constraints at the verb would be similar, except for tense/voice, which we weighted a little more heavily in order to give the model some degree of "bottom-up priority." Also, tense/voice frequency is correlated with transitivity, which is a relevant constraint for the reduced relative ambiguity (MacDonald, 1994; Trueswell, 1996). At the verb, we assigned verb tense/voice a weight of 1/3, and discourse bias, clause bias, and parafoveal support were each assigned weights of 2/9. The input strengths for verb tense/voice were condensed into probabilities using the following equations:

$$\begin{aligned}
P(RR) &= (\log PPart/\log BASE/((\log PPart/\log BASE) \\
&\quad + (\log Past/\log BASE)) \\
P(MC) &= (\log Past/\log BASE/((\log PPart/\log BASE) \\
&\quad + (\log Past/\log BASE))
\end{aligned}$$

We made the simplifying assumption that the input strengths for the clause bias, discourse context, and parafoveal effects of *by* would be the same for each stimulus set. We chose the values for discourse bias and clause bias so that the mean of their probabilities would approximate completion data obtained with these materials using NP V fragments (e.g., *The actress selected* ...) in one-referent and two-referent contexts. The probabilities of reduced relative completions with these materials were 25% and 43% for the one-and two-referent contexts, respectively. The parameters for *by* support were determined by the effects of *by* on gated completions conducted by McRae et al. (1998) when *by* was added to NP V fragments (e.g., NP V completions compared to NP V *by* completions). Each new input (verb, noun, *by*-phrase) was assigned a weight of 1.0, and then all the inputs were renormalized. We assumed that the noun in the *by*-phrase provided support for the RR with a bias of .99, and that the main verb increased this support to 1.0. For regions that received multiple fixations (e.g., the *by*-phrase, which averaged 1.6 first-pass fixations, we multiplied the cycles of competition by the mean number of first-pass fixations.

Figure 4.4 presents processing difficulty as indexed by a reduction effect in ms for first-pass reading times plotted against the model predictions in cycles of competition.

The model provides reasonably good fits to the first-pass reading time data and also makes some interesting fine-grained predictions. At the verb, for instance, the amount of competition should vary as a function of the relative biases provided by the verb in the two-referent contexts. A regression equation predicting reduction effects for individual items from the model's predictions in cycles of competition accounted for 33% of the variance. The prediction improved to 50% of the variance when those verbs with twenty or fewer occurrences per million were excluded. Corpus estimates are less likely to be reliable for these verbs.

To test the generality of the model, we used the same weights and applied the model to two additional experiments using similar materials in which discourse context had much weaker effects. The first was an experiment reported in Spivey-Knowlton et al. (1993). This experiment used word-by-word

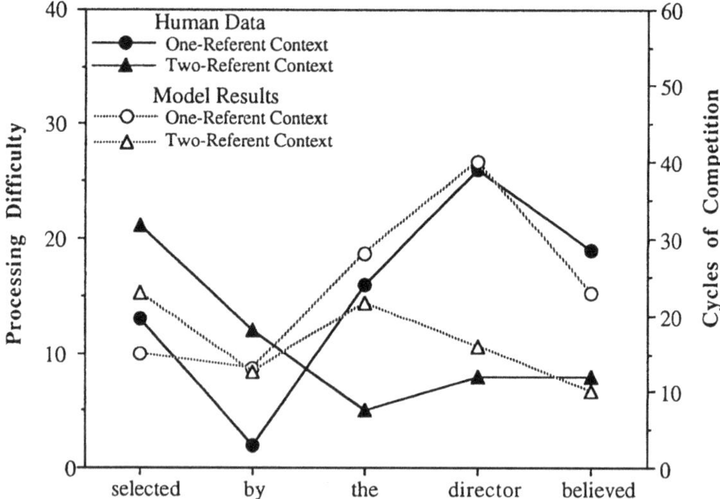

Figure 4.5. The integration-competition model approximates the pattern of processing difficulty across the five critical regions for the two contexts in word-by-word self-paced reading (Spivey-Knowlton et al., 1993, Experiment 3). Processing difficulty is computed as self-paced reading time in the ambiguous reduced relative minus that in the morphologically unambiguous reduced relative for each word. Model results are overlaid on the data to show general correspondence of the patterns. (As the measure of processing difficulty is qualitatively different from that in other simulations, the scale factor for this overlay is not expected to coincide with the others.)

self-paced reading with moving-window presentation and the same materials as the eye-tracking study. With one-word presentation, parafoveal support from the *by* is no longer present at the verb. The model now predicts more competition for two-referent contexts than for one-referent contexts at the verb – exactly the opposite pattern as with parafoveal support. The competition then crosses over, later in the sentence. Figure 4.5 presents the model's predictions for word-by-word self-paced reading and the actual results obtained by the Spivey-Knowlton et al. (1993). While the correspondence is not perfect, the model matches the general pattern in the data.

The same weights were also used to simulate data from an experiment by Murray and Liversedge (1994) in which, paradoxically, the two-referent context actually increased processing difficulty for the reduced relative clause throughout the entire sentence. Verb Voice/Tense frequency information was obtained using the appendices in Liversedge (1994). The materials used dative verbs followed by a definite noun phrase (e.g., *The salesman paid the money put it . . . , The guest grilled the steak said it . . .*). Because dative verbs can be followed by an NP in a reduced relative, we assumed that parafoveal support would be equally biased toward the main clause and reduced relative interpretation. The nouns in the NP were typically biased toward a main clause; correspondingly, this input was given a bias of .75 toward a main clause and .25 toward a relative clause. Similar results would have occurred if we had assumed equal biases from the noun and assumed that *the* provided stronger support for a main clause than for a reduced relative even for dative verbs, which is highly likely. The discourse bias was set to approximate the percentage of main clause and relative clause sentence completions that Murray and Liversedge (1994) report in NP V fragments with one- and two-referent contexts (4% and 10%, respectively). The mean competition for the Verb and NP regions was summed because Murray and Liversedge presented data collapsed across these regions. As in the simulation of the Spivey-Knowlton and Tanenhaus (1994) eye-tracking experiment, we assumed 1.6 fixations in the NP. The model, using the same weights as in the previous simulations, replicated the general pattern in which the supportive (two-referent) context actually increases processing difficulty compared to the one-referent context. The simulation results are plotted in Figure 4.6 along with Murray and Liversedge's (1994) data.

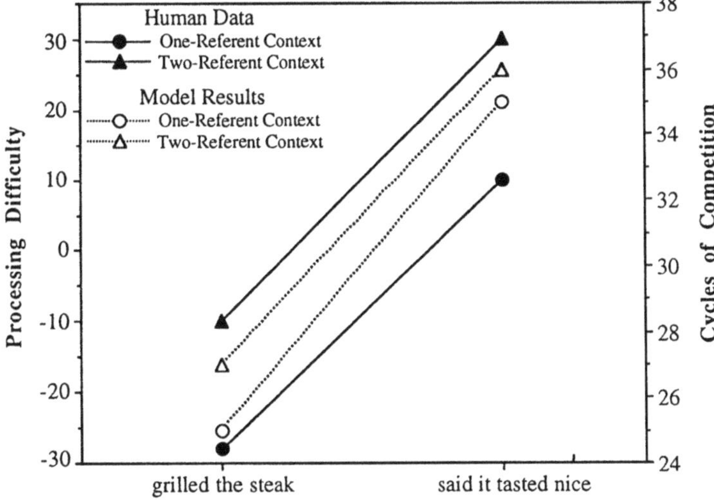

Figure 4.6. The integration-competition model approximates the pattern of processing difficulty across the two critical regions for the two contexts in an eyetracking experiment with a different set of materials (Murray & Liversedge, 1994, Experiment 2). Processing difficulty is computed as first-pass *per-word* reading time in the reduced relative minus that in the full relative, for each region. Model results are overlaid on the data to show general correspondence of the patterns. (As the measure of processing difficulty is qualitatively different from that in other simulations, the scale factor for this overlay is not expected to coincide with the others.)

The simulations we have reported thus far provide support for our claim that salient constraints from discourse are continuously integrated with more local constraints in evaluating syntactic alternatives. Using the same weights and biases that were determined from either corpora or completion norms, we were able to simulate three different data patterns, one that provides clear support for immediate use of discourse constraints and two others that have been used to argue for the delayed use of discourse constraints. As in the case of thematic constraints, the strongest effects of discourse context were found when parafoveal information supported the reduced relative. However, it is important to note that under conditions in which discourse constraints are highly weighted, we would expect to find that discourse context can override even strong local constraints. This claim runs contrary to recent proposals by Britt (1994) and others that discourse contexts can override preferences that involve adjuncts, but not arguments (see Spivey-Knowlton & Sedivy, 1995). The next section provides support for this claim.

4.4.1 Thematic Ambiguities in By*-phrases*

In the previous simulations, stimulus weights were set using a mix of completion data and corpus information. Since completions measure off-line performance, the success of the simulations suggests that it is important to re-evaluate the standard assumption that constraints are integrated differently in on-line processing than in off-line processing. We did this by first independently quantifying the relevant constraints and then establishing weights to model off-line completions. The crucial question was whether the same off-line data simulation weights would successfully model on-line reading times. A full description of the sentence completion and eye-tracking experiments and of the modeling is given in Hanna et al. (1996).

We examined the temporary ambiguities introduced by prepositional *by*-phrases in passive sentences. The preposition *by* is lexically ambiguous, introducing a noun phrase that can be assigned the thematic role of an agent (e.g., *hung by the director*) or a location (e.g., *hung by the entrance*), among others. Discourse constraints were manipulated by using embedded questions to establish a thematic expectation for receiving information about an agent or a location. Example stimuli are shown in (8):

(8) a. Agent Context/Agent Target Noun:
The artist decided to go to the gallery. Once he got there he wanted to know *who* had hung his prize painting. He was pleased to discover that his painting had been hung *by the director* earlier in the week.

Table 4.2. *Percentage of agent and location completions*

	Condition					
	No context Verb + *by*		Agent context Verb + *by*		Location context Verb + *by*	
Completion:	Agentive	Locative	Agentive	Locative	Agentive	Locative
All verbs	76%	19%	93%	6%	50%	48%
Agent-biasing verbs	92%	0%	98%	0%	66%	32%
Location-biasing verbs	38%	59%	64%	34%	18%	82%

b. Location Context/Location Target Noun:
The artist decided to go to the gallery. Once he got there he wanted to see *where* his prize painting had been hung. He was pleased to discover that his painting had been hung *by the entrance* earlier in the week.

Three constraints are relevant to the resolution of this ambiguity: discourse expectation, verb bias, and a contingent frequency bias from the preposition itself. We quantified the strength of the constraints provided by the context and by the verb (in conjunction with its theme) by obtaining ratings for the importance of receiving information about the agent and the location of the relevant event. Ratings were elicited for the agent and location biasing contexts alone (the first two sentences of the stimuli), as well as for the target passive sentences alone (e.g., *The painting had been hung . . .*). These ratings independently quantified the strength of the discourse expectations for individual items as well as for agent and location biasing contexts in general; they also quantified the biases for individual passive verbs. In order to quantify the bias coming from the preposition, an analysis of the Treebank Corpus (Marcus, Santorini, & Marcinkiewicz, 1993) was performed to obtain the frequency with which agentive and locative *by*-phrases occur in passive constructions. Out of over 300 passive sentences containing *by*-phrases, not one introduced a location, while agents were frequent (Hanna, Barker, & Tanenhaus, 1995), indicating that a *by*-phrase following a passive verb provides overwhelming support for the agentive interpretation.

Gated sentence completions were collected and the percentage of agentive, locative, and other completions were recorded for each of twenty-four stimuli in six conditions, crossing the presence of either context or their absence (3 levels) with the presence or absence of the preposition (2 levels). Table 4.2 shows a summary of the completion results with sentence fragments up to and including *by*.

Without the *by*, (fragments like *The painting had been hung . . .*; i.e., the no context condition without the *by*), there was in fact a preference for locative

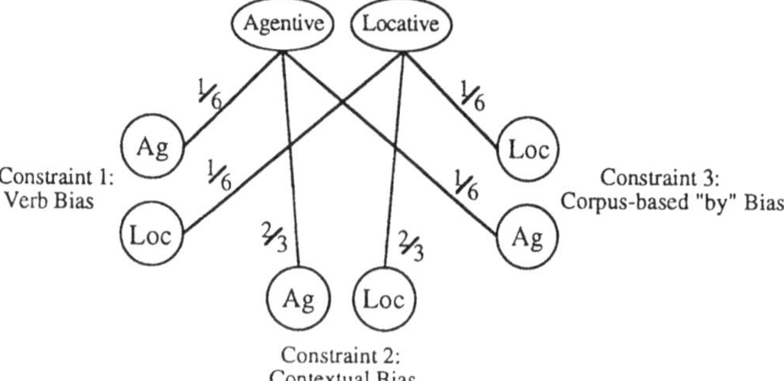

Figure 4.7. Integration-competition architecture for combining constraints to resolve the *by*-phrase ambiguity. All connections are bidirectional. The heavy weighting of Constraint 2 reflects the strong expectations created by the stimulus contexts.

over agentive completions; this reflects a general verb preference in the stimulus set for locations over agents, as was indicated by the importance ratings. With the addition of the preposition to the fragments, an agentive preference was found (Table 4.2), as is consistent with the bias revealed by the corpus analysis. Following an agent context, agentive completions were even more frequent; following location contexts, however, agentive and locative completions were equally probable. Thus, the discourse context bias interacted with the contingent *by* frequency bias. There were also effects of individual verb biases. Using the importance ratings, the stimulus items were divided into the most strongly agent- and location-biasing verbs (as well as an intermediate group). Agent-biasing verbs strengthened the preference for an agent completion in all conditions. Likewise, location-biasing verbs strengthened the preference for a location completion in all conditions.

For simulating the sentence completions with sentence fragments up to and including *by*, the quantified constraints from each context and target sentence (provided by ratings and corpus data) were entered into the model, which is illustrated in Figure 4.7. The model was allowed to iterate for ten cycles. After ten cycles, the activation of the agentive interpretation node indicated the percentage (or probability) of agentive completions for that stimulus item. Figure 4.8 shows the sentence completion data and simulation results for agent- and location-biasing contexts as well as agent- and location-biasing verbs.

This simulation provided a set of weights for the different constraints that could then be used to predict reading times, where the duration of competition (number of cycles) should correspond to mean reading times in the various experimental conditions.

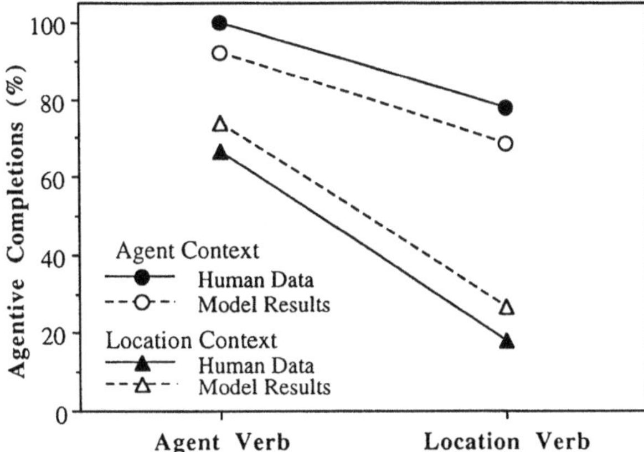

Figure 4.8. Proportion of agent completions for human subjects and model simulations in agent-biasing and location-biasing contexts with agent-biasing and location-biasing verbs.

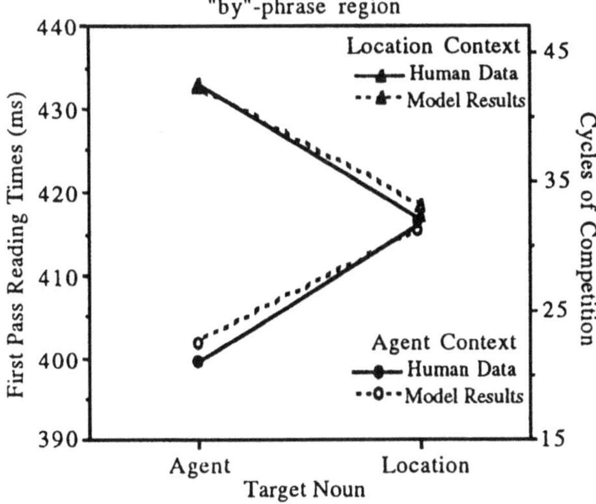

Figure 4.9. First-pass reading times and model predictions at the *by*-phrase region.

In the simulations at the *by*-phrase, the model was first presented with information through the preposition and was allowed to settle into an interpretation. Then information from the noun was introduced, and the model was again allowed to settle into an interpretation. The model simulation (see Figure 4.9) shows that the least competition occurred when the context and target were both consistent with the strong *by*-bias; this was the agentive context–agent target noun condition. The lengthiest competition occurred when a strongly weighted constraint (sentence completions were best fit with context given a weight of 2/3) was pitted against a strongly biased constraint (based on the corpus data, *by* is given a .98 bias for agentive and .02 bias for locative); this is the location context–agent target noun condition. Intermediate degrees of conflict between constraints elicited intermediate competition durations; these were both location target noun conditions. Figure 4.9 presents both the model simulation along with the first-pass reading times at the *by*-phrase, which matched the model predictions. The shortest reading times were found in the agent context–agent target noun condition, the longest reading times occurred in the location context–agent target noun conditions, and the location–target noun conditions showed intermediate times.

It might appear surprising at first that the agent context–location target noun condition should show less competition initially than the location context–agent target condition. Although both targets are incompatible with their contexts, the condition where the target is also compatible with the *by*-bias is showing more competition than the case where the target is incompatible with the *by*-bias. In fact, for many of the items in the agent context–location target noun condition, the model converges relatively quickly (at that point in the sentence) toward an agentive interpretation of the *by*-phrase, the interpretation that is inconsistent with the target. Thus, in this condition, the model would predict that later on in the sentence, as further information provides support in favor of the locative interpretation, there would be especially long reading times as the constraints build up against the agentive interpretation (or probabilistically revise the interpretation). For example, on the next fixation, the target would start to exert a stronger influence since it would again be weighted more heavily that the other constraints when the weights were renormalized.

In fact, the probability of a regressive eye-movement being triggered in the region following the *by*-phrase (see Figure 4.10), was greatest in the agent context–location target condition (total reading times at the *by*-phrase were also the longest in this condition, precisely because readers are more likely to make a regressive eye-movement from the next region). For simulating these results, we assumed that the probability of making a regressive eye-movement is proportional to the size of the change in the probabilities associated with an interpretation node, with large changes corresponding to shifts in the preferred interpretation.

Figure 4.10 plots the actual percentage of regressive eye-movements against the change in the probability of an agent interpretation in the *by*-phrase. The model was allowed to settle into a provisional interpretation with information

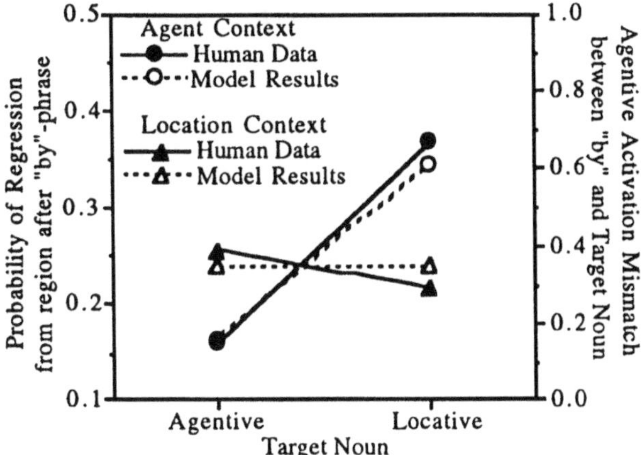

Figure 4.10. Probability of a regressive eye movement being triggered from the region after the *by*-phrase and degree of mismatch between the activation of the target noun at the noun and at the previous fixation.

up to and including the preposition. The activation level of the agent interpretation node was then compared to the incoming information from the noun. As the figure shows, the model does an excellent job of predicting regressive eye-movements, according to this metric. Given these results, it would be straightforward to implement a version of the model that generated regressive eye-movements and made predictions about first-pass reading times and total reading times. It is important to note, though, that there is likely to be a trade-off between whether effects occur primarily in first-pass reading times or in a number of regressive eye-movements. This may account for some of the differences in the results reported by Liversedge et al. (1995) using similar materials. Although their total reading time data are very similar to ours, they obtained a somewhat different pattern of first-pass reading times.

These simulations highlight the important point that inferences based on differences between first-pass and total reading time differences are extremely risky in the absence of a model with an explicit mechanism that maps onto processing difficulty. Despite the fact that the data pattern we observed with offline completions and total reading times differed from the first-pass reading times, the same model with the same parameters and weights simulated both data patterns. The differences we observed are clearly due to differences in the time course with which different constraints exert effects that are detectable in reading times. However, these differences arise from an architecture in which all constraints are simultaneously integrated as they become available.

In sum, the normalized recurrence model fit data from two different types of local ambiguities in which discourse constraints combine with local constraints. The model provided good fits for experimental results showing a data pattern most consistent with the immediate use of local and discourse constraints. Equally importantly, the model, using the same weights but different input values where appropriate (e.g., using different frequency inputs for stimuli with different verbs), also provided good fits to data patterns that have been interpreted as evidence for the delayed use of constraints. These different data patterns fall out naturally from: (a) differences in the strength of the constraints used in different experiments, (b) differences in stimulus presentation, and (c) the nature of the integration mechanism. Moreover, the fact that parameters chosen to model off-line completion data produced excellent fits for on-line reading time data provided counterevidence to the common assumption that constraints are integrated differently in on-line processing compared to off-line processing.

4.5 General Discussion

Researchers in the sentence-processing community continue to invest considerable effort and expense using fine-grained measures such as eye-tracking to discriminate among competing models of ambiguity resolution which make different claims about the early or late use of various information sources during processing. Despite these efforts, our journal pages and review articles are filled with discussions in which authors motivate experiments by noting that whether some constraint is used in initial processing or in reanalysis remains controversial. There are also a plethora of proposals about how to distinguish between those structures that show discourse or semantic context effects and those that do not. This state of affairs is not accidental. In the absence of explicit mechanistic models, it is extremely difficult, if not impossible, to make clear predictions. Our simulations demonstrate that a simple multiple-constraints framework can account for the wide range of data patterns observed in the literature by using a simple mapping of integration time onto processing time and by varying stimulus parameters in principled ways. While that doesn't mean that this type of model is necessarily correct, it does mean that additional architectural assumptions, e.g., proposing processing stages that distinguish between initial structure building and evaluation/revision, cannot be motivated without first falsifying a constraint-based account. That can only be done by meeting the minimal conditions we outlined: (1) specifying and quantifying the relevant constraints, (2) describing an integration mechanism, and (3) specifying a mapping onto processing times that generates clear quantitative predictions.

Some researchers might argue that attention to the level of detail required to meet these conditions shifts the focus away from explorations of the broad principles that underlie sentence processing towards relatively uninteresting questions of empirical detail. However, without taking into account relevant detail, it is not clear that the experimental evidence will bear on the principles that people want to test. In the absence of these procedures, the literature will continue to be equivocal. Constraint-based theorists will be able to account for most data patterns by treating strength and availability of constraints as free parameters. Two-stage theorists will be able to account for most data patterns by treating the time course of revision effects as a free parameter. Different experiments will inevitably come up with different results because the strength of the constraints in the materials will vary across experiments. In the absence of explicit models, using these data to draw inferences about underlying architecture will be as futile as trying to predict the actions of Thomas Hardy's "purblind doomsters" who amuse themselves by "dicing time."

Finally, while our focus here has been on an essentially methodological point, it is worth noting the broader implications of the emerging evidence for probabilistic constraints in processing. In the current modeling, we have abstracted away from details about the underlying representations, assuming localist constraints that are associated with probabilities. In models like these, the probabilities (i.e., conditional or contingent frequencies) are extrinsic to the representations themselves. However, the increasing evidence for probabilistic effects in language processing, and more recently in language acquisition (e.g., Saffran, Aslin & Newport, 1996), strongly encourages approaches in which probabilities are intrinsic to the representations themselves, and structural constraints/knowledge are treated as emergent properties (cf. Tabor et al., 1997). These approaches have the potential to integrate theoretical work in acquisition, representation, and processing in ways that offer a very different perspective than approaches to the architecture of the language processing system that focus on domain-specific principles (cf. Seidenberg, 1997).

References

Altmann, G.T.M, Garnham, A. & Dennis, Y. (1992). Avoiding the garden-path: Eye-movements in context. *Journal of Memory and Language*, 31, 685–712.

Altmann, G. & Steedman, M. (1988). Interaction with context during human sentence processing. *Cognition*, 30, 191–238.

Bates, E. & MacWhinney, B. (1989). Functionalism and the competition model. In B. MacWhinney & E. Bates (Eds.), *The crosslinguistic study of sentence processing* (pp. 157–193). Cambridge, Cambridge University Press.

Bever, T. G. (1970). The cognitive basis for linguistic structures. In J. R. Hayes (Ed.), *Cognition and the development of language* (pp. 279–352). New York, Wiley.

Britt, M. A. (1994). The interaction of referential ambiguity and argument structure in parsing of prepositional phrases. *Journal of Memory and Language*, 33, 251–283.

Burgess, C., Tanenhaus, M., & Hoffman, M. (1994). Parafoveal and semantic effects on syntactic ambiguity resolution. In A. Ram & K. Eiselt (Eds.), *Proceedings of the 16th Annual Conference of the Cognitive Science Society* (pp. 96–99). Hillsdale, NJ: Erlbaum.

Crain, S. & Steedman, M. (1985). On not being led up the garden path. In D. Dowty, L. Kartunnen, & A. Zwicky (Eds.), *Natural language parsing* (pp. 320–358). Cambridge: Cambridge University Press.

Ferreira, F. & Clifton, C. (1986). The independence of syntactic processing. *Journal of Memory and Language*, 25, 348–368.

Frazier, L. (1987). Sentence processing: A tutorial review. In M. Coltheart (Ed.) *Attention and Performance XII* (pp. 559–586). Hillsdale, N.J. Erlbaum.

Frazier, L. (1995). Constraint satisfaction as a theory of sentence processing. *Journal of Psycholinguistic Research*, 24, 437–468.

Frazier, L. & Clifton, C. (1996). *Construal*. Cambridge, MA:MIT Press.

Frazier, L. & Fodor, J.D. (1977). The sausage machine: A new two-stage parsing model. *Cognition*, 6, 291–326.

Frazier, L. & Rayner, K. (1982). Making and correcting errors during sentence comprehension: Eye movements in the analysis of ambiguous sentences. *Cognitive Psychology*, 14, 178–210.

Ford, M, Bresnan, J., & Kaplan, R. (1982). A competence-based theory of syntactic closure. In J. Bresnan (Ed.), *The mental representation of grammatical relations*. Cambridge, MA: MIT Press.

Garnsey, S.M., Pearlmutter, N.J., Myers, E., & Lotocky, M.A. (1997). The contribution of verb bias and plausibility to the comprehension of temporarily-ambiguous sentences. *Journal of Memory and Language*, 37, 58–93.

Hanna, J. E., Barker, C., & Tanenhaus, M. (1995). *Integrating local and discourse constraints in resolving lexical thematic ambiguities*. Poster presented at the Eighth Annual CUNY Conference on Human Sentence Processing.

Hanna, J. E., Spivey-Knowlton, M. J., & Tanenhaus, M. K. (1996). Integrating discourse and local constraints in resolving lexical thematic ambiguities. In G. Cotrell (Ed.), *Proceedings of the Eighteenth Annual Conference of the Cognitive Science Society* (pp. 266–271). Hillsdale, NJ: Earlbaum.

Jurafsky, D. (1996). A probabilistic model of lexical and syntactic access and disambiguation. *Cognitive Science*, 20, 137–194.

Kimball, J. (1973). Seven principles of surface structure parsing in natural language. *Cognition*, 2, 15–47.

Liversedge, S. (1994). Referential context, relative clauses and syntactic parsing. Unpublished Ph.D. dissertation. University of Dundee, Scotland.

Liversedge, S., Pickering, M., & Branigan, H. (1995). *The comprehension of sentences that are ambiguous between agentive and locative interpretations*. Poster presented at the 8th Annual CUNY Sentence Processing Conference.

MacDonald, M. (1994). Probabilistic constraints and syntactic ambiguity resolution. *Language and Cognitive Processes*, 9, 692–715.

MacDonald, M., Pearlmutter, N., & Seidenberg, M. (1994). The lexical nature of syntactic ambiguity resolution. *Psychological Review*, 101, 676–703.

Marcus, M. P., Santorini, B., & Marcinkiewicz, M. A. (1993). Building a large annotated corpus of English: The Penn Treebank. *Computational Linguistics*, 19, 313–330.

Marslen-Wilson, W. (1975b). Sentence perception as an interactive parallel process. *Science*, 189, 226–228.

McRae, K., Spivey-Knowlton, M., & Tanenhaus, M. (1998). Modeling the effects of thematic fit (and other constraints) in on-line sentence comprehension. *Journal of Memory and Language*, 38, 283–312.

Mitchell, D.C. (1989). Verb guidance and other lexical effects in parsing. *Language and Cognitive Processes*, 4, 123–154.

Mitchell, D.C., Corley, M., & Garnham, A. (1992). Effects of context in human sentence parsing: Evidence against a discourse-based proposal mechanism. *Journal of Experimental Psychology: Learning, Memory & Cognition*, 18, 69–88.

Mitchell, D.C., Cuetos, F., Corley, M.M.B., & Brysbeart, M. (1995). Exposure-based models of human parsing: Evidance for the use of coarse-grained (non-lexical) statistical records. *Journal of Psycholinguistic Research*, 24, 469–488.

Murray, W. & Liversedge, S. (1994). Referential context effects on syntactic processing. In Clifton, C., Rayner, K., & Frazier, L. (Eds.), *Perspectives in sentence processing*. Hillsdale, NJ: Erlbaum.

Pearlmutter, N. & MacDonald, M. (1995). Probabilistic constraints and working memory capacity in syntactic ambiguity resolution. *Journal of Memory and Language*, 43, 521–542.

Rayner, K. & Morris, R. (1991). Comprehension processes in reading ambiguous sentences: Reflections from eye movements. In G. Simpson (Ed.), *Understanding word and sentence*. (pp. 175–198) New York: North-Holland..

Rayner, K., Sereno, S., Morris, R., Schmauder, R., & Clifton, C. (1989). Eye movements and on-line language comprehension processes. *Language and Cognitive Processes*, 4, 21–50.

Saffran, J.R. Aslin, R.N., & Newport, E. (1996). Statistical learning by 8-month old infants. *Science*, 274, 1926–1928.

Seidenberg, M.S. (1997). Language acquisition and use: Learning and applying probabilistic constraints. *Science*, 275, 213–215.

Spivey-Knowlton, M. (1994). Quantitative predictions from a constraint-based theory of syntactic ambiguity resolution. In M. Mozer, J. Elman, P. Smolensky, D. Touretzky, & A. Weigand (Eds.), The 1993 Connectionist Models Summer School (pp. 130–137). Hillsdale, NJ: Erlbaum.

Spivey-Knowlton, M.J. & Sedivy, J. (1995). Resolving attachment ambiguities with multiple constraints. *Cognition*, 55, 227–267.

Spivey-Knowlton, M.J. & Tanenhaus, M.K. (1994). Immediate effects of discourse and semantic context in syntactic processing: Evidence from eye-tracking. In A. Ram & K. Eiselt (Eds.). *Proceedings of the 16th Annual Conference of the Cognitive Science Society*, 812–817. Hillsdale, NJ: Erlbaum.

Spivey-Knowlton, M.J. & Tanenhaus, M.K. (1998). Syntactic ambiguity resolution in context: Modeling the effects of discourse context and lexical frequency. *Journal of Experimental Psyshology: Learning,Memory, and Cognition*, 24, 1521–1543.

Spivey-Knowlton, M.J., Trueswell, J.C., & Tanenhaus, M.K. (1993). Context effects in syntactic ambiguity resolution: Discourse and semantic influences in parsing reduced relative clauses. *Canadian Journal of Experimental Psychology*, 37, 276–309.

Stevenson, S. (1994). A competitive attachment model for resolving syntactic ambiguities in natural language parsing. Unpublished Ph.D. dissertation, University of Maryland.

Tabor, W., Juliano, C., & Tanenhaus, M. K. (1997). Parsing in a dynamical system: An attractor-based account of the interaction of lexical and structural constraints in sentence processing. *Language and Cognitive Processes*, 12, 211–271.

Tanenhaus, M.K., Spivey-Knowlton, M.J., Eberhard, K.M., & Sedivy, J.E. (1995). Integration of visual and linguistic information in spoken language comprehension. *Science*, 268, 1632–1634.

Tanenhaus, M.K. & Trueswell, J.C. (1995). Sentence comprehension. In J. Miller & P. Eimas (Eds.), *Handbook of cognition and perception* (pp. 217–262). San Diego, CA: Academic.

Taraban, R. & McClelland, J.L. (1988). Constituent attachment and thematic role assignment in sentence processing: Influences of content-based expectations. *Journal of Memory and Language*, 27, 597–632.

Trueswell, J.C. (1996). The role of lexical frequency in syntactic ambiguity resolution. *Journal of Memory and Language*, 35, 566–585.

Trueswell, J.C., Tanenhaus, M.K., & Garnsey, S.M. (1994). Semantic influences on parsing: Use of thematic role information in syntactic disambiguation. *Journal of Memory and Language*, 33, 285–318.

Trueswell, J.C. & Tanenhaus, M.K., & Kello, C. (1993) Verb-specific constraints in sentence processing: Separating effects of lexical preference from garden-paths. *Journal of Experimental Psychology: Learning, Memory, and Cognition*, 19, 528–553.

5

Late Closure in Context: Some Consequences for Parsimony

GERRY T. M. ALTMANN

5.1 Introduction

We use language, amongst other things, to describe the world in which we live (whether the physical world or the mental equivalent). For us to be able to do this, there must exist an interdependence between the two – we must be able to map whatever representations are evoked by experiencing the world directly onto whatever representations are evoked by hearing (or reading) a description of that world. With respect to language acquisition, it is commonly believed that the interpretation of structure in language and of structure in the world are mutually constraining – without that mutual constraint we could not learn the meanings of verbs or the significance of different sentential structures (e.g., Fisher, Hall, Rakowitz, & Gleitman, 1994; Gleitman, Gleitman, Landau, & Wanner, 1988). Unless our language processing system somehow metamorphoses into an adult state that bears no relationship whatsoever to its younger self, adult sentence processing must respect the interdependence between sentences in the language and events in the world. The process of sentence interpretation is nothing more than the realization of that interdependence, and the realization of the mapping between sentential input and the mental world.

Ambiguity in the language complicates the mapping process, because it allows for more than one possible mapping. The question then is: On what basis do we determine which mapping is intended? On what basis are ambiguities in the language resolved? In this chapter I shall (re)consider this question as it applies to syntactic ambiguities. Syntactic ambiguity is an important testbed on which to test radically different theories of the interrelationship between language and the world. Broadly speaking, a syntactic ambiguity arises when it is unclear which grammatical conventions (or syntactic structures) are being signalled. In principle, these conventions can be specified independently of any world which the language they apply to describes – the syntactic structure of a sentence can be specified without any reference, ordinarily, to the world which that sentence describes, and syntactic ambiguities might therefore be resolved without any such reference. On the other hand, because syntactic ambiguities arise when more than one mapping is possible onto the (mental) world, their resolution could in principle require reference to those alternative worlds ("alternative" by virtue of those alternative mappings).

In this chapter I shall explore one particular theory of sentence processing that makes explicit the link between sentences and the mental worlds they describe. I shall demonstrate that despite its intuitive appeal, it requires a radical theoretical overhaul. The theory in question is the incremental interactive theory of sentence processing developed by Crain & Steedman (1985) and Altmann & Steedman (1988).

5.2 Presupposition and the Resolution of Syntactic Ambiguity

Until the mid-1980s, much contemporary research into the processing of sentences containing syntactic ambiguities had ignored the possibility that syntactic ambiguities are resolved with reference to the kinds of context in which these kinds of sentence could normally be expected to occur. Crain and Steedman (1985) and subsequently Altmann and Steedman (1988) argued that the use of certain kinds of construction presupposes certain kinds of context, and that in the absence of such contexts, these presuppositions are violated. Example (1) exemplifies the problem:

(1) The doctor told the woman that he had given the antibiotics to to return soon to the clinic.

The second *to* in this sentence is problematic for many readers because they interpret the sequence *that he had given the antibiotics to* as a complement clause (what was told to the woman). In fact, it should be interpreted as a relative clause (the woman *that the doctor had given the antibiotics to*). Crain and Steedman (1985) pointed out that the use of a relative clause in an example like this presupposes that there is more than one woman in the context within which such a sentence would be produced, and that within this context there is just one woman of whom it is true that the doctor had given her antibiotics. Using a complement clause in place of the relative clause (that is, intending the sequence *that he had given* ... to be a complement clause) would presuppose that there is just one woman that could be identified from the context in which this sentence was produced.

Crain and Steedman proposed that the human sentence processor obeys a principle of parsimony; it prefers whichever interpretation leaves unsatisfied fewest presuppositions. Altmann (1987) and Altmann and Steedman (1988) described a specific instance of this principle, termed the principle of referential failure, in which the processor attempts to interpret incoming material as a restrictive noun phrase modifier if the current noun phrase cannot identify a unique referent – if *the girl* in (1) does not identify which girl is being referred to, the subsequent *that*-clause will be interpreted as a noun phrase modifier. A variety of studies have found support for such referential principles, although the results are not free of controversy (e.g., Altmann, 1988; Altmann, Garnham, & Dennis, 1992; Altmann, Garnham, & Henstra, 1994; Spivey-Knowlton & Sedivy, 1995; Spivey-Knowlton & Tanenhaus, 1994; Spivey-Knowlton, Trueswell, & Tanenhaus, 1993; but see also Clifton & Ferreira, 1989; Ferreira & Clifton, 1986; Mitchell & Corley, 1994; Mitchell, Corley, & Garnham, 1992; Steedman & Altmann, 1989).

The theoretical significance of the Crain/Steedman/Altmann account is that much emphasis is placed on the notion of presupposition – on what would need to be true in the real or mental world (and known to the hearer/reader) for a sentence to be felicitous (see e.g., Levinson, 1983, for a more formal discussion of presupposition). In other words, and in contrast to other contemporary theories of sentence processing (e.g., Frazier & Clifton, 1996; MacDonald, Pearlmutter, & Seidenberg, 1994a; Trueswell & Tanenhaus, 1994), the interdependence between sentence processing and the mental world, and hence between sentence processing and the extrasentential context on which basis this mental world is constructed, occupies centre stage.

5.3 Presupposition and Late Closure

The majority of studies to have explored context effects on syntactic ambiguity resolution have done so using sentences to which Frazier's minimal attachment principle might be applied (e.g., Altmann, 1988; Altmann et al., 1992; Altmann et al., 1994; Altmann & Steedman, 1988; Ferreira & Clifton, 1986; Mitchell & Corley, 1994; Mitchell et al., 1992; Spivey-Knowlton & Sedivy, 1995; Spivey-Knowlton & Tanenhaus, 1994; Spivey-Knowlton et al., 1993; Trueswell & Tanenhaus, 1991). These were sentences in which a noun phrase could be interpreted as a simple noun phrase, or as the head of a complex noun phrase (compare *the woman* with *the woman with the ear infection* or *the woman that the doctor treated*). Altmann's principle of referential failure (formulated more generally in Altmann & Steedman, 1988, as a principle of "referential support") was developed with such ambiguities in mind. However, these are not the only ambiguities to which the principle might apply. Consider (2):

(2) Sam iced the cake he baked yesterday.

In this example an ambiguity arises because the adverbial phrase *yesterday* can attach either to *baked* or to *iced*. There is a preference, in the absence of any prior context (more of which later) to interpret the adverbial as modifying the most recent verb – a preference that has been succinctly captured in terms of the parsing principles "late closure" (incoming material is incorporated, if possible, within the current clause; e.g., Frazier, 1987) and "right association" (incoming material is attached as low in the parse tree as possible, which in a right-branching language like English means as low and to the right as possible; Kimball, 1973). The incremental interactive hypothesis, as originally formulated by Crain, Steedman, and Altmann, made no specific claims regarding the nature of the contextual information which might influence the resolution of ambiguities such as in (2). The account does nonetheless apply to such cases.[1]

Consider, for example, a case in which (2) is embedded in a context in which Sam had two cakes, one of which he had baked yesterday, and the other of which he had baked some other time. When *the cake* is encountered, a set of cakes will be identifiable from the context, but no single cake will be uniquely identified. According to the referential principles developed by Crain, Steedman, and Altmann, the processor will therefore interpret the subsequent material (*he baked* . . .) as a restrictive modifier (*he baked* could, in the written form, be the beginning of a subsequent sentence, so its interpretation as a *that*-less relative is not, strictly speaking, its only grammatically permissible interpretation). The complex noun phrase *the cake he baked* will still not identify a unique referent within the discourse context because there had been two cakes that Sam had baked. Consequently, *yesterday* will be interpreted as providing further restrictive modification. Its use in this case presupposes an appropriate contrast set – it was the cake baked yesterday, as opposed to any other day.

Consider now a case in which the context does not introduce an appropriate contrast set – a context in which Sam had two cakes, only one of which he had baked himself. When *the cake* is encountered, no single cake will be identifiable and the subsequent sequence *he baked* will be interpreted as a restrictive modifier (as before). *The cake he baked* will referentially succeed (that is, a unique referent will be identified). But now *yesterday* is encountered. Its incorporation within the restrictive relative clause *(that) he baked* would presuppose an appropriate contrast set, and because none is available, this presupposition would be violated. According to Crain and Steedman's (1985) principle of parsimony, this reading should therefore be rejected in favour of the reading that

[1] The referentially-based account also applies to sequences such as *the daughter of the man who was waving her concert programme*, but to date there have been no studies which have embedded such sequences in extrasentential referential contexts.

would involve attachment of *yesterday* to the higher verb *iced*. Such an attachment would provide new information about the icing event. In fact, only by attaching *yesterday* to *iced* would no presuppositions be violated. According to Altmann and Steedman's (1988) account, both attachments would be attempted in parallel, but the low right attachment would be rejected in favour of the high attachment on the presuppositional grounds just outlined.

Sentence (3) is a garden-path sentence equivalent in structure to (2) – attachment of the adverbial to the most recent verb (*washed*) is ungrammatical, and only the alternative attachment to *will brush* is possible. The claim, then, is that it should be possible to construct contexts in which the high attachment to *will brush* is the initially preferred attachment, and in which, consequently, the garden path should be avoided.

(3) Sam will brush the dog he washed tomorrow to make its fur shine again.

In a series of experiments with examples of this kind, we (Altmann, van Nice, Garnham, & Henstra, in 1998) created the two different kinds of context outlined above. Sentences like (3) ("high-attachment" sentences) were preceded by contexts which did not provide the appropriate contrast set (the second of the two contexts mentioned earlier). Sentences like (4) ("low-attachment" sentences) were preceded by contexts that did provide the appropriate contrast set (the first of the two contexts mentioned earlier).

(4) Sam will brush the dog he washed yesterday to make its fur shine again.

In other words, each kind of sentence was preceded by what was intended to be its felicitous context. We monitored subjects' eye movements as they read each context + target passage. We found, to our surprise, that the provision of these felicitous contexts did not eliminate the garden path normally associated with sentences such as (3). The adverb (*tomorrow* or *yesterday*) took longer to read and engendered more leftward regressive eye movements in the high-attachment case (3) than in the low-attachment case (4). In short, the predictions that we had made on the basis of the principle of parsimony were not met.

In fact, the principle of parsimony can be construed as (incorrectly) predicting a garden path in (4) even when there is no context. The *that*-less relative clause *he washed* violates the presuppositions that there exist several dogs, and that they can be contrasted in terms of which were washed by the Sam. The relative clause *he washed yesterday* violates the presuppositions that there exist several dogs washed by Sam, and that they can be contrasted in terms of when Sam washed each one. This last presupposition requires the addition of a temporal dimension to each referent set. If the incorporation of *yesterday* into the *that*-less relative clause therefore violates an additional (temporal) presupposition, the principle of parsimony would predict that this incorporation should be rejected in favour of the higher attachment, which need not violate any more presuppositions than those already violated by the relative clause *he washed*. In (4), though, this high attachment would prove ungrammatical (because of the tense mismatch), and a garden path should ensue. Clearly, it does not. Either this analysis of which interpretation violates fewest presuppositions is wrong (and much depends on whether the incorporation of the adverbial phrase into the relative clause does violate more presuppositions than would be violated if it were not so incorporated), or the principle of parsimony is, once again, flawed.

Irrespective of whether parsimony makes the right predictions in the absence of any context, the fact remains that it failed to predict the persistence of the late-closure preference when examples (3) and (4) were embedded in what should have been their respectively felicitous contexts. Other studies have succeeded in completely reversing the difference between sentences similar to (3) and (4), using contexts such as *Heather wonders when Sam will brush the dog he washed* – the high attachment engendered shorter first-pass reading times in the adverbial region, and fewer regressive eye movements, than the low-attachment target (Altmann et al., in 1998).[2] So the late-closure preference can be overriden, but not in the way that we would have first predicted on the basis of parsimony. So what role is left for parsimony and presupposition?

5.4 Presupposition and Constraint Satisfaction

If a presupposition is simply information that is supposed to be true in the real or mental world (in fact, language users have access only to the mental world), then the principle of parsimony can be (re)interpreted in the following terms: The processor prefers whichever reading can be mapped most closely onto that world. Indeed, it is quite unclear how the processor could prefer anything else. In this sense, the principle of parsimony has intuitive appeal. One prediction that follows from this reinterpretation of the principle of parsimony is that we should

[2] In one experiment, the differences between examples such as (3) and (4) were eliminated. In a second experiment, with sentences such as *Sam will brush the dog he washed in the bath tomorrow* (note the additional prepositional phrase), the difference was reversed. We argue elsewhere (Altmann et al., 1998) that without the additional material between the second verb and the adverbial, the two argument structures are equally active (more or less), and hence equally available – the second because it is the more recent, and the first because of the contextual support it receives. With the additional material, the argument structure associated with *washed* is given time to decay relative to that associated with *brush* (cf. MacDonald et al., 1994) – hence the complete reversal.

prefer alternatives that are more likely to be true (or that are, in some sense, more typical), and there is considerable evidence to suggest that this is the case (see, for example, Trueswell, Tanenhaus, & Garnsey, 1994; Trueswell, Tanenhaus, & Kello, 1993). Nonetheless, the more recent evidence described above damages the empirical credibility of the principle. However, much hinges, as it did in the original formulation of the principle, on the nature of presupposition. Whilst the definition of a presupposition given earlier is relatively straightforward, what is less straightforward is how the processor knows what is, or what is not, presupposed. In other words, it is unclear how the processor knows what should be true in the real or mental world for the current sentence to be felicitous. How does it acquire this knowledge? And how does it in fact apply this knowledge?

It is all very well to say that a context supports the presuppositions associated with the use of a particular syntactic structure, but how is that support implemented within the architecture of the human sentence processing device? One possibility is that a context supports the presuppositions associated with a particular structure if there exists a simple interdependence between some property of that context and the structure which that context supports. In the case of example (1), repeated here, a context would support the presuppositions associated with the relative clause if it introduced more than one woman, and if the doctor had given antibiotics to just one of those women.

(1) The doctor told the woman that he had given the antibiotics to to return soon to the clinic.

In such a situation, there would exist an interdependence between the referential properties of the context (that is, of the mental world that exists on the basis of that context) and the relative clause *that he had given the antibiotics to.* This interdependence would in fact be a statistical dependency between the referential properties of the context and the structural properties of the sentence in question. In this case, the crucial dependency, or contingency, is between a context of a particular kind (containing multiple objects of the same kind – multiple women) and the form of the referring expression that can subsequently be used to refer to one of those objects (a complex noun phrase containing a restrictive modifier – *the woman that* . . .). The term "statistical" is used here to refer to knowledge that is acquired through experience of the frequencies with which particular linguistic forms occur in particular kinds of context – contexts of particular kinds will constrain the range of structures which can be used subsequently to refer to aspects of those contexts. In this sense, and by virtue of the existence of those constraints, the contingency between context and subsequent structure is predictive (if one thing constrains the range of possible other things, it is predictive of them). I shall return to what manner of mechanism might acquire such predictive contingencies in the final section.

If presuppositions are in fact statistical dependencies between the context in which a sentence is produced and that sentence itself, then they are just one of a range of statistically derived constraints that, according to constraint-based theories of sentence processing (MacDonald et al., 1994a; McClelland, St. John, & Taraban, 1989; Trueswell & Tanenhaus, 1994), are applied during sentence processing. According to this approach, sentence processing involves the application, in parallel, of different constraints. These constraints may be syntactic in origin, discourse-based, statistical (or frequency-based), or anything else that can constrain the interpretation of a sentence. In MacDonald et al.'s formulation, the constraints are applied within an interactive activation architecture – argument structures are activated as a function of various interacting variables, such as their frequency of occurrence in the language, the extent to which they receive contextual support, and so on. A variety of empirical results support the view that the availability of alternative argument structures is graded (due to lexical-frequency effects), and that this differential availability determines the extent to which other constraints (referential or pragmatic, for instance) can influence the parsing process (e.g., MacDonald, 1994; MacDonald, Pearlmutter, & Seidenberg, 1994b; Spivey-Knowlton & Sedivy, 1995; Spivey-Knowlton & Tanenhaus, 1994; Trueswell, 1996; Trueswell & Tanenhaus, 1994; Trueswell et al., 1994).

An important component of the constraint satisfaction approach is that constraints are not all-or-none – the stronger the lexical constraints, for example (e.g., frequency of occurrence of one argument structure rather than another), the weaker the potential influence of contextual or pragmatic constraints. Indeed, this premise itself compromises the basic tenet of the presuppositional approach that Crain and Steedman (1985) espoused. There, either an analysis violated more presuppositions than another, or it did not. There was no compromise. The constraint-satisfaction approach, on the other hand, is all about compromise.

Within the constraint-satisfaction model described by MacDonald et al. (1994a), the tendency to associate incoming material with the most recent verb-argument structure (i.e., late closure) arises in English because any earlier argument structure will have become less activated through temporal decay.[3] Any constraints that may increase that earlier structure's activation must necessarily

[3] Not all languages exhibit a preference to associate with the most recent structure (e.g., Spanish – Cuetos & Mitchell, 1988), although all demonstrations of high attachment have involved complex NP constructions (see note 1) and not the adverbial attachment construction tested here.

be pitted against the temporal constraint that, at least in the absence of any explicit prior context, makes the most recent structure the most accessible (recent work in our laboratory suggests that that earlier structure can be made more accessible in appropriate contexts – see note 2).

5.5 On the Derivation of Statistical Constraints

In the case of some of the lexical constraints (MacDonald et al., 1994a; MacDonald et al., 1994b; Trueswell, 1996), the statistics to which the sentence processor is sensitive appear to be based on simple frequency-of-occurrence counts. But if, notwithstanding the closure result described above, the sentence processor is sensitive to the kinds of referential presupposition that Crain, Steedman, and Altmann were concerned with (for supporting evidence see the references cited earlier), how would the processor know which kinds of occurrence it should be counting? This is a problem that applies to any kind of pragmatic constraint, and not simply to the referential constraints. Interestingly, it is a problem that has also been identified as a central flaw in models of language acquisition that rely solely on sensitivity to statistical dependencies (e.g., Pinker, 1987, 1995).

Another way of stating the problem is to ask what drives the statistical mechanism – why gather the statistics in the first place, and where does the gathering stop (that is, which statistics are gathered, and which are not)? One solution is provided in a series of elegant computational simulations described by Elman and colleagues (Elman, 1990a, 1990b, 1995; Elman, Bates, Johnson, Karmiloff-Smith, Parisi, & Plunkett, 1996). Elman devised a neural network (a simple recurrent network, in fact) whose task was to predict what its next input would be. One of the many interesting properties of this network was that it encoded statistical dependencies only insofar as they were predictive. If there were no predictive contingency between two events, the chance co-occurrence of those events would not contribute to the encoded statistics (Altmann, 1997, describes why such a property is inevitable given the prediction task). In a more recent series of simulations, Dienes, Altmann, & Gao (in press), reported in Altmann (1996), (see also Altmann, Dienes, & Goode, 1995) demonstrated how a simple extension to Elman's recurrent architecture (itself a modification of the recurrent architecture developed by Jordan, 1986) could generate mappings between sequential structure presented in one domain (e.g., auditory) and sequential structure presented in another (e.g., visual). It could do so because there existed an interdependence between the structures in one domain and the structures in the other, and because statistics regarding sequential structure in one domain were derived so as to be predictive also of sequential structure in the other.

The lesson to be learned from these simulations is that perhaps the human language device operates according to the following (statistical) principle: Statistics are derived only insofar as they are predictive with respect to variation both in the language and in the world described by that language. After all, the purpose of language, and its relationship to the world it can describe, is to permit exactly such prediction. With regard to the resolution of syntactic ambiguity, we can take as given the existence of predictive contingencies between discourse context and subsequent structure (cf. referential context and simple/complex NPs), and our sensitivity to such contingencies. In this case, what is at issue are the mechanism by which such contingencies are acquired, and the mechanism by which sensitivity to such contingencies is manifested during sentence processing. If the human language-acquisition device obeys the same principles as manifested by Elman's predictive networks, it too would encode statistical dependencies insofar as they were predictive (in this case, of subsequent input). And if the human sentence-processing device obeys the same principles as manifested by Elman's predictive networks, it too would predict one structure rather than another on the basis of prior context if that context was predictive of one rather than the other.

5.6 Conclusions

The idea that language processing is essentially just a matter of predicting what will happen next has a number of important consequences. First, a constraint exists by virtue of having some predictive power. What matters is not so much what the constraint is, but rather how constraining it is. Second, fragments of language cannot be divorced from the context within which those fragments occur. The trick is to discover which aspects of the context are important – that is, which aspects constrain the range of possible predictions. Third, if predictive statistics are derived at the level of representation at which language is mapped onto the (mental) world, then it follows that the factors which govern the interpretation of the world necessarily govern the interpretation of the language used to describe that world. In principle, of course, relevant statistics could be derived at some level of representation that is somehow prior to the level at which language is mapped onto the world. But we already know that statistics must be derived at that higher level, as otherwise the relationship between language and the world would be untenable. It is precisely because that relationship exists that the interpretation of language, and the interpretation of the world which that language can describe, must to some extent be mutually interdependent.

What has this to do with presuppositions? To the extent that presuppositions are simply contextual dependencies, and parsimony is simply the requirement that an interpretation is chosen which best satisfies the constraints, Crain and Steedman (1985) and subsequently Altmann and Steedman (1988) were entirely correct: Context is all-important.

References

Altmann, G. T. M. (1987). Modularity and interaction in sentence processing. In J. Garfield (Ed.), *Modularity in knowledge representation and natural language understanding* (pp. 249–258). Cambridge, MA: MIT Press.

Altmann, G. T. M. (1988). Ambiguity, parsing strategies, and computational models. *Language and Cognitive Processes* 3, 73–97.

Altmann, G. T. M. (1996). Accounting for parsing principles: From parsing preferences to language acquisition. In T. Inui & J. McClelland (Eds.), *Attention and performance XVI*. Cambridge, MA: MIT Press.

Altmann, G. T. M., Dienes, Z., & Goode, A. (1995). Modality independence of implicitly learned grammatical knowledge. *Journal of Experimental Psychology: Learning, Memory, and Cognition* 21, 899–912.

Altmann, G. T. M., Garnham, A., & Dennis, Y. (1992). Avoiding the garden path: Eye movements in context. *Journal of Memory and Language* 31, 685–712.

Altmann, G. T. M., Garnham, A., & Henstra, J. A. (1994). Effects of syntax in human sentence parsing: Evidence against a structure-based proposal mechanism. *Journal of Experimental Psychology: Learning, Memory & Cognition* 20, 209–216.

Altmann, G. T. M., & Steedman, M. J. (1988). Interaction with context during human sentence processing. *Cognition* 30, 191–238.

Altmann, G. T. M., van Nice, K. Y., Garnham, A., & Henstra, J.-A. (1998). Late closure in context. *Journal of Memory and Language* 38, 459–484.

Clifton, C., & Ferreira, F. (1989). Ambiguity in context. *Language and Cognitive Processes*, 4, 77–104.

Crain, S., & Steedman, M. J. (1985). On not being led up the garden path: The use of context by the psychological parser. In D. Dowty, L. Karttunen, & A. Zwicky (Eds.), *Natural language parsing: Psychological, computational, and theoretical perspectives* (pp. 320–358). Cambridge: Cambridge University Press.

Cuetos, F., & Mitchell, D. C. (1988). Cross-linguistic differences in parsing: Restrictions on the use of the Late Closure strategy in Spanish. *Cognition* 30, 73–105.

Dienes, Z., Altmann, G. T. M., & Gao, S.-J. (in press). Mapping across domains without feedback: A neural network model of transfer of implicit knowledge. *Cognitive Science*.

Elman, J. L. (1990a). Finding structure in time. *Cognitive Science* 14, 179–211.

Elman, J. L. (1990b). Representation and structure in connectionist models. In G. T. M. Altmann (Eds.), *Cognitive models of speech processing: Psycholinguistic and computational perspectives* (pp. 345–382). Cambridge, MA: MIT Press.

Elman, J. L. (1995). Language as a dynamical system. In R. F. Port & T. V. Gelder (Eds.), *Mind as motion*. Cambridge, MA: MIT Press.

Elman, J. L., Bates, E. A., Johnson, M. H., Karmiloff-Smith, A., Parisi, D., & Plunkett, K. (1996). *Rethinking innateness: A connectionist perspective on development*. Cambridge, MA: MIT Press.

Ferreira, F., & Clifton, C. (1986). The independence of syntactic processing. *Journal of Memory and Language* 25, 348–368.

Fisher, C., Hall, D. G., Rakowitz, S., & Gleitman, L. R. (1994). When it is better to receive than to give: Syntactic and conceptual constraints on vocabulary growth. *Lingua* 92, 333–375.

Frazier, L. (1987). Sentence processing: A tutorial review. In M. Coltheart (Ed.), *Attention and performance XII: The psychology of reading* (pp. 559–586). Hillsdale, NJ: Erlbaum.

Frazier, L., & Clifton, C. (1996). *Construal*. Cambridge, MA: MIT Press.

Gleitman, L., Gleitman, H., Landau, B., & Wanner, E. (1988). Where learning begins: Initial representations for language learning. In F. Newmeyer (Ed.), *The Cambridge linguistic survey, Vol. III*. Cambridge, MA: Harvard University Press.

Jordan, M. I. (1986). *Serial order: A parallel distributed processing approach*. Technical Report No. 8604, Institute of Cognitive Science, University of California, San Diego, CA.

Kimball, J. (1973). Seven principles of surface structure parsing in natural language. *Cognition* 2, 15–47.

Levinson, S. (1983). *Pragmatics*. Cambridge: Cambridge University Press.

MacDonald, M. (1994). Probabilistic constraints and syntactic ambiguity resolution. *Language and Cognitive Processes* 9, 157–202.

MacDonald, M. C., Pearlmutter, N. J., & Seidenberg, M. S. (1994a). The lexical nature of syntactic ambiguity resolution. *Psychological Review* 101, 676–703.

MacDonald, M. C., Pearlmutter, N. J., & Seidenberg, M. S. (1994b). Syntactic ambiguity resolution as lexical ambiguity resolution. In C. Clifton, L. Frazier, & K. Rayner (Eds.), *Perspectives on sentence processing*. Hillsdale, NJ: Erlbaum.

McClelland, J. L., St. John, M., & Taraban, R. (1989). Sentence comprehension: A parallel distributed processing approach. *Language and Cognitive Processes* 4, 287–336.

Mitchell, D. C., & Corley, M. M. B. (1994). Immediate biases in parsing: Discourse effects or experimental artefacts? *Journal of Experimental Psychology: Learning, Memory, and Cognition* 20, 217–222.

Mitchell, D. C., Corley, M. M. B., & Garnham, A. (1992). Effects of context in human sentence parsing: Evidence against a discourse-based proposal mechanism. *Journal of Experimental Psychology: Learning, Memory and Cognition* 18, 69–88.

Pinker, S. (1987). The bootstrapping problem in language acquisition. In B. MacWhinney (Ed.), *Mechanisms of Language Acquisition* (pp. 399–441). Hillsdale, NJ: Erlbaum.

Pinker, S. (1995). Language acquisition. In L. R. Gleitman & M. Liberman (Eds.), *Language: An invitation to cognitive science*. Cambridge, MA: MIT Press.

Spivey-Knowlton, M., & Sedivy, J. C. (1995). Resolving attachment ambiguities with multiple constraints. *Cognition* 55, 227–267.

Spivey-Knowlton, M., & Tanenhaus, M. (1994). Referential context and syntactic ambiguity resolution. In C. Clifton, L. Frazier, & K. Rayner (Eds.), *Perspectives on sentence processing*. Hillsdale, NJ: Erlbaum.

Spivey-Knowlton, M., Trueswell, J., & Tanenhaus, M. (1993). Context and syntactic ambiguity resolution. *Canadian Journal of Experimental Psychology* 47, 276–309.

Steedman, M. J., & Altmann, G. T. M. (1989). Ambiguity in context: A reply. *Language and Cognitive Processes* 4, 105–122.

Trueswell, J. C. (1996). The role of lexical frequency in syntactic ambiguity resolution. *Journal of Memory and Language* 35, 566–585.

Trueswell, J. C., & Tanenhaus, M. K. (1991). Tense, temporal context, and syntactic ambiguity resolution. *Language and Cognitive Processes* 6, 303–338.

Trueswell, J. C., & Tanenhaus, M. K. (1994). Towards a lexicalist framework of constraint-based syntactic ambiguity resolution. In C. Clifton, L. Frazier, & K. Rayner (Eds.), *Perspectives on sentence processing* (pp. 155–179). Hillsdale, NJ: Erlbaum.

Trueswell, J. C., Tanenhaus, M. K., & Garnsey, S. M. (1994). Semantic influences on parsing: Use of thematic role information in syntactic disambiguation. *Journal of Memory and Language* 33, 285–318.

Trueswell, J. C., Tanenhaus, M. K., & Kello, C. (1993). Verb-specific constraints in sentence processing: Separating effects of lexical preference from garden-paths. *Journal of Experimental Psychology: Learning, Memory and Cognition* 19, 528–553.

Part II

Syntactic and Lexical Mechanisms

6

The Modular Statistical Hypothesis: Exploring Lexical Category Ambiguity

STEFFAN CORLEY AND MATTHEW W. CROCKER

6.1 Introduction

A central topic of debate in the sentence processing community has been whether or not the Human Sentence-Processing Mechanism (HSPM) is composed of a number of articulated modules (Frazier, 1987) or a single homogenous processing unit (Trueswell & Tanenhaus, 1994). This debate is still current; new modular (Frazier & Clifton, 1996; Crocker, 1996; Stevenson, 1994) and interactive (MacDonald, Pearlmutter, & Seidenberg, 1994, Tanenhaus, Spivey-Knowlton & Hanna, this volume) models are being proposed that can explain a larger portion of the data than their predecessors. The modularity question has been inextricably intertwined with our theories of human parsing strategies, since such issues of architecture will determine what kinds of representations and knowledge the parser can bring to bear in making decisions. Rational motivation for a modular parsing subsystem also derives from the fact that current theories of syntax typically posit a restricted and specialised representational framework. A further argument for modularity concerns computational complexity: A module which need only consider restricted knowledge in making decisions can function more rapidly that one which does not.

In this chapter we develop the latter, computational arguments further by considering the role of probabilistic mechanisms within a modular language comprehension system. While the use of frequency information has standardly been associated with nonmodular, interactive architectures (Spivey-Knowlton & Eberhard, 1996), we argue that the use of frequency-based heuristics is in fact a more natural ally of modular systems. In short, truly interactive architectures have the ability to recruit all relevant knowledge in processing, while modular models may be required to approximate this knowledge using probabilistic mechanisms. Indeed, this has emerged as a successful approach in computational linguistics, where statistical techniques are used precisely because the representation and use of full knowledge is intractable (see Charniak, 1993, for discussion).

To investigate this Modular Statistical Hypothesis (MSH) further, we consider an aspect of language processing which has proven itself to be particularly amenable to statistical techniques: lexical category disambiguation. We begin by developing the arguments for the MSH in greater detail and considering some of the current proposals that exploit statistical mechanisms. We then turn our attention to the specific problem of lexical-category resolution, and motivate a particular modular statistical mechanism, the Statistical Lexical Category Module (SLCM). The SLCM is based upon standard part-of-speech tagging technology (Charniak, 1993) constrained by several cognitively motivated factors. The remainder of the chapter is devoted to an examination of how the proposed mechanism fares in dealing with a range of existing findings. In particular, we will show that it provides an extremely simple explanation of some previously problematic data, in addition to being a highly effective mechanism for the problem it is intended to solve in the general case. This model forms a plausible candidate for inclusion in the HSPM. It also demonstrates that a modular model composed of simple statistical (and possibly nonstatistical) components may be preferable to a more interactive approach. We conclude that such simple statistical models, and the MSH itself (see Section 6.2.3), merit further exploration.

6.2 Statistical Mechanisms and Modularity

In this work we assume that the HSPM is at least partially statistical in nature. This assumption is defined by the Statistical Framework:

> Statistical mechanisms play a central role within the human sentence processor.

The specific assumptions embodied by this framework are still the subject of controversy within the sentence-processing literature. Evidence for a statistical position has been produced by researchers advocating the Tuning Hypothesis (Cuetos, Mitchell, & Corley, 1996, and citations therein) and constraint-based positions (MacDonald, Pearlmutter, & Seidenberg, 1994, Tanenhaus, Spivey-Knowlton, & Hanna, this volume). From the constraint-based perspective, statistical effects are simply an unavoidable consequence of micro-level connectionist architectures.[1] However, there is also evidence to suggest that

[1] That is to say, the connectionist mechanisms they assume are inherently sensitive to the frequencies of the data (e.g., utterances) used to train them.

the HSPM does sometimes make decisions that are at odds with the statistical tendencies embodied in language use (Gibson & Schütze, 1996; Mitchell & Brysbaert, 1998; Pickering and Traxler, this volume). Thus an alternative is that the sentence processor makes more selective, or strategic, use of statistical knowledge.

Full consideration of this controversy is beyond the scope of this chapter. Rather, we simply assume the Statistical Framework in general and look at some particular models that are encompassed by it. In particular, we consider whether such statistical models necessarily consist of a single process, drawing on a large range of statistical knowledge (an interactive model), or whether they might be exploited by a number of simpler and more restricted components (a modular model).

There are several reasons why explicitly considering a modular account is worthwhile. If two different types of decisions are dominated by different statistical measures, then a model in which these two decisions are separated into different modules is more predictive. That is, the available set of statistical measures is limited by the modular architecture, on the grounds that if, say, lexical category and syntactic processing are distinct, no cross-module statistical measure would be permitted. It also follows that fewer statistical parameters will be available than in an interactive model, where cross-representational measures might also need to be maintained. As a result, both the learning and processing complexity of the modular account is reduced.

6.2.1 Dominance and the Tuning Hypothesis

One of the issues that divides statistical models is the question of 'dominance' – which statistical measures determine which choices. This is closely related to the so-called grain problem, an issue which is being actively researched by proponents of the Tuning Hypothesis (Mitchell & Cuetos, 1991). The Tuning Hypothesis falls squarely within the Statistical Framework. It makes two central claims:

- In the face of structural ambiguity in the linguistic input, the HSPM makes initial decisions based on statistical information.
- This statistical information is derived from the individual's previous experience of the language.

Tuning maintains that all first-pass structural decisions are made on the basis of statistics accrued during one's linguistic experience, and only on this basis (Cuetos, Mitchell, & Corley, 1996). While the Statistical Framework is designed as a general proposal rather than a testable hypothesis, Tuning makes more specific, predictive, and therefore testable claims. Recent research within the Tuning Hypothesis has been focussed upon the grain problem (Mitchell, Cuetos, Corley, & Brysbaert, 1995; Corley, Mitchell, Brysbaert, Cuetos, & Corley, 1995; Mitchell & Brysbaert, 1998). Consider the sentences in (1) (from Mitchell et al., 1995):

(1) a. Someone stabbed the wife of the football star who was outside the house.
b. Someone stabbed the estranged wife of the moviestar outside the house.

These similar sentences have the same attachment ambiguity – was it the wife or the star who was outside the house?[2] In the former case, the final relative clause (or prepositional phrase) is attached to the first NP, *wife* (high attachment), whereas in the latter it is attached to the second, *moviestar* (low attachment). Such an ambiguity is amenable to resolution by a statistical decision process. For example, statistics could be collated over all occurrences of the sequence NP–PP–RC that the individual has been exposed to. An initial decision would then be made depending on whether the individual had previously heard more occurrences resolved to the high attachment reading or the low one.

However, there are other possible mechanisms, of both finer and coarser grain. One of the finest-grain solutions would be that statistics are collated for all occurrences of these exact words: that is, of all the occasions when the hearer has heard precisely that sentence, how many times was the attachment resolved high versus low? According to this, a different preference might then obtain for the two sentences. A coarse-grain solution, on the other hand, which would entail that a given individual would make the same initial decision when parsing both (1a) and (1b), would be to collate occurrences of NP–NP–modifying constituents.

If a researcher claims that all ambiguity decisions are made on the basis of statistics collated over just one grain of representation, they are arguing that this grain has overall dominance. This is the position of at least one of the Tuning researchers:

> While there is nothing in the current general formulation of the tuning hypothesis to rule out the retention and use of more fine-grained statistics as well as (or instead of) such coarse-grained measures, at least one of the present authors (D.C.M.) favours variants of the model which ignore such information in initial decision-making. (Mitchell et al., 1995, pp. 476–477)

[2] A third possible interpretation of (1b) is that the stabbing occurred outside the house (attachment of the final PP to the VP), but Mitchell et al. do not consider this.

However, dominance is not synonymous with grain. Grain is the structural representation over which statistics are collated – a coarse-grained model makes use of more general representations, whereas a fine-grained model uses more specific ones. On the other hand, a particular set of statistical measures is dominant if the outcome of an ambiguity decision is the same as it would be if these measures were the only ones used in making the decision. If a particular granularity of representation is used to inform a parsing decision, then it follows that statistical measures collated over that level of granularity are dominant for that decision. If a set of statistical measures has dominance, it does not follow that the decision is made at a particular level of grain. The dominant measures may, for instance, have been collated over a number of different grains, or other grains may be taken into account in making the decision, but have a very limited effect.

The opposite of dominance is redundancy. If a possible statistical measure makes no difference to any ambiguity decision, then it is redundant.[3] It makes sense to assume that the HSPM does not collate redundant statistics, particularly if the HSPM is strategic in its use of statistical knowledge. That is, as there are an infinite number of possible statistical measures, the HSPM must in some way determine which ones are worth the required resources to collate. The job of the researcher is therefore to determine which statistics dominate a particular decision process, and which are redundant.

6.2.2 Competition, Sparse Data and Parameters

According to this exposition of the grain argument, ambiguities are resolved absolutely, in accordance with frequencies collated over a particular level of grain, and there is no sense in which different analyses compete. For researchers wishing to propose that more fine-grained statistics are dominant, such a model is immediately problematic. Consider sentence (1a), repeated as (2).

(2) Someone stabbed the wife of the football star who was outside the house.

Mitchell et al. only consider the possibility that statistics are collated for all occurrences of the entire relevant structure. That is, previous exposures to the structural sequence NP–PP–RC may affect the outcome of a future decision, but exposures to intransitive VP–PP–RC will not. How could they? A relative clause cannot be attached to an intransitive VP, and so there is no ambiguity

[3] Note that it is possible for a measure to have a very small influence, and therefore neither dominate nor be redundant.

in the latter case. The problem arises if you wish to argue, for example, that statistics collated at the lexical level are always dominant. It is quite possible that an individual would never have heard *the wife of the football star who* before. In this case they have no previous exposure to exactly this ambiguity, and therefore no statistical data on which to base their decision. Researchers in statistical language modelling often refer to this as the sparse data problem; one solution is to allow competition between different attachments to offer a possible solution.

MacDonald et al. (1994) and Trueswell & Tanenhaus (1994) have proposed models in which lexical statistics are (partially) dominant. Such lexicalist models have been implemented as constraint-based neural networks. When faced with ambiguity, the different possible analyses gain activation based on evidence from the input and previous training data. These analyses are in direct competition. Eventually, the analysis with the greatest activation wins and becomes the currently preferred reading of the sentence. Such a model can be viewed as a statistical model: Choices are informed by frequencies derived from previous exposure to the language during training. However, unlike the model suggested by Mitchell et al. (1995), a number of different frequencies interact to assign activations to competing analysis.

Crucially, in contrast to the Tuning account presented in Section 6.2.1, lexicalist researchers explain a number of ambiguities in terms of previous exposure to the individual words forming the current input, whether or not they occurred in a similarly ambiguous sentence. For example, MacDonald et al. (1994) propose that the dominant statistic in interpreting sentences like (2) is the modifiability of the head noun – *wife* or *football star*. For the sake of argument, let us suppose that 12% of the time *football star* is encountered there is a postnominal modifier, whereas *wife* is only modified on 6% of occurrences. In this case, low attachment should be initially preferred on encountering a sentence such as (2).

Structural statistics may also influence decisions in constraint-based networks (see Mitchell et al., 1995, for further discussion). For example, the HSPM could collate statistics concerning the modifiability of different types of NPs, as well as those concerning specific lexical items. Suppose that NPs in verb object position are modified 30% of the time, but NPs within PPs are only modified 3% of the time. In this case, assuming equal weighting, we would expect the structural statistic to override the lexical one; the initial decision in (2) would be in favour of high attachment.

This interaction of different statistics is what gives constraint-based models their immense power to account for any observations. However, they also rely on a large number of different statistical measures – it is therefore difficult to say which, if any, measures are redundant. The large number of parameters that inform, and may dominate, any decision means that such models tend to be unpredictive.

6.2.3 The Modular Statistical Hypothesis

Let us return to the difference between a modular and an interactive (constraint-based) statistical model. In the former case, we assume that each module has access only to those particular representations that are relevant to its task. This means that it can only use statistical measures which are collated over those representations.

In contrast, a single, interactive decision process has, potentially, access to all levels of linguistic representation (McClelland, St. John, & Taraban, 1989). A truly interactive module, one which also uses nonlinguistic information such as world knowledge, must also have access to appropriate nonlinguistic representations. Statistics may be collated both within and across any of these representations, and there is no principled or practical way for a researcher to decide which measures dominate, and which are redundant.

For example, MacDonald et al. (1994) explicitly tell us that certain ambiguities are decided with reference to particular statistical measures. However, it is by no means clear that the same statistical measures dominate all ambiguities, or that these are the only statistics that play a role in these ambiguities (and that hence all others are redundant). Nor are we told the weights assigned to the different measures, which crucially determines how measures are combined together. Such a model is easily able to account for, or fit, existing data. Indeed, such a model is impossible to refute, as it makes no firm predictions until the dominant statistics and associated weights are determined. If these predictions turn out to be wrong, it is a particular set of weights and statistics that have been refuted, not the model itself. In summary, the single decision process in an interactive model has too many parameters, leading to unpredictiveness. A model with so many degrees of freedom can eschew refutation by simply varying the parameters.

In contrast, the number and type of possible statistical measures used for each decision in a modular model is relatively small. Thus the modular position is computationally simpler with respect to both the amount of statistical knowledge which may be represented, and the amount of experience, or training, required to set such parameters. This in turn means that systematic predictions from such a model are possible. A modular architecture defines which statistical measures may influence which decisions, and perhaps more specifically, which measures may not. Thus the architecture itself is open to falsification, rather than just the particular statistics and weights used by some instance of an interactive architecture. Indeed, from a methodological standpoint, it seems that the only way to satisfactorily prove the interactionist case is to successfully refute the range of more predictive and falsifiable modular theories.

In sum, we have argued that a modular statistical architecture is to be preferred for both methodological and computational reasons. We formalise our position by introducing the Modular Statistical Hypothesis, which refines the Statistical Framework to cover only the space of modular models.

> The human sentence processor is composed of a number of modules, and any statistical mechanisms are restricted to operating within, and not across, modules.

This hypothesis still encompasses a number of possible models, including the coarse-grained architecture proposed by the Tuning researchers (Mitchell et al., 1995). However, unlike the Statistical Framework, it excludes interactive, constraint-based models such as those proposed by MacDonald et al. (1994) and Trueswell & Tanenhaus (1994). In Section 6.3 we develop a partial model that falls within the Modular Statistical Hypothesis, which is more predictive and therefore testable than the Statistical Framework. We demonstrate that the partial model successfully accounts for a range of findings.

If we accept the Modular Statistical Hypothesis, there is another possible way in which statistical architectures may vary – the composition of their modules. While it is traditional for modular models of mind to be split into lexical, syntactic, and semantic components (Forster, 1979), other divisions are possible. Further, one of these modules may again be split into further submodules (Frazier, 1990; Crocker 1996). Lexical-category disambiguation has generally been assumed to lie somewhere between the processes of lexical access and syntactic structure building. In the next section we suggest that lexical category determination may constitute a distinct, modular, decision process.

6.3 Lexical Category Disambiguation

One of the most frequent ambiguities in natural language is lexical category ambiguity. For example, consider the well-known sentences in (3).

(3) a. Time flies like an arrow.
    b. They saw her duck.

In (3a), *flies* is ambiguous between its noun and verb readings – both readings are grammatically possible, but the noun reading is implausible. In contrast,

(3b) is plausible if *her* is read as a possessive pronoun and *duck* as a noun, or if *her* is read as a personal pronoun and *duck* as a verb.

Both (3a) and (3b) are globally ambiguous. However, the majority of lexical category ambiguity is local. For instance, in 4, *her* is disambiguated by the fact that *leave* can only be a verb, not a noun.

(4) They saw her leave.

We argue that lexical category disambiguation has separate status from syntactic parsing – i.e., that it is a separate module. There are a number of reasons for this:

- The statistics relevant to lexical category disambiguation are different from those relevant to parsing (see Section 6.3.1).
- Lexical category ambiguity is typically resolved extremely locally – often by the adjacent words. Structural disambiguation tends to be more long-distance.
- In a serial, bottom-up parser, lexical category disambiguation must occur prior to structure building.
- Lexical category disambiguation is not typically assumed to involve the creation of compositional structure, whereas parsing does, so the output of the two processes is quite different (though see MacDonald et al., 1994, for an opposing view).

In summary, the two are distinct, require different statistics, and generate different output. Given the discussion in Section 6.2, it seems reasonable to hypothesize that these processes identify distinct modules, and in the next sections we outline our proposal for a distinct lexical category disambiguation mechanism.

6.3.1 Statistics and Relevance

If we are to design a lexical-category disambiguation module, the first question must be which statistics dominate, and which are redundant. In order to ensure predictiveness, we must initially assume that a minimal set of statistical measures dominate, and that all others are redundant. This is the most restrictive position. We may then introduce more statistical parameters just in case such a move is warranted by the data; otherwise our simpler model is to be preferred.

In Section 6.2.3 we stated that a module may only make use of statistical measures collated over representations available to that module. For example, as a lexical category disambiguation module must precede syntactic processing, it can make no use of structural statistics. This restriction partially ensures relevance – decisions should be made using statistics collated over structures relevant to that decision. We may therefore rule out the influence of structural or other nonlexical statistics within the lexical category disambiguation module. The question becomes what lexical statistics are relevant?

It seems likely that the HSPM could gather statistics relating individual words to their lexical category – for example, how often the individual has been exposed to the word *flies* as a noun and as a verb. We would expect such a statistic to be dominant.

Beyond that, experimental evidence supports the use of some contextual information (Juliano & Tanenhaus, 1993). At a lexical level, the simplest such statistics are word co-occurrence (e.g., how often the individual is exposed to the sequence *the man*) and category co-occurrence (e.g., exposure to Det–Noun sequences). The latter measure generates fewer parameters and is therefore, by our measure, simpler. It also leads to fewer problems due to sparse data. For example, an individual hearing (5) may have never previously encountered the sequence *pink banana*, but the sequence Adj–Noun will be far more familiar.

(5) Someone gave me a pink banana yesterday.

We therefore hypothesise that word–category and category co-occurrence statistics dominate lexical-category decisions. For the current study, we assume all other statistics are redundant.

6.3.2 The Tagger

Statistical lexical category disambiguation algorithms along the lines we have just described have been well explored in the computational linguistics literature. In particular, there is a range of efficient, accurate, and easily trainable algorithms to perform category disambiguation, a problem typically referred to as part-of-speech tagging (Charniak, 1993).

The job of a tagger is to determine a preferred set of part-of-speech tags (lexical categories) for a given set of words. The simple bigram probabilistic tagger uses the equation (1) to assign a probability to each possible tag sequence (or tag path). In this equation w_i is the word at position i in the sentence (of length n) and t_i is any possible tag for that word[4] – the equation assigns a probability to a given tag path $t_0 \dots t_n$, and we must calculate the probability of

[4] w_0 is a pseudo-word indicating the start of the sentence. t_0 is similarly a pseudo-tag.

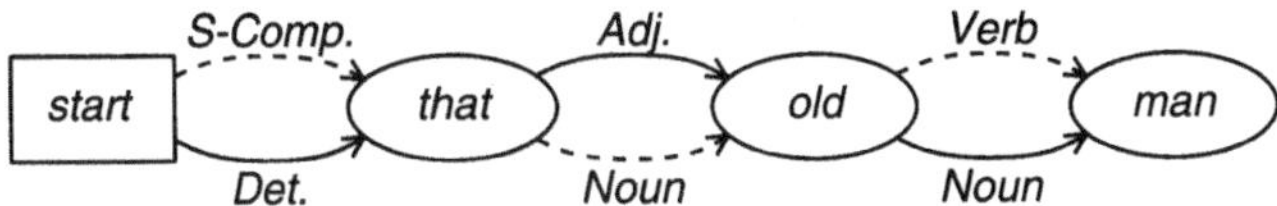

Figure 6.1. Tagging the words *that old man.*

a subset of the possible tag paths to find the preferred one.

$$P(t_0, \ldots t_n, w_0, \ldots w_n) \approx \prod_{i=1}^{n} P(w_i \mid t_i) P(t_i \mid t_{i-1}) \tag{1}$$

The two terms in the righthand side of the equation are the two statistics that we hypothesise to dominate lexical category decisions. $P(w_i \mid t_i)$ – the unigram or word–category probability – is the probability of a word given a particular tag.[5] $P(t_i \mid t_{i-1})$ – the bigram or category co-occurrence probability – is the probability that two tags occur next to each other in a sentence. Estimates for both of these terms are typically based on the frequencies obtained from a relatively small training corpus in which words appear with their correct tags.

This equation can be applied incrementally. That is, after perceiving each word we may calculate a contingent probability for each tag path terminating at that word; an initial decision may be made as soon as the word is seen.

Figure 6.1 depicts tagging of the phrase *that old man*. Each of the words has two possible lexical categories,[6] meaning that there are eight tag paths. In the diagram, the most probable tag path is shown by the sequence of solid arcs, and other potential tag paths are represented by dotted arcs.

The tagger's job is to find this preferred tag path. The probability of a sentence beginning with the start symbol is 1. When *that* is encountered, the tagger must determine the likelihood of each reading for this word when it occurs sentence-initially. This results in probabilities for two tag paths – *start* followed by a sentence complementiser and *start* followed by a determiner. The calculation of each of these paths is shown in Table 6.1.

While *that* occurs more frequently as a sentence complementiser than as a determiner in absolute terms, sentence complementisers are relatively uncommon at the beginning of a sentence. Therefore tag path 2 has a greater probability. This ambiguity is dealt with in more detail in Section 6.4.2.

[5] This may appear counterintuitive, since $P(t_i \mid w_i)$ would seem more natural. See Charniak (1993) for an explanation of how this is derived.

[6] We ignore other, less common possibilities.

Table 6.1. *Tagging* that old man, *stage 1* – that

Path	Probability
1 scomp	$P(\text{“}\textit{that}\text{”}\mid\text{scomp})P(\text{scomp}\mid\text{start})$
2 det	$P(\textit{that}\mid\text{det})P(\text{det}\mid\text{start})$

Table 6.2. *Tagging* that old man, *stage 2* – that old

Path	Probability
1.1 scomp–adj	$P(\textit{old}\mid\text{adj})P(\text{adj}\mid\text{scomp})P(\text{path1})$
1.2 scomp–noun	$P(\textit{old}\mid\text{noun})P(\text{noun}\mid\text{scomp})P(\text{path1})$
2.1 det–adj	$P(\textit{old}\mid\text{adj})P(\text{adj}\mid\text{det})P(\text{path2})$
2.2 det–noun	$P(\textit{old}\mid\text{noun})P(\text{noun}\mid\text{det})P(\text{path2})$

Table 6.3. *Tagging* that old man, *stage 3* – that old man

Path	Probability
1.1.1 scomp–adj–verb	$P(\textit{man}\mid\text{verb})P(\text{verb}\mid\text{adj})P(\text{path1.1})$
1.1.2 scomp–adj–noun	$P(\textit{man}\mid\text{noun})P(\text{noun}\mid\text{adj})P(\text{path1.1})$
1.2.1 scomp–noun–verb	$P(\textit{man}\mid\text{verb})P(\text{verb}\mid\text{noun})P(\text{path1.2})$
1.2.2 scomp–noun–noun	$P(\textit{man}\mid\text{noun})P(\text{noun}\mid\text{noun})P(\text{path1.2})$
2.1.1 det–adj–verb	$P(\textit{man}\mid\text{verb})P(\text{verb}\mid\text{adj})P(\text{path2.1})$
2.1.2 det–adj–noun	$P(\textit{man}\mid\text{noun})P(\text{noun}\mid\text{adj})P(\text{path2.1})$
2.2.1 det–noun–verb	$P(\textit{man}\mid\text{verb})P(\text{verb}\mid\text{noun})P(\text{path2.2})$
2.2.2 det–noun–noun	$P(\textit{man}\mid\text{noun})P(\text{noun}\mid\text{noun})P(\text{path2.2})$

The next word, *old*, is also ambiguous between being an adjective or a noun. There are therefore four possible tag paths up until this point. Table 6.2 shows the calculations necessary to determine the probability of each of them. In this case, old is far more frequently an adjective than a noun, and so this is the most likely reading. As an adjective following a determiner is more likely than one following a sentence complementiser, path 2.1 becomes far more probable than 1.1.

The process is identical when *man* is encountered. There are now eight tag paths to consider, shown in Table 6.3. As *man* occurs more frequently as a noun than a verb, and this reading is congruent with the preceding context, path 2.1.2 is preferred.

So far, we have assumed that it is necessary to keep track of every single tag path. This would make the algorithm extremely inefficient and psychologically implausible, for as the length of the sentence grows, the number of possible tag paths increases factorially. However, a large number of clear losers can rapidly be discarded – in fact, we need only keep track of a fixed number of tag paths (Viterbi, 1967). With this simplification, the algorithm is linear; this means that the amount of work required to determine a tag for each word is essentially constant, no matter how long the sentence is. Indeed, this property contributes directly to the psychological plausibility of this mechanism over more complex alternatives.

Taggers, in general, are extremely accurate (typically over 95%; see Charniak, 1993). However, they have distinctive breakdown and repair patterns. In Sections 6.4 and 6.5, we argue that these patterns are very similar to those displayed by people upon encountering sentences containing lexical-category ambiguities. We therefore propose the existence of a lexical-disambiguation mechanism, functionally equivalent to a part-of-speech tagger, as a distinct component within the HSPM. We will call this module the Statistical Lexical Category Module (SLCM).

6.4 Lexical Category Decisions

6.4.1 Noun-Verb Ambiguities

Following Frazier & Rayner (1987), MacDonald (1993) investigated processing of sentences where a word is ambiguous between noun and verb readings, following another noun.

(6) a. The union told reporters that the *warehouse fires* many workers each spring ...
    b. The union told reporters that the *corporation fires* many workers each spring ...

In (6a), the two words form a plausible noun compound (*warehouse fires*).[7] As all her disambiguations favour a verb reading for the ambiguous word,[8]

[7] It is perhaps important to note that while *warehouse fires* is one of MacDonald's materials, many of the other materials were highly plausible noun compounds such as *fraternity houses* and *computer programs*.

[8] We refer to MacDonald's second experiment. The first is largely concerned with refuting Frazier and Rayner's (1987) experimental materials and is therefore of little relevance here.

MacDonald calls this an unsupportive bias. In contrast, the potential noun compound in (6b) (*corporation fires*) is implausible and so the verb reading is more likely – a supportive bias.

The experiment also included two unambiguous conditions in which the noun compound was ruled out on syntactic grounds. (7a) and (7b) are sample materials for the unsupportive and supportive bias versions of this condition.

(7) a. The union told reporters that the *warehouses fire* many workers each spring . . .
    b. The union told reporters that the *corporations fire* many workers each spring . . .

The critical region is shown in italics. The reading times for the disambiguating region, immediately following the critical region, in each ambiguous condition were compared to the same region in the analogous unambiguous condition. MacDonald's hypothesis was that if bias affects the initial decisions of the HSPM, the decision in the ambiguous unsupportive bias condition (6a) should be in favour of a noun compound reading, and there would therefore be a processing delay when reading the disambiguation.

MacDonald's results confirmed her hypothesis. There was a significant increase in reading time between the ambiguous and unambiguous unsupportive bias conditions, but almost no difference in the supportive bias conditions. That is, the evidence suggests that (6a) is the only case in which the HSPM makes an initial decision in favour of the noun compound reading.

MacDonald did not argue that the initial decisions of the HSPM are based on plausibility per se. Instead, she demonstrated a correlation between unsupportive bias and some fine-grained statistical measures, including word-word co-occurrence frequencies and the head-modifier preference of the first noun (*corporation* or *warehouse*). She suggested that it is on the basis of these statistics that the HSPM makes its initial decisions.

In the SLCM, such fine-grained statistics are redundant. It is therefore clear that the predictions of our model will differ substantially from MacDonald's. The inspection of several corpora for part-of-speech bigrams (i.e., examining the pairwise frequencies of part-of-speech tags, not particular words), reveals that the frequency with which a noun is followed by some other noun is very close to that with which a noun is followed by a verb; this turns out to be true in all corpora we have examined. That is, there is unlikely to be any strong bias from the part-of-speech bigram statistic. The behaviour of the SLCM will therefore depend largely on the category bias of the individual ambiguous words used.

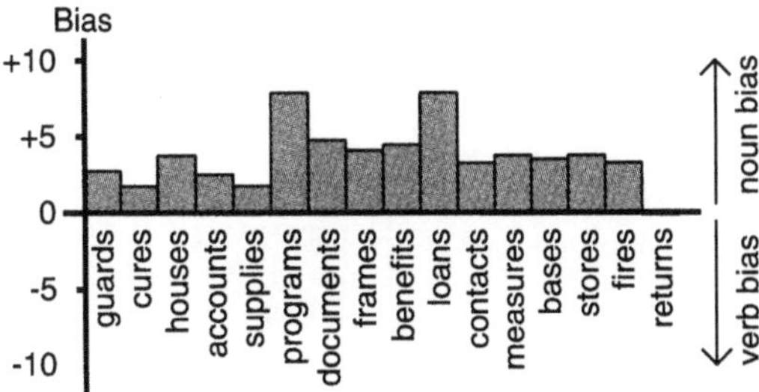

Figure 6.2. Bias of ambiguous words in MacDonald's (1993) experiment.

Figure 6.2 represents the noun-verb bias of each of the ambiguous words in MacDonald's experiment.[9] The data was obtained from a corpus count, and Equation 2 was used to calculate each word's bias from the count.

$$bias = \log\left(\frac{noun/count}{verb/count}\right) \tag{2}$$

It should be clear that the vast majority of MacDonald's experimental materials were strongly biased towards a nominal reading. The initial decision of the SLCM depends on two probabilities – $P(t_i \mid t_{i-1})$, the bigram probability (roughly equal for the noun and verb readings), and $P(w_i \mid t_i)$, the unigram probability, represented as bias in Figure 6.2. The SLCM therefore predicts an initial decision in favour of the noun reading for all of MacDonald's experimental items (with the possible exception of those based on the word *returns*).

However, the initial decision may require revision following analysis by other modules. We would expect, for example, that the ungrammaticality of the noun reading in the unambiguous conditions (7) would result in immediate revision by the parser. The pragmatic implausibility of the supportive bias condition (6b) may have a similar effect. As these revisions are triggered by module-external disambiguation, which is presumably costly, we would expect processing delays as the word is read. On encountering the disambiguating material, the preferred reading would be that the ambiguous word is a verb in all but the ambiguous unsupportive bias condition (6a).

9 The mean bias is 3.69, and the standard deviation is 1.97. This data was obtained from the British National Corpus (BNC), which contains over 100 million words of British English. The frequencies are based on the plural noun and singular present tense form (i.e., *-s*) of the noun and verb usages, respectively (the alternative spelling *programmes* was included in the count for *programs*). However, even if we include both base and plural forms, the results are similar (mean 2.66, standard deviation 1.79). Searching smaller corpora of American English (SUSANNE and part of the Treebank Corpus) also gives very similar results.

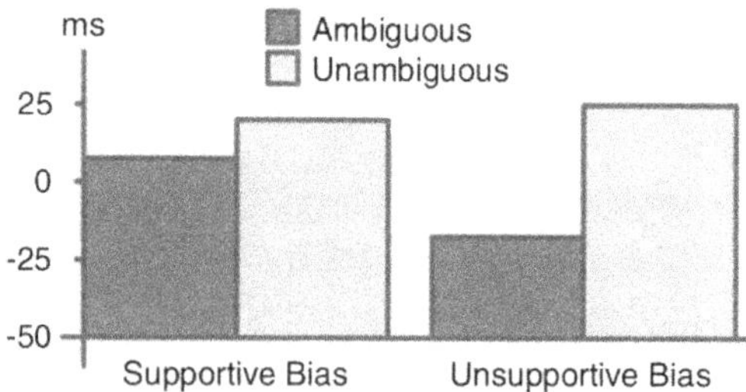

Figure 6.3. Length-adjusted reading times for the ambiguous word from MacDonald (1993).

These predictions partially agree with MacDonald's reported findings. We predict a similar pattern of results to MacDonald's in the disambiguating region. However, we also predict processing delays on the ambiguous word in three out of the four conditions. Fortunately, MacDonald reported the reading times for the ambiguous word (shown in Figure 6.3).

In the unambiguous conditions (7) and in the supportive ambiguous condition (6b), there is a significant increase in reading time compared to the unsupportive ambiguous condition (6a). MacDonald attributes this to the overhead of building the more complex verb phrase structure and calls it a reverse ambiguity effect (MacDonald, 1994). However, this processing delay is directly predicted by our model. A wrong initial decision, noun–noun over noun–verb, is predicted, and the necessary subsequent revision forced by module-external syntactic constraints explains the increased reading times. This explanation follows directly from the modular lexical category decision mechanism we have outlined.

6.4.2 **That** *Ambiguity*

The evidence from MacDonald (1993) supports the use of unigram statistics in the SLCM. However, since noun–verb and noun–noun sequences have similar likelihood, the bigram measures of the SLCM have no effect on the decision process in this case. Juliano & Tanenhaus (1993) have published findings that support the use of bigram statistics, and we examine these next.

Juliano and Tanenhaus investigated the initial decisions of the HSPM when faced with the ambiguous word *that* in two contexts – sentence-initially and following a verb. They forced disambiguation by manipulating the number of the following noun.

(8) a. The lawyer insisted *that experienced diplomat* would be very helpful.
b. The lawyer insisted *that experienced diplomats* would be very helpful.

(9) a. *That experienced diplomat* would be very helpful to the lawyer.
b. *That experienced diplomats* would be very helpful made the lawyer confident.

In (8a) and (9a), *that* must be a determiner, as the following noun is singular and a singular noun cannot occur without a determiner. In contrast, the plural noun in (8b) and (9b) forces the complementiser reading, as the determiner reading of *that* leads to a number disagreement with *diplomats*.

If the initial decision of the HSPM is different when faced with *that* in two different sentence positions, then lexical-category disambiguation must be context-dependent. The unigram statistic is context-independent, so this would provide evidence that there is at least one other statistic interacting with it. Evidence in favour of context dependence would be given by a delay in reading the disambiguation in the determiner condition (compared to the sentence complementiser condition) in one of the two sentence positions, but a delay in reading the sentence complementiser in the other.

This is exactly what Juliano and Tanenhaus found. The disambiguating region took longer to read in the determiner reading compared to the sentence complementiser reading following a verb, but the effect was reversed sentence-initially. This provides evidence that there is an initial preference for the sentence complementiser reading following a verb (8), but for the determiner reading sentence-initially (9).

This evidence supports the dominance of a context-dependent statistical measure in the SLCM, alongside the unigram probability – but is the bigram probability the right measure? It is the simplest statistic (see Section 6.3.1) in the sense that it requires fewer parameters than part-of-speech trigrams or word bigrams, and it should therefore be preferred if it is sufficient to account for the data. It is also compatible with our analysis of MacDonald's (1993) result.

On first glance, it would seem that bigram probabilities can easily explain Juliano and Tanenhaus's data. The data follow a regular pattern in the language – complementisers are more frequent following a verb than sentence-initially, and determiners are more frequent sentence-initially than following a verb. Table 6.4 lists the relevant statistics.

As Table 6.4 shows, the bigram probability on its own is not sufficient to account for the data. While the pattern in the language is as predicted, in both sentence positions a determiner is more likely than a complementiser. However, the decision of the SLCM is based on the interaction of these and the unigram statistics, and the latter are biased the other way ($P(\mathit{that}|\text{comp}) = 1.0$, $P(\mathit{that}|\text{det}) = 0.171$). To determine the SLCM's decision for the four

Table 6.4. *Estimated bigram probabilities for Comp and Det sentence-initially and following verb (from British National Corpus)*

Tag_{i-1}	$P(\text{comp}\mid\text{tag}_{i-1})$	$P(\text{det}\mid\text{tag}_{i-1})$
Initial	0.0003	0.0652
Verb	0.0234	0.0296

Table 6.5. *Estimated tag-path probabilities for the four conditions*

(8a)	$P(\textit{that}\mid\text{det})P(\text{det}\mid\text{verb})$	$.171 \times .0296$	.0051
(8b)	$P(\textit{that}\mid\text{comp})P(\text{comp}\mid\text{verb})$	$1.0 \times .0234$	**.0234**
(9a)	$P(\textit{that}\mid\text{det})P(\text{det}\mid\text{initial})$	$.171 \times .0652$	**.0111**
(9b)	$P(\textit{that}\mid\text{comp})P(\text{comp}\mid\text{initial})$	$1.0 \times .0003$	.0003

conditions in (8) and (9), we compute the following corresponding values for each item in Table 6.5.

The unigram bias is strong enough to overcome the comparatively weak bigram bias following a verb, and so an initial decision in favour of the sentence-complementiser reading is preferred. However, the far stronger sentence-initial bigram bias dominates the unigram bias, and so in this case the initial decision favours the determiner reading. These predictions match Juliano and Tanenhaus's results and so provide some evidence for the use of both unigram and bigram statistics in lexical-category disambiguation.

6.5 Lexical Category Reanalysis

The results reported so far demonstrate that the initial decisions made by the SLCM match some established experimental results. The equations on which a tagger (and therefore the SLCM) is based, however, are not inherently directional. While most tagging algorithms work left to right in computing the probabilities of the possible tag paths, right context can affect which tag path ultimately has the highest probability. If, for example, we created a tagger based on these equations that made category decisions right to left, the final decision would be exactly the same as those made by a left-to-right tagger.

This directional independence is achieved by efficient mechanisms for re-assigning category tags on encountering further input; this can be considered a form of reanalysis within the tagger. Of course, in the HSPM as a whole, lexical categories may also be disambiguated module-externally. For example, incompatibility of a lexical category with the current syntactic context might force reanalysis of the category, and such reanalysis is predicted to be more costly than module-internal revisions. In this section, we explain exactly how reanalysis may occur within the SLCM and what the limitations of such a mechanism are. We then explore whether such reanalysis capabilities may be sufficient to explain existing experimental data.

6.5.1 How Reanalysis Works in a Tagger

We have already discussed how a tagger assigns a probability to a tag path (see Section 6.3.2). In our example, the tagger always chose the correct tag on first encountering the data. However, this is frequently not the case. Consider, for example, sentence 10.

(10) The young are often rebellious.

The word *young* is more frequently an adjective than a noun and, in this context, that would be the initial decision of a tagger. However, in this case the tagger would revise its initial decision on encountering the next word. How does this work?

Let us assume that the tagger has already made decisions for *the young*, and that Det–Adj is the preferred tag path over Det–Noun. The next step is to calculate the likelihood of each tag path including *are*. However, what happens when $P(\text{verb}|\text{noun})$ – the probability of a verb following a noun – is significantly greater than $P(\text{verb}|\text{adj})$ – the probability of a verb following an adjective? The answer is that if Equation (3) is true, the most likely tag path will now be the one in which *young* is a noun.

$$\frac{P(\text{verb}|\text{noun})}{P(\text{verb}|\text{adj})} > \frac{P(\textit{young}|\text{adj})P(\text{adj}|\text{det})}{P(\textit{young}|\text{noun})P(\text{noun}|\text{det})} \tag{3}$$

This occurs because the greater probability of $P(\text{verb}|\text{noun})$ over $P(\text{verb}|\text{adj})$ causes the previously dispreferred tag sequence, Det–Noun, to become preferred. This demonstrates how the tagger may revise (effectively by reranking the tag sequences) a previous decision when a previously less likely tag path becomes more likely. As the SLCM is functionally equivalent to a tagger, it will exhibit identical repair characteristics.

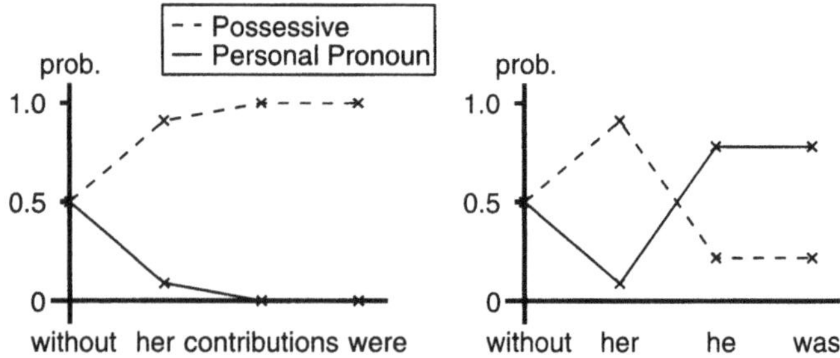

Figure 6.4. *Her* ambiguities.

However, a tagger's ability to change its preferred tag path is extremely limited. In a bigram model,[10] the tagger may only choose a tag path that results in a new tag if:

- the tag to be changed is the one which was most recently determined, or
- the new tag path also involves a change to the tag of the following word (which must also fulfill these conditions).

These conditions mean that any number of tags may be revised provided all tags between the leftmost revised tag and the current tag are also revised. In practise it is very rare for more than a single tag to be altered.

6.5.2 Reanalysis within the SLCM

While the example in Section (6.5.1) is contrived, the sentences in (11) are examples of where such reanalysis may really occur.

(11) a. Without her contributions were lost.
b. Without her he was lost.

According to Pritchett (1992), informants reported a conscious garden-path effect on reading sentence (11a). However, (11b) produced no such problems. We created a computational implementation of the SLCM and trained it on data from the SUSANNE Corpus (Sampson, 1995). We then tested it on each of these two sentences. Figure 6.4 is a plot of the probabilities assigned by the SLCM to each of the two most likely tag paths after each word.[11]

[10] In an n-gram model, where n is greater than or equal to 2, one of the next $n - 1$ tags must also have been changed.

[11] The probabilities in Figures 6.4 and 6.5 have been scaled to add up to 1.

In both sentences, the SLCM's initial decision when it encounters the word *her* is in favour of the possessive reading. However, in (11b) the next word is *he*, which is unambiguously a personal pronoun. The sequence possessive–personal pronoun is extremely unlikely, whereas the alternative personal pronoun–personal pronoun path is more probable. The SLCM's initial decision is therefore revised upon hearing the word *he*. This fits with the lack of conscious processing difficulty experienced by Pritchett's informants.

In contrast, SLCM reanalysis does not occur in (11a). The sequence possessive–noun is more frequent than the alternative personal pronoun–noun path. Possessive remains the preferred reading for *her*, and it is left to post-SLCM syntactic processing to detect and correct the anomaly. This explains the conscious processing difficulty experienced by Pritchett's informants.

Unfortunately, we know of no relevant experimental evidence regarding *her* ambiguities, so these results are not fully tested (though see Clifton, this volume, and Clifton, Kennison, & Albrecht, 1997, for some discussion). In the remainder of this section we examine two ambiguities for which experimental evidence has been published and demonstrate how they could be explained in terms of reanalysis within the SLCM.

6.5.3 Post-Ambiguity Constraints

MacDonald (1994) investigated a number of contextual manipulations which can make main verb/reduced relative ambiguities easier to parse.[12] Among these were post-ambiguity constraints.

(12) a. The sleek greyhound *raced* at the track won four trophies.
b. The sleek greyhound *admired* at the track won four trophies.
c. The sleek greyhound *shown* at the track won four trophies.

(13) The sleek greyhound raced at the track all day long.

Sentences (12a) and (12b) are locally ambiguous between two interpretations. Either the first verb is a main verb (as in (13)), or it introduces a reduced relative. Both sentences are disambiguated towards the reduced-relative reading. For sentences like (12a), MacDonald found a significant processing delay when reading the disambiguating region, the verb phrase *won four trophies*, compared to the unambiguous version (12c); there was no such delay on reading sentences similar to (12b). However, the ambiguous region of (12b) (*admired at the track*) took longer to read than that of (12a).

[12] Readers should also see Merlo and Stevenson (this volume) for a more detailed lexicosyntactic explanation of reduced-relative ambiguities.

What is the difference between these sentences? In (12b), the ambiguous verb (*admired*) is strongly biased towards being transitive (in its main-verb reading), whereas in (12a) the verb (*raced*) is biased towards intransitivity. In the unambiguous case (12c), the first verb can only be a past participle, and so a main verb reading is ruled out on syntactic grounds.

MacDonald argues that individuals initially prefer the main-verb reading in both the ambiguous cases. However, when a transitive verb is not immediately followed by a noun phrase, a strong constraint is violated. This post-ambiguity constraint means that the analysis is revised during the ambiguous region in (12b) – hence the processing delay in this region. As the reduced-relative reading is already preferred on encountering the disambiguation, there is no difficulty in processing this region.

In contrast, the intransitive verb in (12a) is consistent with a following prepositional phrase. In this case there is no reanalysis during the ambiguous region, and therefore no processing delay. When the disambiguation is read the main-verb analysis is still preferred. This leads to a serious (perhaps conscious) garden path and severe processing delay.

So far, our examples have been of what MacDonald called good constraints – that is, the word following the verb unambiguously signals that the next phrase is not a noun phrase. MacDonald also tried poor constraints, as in (14).

(14) The sleek greyhound *admired* all day long won four trophies.

In this case the material following the ambiguous verb (*all day long*) could be a noun phrase until the third word is encountered. This poor constraint proved less helpful to the subjects – reading time in the disambiguating region was still significantly greater than in the unambiguous case.

This behaviour appears to fit well with a model dominated by lexical category co-occurrence statistics, provided the lexical category tags include transitivity information. If a transitive verb is followed by a word that cannot introduce a noun phrase, then an alternative analysis may be sought. In terms of the SLCM, this would occur if the probability of a transitive verb being followed by a word of the same category as the constraining word was much lower than that of a past participle being followed by a word of that category. We tested whether the SLCM could explain MacDonald's results by retraining a tagger on data that includes such transitivity tags.

Most large corpora do not distinguish transtive and intransitive verbs in their part-of-speech tags. The markup in the SUSANNE Corpus (Sampson, 1995) is very detailed, however, including both syntactic structure and logical structure. Whilst verbs are not directly marked as being used transitively or intransitively,

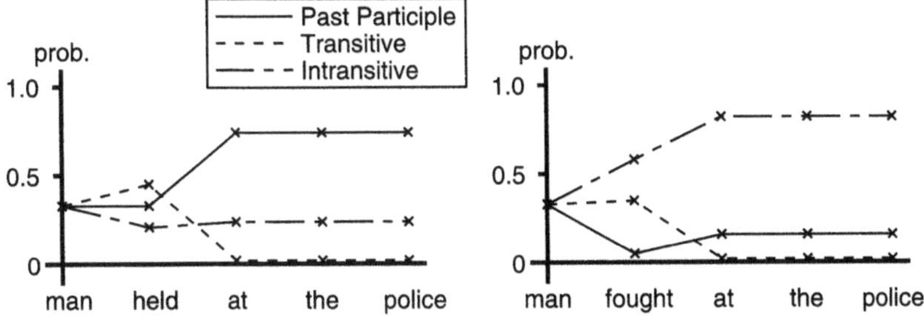

Figure 6.5. Behaviour of the SLCM with transitive and intransitive verbs.

there is sufficient syntactic information to allow the tag assigned to each verb to be automatically altered to include this information. We performed this alteration and used the new corpus to train the SLCM.

This transitivity marking is dependent on the SUSANNE Corpus, and this corpus is quite small. As a result, we found that there were insufficient lexical statistics to reliably tag the same sentences used by MacDonald. We therefore constructed some new materials that are similar to MacDonald's, but are composed of words that were comparatively frequent in our training corpus.

(15) a. The man held at the police station fainted.
b. The man fought at the police station fainted.

(15b) is equivalent to (12a) in that the ambiguous verb (*fought*) is frequently intransitive. The verb in (15a) (*held*), however, is strongly biased towards a transitive reading, mirroring (12b). We fed these two sentences through the SLCM implementation; the results are shown in Figure 6.5.

For (15a), the SLCM initially prefers the transitive reading. However, a transitive verb followed by a preposition is sufficiently improbable that the SLCM revises its initial analysis to prefer a reduced-relative reading. Therefore the predictions of a model that includes the SLCM are increased reading time in the ambiguous region, but no reading time penalty in the disambiguating region.

For (15b), the intransitive reading is initially preferred. An intransitive verb followed by a preposition is not particularly unlikely, so there is no reanalysis. A model including the SLCM therefore predicts no increased reading time in the ambiguous region. However, the preferred reading is not consistent with the disambiguating region, and so there will be a reading time penalty when the disambiguation is read.

These predictions, based on the dominance of two very simple statistics, exactly agree with MacDonald's (1994) results. It seems that our proposed

SLCM offers a simple explanation of the mechanism behind post-ambiguity constraints. It has an advantage over more complex models in that it has very few parameters and is highly predictive.

6.6 Conclusions

Statistical mechanisms have tacitly been associated with constraint-based, interactionist models. In the first half of this chapter, however, we argued against such an assumption. Even if we accept that the HSPM makes use of statistical mechanisms, there are good reasons to prefer a modular position.

Statistical mechanisms are in fact a natural ally of modular architectures: They provide near optimal heuristic knowledge in the absence of full knowledge. In the case of lexical category disambiguation, statistical mechanisms perform extremely well, are easily trained, and are computationally efficient. We also prefer the modular statistical position on more theoretical grounds. Because it is simpler and more restricted, it has greater predictiveness and constitutes a refutable theory. The decision process in an interactive model is influenced by a large number of statistical parameters, and there is no principled way to determine the combinatorial contribution of each of these. In contrast, a modular model is informationally simple; few parameters may influence each decision and the contribution of each of these is therefore easier to determine. Indeed, even if the degree of modularity turns out to be weaker than that proposed here, we feel that our approach will lead to better motivated, simpler, and more predictive characterisations of the statistical language processing mechanism and its architecture.

In a constraint-based model, the use of statistics follows unavoidably from other architectural assumptions. In the modular case, the use of statistics is more strategic: Whether to use statistics is a choice that must be made independent of the overall architecture. As statistics are associated with both processing and memory costs, we suggest that the processor employs statistical parameters more judiciously – only when the benefit outweighs the disadvantages. Our research strategy should therefore be to create models that make very simple use of statistics and test these.

In the second half of this chapter, we introduced such a model. The SLCM is a presyntactic module that arbitrates lexical category ambiguities. To do so, it makes use of word-category and category-category co-occurrence statistics. We demonstrated that this model can account for data that has previously been taken to support constraint-based architectures. The explanation we offer is simpler than the high-level constraints proposed by a number of researchers. It also avoids the necessity of assuming arbitrary processing delays when constructing complex representations. However, there are two further messages this model offers, which affect modular and interactive researchers alike:

- The model demonstrates how powerful very simple statistical models can be; researchers have suggested that fairly complex statistical interactions are necessary to explain existing data, without fully exploring simpler architectures. If we are to fully understand the power and predictions of statistical models, we have to actually construct them as well as argue over philosophies.
- Suggesting that lexical category disambiguation is a presyntactic process brings much accepted data about the behaviour of the parser into question. Many putatively syntactic ambiguities explored in the literature manipulate representations that could form part of a lexical category, such as subcategorisation information. If we are to fully understand the behaviour of the parser, we must first determine which representations are lexical and which are syntactic.

In conclusion, we suggest that there is good reason to adopt the Modular Statistical Hypothesis on empirical, theoretical, computational, and methodological grounds. The SLCM provides concrete instantiation of this approach and demonstrates that relatively simple statistical mechanisms can successfully explain a broad range of findings which have been previously used to motivate more complex and unconstrained accounts.

References

Charniak, E. (1993). *Statistical language learning*. Cambridge, MA: MIT Press.

Clifton, C., Kennison, S., & Albrecht, J. (1997). Reading the words her, his, him: Implications for parsing principles based on frequency and structure. *Journal of Memory and Language* 36, 276–292.

Corley, M., Mitchell, D. C., Brysbaert, M., Cuetos, F., & Corley, S. (1995). Exploring the role of statistics in natural language processing. In A. I. C. Monaghan (ed.), *Proceedings of CSNLP 95*. Dublin: Dublin City University.

Crocker, M. W. (1996). *Computational psycholinguistics: An interdisciplinary approach to the study of language.* Studies in theoretical psycholinguistics 20. Dordrecht: Kluwer Academic Publishers.

Cuetos, F., Mitchell, D. C., & Corley, M. M. B. (1996). Parsing in different languages. In M. Carreiras, J. García-Albea, & N. Sabastían-Gallés (eds.), *Language Processing in Spanish*, 145–189. Mahwah, NJ: Erlbaum.

Forster, K. I. (1979). Levels of processing and the structure of the language processor. In W. Cooper & E. Walker (eds.), *Sentence processing: Psycholinguistic studies presented to Merrill Garrett*, 27–85. Hillsdale, NJ: Erlbaum.

Frazier, L. (1987). Theories of sentence processing. In J. Garfield (ed.), *Modularity in knowledge representation and natural language processing*, 291–308. Cambridge, MA: MIT Press.

Frazier, L. (1990). Exploring the architecture of the language system. In G. Altmann (ed.), *Cognitive models of speech processing: Psycholinguistic and computational perspectives*, 409–433. Cambridge, MA: MIT Press.

Frazier, L. & Clifton, C. (1996). *Construal.* MIT Press.

Frazir, L. & Rayner, K. (1987). Resolution of syntactic category ambiguities: Eye movements in parsing lexically ambiguous sentences. *Journal of Memory and Language* 26, 505–526.

Gibson, E. & Schütze, C. T. (1996). The relationship between the frequency and the perceived complexity of conjunction attachments: On-line evidence. Poster presented at the 9th Annual CUNY Conference on Sentence Processing.

Juliano, C. & Tanenhaus, M. K. (1993). Contingent frequency effects in syntactic ambiguity resolution. In *Proceedings of the Fifteenth Annual Conference of the Cognitive Science Society*, 593–598. Hillsdale, NJ: Erlbaum.

MacDonald, M. C. (1993). The interaction of lexical and syntactic ambiguity. *Journal of Memory and Language* 32, 692–715.

MacDonald, M. C. (1994). Probabilistic constraints and syntactic ambiguity resolution. *Language and Cognitive Processes* 9, 157–201.

MacDonald, M. C., Pearlmutter, N. J., & Seidenberg, M. S. (1994). The lexical nature of syntactic ambiguity resolution. *Psychological Review* 10, 676–703.

McClelland, J., St. John, M., & Taraban, R. (1989). Sentence processing: A parallel distributed processing approach. *Language and Cognitive Processes* 4, 287–335.

Mitchell, D. C. & Brysbaert, M. (1998). Challenges to recent theories of cross-linguistic variation in parsing: Evidence from Dutch. In D. Hillert (ed.), *Sentence processing: A cross-linguistic perspective*, 313–335. San Diego, CA: Academic.

Mitchell, D. C. & Cuetos, F. (1991). The origins of parsing strategies. In *Current issues in natural language processing.* Houston, TX: Center for Cognitive Science. University of Houston, Texas.

Mitchell, D. C., Cuetos, F., Corley, M. M. B., & Brysbaert, M. (1995). Exposure-based models of human parsing: Evidence for the use of coarse-grained (non-lexical) statistical records. *Journal of Psycholinguistic Research* 24, 469–488.

Pritchett, B. L. (1992). *Grammatical competence and parsing performance.* Chicago, IL: University of Chicago Press.

Sampson, G. (1995). *English for the computer: The SUSANNE corpus and analytic scheme.* Oxford: Clarendon Press.

Spivey-Knowlton, M. & Eberhard, K. (1996). The future of modularity. In G. W. Cottrell (ed.), *Proceedings of the Eighteenth Annual Conference of the Cognitive Science Society*, 39–40. Hillsdale, NJ: Erlbaum.

Stevenson, S. (1994). Competition and recency in a hybrid network model of syntactic disambiguation. *Journal of Psycholinguistic Research* 23, 295–322.

Trueswell, J. C. & Tanenhaus, M. K. (1994). Toward a lexicalist framework for constraint-based syntactic ambiguity resolution. In C. Clifton. L. Frazier, & K. Rayner (eds.), *Perspectives on sentence processing*, 155–179. Mahwah, NJ: Erlbaum.

Viterbi, A. (1967). Error bounds for convolution codes and an asymptotically optimal decoding algorithm. *IEEE Transactions of Information Theory* 13, 260–269.

7
Lexical Syntax and Parsing Architecture

PAOLA MERLO AND SUZANNE STEVENSON

7.1 Introduction

Traditionally, accounts of cognitive abilities have proposed inherent restrictions on cognitive architecture as the underlying cause of observed patterns of human behaviour. Models of the human sentence-processing mechanism (HSPM) have largely fallen within this architectural paradigm, attributing interpretation preferences and processing breakdown to limitations on computational resources or on the interface between cognitive modules (e.g., Crocker, 1992; Frazier and Fodor, 1978; Gibson, 1991; Lewis, 1993; Marcus, 1980). Recently, in conjunction with advances in connectionism, research in cognitive modelling has seen a surge of interest in the role of environmental factors in determining crucial properties of intelligent behaviour. In contrast to a highly constrained underlying architecture, relatively unrestricted cognitive mechanisms are proposed, whose precise behaviour is determined by their adaptation to specific experiences. Within sentence-processing research, this approach is exemplified by the constraint-based paradigm (e.g., MacDonald, 1994; MacDonald, Pearlmutter, and Seidenberg, 1994; Spivey-Knowlton, Trueswell, and Tanenhaus, 1993; Trueswell, 1996; Trueswell, Tanenhaus, and Garnsey, 1994; but see also Mitchell, Cuetos, Corley, and Brysbaert, 1995), which proposes that exposure to the linguistic environment, rather than internal architectural properties, is primarily responsible for the specific behaviours of the HSPM. In constraint-based models, individual lexical entries play a central

We thank Charles Clifton, Sven Dickinson, Uli Frauenfelder, Jane Grimshaw, Maryellen MacDonald, Luigi Rizzi, Mike Tanenhaus, John Trueswell, and anonymous reviewers for helpful comments and discussion on earlier drafts of this manuscript. Thanks also are due our informants at the Rutgers Center for Cognitive Science (RuCCS) and at the University of Geneva for volunteering their time. This work was begun under the generous financial and administrative support of RuCCS. It was completed while the first author was a visiting scientist to the Institute for Cognitive Science at the University of Pennsylvania, on Swiss National Science Foundation fellowship 8210-46569, and while the second author was supported by the U.S. National Science Foundation, under grant IRI-9702331. The support of these institutions is gratefully acknowledged.

role as the repository of experiential knowledge, and lexical frequencies are a primary determinant of human behaviour. In particular, the operation and outcome of the HSPM are determined almost entirely by the differential frequencies among alternative interpretations.

In contrast to this recent trend, we have argued that restrictive architectural assumptions are necessary to an explanatory account of the HSPM (Stevenson and Merlo, 1997). Our work has focussed on reduced relative clauses, investigating the sharp contrast in acceptability between the following sentences:

(1) The horse raced past the barn fell. (unacceptable)

(2) The butter melted in the microwave was lumpy. (easily interpreted)

Until the final verb of each sentence, which is the actual main verb, the first verb (*raced, melted*) can be interpreted as either a past-tense main verb or as a past participle within a reduced-relative construction (i.e., *the horse* [*that was*] *raced past the barn*). These sentences are thus said to contain a main verb/reduced relative (MV/RR) ambiguity. In general, the main-verb interpretation is preferred, but the reduced-relative interpretation is necessary for a coherent analysis of the complete sentence in both (1) and (2). In (1), the strength of preference for the main verb interpretation of *raced* leads to breakdown when the verb *fell* is processed. By contrast, although sentence (2) contains a different verb (*melted*) with exactly the same type of MV/RR ambiguity, it is easily understood. The striking effect of individual verbs on the processing of this ambiguity has been argued to support a constraint-based account in which verb-specific frequency information is largely responsible for the variability of processing difficulty in this construction (e.g., MacDonald, Pearlmutter, and Seidenberg, 1994; Trueswell, 1996).

We find the lack of restrictiveness in the frequency-based accounts to be unsatisfactory, since the underlying cause of the differential frequencies themselves remains unexplained. We instead pursue the following two-pronged approach to explaining the differential difficulty in processing these types of sentences. First, we observe that the ease or difficulty of processing a reduced relative clause is correlated with the lexical semantic class of the verb within the construction (e.g., *raced* or *melted*). Based on lexical and syntactic properties, we propose that verbs of the unergative class (such as *race*) have a more complex transitive structure than other optionally transitive verbs (such as *melt*). The analysis is supported by acceptability judgments which reveal a bimodal distribution for reduced-relative constructions, with the unergative verb class causing processing difficulty, and other optionally transitive verbs yielding easy processing. Second, we present the architectural properties of the competitive attachment parser – a computational model of the HSPM – that are relevant to the analysis of reduced-relative constructions. We show that inherent restrictions on the parsing mechanism interact with the proposed syntactic analysis to precisely account for the difficulty of unergative reduced relatives in contrast to other verb types. Through this demonstration, we hope to convey the continued importance of investigating restrictive architectural assumptions in order to progress beyond descriptions of human behaviour, to deeper insights into the mechanisms that underlie language processing.

7.2 Verb Classes and Lexical Syntax

We begin our account with the observation that the prototypically difficult reduced relatives, *The horse raced past the barn fell* and *The boat floated down the river sank* both contain a manner of motion verb (*raced, floated*) in its transitive usage. Manner of motion verbs have an intransitive/transitive alternation, in which the intransitive form is classified as unergative (Levin, 1993; Levin and Rappaport Hovav, 1995) and the transitive form is the causative counterpart of the intransitive. We tested our intuitions about the difficulty of unergatives in the reduced relative construction by asking naive informants for acceptability judgments on sentences with reduced relative clauses containing verbs from this class, exemplified in (3).

(3) a. The clipper sailed to Portugal carried a crew of eight.
   b. The troops marched across the fields all day resented the general.
   c. The greyhound run around the track all day was tired.

Most informants find these sentences very difficult. One conjecture is that the difficulty of unergative verbs in the reduced-relative construction derives from the fact that the sentence has a complex causative semantics. As a comparison group, we chose the unaccusative verbs, another well-defined verb class that displays a similar intransitive/transitive alternation related by causativisation (Levin, 1993). Examples are given in (4). Informants found these sentences mostly easy.

(4) a. The witch melted in the Wizard of Oz was played by a famous actress.
   b. The genes mutated in the experiment were used in a vaccine.
   c. The window broken in the soccer game was soon repaired.

Clearly, judgments on the difficulty of reduced relatives containing unergative versus unaccusative verbs show a patterning of responses along verb class lines:

unergative verbs are difficult, while unaccusatives are easy.[1] Looking at the individual verbs, we can summarize the results as follows. In the unergative group, *advance*, *glide*, *march*, *rotate*(I),[2] *sail*, and *run* were judged unacceptable, whereas *shrink*, *fly*(I), *withdraw*, and *walk* were judged mostly unacceptable. In the unaccusative group, *melt*, *mutate*, *pour*, *rotate*(N), *begin*, and *freeze* were judged slightly degraded. *reach*, *break*, *grow*, and *fly*(N) were judged perfect.

First, all of the (mostly or completely) unacceptable verbs belong to the unergative group, while all of the easy verbs (i.e., perfect or only slightly degraded) belong to the unaccusative group.[3] Second, the ease or difficulty of the reduced relative construction appears to be relatively insensitive to the ambiguity of the past participle. Even unergative verbs whose past tense/past participle forms are not ambiguous cause difficulty in a reduced relative clause (for example, *run* and *withdraw*).

The remainder of this section develops our analysis of the lexical structure of unergative and unaccusative verbs and of the ensuing syntactic consequences of the proposed structures.

7.2.1 Lexical Structure

Sentences (5) and (6) exemplify the manner of motion and sound emission verbs that form the subclass of unergative verbs that occur in an intransitive/transitive alternation.

(5) a. The horse raced past the barn.
    b. The jockey raced the horse past the barn.

(6) a. The lion jumped.
    b. The trainer jumped the lion through the hoop.

As noted earlier, the transitive (b) form of each sentence is the causative counterpart of the intransitive (a) form (see Brousseau and Ritter, 1991, and Hale

[1] A complete list of the sentences used is reported in Stevenson and Merlo (1997).

[2] Two of the verbs, *rotate* and *fly*, were used in two different reduced relatives in which the modified noun differed according to its semantic properties of motion. An I designation means that the verb occurred with an argument with inherent motion (e.g., a bird); an N means that it occurred with an argument with non-inherent motion (e.g., a kite). Classification of verbs as unergative or unaccusative depends on the lexical semantics of the verb and its arguments taken together. Manner of motion verbs with an object of inherent motion are classified as unergative, and with an object of non-inherent motion are classified as unaccusative (Levin, 1993).

[3] Another difference seems to characterize easy and difficult garden paths, namely that easily processed verbs are those that have an adjectival passive form (Bresnan, 1982; Levin and Rappaport, 1986). However, when applying the standard tests for adjectival passives, this distinction did not correctly characterize the differential processing difficulty found here.

and Keyser, 1993, but also cf. Levin and Rappaport Hovav, 1995). That is, the syntactic subject of the intransitive form becomes the object of the transitive form, and the transitive subject is the causer of the action.[4] Unaccusative verbs can similarly occur in an intransitive/transitive alternation related by causativisation, as shown in (7) and (8).

(7) a. Butter melted in the pan.
    b. The cook melted the butter in the pan.

(8) a. Rice grows in Northern Italy.
    b. Farmers grow rice in Northern Italy.

However, despite the superficial similarity between the causative alternation in (5)/(6) compared to (7)/(8), there are several crucial differences between unergatives and unaccusatives, which lead us to postulate a different lexical, and consequently syntactic, structure.

First, the subject of an intransitive unergative, such as *the horse* in (5a), is an Agent, while the subject of an intransitive unaccusative, such as *the butter* in (7a), is a Theme (or Patient). This theta-role difference has interesting consequences for the causative alternation of these verbs. Conceptually, causativization involves the insertion of a Causal Agent into the existing argument structure. The causativization of an unaccusative, such as *melt* in (7b), yields a transitive form whose subject is a Causal Agent (*the cook*) and whose object is a Theme (*the butter*). By contrast, the causativization of an unergative, such as *race* in (5b), yields a transitive form whose subject is again the Causal Agent (*the jockey*), but whose object in this case is itself an Agent as well (*the horse*). That is, although the subject NP *the jockey* is the agent of the causing action, the object NP *the horse* is the agent or actor of the actual racing. These relationships are perhaps even more evident in the sentence *The trainer jumped the lion through the hoop*, in which *the lion* is clearly the agent of *jump*.

The transitive form of an unergative, then, is unusual in that it has an argument structure with two agentive theta roles (Causal Agent, Agent).[5] The peculiarly agentive nature of the object of manner of motion verbs has been remarked before (Cruse, 1972; Hale and Keyser, 1987), and is confirmed by the fact that the causer argument can only be a true agent, never an instrument or a natural

[4] Sound emission verbs, such as *ring* and *buzz*, show the same linguistic and processing properties of manner of motion verbs. Although we do not discuss them directly, the analysis we develop below applies also to the sound emission verb-class.

[5] Several accounts describe the object of the verb as a Theme (Levin and Rappaport Hovav, 1995; Harley, 1995). We think that this approach is seriously flawed, as it voids the notion of theta role of any semantic sense, since the object has a clear agentive role in the action.

force (Cruse, 1972; Levin and Rappaport Hovav, 1995); compare the unergatives in (9) (from Levin and Rappaport Hovav, 1995) with the unaccusatives in (10).

(9) a. *The downpour marched the soldiers to the tents.
b. *The firecracker jumped the horse over the fence.

(10) a. The ice storm froze the pipes.
b. The radiation mutated the genes.

This pattern suggests that the object of an unergative cannot be subordinated to a subject that receives a lesser role in the thematic hierarchy (Jackendoff, 1972).

The causative alternation of unergatives and unaccusatives also presents differences in productivity, within the same language and cross-linguistically. Several languages (such as Italian or French) do not permit unergative verbs to transitivize, and those that do, such as English, appear to do so in a limited way. For instance, in English only a subset of unergative verbs can be used transitively. If we consider the previous observation that the object of a transitive manner of motion verb is peculiarly agentive, we can consider this limited productivity as a special case of a more general restriction on the mapping between thematic relations and grammatical functions. Belletti and Rizzi (1988) argue that the Agent theta role seems to have a special status in the mapping of theta roles to syntax. They observe that psych verbs in Italian belong to three different syntactic subclasses, which have all the mappings of the Experiencer–Theme pair onto syntactic configurations. Consider the examples in (11), where the Experiencer can be the subject (a), the object (b), or the indirect object (c), and the Theme can be the subject (b,c) or the object (a).

(11) a. Gianni teme i serpenti.
'Gianni fears snakes.'
b. L'esame preoccupa Gianni.
'The examination worries Gianni.'
c. A Gianni piace il gelato.
'Gianni likes ice cream.' (literally, *To Gianni pleases ice cream*)

However, there is no verb that has a similar alternation between Agent, Theme. If there is an Agent, it must be the theta role that is mapped onto the external argument position, i.e., the subject.

Finally, there is a clear morphological difference in the formation of the causative form in those languages that allow both classes of verbs to causativize morphologically, such as Hebrew. As observed in Levin and Rappaport Hovav (1995), unaccusatives show morphological marking of the intransitive member of the pair. Moreover, this pattern of causativization is productive and unmarked. On the other hand, unergative causatives show that the transitive form is morphologically derived from the intransitive, which is itself underived. Levin and Rappaport Hovav conclude from this that unergative verbs are formed by a different causativisation process than the one that applies to unaccusatives.

We can provide a unified explanation of these linguistic facts by extending Hale and Keyser's (1993) approach to lexical syntax and thematic roles. The main claim of Hale and Keyser's work is that thematic roles do not exist as an independent linguistic entity, but are in fact simply notational shorthands for certain structural relations between lexical categories at the lexical level. By reducing thematic roles to the cross-product of lexical categories and structural configurations, they explain why the number and type of thematic roles is so limited and so uniform across languages.

Before presenting the technical details of our proposal, we might want to consider the theoretical import of a purely formal approach, given that semantic factors are clearly relevant to the classification of verbs as unergative or unaccusative (cf. note 2 regarding the ambiguous verbs *fly* and *rotate*). We follow the view that a linguistic theory that does not make reference to thematic roles directly is more restricted than is one that does. For example, the lexical structural approach of Hale and Keyser (1993) accounts for distributional properties of lexical items in English (for example, why causativisation of unergatives is so limited), which would remain unexplained under a purely semantic account. The explanation is available at no extra theoretical cost, as a mapping between argument structure and syntactic structure is independently needed for the definition of the syntax-semantics interface. In other words, there has to be a set of linking rules between roles and grammatical functions which determines for a given lexical entry what argument becomes the subject, and which the object, for instance.

On this view, the apparent sensitivity of certain grammatical processes to thematic content, although empirically correct, is epiphenomenal. Moreover, a syntactic account is more general, as it is supported by a vast body of studies showing that the lexical semantics of unaccusative and unergative verbs entails different syntactic behaviour, for instance in the distribution of partitive and reflexive clitics in Romance languages (Belletti and Rizzi, 1988; Burzio, 1981), in the alternation of auxiliary verbs (Burzio, 1981, 1986), and in the form of resultative constructions (Levin and Rappaport Hovav, 1995).

Thus, we follow Hale and Keyser (1993) in assuming that each thematic role corresponds to a given structural configuration within a lexical semantic structure. Consequently, the difference in theta-assignment noted earlier is evidence of a difference in underlying lexical structure. Hale and Keyser argue that the lexical entry of a verb captures its lexical semantics in a syntactic structure within the lexicon. The syntactic nature of the lexical entry allows the application of syntactic processes at the level of lexical representation. Verb forms may be created through the combination of lexical items with abstract verbal morphemes, such as DO, BECOME, and CAUSE. The combination operation is one of syntactic head movement within the lexical structure; see Figure 7.1, left panel.

For example, an intransitive unaccusative verb such as *melt*, which expresses a change of state, consists of an adjectival head *melted* that incorporates into the abstract verbal head BECOME. On the other hand, an intransitive unergative verb such as *race*, which expresses an activity, is generated by the lexical incorporation of a noun *race* into the abstract verbal head DO. Theta roles are assigned in these structures as follows. The specifier position of the BECOME morpheme is designated in the lexical structure as the theme of the incorporated verb, by predication with the adjectival phrase in complement position (see Figure 7.1). However, the specifier of the abstract verb DO is left empty, because the agent of the activity cannot be in a predication relation with the NP in complement position, as an NP is not a predicate. The agent of the *race* activity must be inserted at the syntactic level, where it is related to the verb by predication; it is therefore not mapped from the lexicon, but is instead projected by a syntactic rule in virtue of the Extended Projection Principle (Chomsky, 1981). It is a true external argument in the sense that it is external to the lexical structure.

The causative counterpart for each of these types of verbs requires further incorporation with the abstract verbal morpheme CAUSE. In the case of the unaccusative verb *melt*, the incorporation can occur within the lexicon: because the argument structure of the verb is complete, the entire VP can act as an argument to the CAUSE morpheme. Specifically, Hale and Keyser propose that because the *theme* argument of *melt* (that is, BECOME + *melted*) is internal to the VP headed by BECOME in the lexical entry, the VP can be further embedded as the complement of another verb. Figure 7.1 shows the lexical derivation of the causative form of *melt*. By contrast, an unergative verb like *race* cannot be causativized in the lexicon, because not all its arguments have been assigned. Since the Agent argument is missing from the lexical structure, the VP for *race* cannot be further embedded as a complement to another verbal head. Hale and Keyser (1993) do not address the problem that, nevertheless, a causative form for a subset of these verbs does occur, as evidenced by the transitive alternations in (5) and (6).

It is therefore necessary to extend Hale and Keyser's account to deal with transitive unergatives. We propose that an operation of syntactic causativization may apply in the case of an unergative verb. For the transitive use of *race*, for example, both the abstract morpheme CAUSE and the incorporated activity verb

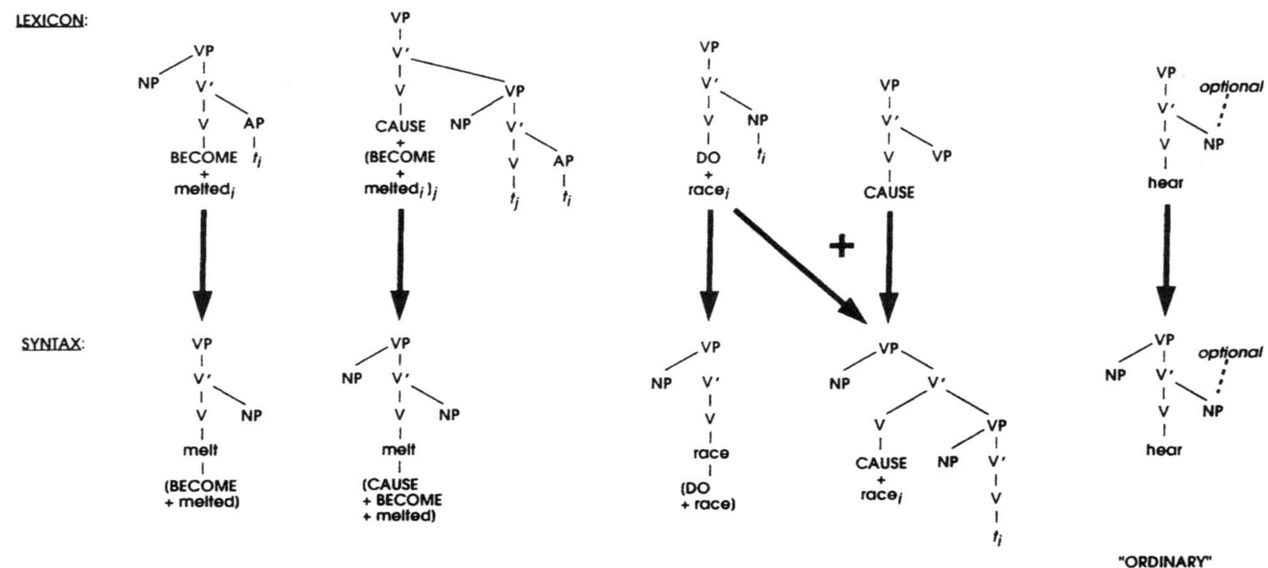

Figure 7.1. Lexical entries, showing verb incorporation for various verb types, and their corresponding syntactic structures.

race (DO + *race*) must be projected onto the syntax. There, the Agent of the racing action can be inserted into the specifier position of the verb *race*. The abstract verb CAUSE takes the VP headed by *race* as its complement, and a Causal Agent is inserted into its specifier position. The explicit combination of the two verbs in the syntax is responsible for producing the two [spec, VP] positions that are necessary for the two external (agentive) theta roles.[6] As can be seen in Figure 7.1, bottom panel, the syntactic operation of causativization entails that the syntactic representation of the transitive form of unergatives is more complex than a simple VP.

For verbs that do undergo incorporation within the lexicon, we assume that while the structure of a lexical entry is visible to lexical operations, these articulated lexical structures are not visible to the syntactic level of processing.[7] Specifically, a verb that results from lexical incorporation – a sequence of head movements within a nested predicate argument structure – appears in the syntax in a conflated form, within a simple VP. Figure 7.1 illustrates this relation between the underlying (articulated) lexical structures, and the resulting syntactic structures of various verbs.

This linguistic analysis, which posits lexical and syntactic differences between unergative and unaccusative verbs, constitutes the first part of our explanation of the differential difficulty of reduced relative clauses, by entailing that the transitive form of an unergative verb is structurally more complex than that of an unaccusative verb. In order to complete our account, we must exhibit a processing model whose crucial properties are justified on purely computational grounds, and whose interaction with the proposed linguistic representation gives rise to the observed behaviour in processing reduced relative clauses. We do so in the next sections.

7.3 The Competitive Attachment Architecture

The competitive attachment model is a hybrid connectionist parser that integrates simple symbolic processing with numeric spreading activation, within a network of processing nodes that directly represents syntactic structures. The model dynamically builds a parse tree by activating processing nodes in response to the input, whose attachments within the tree structure are incrementally

[6] The specifier position of an XP will be referred to throughout the paper as "[spec, XP]".

[7] Here again our proposal deviates from that of Hale and Keyser, 1993. The topological approach to the mapping of thematic roles adopted here (modifying Baker, 1988, and Hale and Keyser, 1993) is the simplest one, where the Theme is always an object and the Agent always a subject at the relevant level of representation, D-structure.

established through distributed network computation. Symbolic feature processing determines the grammaticality of potential phrase structure attachments, based on Government-Binding theory (Chomsky, 1981; Rizzi, 1990). Numeric spreading activation weighs the relative strengths of the valid attachment alternatives and focuses activation onto the preferred structures. Competition for activation is the crucial mechanism for resolving ambiguity.

The architecture is constrained by several computationally motivated restrictions arising from the requirements of the dynamic network creation and competitive activation processes of the model. These restrictions define a precise range of structural hypotheses that can be represented within the network. In particular, the constraints on the parsing architecture generally limit the occurrence of empty nodes, but also, perhaps surprisingly, dictate the presence of empty structure in certain configurations. Because empty structure (empty operators and traces) plays an important role in the syntactic analysis of reduced relative clauses, the constraints on empty structure in the model are of central concern.

Here we will first present the basic network creation and numeric competition processes within the parser and then turn to the precise architectural restrictions regarding empty nodes and phrases. We conclude the section with a description of the syntactic projection of verb classes within the model.

7.3.1 Overview of the Competitive Attachment Process

The network of alternative parse-tree structures is dynamically created by activating two types of processing nodes: one corresponding to the phrasal nodes of a standard parse-tree representation, and one corresponding to the links or attachments between the phrases. Phrasal nodes are activated from a pool of $\bar{X}$ templates, and their symbolic features are initialized based on an input token's lexical entry. Figure 7.2 shows a sample $\bar{X}$ template and its instantiation. Attachment nodes are established between two phrasal nodes that are potential sisters in the parse tree; Figure 7.3 shows the resulting representation of basic $\bar{X}$ relations in the network.

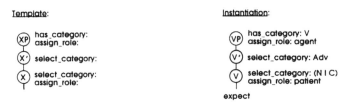

Figure 7.2. An $\bar{X}$ template and its instantiation as a verb phrase.

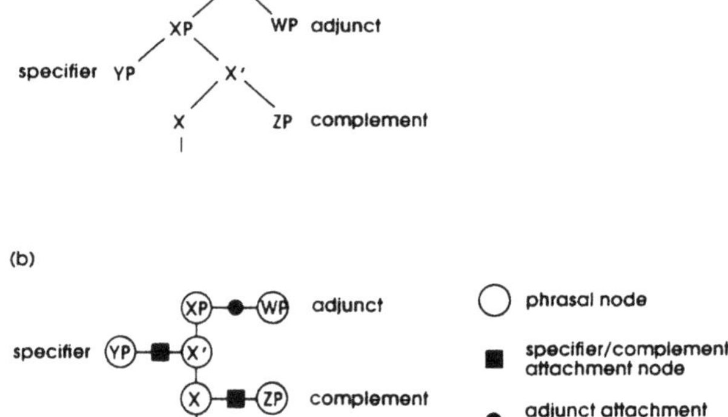

Figure 7.3. (a) The structure of an $\bar{X}$ phrase and (b) its representation in the competitive attachment network.

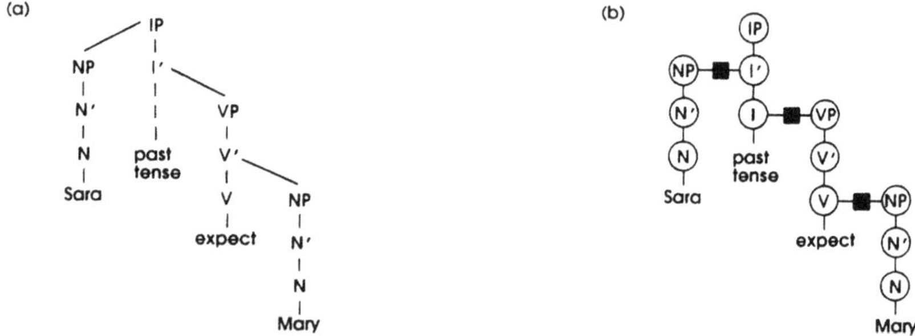

Figure 7.4. (a) An example parse tree and (b) its network representation.

When an input token is read, the parser activates the appropriate phrasal nodes. For an ambiguous input token (that is, one with more than one lexical entry), multiple syntactic phrases are activated, each in proportion to the strength of the corresponding lexical entry. After activating the appropriate phrasal nodes, the parser allocates the attachment nodes to represent the potential attachments between the new phrasal nodes and the existing network. Then, each processing node iteratively updates and outputs its symbolic features and numeric activation until the network settles into a stable state representing the attachment decisions for each of the new phrases. Figure 7.4 shows the final parse tree for a complete sentence, and the corresponding network structure.

Two types of competitions occur during the network processing described above. Attachment competition is a competition at a phrasal node for the best attachment to activate. Since multiple attachments for a phrasal node may be grammatical, a competitive output function (Reggia, 1987) weighs the evidence for an attachment and proportionately allocates activation from the phrasal node to its attachment nodes. When the network stabilizes, the set of active attachment nodes for each syntactic phrase represents the current parse-tree attachments for that phrase; inactive attachment nodes connected to that phrase are deleted. Lexical competition arises when an input token has more than one possible syntactic projection. The activation level of each possible phrase is determined in part by the level of activation of its attachments, and in part by the activation it receives from the input token. As in attachment competition, the input token uses a competitive output function that proportionately divides activation among the recipient nodes – in this case, the possible phrases for the input. This lexical competition determines which of the multiple possible phrases will be most highly activated by the input token.

7.3.2 Architectural Restrictions and Empty Structure

In order for a particular network configuration to represent a valid partial parse tree, each phrasal node must activate a certain number of attachment nodes to satisfy its grammatical properties. For example, an I′ node must activate a single attachment to a subject phrase, and a V node that represents an obligatorily transitive verb must activate a single attachment to a complement phrase. However, the competitive attachment mechanism is quite limited in its ability to activate a precise number of attachment nodes. Specifically, the competitive function, which determines the amount of activation to output to attachment nodes, cannot be successfully parameterized to activate a variable number of attachments, an ability that appears necessary even in the most straightforward cases. For example, in processing a simple sentence with an obligatorily transitive verb, the V node must initially activate zero attachment nodes, since its complement phrase will not have been reached yet in the input. Once the complement phrase is activated, the V node will then need to activate a single attachment node to it. But while the competitive output function can be tuned to effectively activate exactly one attachment, it cannot be adjusted to allow the activation of zero attachment nodes at one point in processing, and one attachment node at another.

Since the competitive function can bring about activation of one attachment node, but not zero or one, those phrasal nodes that license an attachment must have an attachment node to activate at all times. To accommodate this, such a phrasal node automatically posits an attachment to an empty node. Each phrasal node that licenses an attachment thus has a dummy node to attach to even when no overt phrase is available. Furthermore, to maintain uniformity of numeric

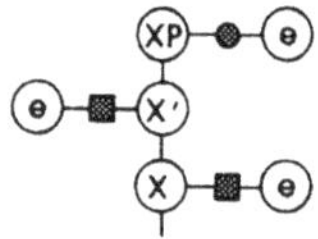

Figure 7.5. Empty nodes are activated in conjunction with every phrase, at each attachment site.

processing across all phrasal nodes, every phrasal node activates an attachment to an empty node. In the case where an attachment is prohibited at a node, or simply not required, an empty node is interpreted in the network as an explicit representation of the lack of an attachment. Figure 7.5 shows the empty nodes that are activated with an $\bar{X}$ template; each attachment site connects to an attachment node that in turn connects to an empty node. (Empty nodes are labeled "e" in the figures and are omitted in remaining figures where they are irrelevant.)

Because empty nodes occur at all possible attachment sites, they can be used to represent null elements required in a parse – i.e., the empty categories or traces of Government-Binding theory. For example, in the reduced-relative construction, empty nodes are needed to represent both the trace of passive movement, and the empty operator in the specifier of the relative clause. The role of an empty node as an empty category is determined within the network by the attachment and binding relations in which the node participates. Note, however, that the activation of empty structure is quite restricted, in that each empty node is a single dummy phrasal node. A empty node cannot have an articulated phrasal structure, which could in turn recursively activate additional empty structure. This restriction is necessary to curb the potential explosion of nested empty structure, which could quickly exhaust the available processing nodes in the parser. Thus, two fundamental aspects of the competitive attachment architecture – the numeric competition process and the dynamic activation of structure – lead to the necessity of allocating empty structure, which is restricted to being a single processing node.

The status of an empty node as a default phrase to attach to entails that it initially has only minimal activation. If the empty node occurs at a site that does not require an attachment (e.g., as the complement to an intransitive verb), then it represents a valid non-attachment and quickly becomes fully activated. If the empty node attaches to a site that does require an attachment (e.g., as the specifier of an I′, or the complement of an obligatorily transitive verb), then there are several possible outcomes. Often the default attachment to an empty node is later replaced by an attachment to an overt phrase that is subsequently projected from the input; in this case, the empty node is fully deactivated. However, as noted earlier, an empty node may participate in the parse-tree structure by representing an empty category. The coindexation of an empty node licenses the node as an empty category and instantiates its symbolic features, thereby increasing its activation level. Conversely, if an empty node occurs in a position that requires an attachment and is not coindexed, it will remain only weakly activated.

7.3.3 The Projection of Lexical Structure

The bottom-up nature of the competitive attachment model entails that syntactic structure is projected from a lexical item, where projection can require the activation of potential extended projections. The activation of a number of extended projections for a verb reflects the potential "stacking" of functional projections over the primary lexical projection of a word (Grimshaw, 1991, 1997). A verb, for example, will activate three extended projections: a VP, an IP–VP, and a CP–IP–VP. The three potential extended projections will compete for activation from the single verb that initiated their activation, and they must also compete for attachments to the existing and developing partial parse tree structures. The linguistic account presented in Section 7.2 entails that the internal structure of the VP of the extended projection encodes features from the predicate argument structure of the verb; that is, the VP of each extended projection has the specifier and complement requirements determined by the lexical features of the (possibly incorporated) verb. Initially, the specifier and complement sites will have attachments to empty nodes, as described earlier. The lexical information associated with the verb will constrain the interpretation of the empty nodes.

For a conflated verb, such as *melt*, the structure of the VP is based on the position of the verb following incorporation within the lexical structure. The form of *melt* created from the incorporation of BECOME and *melted* projects a VP that has a single internal argument and no external argument. The NP that occurs in the [spec,VP] of the abstract element BECOME is realized in the syntax as a direct object of the conflated verb. Thus, this form of *melt* will have an empty node in the complement attachment position whose category is set to NP by the V node. Since it has no external argument, the empty node attached to the V′ has its category set to NONE. The form of *melt* created from incorporation of CAUSE, BECOME and *melted* also projects a VP with a single internal argument. Again, the internal NP argument is realized in the syntax as a direct object of the conflated verb. The difference between this form of *melt* and the intransitive form is that this form also has an external argument to assign (the Causal Agent). Here the empty node attached to the V′ has its category set to NP.

Unergative verbs are distinguished from unaccusative verbs in that the lexical rule of causativization cannot apply, as described in Section 7.2. The only lexical

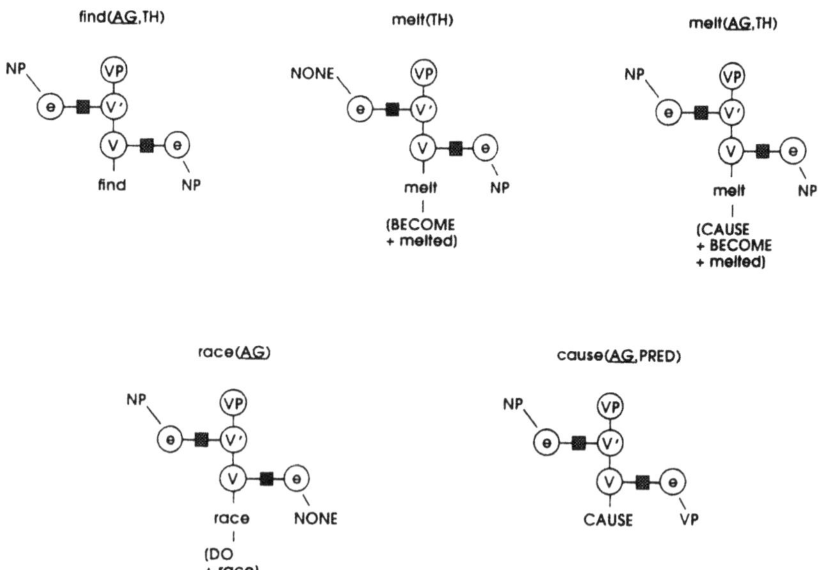

Figure 7.6. The VP structures initially activated by the parser in response to various types of verbs.

form available for a verb such as *race* is the intransitive. An unergative verb therefore projects a VP in which the specifier position must be filled by an NP subject, but the complement position is required to be empty. Thus, as shown in Figure 7.6, the category of the empty node attached to the V node is NONE. In order for an unergative verb to be used in the transitive alternation, it must be combined in the syntax with the abstract causative morpheme CAUSE.[8] The processing consequences of syntactic causativization will be discussed in the next section.

7.4 Verb Classes and Processing Results

This section presents the central results of the paper: the consequences of our linguistic analysis and processing model for the interpretation of reduced relative clauses. It is here that we demonstrate the effects of the architectural restrictions regarding empty nodes and empty phrases in the model. Recall that these constraints are motivated by a convergence of restrictive compu-

[8] We assume that CAUSE is linked in the lexicon to the unergative verbs with which it can so combine, since the ability to be causativised, even under the general syntactic operation, is an idiosyncratic property of verbs.

tational assumptions. The results therefore arise from the interaction of our lexical-syntactic proposal with independently justified properties of our parsing architecture.

In what follows, we assume that a verb with a main verb/past participle ambiguity has three lexical entries that are homophonous: the simple past tense, the active past participle, and the passive past participle. Since the active past participle will never be grammatical in the examples considered here, we will only be concerned with the simple past and the passive participle alternatives. We also assume that a reduced relative clause is a CP–IP–VP projection with an empty operator in [spec, CP]. The empty operator in the competitive-attachment parser is realized as an empty node in [spec, CP] that binds an empty node in [spec, IP], which in turn binds an empty node complement of the VP. (Note that other linguistic analyses are possible (e.g., Siloni, 1994), and that whether the reduced relative is assumed to be a CP, IP, VP, or even a DP is irrelevant for the results here.) To simplify the presentation, only highly activated extended projections will be shown in the figures.

7.4.1 Obligatorily Transitive Verbs

First consider a reduced-relative construction with an obligatorily transitive verb, as in *The bird found in the room died*, whose syntactic structure is shown in Figure 7.7. At the point that *found* is processed, the main-verb alternative will highly activate an IP–VP projection, to which the NP *the bird* attaches in subject position. The passive past participle reading will highly activate a CP–IP–VP

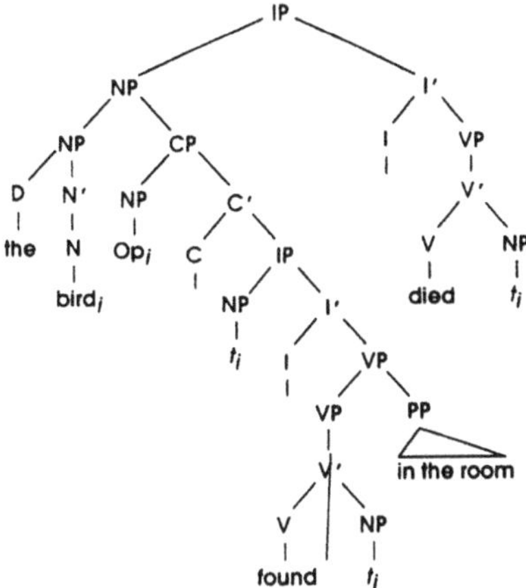

Figure 7.7. The syntactic structure for a reduced relative construction, in *The bird found in the room died.*

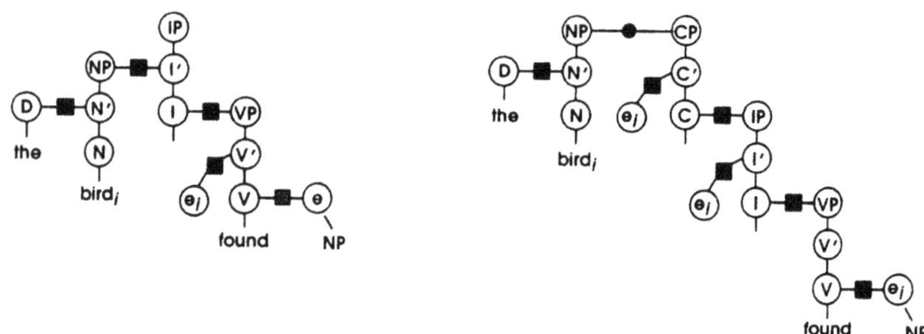

Figure 7.8. The two best competitors activated in response to the input *the bird found.*

projection, which has an empty node in [spec, CP] that can participate in a predication relation with the noun *bird.* The empty node in [spec, CP] can also bind the empty node in [spec, IP], which in turn can bind the empty node that is complement to the V node. This establishes the empty node in [spec, CP] as an empty operator, leading to a grammatical reduced relative construction.

Figure 7.8 illustrates these two competing alternative interpretations: (1) the IP–VP projection corresponding to the main verb lexical entry of *found,* which has the NP *the bird* attached as its subject, and has an empty node as the complement of the VP; (2) the CP–IP–VP projection corresponding to the passive past participle lexical entry of *found,* which modifies the NP *the bird.* Neither alternative emerges as a clear winner. The first has an empty node in a required complement position, which cannot become fully activated. The second is waiting on a (presumably required) predicate. (Currently in the model, this expectation for a predicate is implemented by favoring root nodes that are extended projections of a verb.) The closeness of the competition allows context and theta-role compatibility to influence preferences throughout the processing of the postverbal PP (MacDonald, 1994; Trueswell, Tanenhaus, and Garnsey, 1994). But when the final verb *died* is processed, the only grammatical alternative is for the NP *the bird,* which is modified by the reduced relative clause, to combine with the IP–VP extended projection of *died,* yielding the correct structure for the sentence, shown in Figure 7.9.

7.4.2 Unergative Verbs

The ease of a reduced-relative construction with an obligatorily transitive verb has received a great deal of attention because of the stark constrast with the prototypical garden-path sentence, *The horse raced past the barn fell.* Figure 7.10 shows the syntactic structure of the latter sentence, under our analysis of the transitive alternative of *race* as an explicit syntactic causative. The proposed

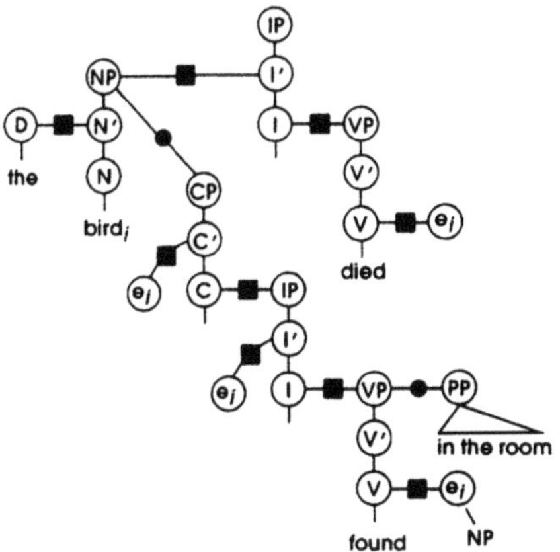

Figure 7.9. The final network configuration for *The bird found in the room died.*

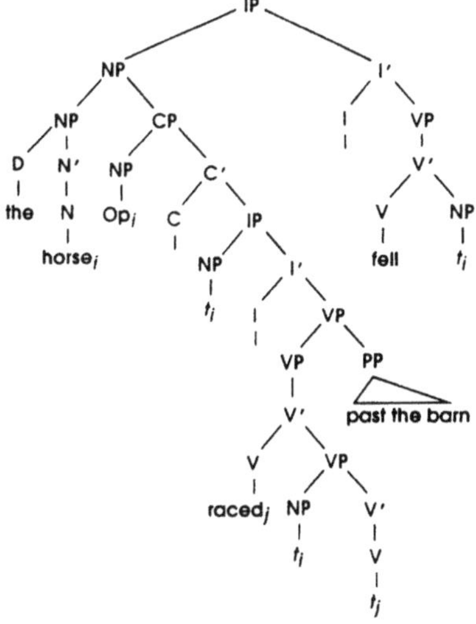

Figure 7.10. The syntactic structure for *The horse raced past the barn fell.*

structure is clearly more complex – in terms of both number of nodes and number of binding relations – than that of a reduced relative with a simple transitive verb such as *found* (compare Figure 7.10 with Figure 7.7). The passive participle *raced* requires a VP complement with two traces. One trace within the complement VP, t_i, is the trace of the NP movement of the passive construction; it is in the [spec, VP] position and is bound by the empty operator, through the trace in [spec, IP]. The other trace within the complement VP, t_j, is the trace of verb movement resulting from the syntactic incorporation of the verb with the

CAUSE morpheme; it occurs in the embedded V and is bound by *raced*. Thus the structure not only contains an empty VP complement, but one which has internal structure with two traces.

We can now examine how this structural analysis affects the competitive-attachment model in its processing of an MV/RR ambiguity with an unergative verb. The two best competitors of the possible extended projections of the main verb reading of *raced* are the two IP–VP forms corresponding to the intransitive reading and the causative reading; these are shown in Figure 7.11. In contrast to the main verb reading of *found*, the empty node that is sister to V in the intransitive form of *raced* is specified to be empty, so it becomes fully activated. The causative form, however, is similar to the main-verb reading of *found* in having a sister to the V node that cannot remain empty. Since the empty node is not bound, this structure has less activation and is less preferred.

For the past-participle reading, the most highly activated extended projection is the CP–IP–VP of the causative form, shown in Figure 7.12. This structure has empty nodes in the same positions as in the reduced-relative form of *found*,

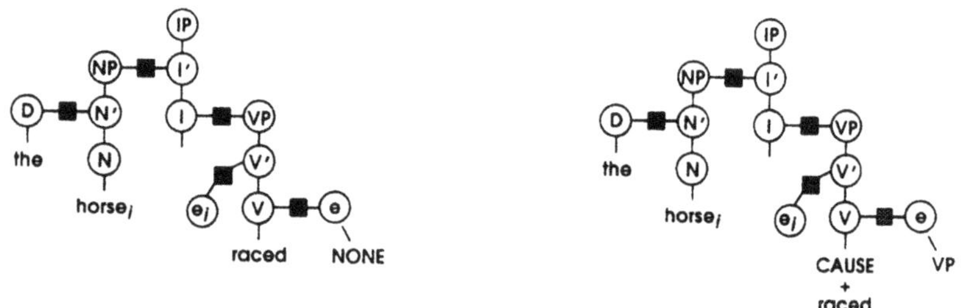

Figure 7.11. The two best competitors of the set of extended projections within the network corresponding to the main verb reading of *raced*.

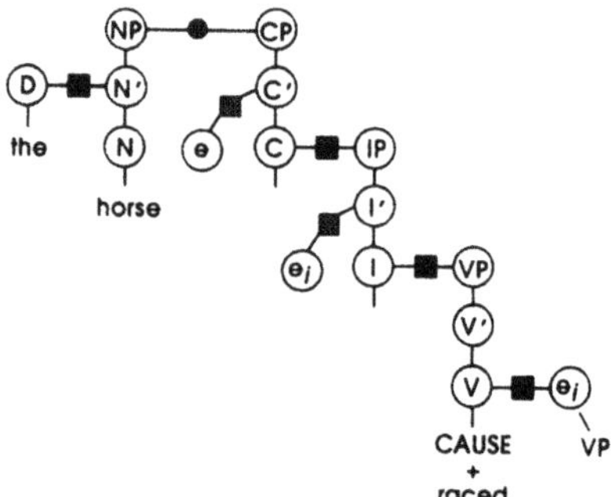

Figure 7.12. The best competitor of the set of extended projections within the network corresponding to the causative past participle reading of *raced*.

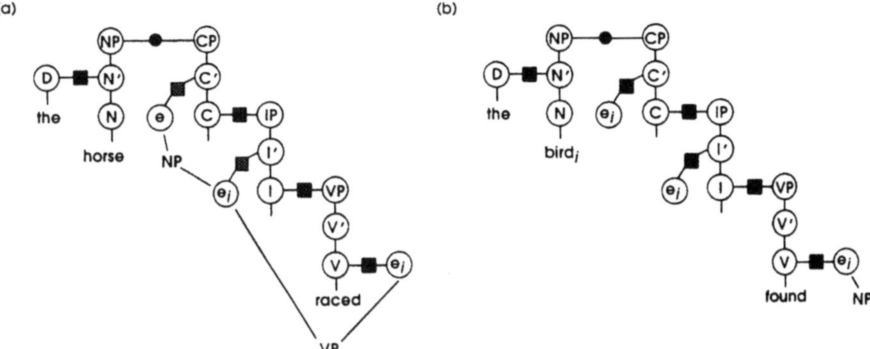

Figure 7.13. The invalid binding relations established in the reduced relative structure for *raced*. The [spec, CP] must be an NP, and the empty complement must be a VP. To be bound by the [spec, CP] and to bind the empty complement, the empty node in [spec, IP] would have an incompatible category specification – both NP and VP.

but the result is very different with the verb *raced*. In the network for *found* (see Figure 7.9), the empty node that is sister to the verb can represent the trace of passive movement, thereby successfully participating in a chain headed by the empty node in [spec, CP], leading to a valid reduced relative structure. In the network for *raced*, however, the empty node that is sister to the verb stands in the place of a VP in the syntactic structure – one that has articulated empty structure. Since the network is only able to allocate a single empty node in the position in which an articulated empty phrase occurs in the syntactic structure, it is unable to encode the binding relations that are necessary to successfully represent a reduced relative clause.

Specifically, in Figure 7.12, the empty node in [spec, IP] binds the complement of the verb, but this establishes a VP chain.[9] To bind the empty node in [spec, IP], the empty operator in [spec, CP] would inherit the V category of the chain. But, to be in a predication relation with the noun being modified by the reduced relative clause, it is required to have category N. The empty node in [spec, CP] cannot participate in both relations, or an incompatible category specification will be made, as shown in Figure 7.13. Thus, there is no way to establish grammatical binding relations among the empty nodes in this extended projection. The CP–IP–VP decreases markedly in activation, since its $\bar{X}$ phrases contain empty nodes that cannot become fully activated; it is therefore unable to compete with the highly activated alternative, that of the main-verb

[9] Alternatively, the empty node in [spec, IP] may not be able to participate in a VP chain. In either case, a valid chain including the [spec, CP], [spec, IP], and complement of V cannot be formed.

intransitive reading. The main-verb IP–VP structure therefore wins the competition for activation, and the past-participle structures become inactive.

Although we have described the outcome for the reduced-relative structure in this example in terms of a competition with the main-verb reading, it is crucial to note that the prognosis for an unergative reduced relative in this account is far bleaker than this may imply. In fact, the parser is simply unable to activate the structure needed for a grammatical analysis of this sentence. Recall our observation that the reduced-relative construction with an unergative verb requires that the verb take an empty VP complement, which must have articulated structure in order to support the right binding relations. This structural requirement arises from the fact that in order to be interpreted as a transitive verb, a syntactic operation is required to combine the unergative verb with the CAUSE morpheme. It is this fact of having an explicit causative structure in the syntax that causes the processing difficulty. The architecture of the competitive-attachment parser limits its abilities to activate empty structure, as explained in Section 7.3. Here the parser can only activate a single empty node, attached to the V node for the incorporated verb, that stands in the position of the VP complement. The parser cannot activate a full projection for the empty embedded VP, which would be necessary to establish the correct empty nodes for the traces of the NP and V movements. Specifically, the parser has independently motivated constraints on the activation of empty structure that render it unable to activate an empty projection which has no overt elements or features to attach to it, which is precisely what is required in this case. The CP–IP–VP that it activates, as in Figure 7.13, is as close as it can come. Thus, it is not the case that the reduced-relative structure merely loses the competition for activation. Rather, the model predicts a severe garden path, in which a grammatical structure for the reduced-relative interpretation is completely unavailable within the normal operation of the parser.

7.4.3 Unaccusative Verbs

This account differs from theories that attribute the difference between easy and hard MV/RR ambiguities to the distinction being verbs that are obligatorily transitive (like *found*) versus optionally intransitive (like *raced*) (e.g., Gibson, 1991; Pritchett, 1992). Such a distinction is not empirically adequate. For example, unaccusative verbs, such as *melt*, are also optionally intransitive, but are easily processed in the reduced-relative construction, even when they have an MV/RR ambiguity. The crucial distinction between the unergatives and unaccusatives is that the unaccusatives undergo causativisation in the lexicon, while the unergatives require a syntactic causative operation.

Figure 7.14. The two best competitors of the set of extended projections within the network corresponding to the main-verb reading of *melt.*

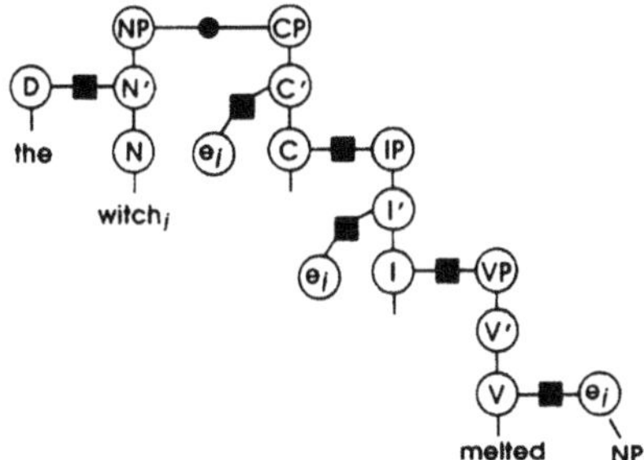

Figure 7.15. The best competitor of the set of extended projections within the network corresponding to the causative past-participle reading of *melt.*

For example, consider *The witch melted in the movie deserved her fate*. Like *raced, melted* has both an intransitive reading and a causative transitive reading. Unlike *raced*, the two readings correspond to two different lexical entries for the verb, as shown earlier in Figure 7.1 When structure is activated based on the main verb entries, the parser ends up with the two competing IP–VP structures shown in Figure 7.14: (1) the intransitive form in which the verb has an empty node in its complement position bound by the subject NP *the witch* (the object of an intransitive unaccusative moves to subject position in the syntax since the verb has no external argument), and (2) the causative form in which the V node has an empty complement that needs to be bound. The latter structure is somewhat less preferred because of the unbound trace. The past participle reading leads to one extended projection, the CP–IP–VP shown in Figure 7.15, which is exactly identical to the reduced relative structure for a simple transitive verb like *found*. This structure is also slightly less preferred than the main-verb intransitive reading, because the NP *the witch* needs a predicate. But although there are incomplete relations, there is not the problem that arises in the unergative case, in which the parser is unable to complete the necessary structures at all, even with additional input. For each of the unaccusative interpretations, the parser can activate and attach the structures it needs when given additional compatible input.

7.4.4 Discussion

We have shown that, together, our lexical structural analysis and the processing principles of the competitive attachment model account for the severe difficulty of reduced relatives with unergative verbs as well as for the ease of interpretation of reduced relatives with simple transitive verbs and unaccusative verbs. A garden-path effect only arises in the very narrow class of unergative verbs that have a transitive alternation. Note that this explanation of difficulty in processing the MV/RR ambiguity with unergative verbs like *raced* has the following consequences. First, it predicts that even unambiguous reduced-relative constructions will be very difficult with unergative verbs, because the structure of the embedded VP cannot be built under the restrictions of the competitive-attachment model. That is, the difficulty does not stem from the ambiguity but rather from the inability of the parser to activate the correct reduced-relative structure for an unergative verb. This is compatible with the observation that difficulty persists even when the reduced relative occurs in a fully disambiguating context, such as in object position (cf. *I groomed the horse raced past the barn*). The account also conforms with the pattern of acceptability judgments presented in Section 7.2, which reveal that unergative verbs in a reduced-relative construction cause processing problems even when the past participle is not ambiguous. Second, our explanation predicts that the passive of a causative unergative should also disrupt normal processing. Since the grammatical structure for a passive unergative includes an empty embedded VP, just as in the reduced relative, the parser should experience the same difficulty in its processing. While the model appears overly strong in this prediction (cf. (7)), we note that passive unergatives are often awkward (cf. (8)).

(7) The schooner was sailed through the narrow channel with difficulty.

(8) ?? The lions were jumped through the hoop after the elephant act.

The evidence indicates some peculiarity with unergatives in the passive and encourages future research into the range of difficulty that is exhibited.

7.5 Conclusion

In conclusion, we have proposed a lexical-structural account for the differential difficulty of reduced relative clauses. We make the novel observation that extreme garden-path effects in this construction appear to be limited to manner of motion/sound emission verbs, a subclass of intransitive verbs with peculiar properties. We have proposed a lexical and syntactic analysis of these unergative verbs that in conjunction with a specific model of processing – the competitive attachment model (Stevenson, 1994) – produces the right description of the data. In our account, the linguistic representation is mapped onto an isomorphic network structure built by the parser, in which structure building is restricted. Our explanation of the difficulty of unergative reduced relatives relies crucially on the interaction of computationally justified architectural features of the processor and specific lexical representations, supported by independent principles of linguistic theory.

This proposal gives prominence to structural information stored in the lexicon, which determines the syntactic structure of verbal projections. In this way it is able to make finer-grained distinctions than either structure-based proposals which rely only on general syntactic information (e.g., Ferreira and Clifton, 1986; Frazier, 1978; Frazier and Fodor, 1978), or those accounts based on the distinction between obligatorily and optionally transitive verbs (Gibson, 1991; Pritchett, 1992). Many other proposals that have discussed the resolution of MV/RR ambiguity are not equipped to explain the difference between verb classes within the same structural ambiguity (Crain and Steedman, 1985; Altmann and Steedman, 1988; Gilboy, Sopena, Clifton, and Frazier, 1995).

Unlike many constraint-based approaches – which often ascribe subclass phenomena to the interaction of frequency and pragmatic/semantic effects (Spivey-Knowlton and Sedivy, 1995) – our proposal is not purely lexicalist, but exploits structural information shared by several lexical items forming a subclass. Moreover, many constraint-based proposals downplay the role of structure building as a source of complexity, and instead capitalize on the differential frequencies of lexical items as the main predictor of processing load (MacDonald, 1994; Trueswell, 1996). Structural complexity comes into play indirectly, because the simpler representation usually corresponds to a global bias in the processing network, and it interacts with item-specific biases in the resolution of ambiguity. No constraint is, in principle, qualitatively different from the others. This approach then predicts that any difficulty posed by a constraint can be eliminated, if the opposing constraints are appropriately manipulated.

By contrast, we specify a constraint-integration algorithm – defining what lexical constraints come into play and how they interact – where not all constraints have the same importance. Structural complexity is given a special status by being defined implicitly by the architectural design: certain structures cannot be computed. In the current model, structural complexity alone can cause failure to interpret a sentence even when all other factors would help its correct interpretation. This phenomenon is clearly observable when the sentence is not ambiguous. In general, the model predicts categorial processing effects, which are not predicted by other constraint-based models.

This approach accounts for the sharp distinctions between unergative reduced relatives and reduced relatives with other verbs, since the parser cannot process reduced relative clauses of unergative verbs due to its limited ability to project empty nodes and to bind them in the structure. For other verbs, such as obligatorily transitive verbs, where the lexical and syntactic competitors in the analysis are more evenly weighted, there is no processing breakdown, and the model can be influenced by frequency, pragmatic, and semantic factors. The proposal thus reconciles results that point toward an architecture where several constraints are simultaneously at play, with results that indicate sharp and irrecoverable breakdown.

References

Altmann, G. and M. Steedman (1988). Interaction with context during human sentence processing. *Cognition* 30, 191–238.

Baker, M. (1988). *Incorporation.* Chicago, IL: University of Chicago Press.

Belletti, A. and L. Rizzi (1988). Psych verbs and θ theory. *Natural Language and Linguistic Theory* 6, 291–352.

Bresnan, J. (1982). The passive in lexical theory. In J. Bresnan (Ed.), *The mental representation of grammatical relations*, 3–86. Cambridge, MA: MIT Press.

Brousseau, A.-M. and E. Ritter (1991). A non-unified analysis of agentive verbs. In D. Bates (Ed.), *West Coast Conference on Formal Linguistics 20*, 53–64. Stanford, CA: CSLI.

Burzio, L. (1981). *Intransitive verbs and Italian auxiliaries.* Ph.D. thesis, MIT.

Burzio, L. (1986). *Italian syntax.* Dordrecht: Kluwer.

Chomsky, N. (1981). *Lectures on Government and Binding: The Pisa lectures.* Dordrecht: Foris.

Crain, S. and M. Steedman (1985). On not being led up the garden path: The use of context by the psychological parser. In D. R. Dowty, L. Karttunen, and A. M. Zwicky (Eds.), *Natural language processing: Psychological, computational, and theoretical perspectives,* 320–358. Cambridge: Cambridge University Press.

Crocker, M. W. (1992). *A logical model of competence and performance in the human sentence processor.* Ph.D. thesis. University of Edinburgh.

Cruse, D. A. (1972). A note on English causatives. *Linguistic Inquiry* 3, 520–528.

Ferreira, F. and C. Clifton (1986). The independence of syntactic processing. *Journal of Memory and Language* 25, 348–368.

Frazier, L. (1978). *On comprehending sentences: Syntactic parsing strategies.* Ph.D. thesis, University of Connecticut. Available through the Indiana University Linguistics Club, Bloomington, IN.

Frazier, L. and J. D. Fodor (1978). The sausage machine: A new two-stage parsing model. *Cognition* 6, 291–325.

Gibson, E. (1991). *A computational theory of human linguistic processing: Memory limitations and processing breakdown.* Ph.D. thesis, Carnegie-Mellon University.

Gilboy, E., J.-M. Sopena, C. Clifton, and L. Frazier (1995). Argument structure and association preferences in Spanish and English complex NPs. *Cognition* 54, 131–167.

Grimshaw, J. (1991). Extended projection. Manuscript, Brandeis University.

Grimshaw, J. (1997). Projection, heads and optimality. *Linguistic Inquiry* 28, 373–422.

Hale, K. and J. Keyser (1987). A view from the middle. Lexicon Project Working Papers 10, MIT.

Hale, K. and J. Keyser (1993). On argument structure and the lexical representation of syntactic relations. In K. Hale and J. Keyser (Eds.), *The view from Building 20*, 53–109. Cambridge, MA: MIT Press.

Harley, H. (1995). *Subjects, events and licensing.* Ph. D. thesis, MIT.

Jackendoff, R. (1972). *Semantic interpretation in generative grammar.* Cambridge, MA: MIT Press.

Levin, B. (1993). *English verb classes and alternations.* Chicago, IL: University of Chicago Press.

Levin, B. and M. Rappaport (1986). The formation of adjectival passives. *Linguistic Inquiry* 17, 623–661.

Levin, B. and M. Rappaport Hovav (1995). *Unaccusativity.* Cambridge. MA: MIT Press.

Lewis, R. (1993). *An architecturally-based theory of human sentence comprehension.* Ph.D. thesis, Carnegie Mellon.

MacDonald, M. C. (1994). Probabilistic constraints and syntactic ambiguity resolution. *Language and Cognitive Processes* 9, 157–201.

MacDonald, M. C., N. Pearlmutter, and M. Seidenberg (1994). The lexical nature of syntactic ambiguity resolution. *Psychological Review* 101, 676–703.

Marcus, M. (1980). *A theory of syntactic recognition for natural language.* Cambridge, MA: MIT Press.

Mitchell, D. C., F. Cuetos, M. M. B. Corley, and M. Brysbaert (1995). Exposure-based models of human parsing: Evidence for the use of coarse-grained (non-lexical) statistical records. *Journal of Psycholinguistic Research* 24, 469–488.

Pritchett, B. (1992). *Grammatical competence and parsing performance.* Chicago, IL: University of Chicago Press.

Reggia, J. (1987). Properties of a competition-based activation mechanism in neuromimetic network models. In *Proceedings of the First International Conference on Neural Networks*, vol. 2, 131–138. New York: IEEE.

Rizzi, L. (1990). *Relativized Minimality.* Cambridge: MIT Press.

Siloni, T. (1994). *Noun phrases and nominalizations.* Ph.D. thesis, University of Geneva.

Spivey-Knowlton, M. J. and J. C. Sedivy (1995). Resolving attachment ambiguity with multiple constraints. *Cognition* 55, 227–267.

Spivey-Knowlton, M. J., J. C. Trueswell, and M. K. Tanenhaus (1993). Context effects in syntactic ambiguity resolution: Discourse and semantic influences in parsing reduced relative clauses. *Canadian Journal of Experimental Psychology* 47, 276–309.

Stevenson, S. (1994). *A competitive attachment model for resolving syntactic ambiguities in natural language parsing.* Ph.D. thesis, University of Maryland, College Park. Available as technical report TR-18 from Rutgers Center for Cognitive Science, Rutgers University.

Stevenson, S. and P. Merlo (1997). Lexical structure and parsing complexity. *Language and Cognitive Processes* 12, 349–399.

Trueswell, J. C. (1996). The role of lexical frequency in syntactic ambiguity resolution. *Journal of Memory and Language* 35, 566–585.

Trueswell, J. C., M. K. Tanenhaus, and S. M. Garnsey (1994). Semantic influences on parsing: Use of thematic role information in syntactic ambiguity resolution. *Journal of Memory and Language* 33, 285–318.

8

Constituency, Context, and Connectionism in Syntactic Parsing

JAMES HENDERSON

8.1 Introduction

As is evident from the other chapters in this book, ambiguity resolution is a major issue in the study of the human sentence processing mechanism. Many of the proposed models of ambiguity resolution involve the combination of multiple soft constraints, including both local and contextual constraints. Finding the best solution to multiple soft constraints is exactly the kind of problem that connectionist networks are good at solving, and several models have used them in one way or another. The difficulty has been that standard connectionist networks do not have sufficient representational power to capture some central properties of natural language (Fodor and Pylyshyn, 1988; Fodor and McLaughlin, 1990; Hadley, 1994). In particular, standard connectionist networks cannot represent constituency. Thus, they cannot capture generalizations over constituents, and in learning they cannot generalize what they have learned from one constituent to another. Since regularities across constituents are fundamental and pervasive in all natural languages, any computational model that predicts no such pattern of regularities cannot be adequate as a complete model of sentence processing. To address this inadequacy without losing their advantages, the representational power of connectionist networks needs to be extended.

This chapter discusses exactly such an extension to connectionist networks. Temporal synchrony variable binding (Shastri and Ajjanagadde, 1993) gives connectionist networks the ability to represent constituency, and thus to capture and learn generalizations over constituents. By doing so, this extension makes a complete connectionist model of the human sentence processing mechanism possible.

One desirable side effect of adding the representation of constituency to connectionist models is that it makes them more similar to symbolic models of sentence processing. However, there is one big difference. Symbolic models rely heavily on structural relationships between constituents and generally ignore contextual information. Temporal synchrony variable binding (TSVB) networks cannot in general represent relationships between constituents and rely heavily on contextual information. This chapter argues that the connectionist approach put forward here actually provides a better account of the linguistic data than the traditional symbolic approach. In particular, we discuss how the lack of relationships between constituents predicts some significant constraints on unbounded dependencies.

The rest of this chapter begins with a discussion of standard connectionist networks and how they represent contextual information. Section 8.3 then discusses the role of constituency in symbolic linguistic theories, with particular attention to the property of systematicity (Fodor and Pylyshyn, 1988). TSVB is presented in Section 8.4; TSVB networks can represent constituents and account for systematicity. Section 8.5 then discusses the inability of TSVB networks to represent structural relationships, and to what extent information about such relationships can be represented using the combination of contextual and constituency information. As discussed in Section 8.6, the generalizations that symbolic linguistic theories express using structural relationships can be captured without explicitly representing these relationships. Section 8.7 then focuses the discussion on recovering unbounded dependencies within this account, which explains some significant constraints on unbounded dependencies, in particular the limited possible violations of wh-islands. Section 8.8 concludes this chapter.

8.2 Context in Connectionist Networks

As discussed in Chapter 1 of this volume, human sentence processing is a highly incremental process. Words are encountered sequentially, and information about the sentence is calculated incrementally as each word is encountered. Early work on sentence processing in connectionist networks did not take advantage of this property. A sentence was presented to the network via a fixed set of input units, with different units for each word position in the sentence (Cottrell, 1989; Fanty, 1985; Selman and Hirst, 1987). Because the number of such units in a network is fixed, such a representation puts a bound on the length of sentences that it can handle. While arguments for some such bound can be made, this problem is symptomatic of one that is much more fundamental: the inability to represent generalizations across word positions. Because each word position has its own input units, and thus its own links to the rest of the network, there is no a priori reason why the same word occurring in similar contexts at different positions should be treated the same. It's as if *the* occurring in position 5 is a totally different word from *the* occurring in position 6. Without the ability to represent such generalizations across word positions, learning the generalizations necessary for sentence processing would be completely intractable.

The answer to the problems of both incremental processing and generalizing across word positions came with developments in recurrent networks. A recurrent network can maintain a memory of its previous inputs because it has cycles in its links. Activation patterns flow around the link cycles and are available when processing the next input. Thus, the words of a sentence can be input sequentially, and the network's pattern of activation incrementally builds up a representation of the sentence. This allows arbitrarily long sentences to be processed, since the network can simply be run for as many time steps as there are words in the sentence. More fundamentally, because the same set of units and links are being used at each step, and thus for each word position in the sentence, such recurrent networks inherently represent generalizations across word positions. This allows information that is learned about a word and context at one word position in a sentence to be generalized to other word positions, thereby greatly reducing the amount of data needed for learning.

The most popular form of network for modeling sentence processing is the simple recurrent network (SRN) (Elman, 1990). An example SRN is shown in Figure 8.1. After each word is input, activation spreads from the input units and the context units through the hidden units (shown in the middle of the network) to the output units. As the activation spreads, it is modified by the network's link weights and unit functions, thereby computing the desired output. When this computation step is finished, the activation of the hidden units is copied to the context units, the next word is presented on the input units, and this new pattern of activation spreads through the network.

In Elman's models of sentence processing, the pattern of activation that is copied to the context units forms a distributed representation of the context provided by the previous words in the sentence. While this pattern of activation changes as the words of the sentence are sequentially input, the pattern of link weights that apply to the context and input word stays the same. Thus because

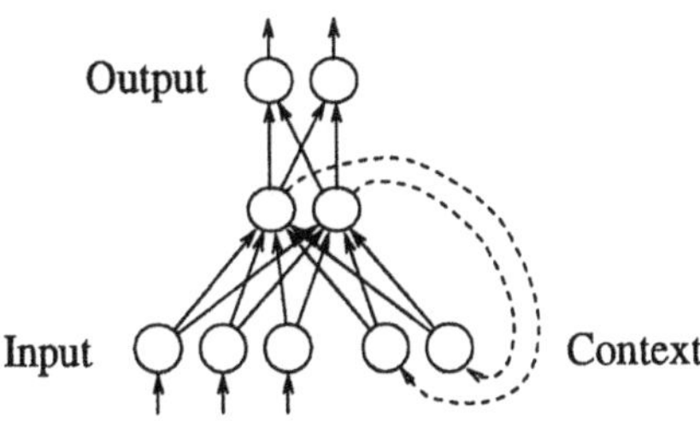

Figure 8.1. A simple recurrent network.

the link weights determine the network's computations, these networks capture generalizations across word positions, as discussed earlier.

8.3 Constituency in Linguistic Theories

Regularities across the positions of individual words are not the only kind of regularity found in natural language sentences. Groups of words also participate in regular patterns. These groups of words are the sentence's constituents. For example, a group of words that make up a noun phrase constituent can appear in a sentence virtually anywhere that any other noun phrase can appear. The pattern of where noun phrases can appear is regular, despite the fact that there is a huge variety of sequences of words that can make up a noun phrase. The prevalence of regularities across constituents (or more generally, across entities) is what Fodor and Pylyshyn (1988) called systematicity. Systematicity is clearly evident in natural language sentences as well as in a wide variety of other cognitive phenomena such as vision and high level reasoning.

Symbolic theories of language account for systematicity by representing generalizations in terms of constituents. This general information is then compositionally combined to form the analysis of a specific sentence. The compositionality of the combination process ensures that the theory's generalizations apply equally across constituents, thereby capturing regularities across constituents. For example, the representation of the constraint that a noun phrase's determiner and head noun must agree in number can be specified in terms of a noun phrase constituent that does not specify whether it is a subject or an object. This single generalization can then be applied to either a subject or an object noun phrase.

The simplest and most typical example of a representation of linguistic generalizations is context-free grammars (CFGs). For each type of constituent, a CFG defines the sequences of constituents that it can be composed of. These generalizations are independent of the context in which the constituent appears. The application of these generalizations defines a hierarchical structure, namely the phrase structure tree of the sentence. Most models of human sentence processing explicitly represent and manipulate a sentence's phrase structure tree. To do this they not only need to represent information about individual constituents, they also need to represent information about structural relationships between constituents. As with individual constituents, this allows these models to capture generalizations over relationships between constituents. For example in most models of English, the parent-child relationships in a phrase structure tree are not allowed to cross, no matter where these relationships appear in the tree. As will be argued in Sections 8.6 and 8.7, generalizations like these aren't actually necessary, because the desired generalizations can be captured without explicitly representing relationships between constituents.

8.4 Constituency in Connectionist Networks

In an SRN, the pattern of activation on the context units is the only representation of the state of the sentence processing mechanism. Because this is an unstructured distributed representation, SRNs have a representation of the sentence as a whole, but don't explicitly represent individual constituents. They can represent information about specifically identifiable constituents, but this information does not generalize across multiple constituents, as is required to account for the prevalence of regularities across constituents. For Elman's (1991) experiments this is not very important. The output of his networks is a prediction of the next word of the sentence. Such a task does not require keeping track of very many distinct constituents, and thus relearning generalizations for each required distinction is not much of a cost, particularly for the sentences he uses. This would not be the case for more complex tasks, such as sentence interpretation, where the output itself requires distinguishing between many constituents.

We can find a connectionist account of generalizations over constituents by considering how SRNs succeed in capturing generalizations over word positions. As discussed in Section 8.2, SRNs represent the position of each word in a sentence by inputting the words sequentially in time. Because time is being used to represent word positions, the network's activation patterns can represent position-dependent information about specific words and contexts in a sentence, while the network's link weights can capture position-independent generalizations that can be dynamically applied to these activation patterns. SRNs inherently generalize across word positions because the same pattern of link weights is used at every time, and therefore for every word position. If a connectionist network can also use time to represent multiple constituents, then it will also inherently generalize across constituents, and thereby account for the prevalence of regularities across constituents in natural language. Temporal synchrony variable binding (TSVB) provides just such a mechanism.

TSVB (Shastri and Ajjanagadde, 1993) is a method for using time to represent both sequences and entities. For sentence processing, the sequences are the words of the sentence and the entities are the constituents. To use the time dimension in both these ways, TSVB uses units that pulse, rather than producing sustained output. Sequences of pulses provide for two notions of timing: a course-grained notion, called the period, and a fine-grained notion, called the phase. The period specifies what number a pulse is in the sequence, and the phase specifies whether two pulses in the same period are precisely synchronous or not. If two pulses occur synchronously (i.e., in the same phase), then they are representing information about the same constituent. Periods are simply analogous to the computation steps of SRNs and are therefore used to represent the positions of the words in a sentence. Thus, TSVB networks incrementally process each word of a sentence, and for each word, they cycle through the set of constituents one at a time. This is the dual use of time that we required to ensure that the network can capture generalizations over both word positions and constituents.

TSVB is an extension of SRNs, and as such it does not lose their ability to represent context. This is done by simply having some units in the network to which TSVB has not been applied. In other words, some units produce sustained output across a whole period, rather than pulsing in individual phases within a period. As in SRNs, these units represent information about the context as a whole, rather than information about individual constituents within the context. We will call these nonpulsing units context units, and the pulsing units constituency units.

As in all connectionist networks, computation in TSVB networks is done by propagating activation across weighted links and through unit functions. This propagation occurs independently in each phase in each period. Learning changes the pattern of link weights, thereby changing the propagation of activation, and thus changing the computation. What is different about TSVB networks is the way activation is stored and used across time. For a pulsing unit (i.e., a constituency unit), the current output activation is determined by the activation it received in the same phase one period earlier. This means that information about a constituent will only affect a constituency unit's activation for that same constituent. Thus constituency units cannot transfer information between constituents. For a nonpulsing unit (i.e., a context unit), the current output activation is determined by the sum of the activation it has received over the last period. This means that information about one constituent can affect a context unit's output for all the constituents. Thus context units allow information to be transferred between constituents. However, with this method the constituent receiving the information will not know the identity of the constituent sending the information. This property will be crucial in our discussion of the implications of TSVB networks for sentence processing.[1]

We have seen that TSVB networks' representations of contexts and constituents allows them to capture generalizations across both of these, but there

[1] For a more thorough presentation of TSVB, and how it can be used to implement a syntactic parser, see Henderson (1994a,b).

has been no mention of the hierarchical structure that is so integral to the classical linguistic notion of constituency. To claim that TSVB networks could represent this structure, it would be necessary to show that they can generalize across the structural relationships between constituents that define it. To generalize across relationships between constituents, it is not sufficient to generalize across each constituent independently; the network must generalize across pairs of constituents. Without additional extensions, TSVB networks cannot generalize across pairs of constituents. To do so would require a third independent temporal dimension, which simple sequences of pulses does not provide. Using a spatial dimension (different sets of units for different instances of a relationship, as is done in tensor product variable binding (Smolensky, 1990)) would not result in the appropriate generalizations because the different units would have different link weights applied to them and thus would not necessarily learn the same generalizations. The only other alternative is to use the activation level dimension, but it isn't clear how to encode two independent dimensions in one activation level in such a way as to result in the appropriate generalization. Attempts to use activation levels to represent simple entities have not resulted in such generalization (Henderson, 1994b). Thus, we must say that TSVB networks have a notion of constituency that does not include any hierarchical structure.

8.5 Context versus Structure

As can be seen from the previous sections, the main difference between the representations supported by TSVB networks and the representations used by symbolic linguistic theories of syntactic parsing is that TSVB networks represent constituents and context, but symbolic theories represent constituents and structural relationships.[2] This raises the question to what extent TSVB networks can represent and process the information that symbolic theories represent using structure, and to what extent TSVB networks are constrained by their inability to do so. This section will characterize these abilities and constraints. The next two sections will then explore their empirical consequences for modeling human sentence processing, and human syntactic parsing in particular.

While TSVB networks cannot generalize over both the constituents in a relationship, they can generalize over one of them by using context units to represent information about the other constituent. As mentioned earlier, context units can

[2] Of course there is also the standard distinction between connectionist and symbolic representations, namely continuous versus discrete values. This is an important difference, but it has been discussed extensively elsewhere, and it is not an issue that is particular to TSVB.

be used to transfer information from one constituent's phase to another constituent's phase. Once information about both constituents is represented in the same phase, calculations that involve a relationship between these constituents can be performed. However, this calculation will only know the properties of the constituent that is represented in the context units; it will not know the constituent's identity. The calculation needs to know the constituent's identity so that the results of the calculation can be transfered back to the constituent. Thus, this method will only work if the constituent's identity can be uniquely determined beforehand. In other words, at the time of the calculation one of the two constituents in the relationship needs to be uniquely identifiable. More generally, all but one of the constituents involved in a calculation must be uniquely identifiable at the time of the calculation. This is the central constraint that we will be exploring in the rest of this chapter.

It is worth noting that although one of the constituents in any relationship needs to be uniquely identifiable at any given time, this may be a different constituent at different times. As an example, we will be arguing that fillers for unbounded dependencies are such a special constituent, but there is no problem with processing one unbounded dependency at the beginning of a sentence and then processing another at the end. Thus, the calculation of unbounded dependencies does generalize over fillers, as well as over potential gaps, but it does so in a constrained way. Essentially, we are using one of our two time dimensions to generalize over both the second constituent in a relationship and word positions (or more generally, computation steps). Using the same dimension to represent these two a priori independent dimensions makes the prediction that they are not in fact independent, but that one can be predicted from the other. In particular, if you know the position in the computation, then you know the constituent in the relationship (i.e., the constituent is uniquely identifiable). Thus the incremental nature of sentence processing will be crucial to the linguistic predictions that this constraint makes. The next section begins the discussion of these predictions.

8.6 Replacing Structural Relationships

Given that all the current major theories of natural language syntax are expressed in the symbolic paradigm, proposing an alternative connectionist model of sentence processing requires an explanation of how the empirical coverage of these symbolic theories can be matched by this connectionist approach. As has been discussed in the preceding sections, this requires an explanation of how the uses of structural relationships in symbolic theories can be replaced by the combination of context and constituency. This section will first discuss the mapping from declarative linguistic theories to the processing model proposed in this connectionist work. Then it will discuss the specifically linguistic aspects of this conversion.

Most linguistic theories of syntax are declarative, in that they describe a single static representation of the syntax of a sentence. Processing models such as the one being proposed here, on the other hand, are procedural, in that they describe a sequence of representations that are passed through in analyzing the syntax of a sentence. As discussed in the previous section, the temporal nature of this sequence is crucial to the predictions of this model. The basic principle that this model uses to map from declarative theories to a procedural one is that the parser be optimally incremental: at each point in the parse it represents all that is known and only what is known. This principle cannot be followed precisely, due to processing constraints such as the one being explored here, but it provides a useful ideal.

Because words are the source of the new information during parsing, the principle of optimal incrementality leads to the parser using a lexicalized grammar. Each grammar entry specifies what is known about the syntax of the sentence given the presence of the grammar entry's word. The influence of the information from the preceding words on the information from the new word is handled through disambiguating between the multiple grammar entries for the new word (if necessary), and through the choice of which constituents in the parse of the preceding words should be modified by information in the chosen grammar entry. By adding information to constituents already in the parse, the parser is in effect equating these constituents with constituents from the grammar entry, thereby unifying the information about the equated constituents. Thus the equation of constituents is the basic combination operation used by this parser. This equation mechanism (and its implied unification) is analogous to the way feature-based grammar formalisms, such as LFG (Kaplan and Bresnan, 1982), HPSG (Pollard and Sag, 1987), and FTAG (Vijay-Shanker, 1987), combine information from different grammar entries. Equation is also used within the current parse, to perform delayed attachments or fill gaps for unbounded dependencies.

As an example of how this parsing model works, consider the parse illustrated in Figure 8.2. The parser begins with the information that it is looking for a sentence, represented by the initial S constituent. The grammar entry for *who* is then added to the parser state with its S equated with the parser state's S. While the parser does not actually represent all the phrase structure information depicted, its representations are sufficient to enforce the desired parser-internal

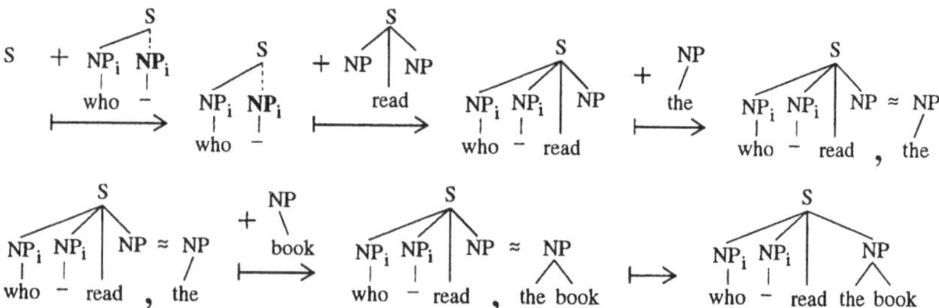

Figure 8.2. A parse for the sentence "Who$_i$ $-_i$ read the book?".

implications of all this information, as discussed later on. The grammar entry for *read* is then added with both its S and its subject NP equated with constituents in the parser state, using a special subject gap filling rule, as discussed in the next section. When *the* is encountered, the parser isn't sure if this is the beginning of the object NP or of a subconstituent of the object NP (as in *the author's book*), so it delays this attachment decision using a list of tree fragments, with the possible equation recorded. The grammar entry for *book* is then attached to the rightmost tree fragment, at which point the parser can decide to commit to the delayed attachment, thereby completing the parse. Note that this parser uses an extremely compact notion of constituency, similar to that used in dependency grammars (Hudson, 1984; Melčuk, 1988). This helps minimize the need for information about relationships between constituents.

The output of the parser is simply the sequence of grammar entries that it uses and the constituent equations it performs. This is the derivation history of the parse, and it is adequate to reconstruct the full parse of the sentence. Strictly speaking, this derivation history does not have to include any information that is not added to the parser state, and thus any constraints on the parser's output are subsumed under constraints on the parser state. However, it is possible to interpret the parser's output in a more semantically informative way, such as would be provided by a phrase structure tree. Given that different constituents in a single grammar entry have different semantic roles, there is no need for semantic relationships to generalize across constituents within a grammar entry. Thus, because only one grammar entry is used at a time, the constraint on the representation of relationships does not restrict this semantic output. So as to reflect this output information, the figures used in this chapter depict phrase structure relationships, even though this information is not stored in the parser's internal representations.

Now we are left with the task of showing how the parser can represent in its state the information that is needed for parsing without using relationships that must generalize over both their constituents.[3] The relationships which symbolic linguistic theories use can be reduced to three structural relationships: immediate dominance (i.e., the parent–child relationship), linear precedence (i.e., sequential ordering), and dominance (i.e., the ancestor relationship). Immediate dominance and linear precedence are used to specify generalizations about word order. The constituents that are immediately dominated by a given constituent are required to be contiguous, and their ordering is required to be consistent with the linear precedence constraints. Because the parsing process is required to produce a single tree, immediate dominance is also used to express the fulfillment of the expectation that a constituent will find some role to play in the sentence. If a constituent does not yet have an immediate parent, then it has not yet found its role in the sentence. Dominance is implicit in any chain of immediate dominance relationships, but it is used explicitly to express constraints on unbounded dependencies.

The uses of immediate dominance are not particularly problematic given TSVB networks' representational abilities. Having or not having an immediate parent is a property of an individual constituent, so enforcing the requirement that all constituents play some role in the sentence can be done independently for each constituent. For the requirement that the children of a given constituent be contiguous, there are some circumstances in which this constraint actually should not be enforced, even for a strongly ordered language like English. For example, sentence (1) is perfectly acceptable, despite the fact that the object noun phrase is interrupted by an adverb from the main clause.

(1) I met a man yesterday who I hadn't seen in years.

The remaining cases can be enforced using a bounded list of rooted tree fragments, which was illustrated in Figure 8.2. The children of the root of the most recent tree fragment must be completely parsed before parsing any earlier tree fragments is resumed, thereby forcing their contiguity. All calculations involving tree fragments are specific to the most recent tree fragment, whose root is unique.

The majority of linear precedence relationships involve words and can thus be enforced without involving more than one constituent. They can be enforced as constraints on when the word can be added to a constituent. For example, the fact that determiners precede the head of a noun phrase can be enforced by

[3] Most of the methods described in this section and the next are specified in more detail in Henderson (1994b). These methods have all been implemented in a working and extensively tested TSVB network parser.

not allowing a determiner to be added to a noun phrase which already has its head. Having a head is represented as a property of a constituent, and the grammar entry for determiners restricts its application to noun phrases that do not have this property. Another class of linear precedence relationships is used to express ordering between subjects and other constituents. Because unattached subjects always occupy a position in the list of tree fragments discussed in the previous paragraph, the tree fragment list can be used to enforce such ordering constraints. These methods leave only one class of linear precedence relationships unenforced (at least for English), namely those between the two objects of ditransitive verbs. This relationship can be represented as long as the second object is unique during the parsing of the first object. This predicts that only one such ordering constraint will need to be enforced at any one time. Sentences (2)–(4) illustrate cases where one, two, and three such relationships, respectively, need to be simultaneously enforced. The case with two relationships (sentence (3)) is surprisingly awkward, but not unacceptable. Because there are two second objects during the parsing of the two first objects, this representation predicts that something will go wrong in this case, although it doesn't predict what. Because there is only this one limited type of sentence that causes a problem, and because even these sentences are of questionable acceptability, any number of alternative strategies would be adequate to explain this particular data. These strategies would not, however, generalize to the case which require three relationships (sentence (4)). Such sentences are clearly unacceptable, as is predicted by TSVB networks' limited ability to represent information about linear precedence relationships between constituents.

(2) John gave the man money to buy roses with.

(3) ?John gave the man who bought the woman roses money to buy them with.

(4) #John gave the man who bought the woman who told Mary stories roses money to buy them with.

As we've seen, the necessary information about immediate dominance and linear precedence relationships can be adequately represented using fairly simple mechanisms that do not require generalizing over pairs of constituents. The situation becomes more complicated for dominance relationships, because they are not local relationships between constituents. Checking a dominance relationship requires checking a chain of immediate dominance relationships. Such an unbounded relationship is necessary for expressing information about unbounded dependencies, such as those given in (5)–(7) (see Section 8.7). However, there are many seemingly idiosyncratic constraints on unbounded dependencies that are not predicted by a completely general representation of dominance relationships, such as those illustrated in (8)–(12)(again, see Section 8.7). Because of the complexity of this phenomena, unbounded dependencies have been extensively studied in linguistics, starting with Ross (1967). Some of the constraints that have been the most troublesome for declarative linguistic theories are predicted by the fact that TSVB networks cannot enforce dominance relationships in a completely general way. The next section will discuss these predictions.

8.7 Predictions for Unbounded Dependencies

Unbounded dependencies are relationships between a filler, such as *who* or *how*, and a missing constituent that is semantically related to the filler, called the gap. In (5), *which book* is the filler and the gap, indicated by underlining, is the object of *read*. The relationship between these constituents is denoted by the shared subscript i.

(5) Which$_i$ book did Mary say John read $\_\,_i$?

The main syntactic constraint on this relationship is that the clause containing the filler must dominate the gap. This allows the gap to be embedded within many intervening constituents, such as that for *read* in (5). For a TSVB network to calculate these dominance relationships, they have to be inherited across the intervening constituents one at a time. This implies a mechanism similar to the slash passing used in GPSG (Gazdar et al., 1985) and HPSG (Pollard and Sag, 1987). Whenever the root of a grammar entry is equated with a dominated constituent, the parser must calculate that any children in the grammar entry are also dominated by the same filler constituent. By performing this calculation when the grammar entry is added, we know that the intervening constituent (the grammar entry root) will be uniquely identifiable. This leaves the filler constituent and the child constituent, one of which must be unique at the time of the calculation in order to prevent confusion about which filler dominates which child. Because there appear to be grammar entries that have multiple children that can contain gaps, we must claim that it is the filler that is always uniquely identifiable at the time. This makes strong predictions about the interaction between multiple fillers in the same sentence, as will be discussed directly. But first we will expand on the precise mechanism that has been developed for parsing unbounded dependencies.

The mechanism that has been developed for parsing unbounded dependencies within the constraints imposed by TSVB networks is based on the analysis given in Kroch, 1989, where constraints from Government-Binding theory (Chomsky,

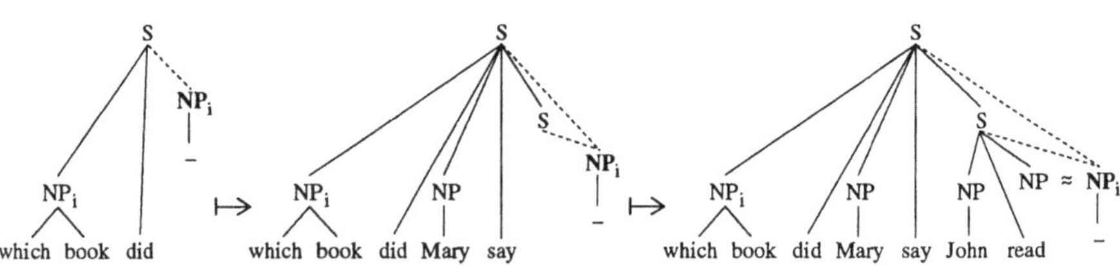

Figure 8.3. An illustration of three states of the parser during the parse of sentence (5).

1981) are expressed in the Tree Adjoining Grammar (TAG) framework (Joshi, 1987). In accordance with the TAG framework, Kroch's analysis divides the constraints on possible unbounded dependencies into a local component and a recursive component. Accordingly, the TSVB mechanism uses two rules, one for calculating what constituents the dependency can cross, and one for calculating where the dependency can end (i.e., the gap site). The application of both these rules is illustrated in Figure 8.3. Adopting the movement terminology commonly used for these dependencies, the parser uses a trace constituent to represent information about the filler and tries to equate this constituent with the constituent at the gap site. The first movement rule calculates what constituents the trace could be dominated by (shown first), and the second movement rule calculates what constituents the trace could be equated with (shown second).

Both dominance and equatability are relationships between constituents, so both movement rules are restricted by the constraints imposed by TSVB networks. As further discussed later on, these rules calculate these relationships based on properties of a trace, a grammar entry's root, and that grammar entry's other constituents. The rules can be implemented without actually using relationships as long as both the trace and the grammar entry's root are uniquely identifiable when the rules apply. This allows the movement rules to apply to each nonroot constituent in the grammar entry, with information about the root and information about the trace represented as contextual properties. To ensure that the trace is uniquely identifiable, we simply need a property that identifies a unique trace at any given time. The movement rules can only apply to this one trace, called the current trace. In the figures, this distinguished constituent is shown in boldface. To ensure that the grammar entry's root is uniquely identifiable, the rules need to apply as the grammar entry is being added to the parser state. Only one grammar entry is added to the parser state at a time, and grammar entries have unique roots.

The dominance calculating rule tests to see if the root of the next grammar entry is being equated with a constituent that potentially dominates the current trace. If so, it predicates this property of other constituents in the grammar entry. This has the effect of iteratively inheriting the property 'potentially dominates current trace' down the phrase structure tree. In the second state illustrated in Figure 8.3, the dominance rule has just applied to the grammar entry for *say*, thereby calculating that the trace could be dominated by the sentential object of *say*. Similarly, the equatability rule tests to see if the root of the next grammar entry is being equated with a constituent that potentially dominates the current trace. If so, it tests constituents in the grammar entry to see if they could be equated with the trace. Constituents which are equatable are recorded as being so. In the third state illustrated in Figure 8.3 the equatability rule has just applied to the grammar entry for *read*, thereby calculating that the object of *read* can be the trace's gap site. The actual equation of the trace with the gap site is done when there is sufficient evidence to commit to this analysis, using another rule which also can only apply to the current trace.

In addition to these two movement rules, there is a mechanism for filling subject gaps, as was illustrated in Figure 8.2. Given that all the relevant information about the current trace is available as contextual properties, it is possible to test its equatability with the verb's subject at the same time as testing equatability for the verb's S. If a constituent in the parser state is compatible with the verb's sentence constituent, and if this constituent dominates the current trace, and if the current trace is compatible with the verb's subject constituent, then the verb's grammar entry is added to the parser state with the matching constituent as its sentence and the current trace as its subject. The current trace has then been equated with its gap site.

Dominance relationships are not the only constraints on unbounded dependencies. Most of the other constraints can be captured in a TSVB network parser simply by compiling them into the grammar entries. Some constituents are specified as being possible gap sites, and some constituents are specified as allowing unbounded dependencies to cross them (i.e., they are not barriers) (Chomsky, 1986). These specifications are checked by their respective movement rules, thereby enforcing the constraints. However, this method is not sufficient to account for the limited possible violations of wh- islands. In the present model, these constraints are accounted for by the constraints imposed by TSVB networks on the parsing mechanism. This explanation is particularly interesting because Kroch (1989) also cannot account for these phenomena within his declarative framework (TAG), but is forced to impose an external constraint on TAG derivations. Thus we see that by accounting for these phenomena within a processing model, we can greatly simplify the competence theory.

As mentioned earlier, the interesting predictions of TSVB's constraints on the representation of relationships arise for sentences that include more than one filler. In general, one filler cannot have its gap within the clause of another filler. Examples of this situation are shown in (8)–(12).

(6) Who$_i$ $-_i$ knew which$_j$ book Mary read $-_j$?

(7) Which$_i$ book did the man who$_j$ Mary met $-_j$ read $-_i$?

(8) ?Which$_i$ book did Mary know who$_j$ $-_j$ read $-_i$?

(9) ??Which$_i$ book did Mary know who$_j$ $-_j$ said John read $-_i$?

(10) Which$_i$ book did Mary know how$_j$ to $-_j$ read $-_i$?

(11) #Which$_i$ book did Mary know who$_j$ John said $-_j$ read $-_i$?

(12) #Who$_i$ did Mary know which$_j$ book $-_i$ read $-_j$?

Because of this constraint, clauses that include fillers are called wh-islands (Ross, 1967). For example in (8), the gap site for *which book* is located within the wh- island introduced by *who*. Given the constraints imposed by TSVB networks, the explanation of this difficulty is straightforward. Because only one trace can be processed at any one time, the processing of the first trace is interrupted by the processing of the second trace and therefore has difficulty finding its gap site within the phrase of the second trace. To make this intuition more precise, we'll have to look in detail at the time course of processing in these cases.

The clearest example of a wh-island is (12). When *read* is input to the parser there are two traces, one for *who* and one for *which book*. Because the trace for *which book* was introduced more recently, it is the current trace.[4] However, the grammar entry for *read* needs to apply the subject gap filling mechanism to the trace for *who*. This cannot happen because this trace is not the current trace. Thus, the parser is stuck in a state where it cannot proceed, and the model correctly predicts that the sentence is unacceptable.

The interesting thing about wh-islands is that in some cases it is fairly acceptable to violate them. Sentence (10) is the best example of this (discussed directly), although to many people (8) and even (9) still aren't as bad as (11) or (12). As illustrated in Figure 8.4, the second trace in (8) and (9) is the subject of *read*, so there is no problem with filling that gap when the grammar entry for *read* is added to the parser state. However, there is a problem when a movement rule needs to apply to the trace of *which book*. The movement rules need to apply when the grammar entry is being added in order to take advantage of the uniqueness of the current grammar entry's root, but the trace of *who* is still the

[4] It is necessary for the most recently introduced trace to be specified as the current trace to allow sentences like (7) to be parsed.

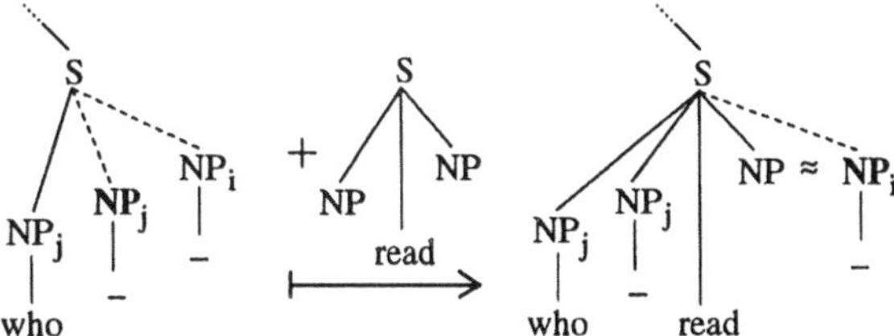

Figure 8.4. An illustration of how *read* in sentence (8) could be parsed using a delayed version of the equatability calculating movement rule. Only the wh-island is shown.

current trace until after the combination occurs. Thus the normal movement rules cannot apply to the trace of *which book.* This timing problem can be solved by delaying the application of the movement rule until after the trace of *which book* becomes the current trace, but before the next grammar entry is added. This is the process illustrated in Figure 8.4 for the equatability movement rule. However, this delay would have to be learned, and the circumstances in which this would be useful (i.e., wh-island violations) are very rare. As it turns out, this flexibility in the model fits with the variability of the acceptability of these sentences. Kroch (1989) reports sentences like (8) to be acceptable. This could be accounted for using a delayed version of the equatability rule. On the other hand, many nonlinguists find such sentences unacceptable. This could be accounted for using the normal version of this rule. Similarly, the unacceptability of sentences like (9) (as Kroch (1989) reports them to be) could be accounted for with the normal version of the dominance rule. This account predicts that it should be possible, with practice, to understand sentences like (9) by using a delayed version of the dominance rule. The fact that to some people (9) is not completely unacceptable seems to support this prediction. Thus, the model provides an account of the marginal nature of (8) and (9), as contrasted with the complete unacceptability of (11) and (12).

Sentence (10) is very similar to (8) except that the second wh-filler (*how*) introduces an adverb trace rather than a noun phrase trace. Because adverbs are optional modifiers, their grammar entries specify their own relationship to the sentence they modify (in accordance with the principle of optimal incrementality). Thus, the adverb trace is looking for a sentence constituent that its sentence constituent can equate with, not an adverb constituent. Given the absence of syntactic information that could prevent the adverb trace from attaching to a sentence, and given that *how to* is relatively common, the parser could decide to choose the sentence for *to read* as soon as *to* is input. In this case, the processing of the second trace will be completely finished by the time *read* is input. Thus, there will be no interference when the movement rule needs to apply to

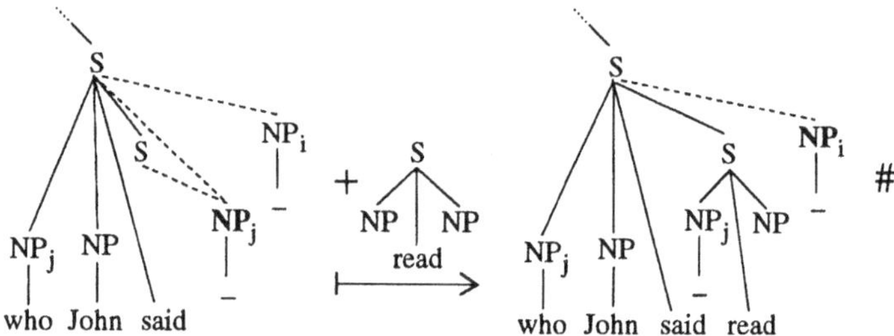

Figure 8.5. An illustration of two states of the parser during the failed parse of sentence (11). Only the wh-island is shown.

the grammar entry for *read* and the trace for *which book*, and the sentence is predicted to be acceptable.

Sentence (11) resembles (8) in that *which book* has its gap within the wh-island in the same way. The difference is that the trace within the wh- island is not immediately equated with its subject gap. This trace must first be passed to the object of *said*, as illustrated on the left in Figure 8.5. Then the grammar entry for *read* can use the subject gap filling mechanism, thereby allowing the trace for *which book* to become the current trace. However, the root of this grammar entry is not specified as dominating this trace, so the movement rules do not apply. The problem arises because both traces needed to be passed to the object of *said* when the grammar entry for *said* was added. But because of the constraints imposed by TSVB networks, the movement rules can only apply to one trace at a time. Thus, it is impossible for a TSVB network parser to compute the necessary dominance information for both traces. This accounts for the complete unacceptability of (11). Note that a simple constraint against crossing dependencies (Fodor, 1978; Pesetsky, 1982) fails to predict the contrast between (11) and (8).

The above model is based on a particular linguistic analysis, that of Kroch, 1989, and involves a particular language, English. However, it is not this particular model that is of interest here, but the general predictions of the constraints imposed by TSVB networks. For example, although in this model a trace can only be used to fill one gap, the model could be extended to cover cases where there is more than one gap for each filler. It would simply be necessary to continue to look for equatable constituents after one gap has been found. Such phenomena include parasitic gaps and gaps within conjunctions. More problematic, however, are languages where there are different fillers for each gap, but where these dependencies are not constrained as in English wh-islands. Examples of this are rare, but Scandinavian languages are reported to have this property (Engdahl, 1982). One possibility is that in these languages it is not the fillers that are uniquely identifiable when the unbounded dependencies are calculated, but the gaps. This would result in a system more similar to that for resolving pronoun reference, such as that proposed by Ejerhed (1982). As Ejerhed puts it (assumption B′, p. 105), "the assignment of fillers to gaps in not an anticipatory but a backwards looking process that is driven by gaps needing antecedents." Thus there would be no need for the slash-passing style mechanism proposed here for English, and thus there would be no interference between multiple such calculations, as was used to predict wh-islands.

In this section we have concentrated on one particular linguistic phenomenon, wh-islands. This phenomenon is particularly interesting because the seemingly idiosyncratic pattern of acceptable and unacceptable violations of wh- islands makes it difficult to incorporate this phenomenon into a competence theory of constraints on possible unbounded dependencies. We have succeeded in deriving this idiosyncratic pattern from the inherent computational limitations of TSVB connectionist networks.

8.8 Conclusion

In this chapter we've shown how standard connectionist networks can be extended to enable them to capture the kinds of linguistic generalizations that symbolic theories of syntactic parsing have found to be central to the nature of language. In the process we've derived computational constraints on syntactic parsing that predict some significant linguistic data.

Symbolic linguistic theories express generalizations about syntax in terms of constituents, thereby accounting for the prevalence of regularities across constituents in natural language (i.e., systematicity (Fodor and Pylyshyn, 1988)). These regularities can be accounted for within a connectionist framework by extending standard recurrent networks with TSVB (Shastri and Ajjanagadde, 1993). This extension allows connectionist networks to capture generalizations over constituents, while keeping their ability to capture generalizations over holistic contexts. However, it does not in general allow networks to capture generalizations over structural relationships between constituents. This is in contrast to symbolic theories, which typically express generalizations in terms of a hierarchical structure of constituents. We have shown that the desired generalizations that symbolic theories express using structure can be captured using only the combination of context and constituency, and that this approach avoids the undesirable overgeneralizations which result from the structure-based approach. In particular, this chapter has concentrated on how this connectionist model predicts the limited possible violations of wh-islands.

By this point, it should be clear that both connectionist computational models and symbolic linguistic models capture important aspects of the human sentence processing mechanism. It should also be clear that they are both inadequate for a complete model of it. The work presented in this chapter goes some way towards reconciling these two rather different perspectives and integrating their complementary strengths. We hope that future work will be successful in building on this synthesis.

References

Chomsky, N. (1981). *Lectures on Government and Binding*. Foris, Dordrecht.

Chomsky, N. (1986). *Barriers*. MIT Press, Cambridge, MA.

Cottrell, G. W. (1989). *A connectionist approach to word sense disambiguation*. Morgan Kaufmann, Los Altos, CA.

Ejerhed, E. (1982). The processing of unbounded dependencies in Swedish. In Engdahl, E. and Ejerhed, E., editors, *Readings on unbounded dependencies in Scandinavian languages*, 99–149. Almqvist & Wiksell, Stockholm.

Elman, J. L. (1990). Finding structure in time. *Cognitive Science*, 14:179–212.

Elman, J. L. (1991). Distributed representations, simple recurrent networks, and grammatical structure. *Machine Learning* 7:195–225.

Engdahl, E. (1982). Restrictions on unbounded dependencies in Swedish. In Engdahl, E. and Ejerhed, E., editors, *Readings on unbounded dependencies in Scandinavian Languages*, 151–174. Almqvist & Wiksell, Stockholm.

Fanty, M. (1985). Context-free parsing in connectionist networks. Technical Report TR174, University of Rochester, Rochester, NY.

Fodor, J. A. and McLaughlin, B. (1990). Connectionism and the problem of systematicity: Why Smolensky's solution doesn't work. *Cognition* 35:183–204.

Fodor, J. A. and Pylyshyn, Z. W. (1988). Connectionism and cognitive architecture: A critical analysis. *Cognition* 28:3–71.

Fodor, J. D. (1978). Parsing strategies and constraints on transformations. *Linguistic Inquiry* 9:427–474.

Gazdar, G., Klein, E., Pullum, G., and Sag, I. (1985). *Generalized Phrase Structure Grammar*. Harvard University Press, Cambridge, MA.

Hadley, R. F. (1994). Systematicity in connectionist language learning. *Mind and Language* 9:247–272.

Henderson, J. (1994a). Connectionist syntactic parsing using temporal variable binding. *Journal of Psycholinguistic Research*, 23:353–379.

Henderson, J. (1994b). *Description based parsing in a connectionist network*. Ph.D. thesis, University of Pennsylvania. Technical Report MS–CIS–94–46.

Hudson, R. (1984). *Word grammar*. Blackwell, Oxford.

Joshi, A. K. (1987). An introduction to Tree Adjoining Grammars. In Manaster-Ramer, A., editor, *Mathematics of language*, 87–115. Benjamins, Amsterdam.

Kaplan, R. and Bresnan, J. (1982). Lexical functional grammar: A formal system for grammatical representation. In Bresnan, J., editor, *The mental representation of grammatical relations*, 173–281. MIT Press, Cambridge, MA.

Kroch, A. (1989). Asymmetries in long distance extraction in a Tree Adjoining Grammar. In Baltin, M. and Kroch, A., editors, *Alternative conceptions of phrase structure*, 66–98. University of Chicago Press, Chicago.

Melčuk, I. (1988). *Dependency syntax: Theory and practice*. SUNY Press, Albany, NY.

Pesetsky, D. (1982). *Paths and categories*. Ph.D. thesis, M.I.T. Distributed by MIT Working Papers in Linguistics, Dept. of Linguistics and Philosophy, MIT.

Pollard, C. and Sag, I. A. (1987). *Information-based syntax and semantics. Vol. 1: Fundamentals*. Center for the Study of Language and Information, Stanford, CA.

Ross, J. (1967). *Constraints on variables in syntax*. Ph.D. thesis, M.I.T.

Selman, B. and Hirst, G. (1987). Parsing as an energy minimization problem. In Davis, L., editor, *Genetic algorithms and simulated annealing*, 141–154. Morgan Kaufmann, Los Altos, CA.

Shastri, L. and Ajjanagadde, V. (1993). From simple associations to systematic reasoning: A connectionist representation of rules, variables, and dynamic bindings using temporal synchrony. *Behavioral and Brain Sciences* 16:417–451.

Smolensky, P. (1990). Tensor product variable binding and the representation of symbolic structures in connectionist systems. *Artificial Intelligence*, 46:159–216.

Vijay-Shanker, K. (1987). *A study of Tree Adjoining Grammars*. Ph.D. thesis, University of Pennsylvania.

Part III

Syntax and Semantics

9

On the Electrophysiology of Language Comprehension: Implications for the Human Language System

COLIN BROWN AND PETER HAGOORT

This chapter is on syntactic and semantic processes during on-line language comprehension. We present event-related brain potential (ERP) data from a series of experiments using both written and spoken input, focussing mainly on sentence processing. The data are discussed in terms of the constraints that they impose on the architecture of the human language system, in particular with respect to the separation of syntactic and semantic knowledge bases.

The issue of the separation of different linguistic knowledge sources is an underlying theme in much psycholinguistic research and is especially relevant for a number of contrasting models on parsing. Although linguistic theory has to a large extent postulated distinct representational systems for structure and meaning, psycholinguistic models of the parsing process differ in their assumptions about the separability of syntactic and semantic knowledge bases and of the processing operations that tap into these bases.

One class of models – referred to as garden-path models in the literature – posits a separate syntactic knowledge base. This linguistic knowledge is used for the computation of a separate intermediate level of representation for the syntactic structure of a sentence. Garden-path models claim that the construction of an intermediate syntactic level is a necessary and obligatory step during sentence processing, if not for all structural assignments, then at least for a significant subset of them (e.g., Clifton & Ferreira, 1989; Frazier, 1987; Frazier & Clifton, 1996; Friederici & Mecklinger, 1996; Rayner, Garrod, & Perfetti, 1992). In terms of the operational characteristics of the system, it is posited that nonsyntactic sources of information do not affect the parser's initial structurally based analysis. Instead, these sources serve to confirm or disconfirm the first parse.

Another class of models (known as interactionist models, originating in part from the connectionist tradition), does not contain any independent status for (intermediate) products of syntactic computation (e.g., Bates, McNew, MacWhinney, Devescovi, & Smith, 1982; Elman, 1990; McClelland, St. John, & Taraban, 1989; Taraban & McClelland, 1990). The McClelland et al. (1989) sentence processing model, for example, posits a single, undifferentiated representational network, in which syntactic and semantic constraints (among others) combine to influence a single representation. In line with this architectural assumption, the on-line comprehension process is characterized as fully interactional, with all sources of information immediately affecting the analysis process.

More recently, other kinds of interactive models have been proposed, known as constraint-satisfaction models (e.g., Boland, Tanenhaus, & Garnsey, 1990; MacDonald, Pearlmutter, & Seidenberg, 1994; Spivey-Knowlton & Sedivy, 1995). In these models, lexical factors play a central role, and the importance of lexically represented information such as verb frequency and conceptual-semantic knowledge is emphasized. Some proponents of these lexicalist models argue that "there is no need for either an initial category-based parsing stage or a separate revision stage" (Tanenhaus & Trueswell, 1995, p. 233), thereby not assigning any specific primacy to syntactic information and syntactic processes. Note that in this approach a separate syntactic stratum can be part of the model (although the architectural aspects of constraint-based models remain at present somewhat underspecified, cf. Tanenhaus & Trueswell, 1995; but see MacDonald et al., 1994). Therefore constraint-based models share at least some representational assumptions with garden-path models.

The clearest representational contrast, then, emerges between the garden-path and interactionist models. These two contrasting classes of models imply quite different architectures underlying sentence processing. One assumes some form of compartmental representation along the lines of basic linguistic distinctions. The other opts for a combined system that does not differentiate at the representational level. Although many aspects of language are involved in sentence processing, a major representational distinction between the two approaches concerns the disputed separation of syntax and semantics, and their related processes. It is this issue that we will address on the basis of the available ERP results. Constraint-based models sit somewhere in between the garden-path and interactionist models. On the one hand, the constraint-based approach proposes at least partly separate representations, but on the other hand, the processing operations are highly interactive.

It is important to reiterate that the representational dispute shares roots with an ongoing debate on the autonomous or interactive processing nature of the parser. Autonomists claim that in sentence comprehension a syntactic parse is first performed, based on syntactic principles only, before other kinds of information (such as that derived from semantics and pragmatics) are brought to bear on the comprehension process (e.g., Ferreira & Clifton, 1986; Frazier, 1987, 1990; Rayner, Carlson, & Frazier, 1983; Rayner et al., 1992). In contrast, interactionists state that nonsyntactic sources of information are used either to direct the parser's initial analysis (e.g., Bates et al., 1982; Holmes, 1987; McClelland et al., 1989), or to immediately evaluate the product of syntactic analysis on a word-by-word basis, as part of the process of constructing a semantic representation of the input (e.g., Altmann & Steedman, 1988; Crain & Steedman, 1985).

Clearly, anyone of the autonomist persuasion has to be committed to a separate level of syntactic representation during sentence processing. An interactionist account of parsing does not by necessity have to posit such a separate level. Given that under this view syntactic information is directly integrated with semantic and pragmatic information, there is little reason to presuppose separate representational tiers during processing. This is the position advocated by Bates, Elman, McClelland, and their coworkers. Constraint-based theorists such as MacDonald, Tanenhaus, Trueswell, and their colleagues are less radical in their architectural assumptions. They reserve an important role for syntactic representations, but at the same time emphasize the dynamic aspects of the constraint-satisfaction process. This process is characterized by competition among incompatible alternatives (e.g., multiple parses), based on both linguistic and nonlinguistic information. An important difference from the garden-path models is that constraint-based models do not assign any primacy to syntactic computations or to syntactic structure building.

In sum, the different architectural assumptions just outlined also relate to different positions concerning the nature of the processing mechanisms that are operative during on-line sentence processing. Therefore, data that bear on the representational debate on syntax and semantics can also have implications for the autonomous versus interactive processing debate. This is what makes the syntax-semantics interface such an important meeting ground for central issues in parsing research.

In the following, we will discuss several ERP experiments on on-line semantic and syntactic processing during language comprehension. Since extensive overviews of the literature on ERPs and language are already available (cf. Kutas & Van Petten, 1988, 1995; Osterhout & Holcomb, 1995; Van Petten & Kutas, 1991), we have chosen to focus on a set of results – primarily from our own laboratory – that provide a clear basis for the points about the architecture of the sentence processing system that we will be making further on in this chapter. Our main claim will be that distinct electrophysiological signatures can be found for semantic and syntactic processes, and, hence, that the ERP data provide evidence for the existence of different brain states for parsing and semantic processing.

We precede the discussion of the ERP results by a short section on the ERP method and the relevance of ERPs for sentence processing research in particular.

9.1 Event-related Brain Potentials and Language Research

Event-related brain potentials (or ERPs) are part of the brain's overall electrical activity, the electroencephalogram (or EEG). ERPs recorded from the scalp reflect the summation of postsynaptic activity in a group of synchronously firing neurons, all having approximately the same geometric (usually parallel) configuration, and the same orientation with respect to the scalp (for detailed discussion of the physiology of ERPs, see Allison, Wood, & McCarthy, 1986; Nunez, 1981, 1990; Picton, Lins, & Scherg, 1995; Wood, 1987). In contrast to the continuously fluctuating voltage variation over time that constitutes the EEG, ERPs represent a series of voltage changes within the EEG that are time-locked to the presentation of an external stimulus. Because the size of the voltage changes in ERPs is small in comparison with the fluctuation of the EEG (1 or 2 microvolts for ERPs, in comparison to between 10 and over a 100 microvolts for the EEG), it is a standard usage in cognitive ERP research to compute an averaged ERP. This average is calculated over a number of EEG epochs, each of which is time-locked to repetitions of the same event. What is repeated can be the exact same stimulus, but more often is different tokens of the same type. The assumption that motivates signal averaging is that the electrical activity that is not related to the processing of the external stimulus varies randomly over time across the individual epochs. The effect, then, of averaging individual time-locked ERP waveforms is that the randomly distributed voltage fluctuations will tend to average to zero, leaving a residual waveform that reflects the activity that is largely invariant over time and between separate eliciting events of the same type. In language research, an acceptable signal-to-noise ratio can be achieved by averaging over anything between roughly 25 and 60 or more trials, depending on the particular issue under investigation.

Within the series of voltage changes that make up an averaged ERP, a number of positive and negative polarity peaks, more commonly called components, can be identified. In the psychophysiological literature these components are broadly categorized into exogenous and endogenous ones. Exogenous components are particularly sensitive to the physical parameters of the external stimulation and are thought to be relatively insensitive to cognitive factors. In contrast, endogenous components vary as a function of specifically cognitive aspects such as task relevance and attention, and are not contingent upon aspects of the physical stimulation.[1]

Exogenous components are sometimes referred to as early components, reflecting the fact that they occur in the first part of the ERP waveform. To a rough first approximation, the endogenous components that are of interest for language researchers do not emerge until some 150 ms after stimulation.

Although the identification of endogenous components in particular remains a controversial issue (cf. Coles & Rugg, 1995), there are only three basic defining ingredients: polarity, latency, and distribution. Polarity has two values, negative or positive, and components are appropriately labelled by either an N or a P. Latency (in almost all cases of the peak of a component) is measured in milliseconds and can range from just a couple of milliseconds (as with very early auditory components) to several hundreds of milliseconds. Components are additionally labelled according to the latency in milliseconds at which their amplitude reaches its maximum. For example, N400 refers to a negative polarity component with a peak value at approximately 400 ms after stimulus onset. In a few cases, components have received functional labels, intended to reflect the process they are thought to be a manifestation of (e.g., the mismatch negativity, see Näätänen, 1992). In addition to their polarity and latency, components are also characterized by their distribution over the scalp, or scalp topography. This refers to the pattern of latency and peak amplitude values over electrode sites. As a rule, an ERP experiment entails the registration of activity from a number of electrodes, distributed in a more or less even fashion over the scalp. Many components (both exogenous and endogenous) show a graded distribution of amplitude values over electrode sites, and this distribution can serve as one of the ways in which to distinguish between components, especially if the temporal windows within which components occur partly overlap in time. It is, however, very important to note that the activity at any particular electrode site on the scalp cannot be taken to originate in the brain tissue directly underlying that site: Scalp topography does not provide a map of neuronal localization. This is due, among other things, to the volume conduction properties of the brain and its surrounding matter, which enable electrical activity generated in one area of the

[1] The exogenous-endogenous distinction is less clear than this brief description suggests. Many components that were first thought to be either strictly exogenous or endogenous have since been shown to be open to the influence of physical or cognitive factors. However, the distinction is still helpful, and under appropriately operationalized experimental conditions, the separation into exogenous and endogenous components can be largely upheld. See Rugg and Coles (1995) for an excellent discussion of this and related issues.

brain to be registered at locations at considerable distance from the generator site.

There are several advantages to using ERPs in the investigation of sentence processing. The first concerns the multidimensional nature of ERPs. Brain potentials can independently vary according to their polarity, latency, amplitude, and scalp topography. This provides a rich basis for distinguishing among separate processing events. One particularly interesting possibility is that ERPs can in principle establish a truly qualitative distinction among processes. On the basis of our knowledge of the physiological origins of ERPs, it is reasonable to assume that certain different types of ERP peaks (e.g., those of opposite polarity) are generated by separate, or at least not entirely overlapping, neural systems. This implies that under appropriately operationalized experimental conditions, we can infer from the presence of qualitatively different electrophysiological profiles that distinct language processes are operative (cf. Kutas & King, 1995; Osterhout & Holcomb, 1995).

A second advantage of ERPs is that they provide a continuous, real-time measure of the language comprehension process. This enables the uninterrupted measurement of activity throughout and even beyond the entire processing of a sentence or discourse. Therefore, it is possible to not only assess the immediate impact of an experimental manipulation (e.g., the presentation of a syntactic anomaly), but also the consequences of this manipulation for the processing of further incoming material.

A third appealing feature of ERPs for sentence processing research is that robust, statistically reliable, and replicable effects can be obtained in the absence of additional task requirements (a feature that ERPs share with eye-movement registration). In most of the experiments that we will report on here, subjects were only instructed to attentively read or listen to the sentences they were presented with. No extraneous task demands were imposed. The advantage here is that we are not plagued by the uncertainties that can accompany reaction-time research on sentence processing, where we always have to take into account the possibility of contamination due to task effects.[2] Of course, by not having the subjects perform any overt task during ERP registration, we are open to the criticism that we have no control over exactly what the subjects are doing during the experiment. However, we would argue that with attentive and cooperative subjects, who are instructed to comprehend the sentences they hear or

[2] A further advantage is that by avoiding an overt task it becomes possible to test subject groups who cannot cope with additional task demands at the same time as adequately processing linguistic stimuli. See Hagoort, Brown, and Swaab (1996) for an example of ERP registration in aphasic patients with severe comprehension deficits.

read, the main task that these subjects are engaged in is the normal process of comprehension. It is, after all, quite difficult if not impossible to not process and understand language when it is presented within the focus of attention (cf. Fodor, 1983). Moreover, in many cases the proof of the pudding is in the eating. That is, if in the absence of extraneous task demands we obtain clear effects as a function of our experimental manipulations, and if these effects can be sensibly interpreted in terms of a priori predictions based on a sufficiently articulated model, then it seems reasonable to claim that we have succeeded in obtaining meaningful insights into on-line sentence processing.

9.2 Semantic Processing and Electrophysiology

In 1980, Marta Kutas and Stephen Hillyard reported a finding that provided the starting point for what has since become a very active research area on the electrophysiology of language comprehension (Kutas & Hillyard, 1980). They presented subjects with written sentences that ended in a semantically congruous or incongruous word. The ERP elicited by the incongruous ending showed a monophasic component with a negative polarity that reached its maximal amplitude at approximately 400 ms after presentation of the sentence-final word. The congruous last word of the sentence elicited the same component, but its amplitude was significantly smaller than with the incongruous ending. In accordance with its polarity and peak latency, Kutas and Hillyard termed the component the N400. The difference in amplitude between the two conditions is referred to as the N400 effect. An extension of the seminal 1980 result is shown in Figure 9.1, from the work of Kutas, Lindamood, and Hillyard (1984). The figure shows data from one representative electrode site on the scalp, labelled Pz, which is located over the central midline on the back of the head. In the Kutas et al. experiment, the sentence ended in three different ways: (1) on a word that was entirely congruous with the preceding context (the best completion condition), (2) on a word that was semantically related to the congruous ending, but that was nevertheless anomalous with respect to the meaning of the preceding sentence (related anomaly), or (3) on a word that had no relation with either the best completion or the sentential context (unrelated anomaly).

The waveforms show a series of voltage fluctuations. The effect of the physical stimulation can be seen in the exogenous potentials that are present in roughly the first 150 ms of the waveform. There is an early negative polarity peak at about 100 ms, immediately followed by a positive polarity peak. This so-called N1-P2 complex is a characteristic exogenous ERP profile that is invariably elicited by visual stimulation. The exogenous nature of this complex is underscored by the fact that it is identical in all three experimental conditions.

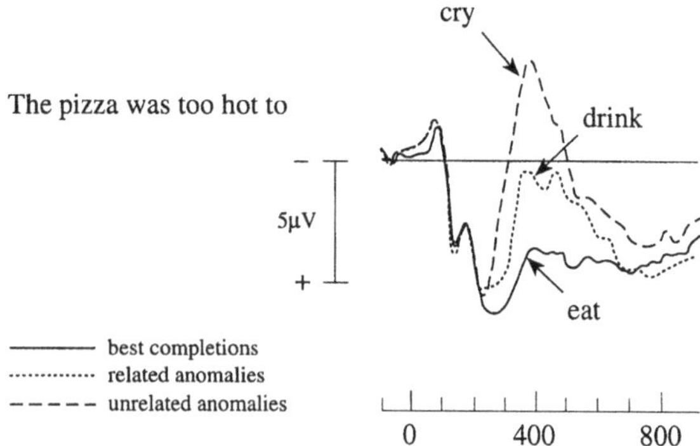

Figure 9.1. Grand average ERPs at electrode site Pz for three visually presented different sentence-final completions preceded by the same sentence. The solid line is the waveform for words that best completed the sentences. The dotted line is the waveform for words that did not fit the sentential contexts, but that were semantically related to the best completions. The dashed line is for words that did not fit the preceding contexts and that were not related to the best completions. In this figure, and all following figures, negative voltage values are plotted upwards, and the time axis is in milliseconds. Figure adapted from Kutas, Lindamood, and Hillyard, ©1984 The Psychonomic Society.

More important for our present purpose is the clear N400 component that is present in each condition. The onset of the N400 is at about 250 ms, with its characteristic peak at 400 ms. As can be clearly seen in the figure, the amplitude of the N400 is modulated as a function of the semantic match between the sentence-final word and the preceding context. The smallest N400 is elicited by the best completions, and the largest by the unrelated anomalies. The amplitude of the N400 to the related anomalies lies in between, reflecting the partial semantic match with the best completion. What these data demonstrate is that modulations in the amplitude of the N400 can be brought about by manipulating the semantic appropriateness of words with respect to the context in which they appear.

In the early research on the N400, semantic incongruities were used to assess the sensitivity of the N400 to contextual information. Subsequent research has shown that the N400 is also elicited in and modulated by more subtle semantic contexts. Figure 9.2 shows an example from our own work (Hagoort & Brown, 1994), in which we manipulated the cloze probability of words (that is, the extent to which a particular word is expected to occur in a sentence, based on the information conveyed by the sentence preceding that word). Compare the sentence *Jenny put the sweet in her mouth after the lesson* with *Jenny put the sweet in her pocket after the lesson.* Here, we contrast the ERP elicited by the word *mouth*, which is expected given the context (the high cloze condition), with

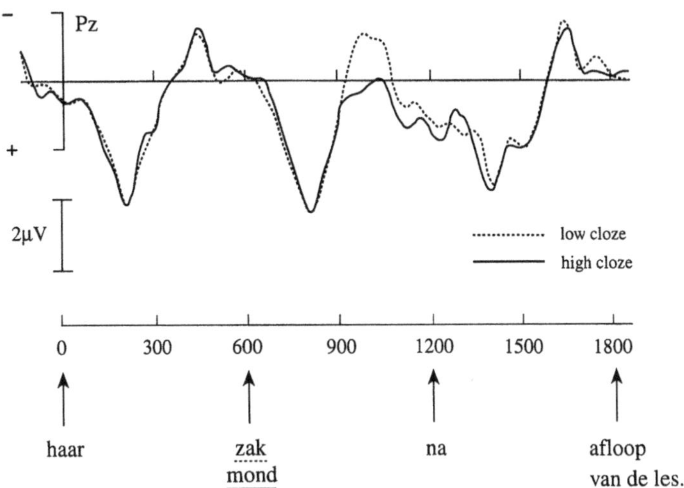

Figure 9.2. Grand average ERPs at electrode site Pz for visually presented less expected (Low Cloze, dotted line) and more expected (High Cloze, solid line) words in mid-sentence position. Presentation onset of the critical words is at 600 ms. In the figure, the critical words are preceded and followed by one word. The translation of the example sentence is *Jenny put the sweet in her pocket/mouth after the lesson.* Figure adapted from Hagoort and Brown, © 1994 Erlbaum.

the word *pocket*, which is less expected (low cloze). Note that in both cases the words are entirely acceptable continuations of the sentence. It just happens to be the case that when presented with the sentence preceding the high and low cloze words, more people choose *mouth* as a more likely continuation than *pocket*.

As can be seen in Figure 9.2, both the high and the low cloze words elicit the N400 component, but with a significantly larger amplitude in the low cloze condition. This demonstrates that the N400 is not a simple incongruity detector, but can reflect quite subtle aspects of ongoing semantic processing.

The majority of N400 research has used visual presentation. However, the elicitation of the N400 is not modality-dependent (cf. McCallum, Farmer, & Pocock, 1984; Connolly & Phillips, 1994), although its latency characteristics can differ depending on whether written or spoken language stimulation is used. In particular, it has been claimed that the onset of the N400 effect can be earlier with spoken input (cf. Holcomb & Neville, 1990; but see Connolly & Phillips, 1994, Hagoort & Brown, 1997). Figure 9.3 gives an example from our own work. Subjects heard naturally produced connected speech, in which in half of the sentences a semantic anomaly occurred in sentence-medial position.

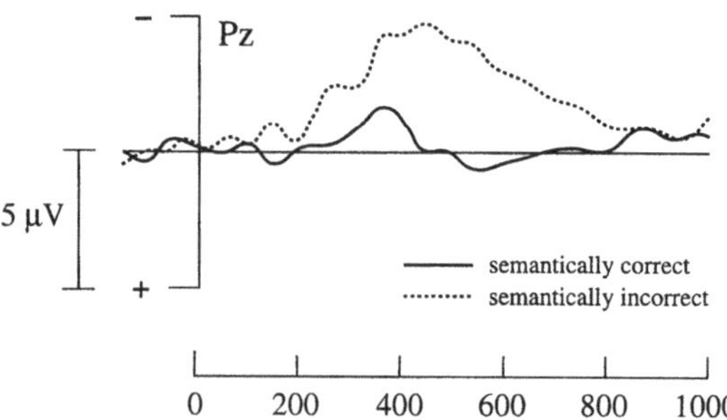

Figure 9.3. Grand average ERPs at electrode site Pz for semantically incorrect (dotted line) and correct (solid line) words occurring in mid-sentence position in naturally produced connected speech. The onset of the critical words is at 0 ms in the figure.

The waveforms in Figure 9.3 look quite different from those in the previous figures. The early exogenous stimulus components that can be seen in visually elicited ERPs are not discernable. This is due to the continuous physical stimulation by the speech signal, which gives rise to a series of temporally overlapping stimulus components. This overlap, in combination with the refractory period of auditory evoked potentials, leads to a smearing of the exogenous potentials, which in turn results in the relatively smooth morphology of the initial part of the waveform. Nevertheless, the waveforms clearly show an effect of the semantic anomaly, with a significant negative shift for the anomalous compared to the congruent condition. Based on its temporal properties and its distribution over the scalp (for expository purposes, we show only one electrode site here), it is clear that the difference between the anomalous and the incongruous condition can be classified as an N400 effect.

An additional observation on the modality independence of the N400 comes from work by Kutas, Neville, and Holcomb (1987). These researchers compared the N400 response to semantic anomalies during reading, listening, and signing. In the signing condition, the subjects were congenitally deaf users of American Sign Language (ASL). When presented with a semantic anomaly in ASL, these subjects showed a reliable N400 effect that was comparable to the N400 effects of the subjects who participated in the reading and listening conditions. This attests to the sensitivity and the validity of the N400 as an index of semantic processing during language comprehension (see Neville, Coffey, Lawson, Fischer, Emmorey, & Bellugi, 1997, for further, confirmatory evidence on ERP language effects in users of ASL).

Since the original report on the N400, a host of experiments has been performed on the conditions under which this component is elicited and modulated. We have discussed only a couple of experiments, focussing on the N400 in sentential contexts. In addition to the sentential work, a considerable amount of research has focussed on the N400 in single-word and word-word contexts. The net result of this wide-ranging research program is too extensive to discuss here (we refer the reader to the literature reviews mentioned earlier), but we conclude this section by briefly listing some of the major characteristics known to hold for the N400, focussing on those aspects that are particularly relevant for sentence processing research.

1. Each open class word as a rule elicits an N400.
2. The amplitude of the N400 is inversely related to the cloze probability of a word in sentence context. The better the fit between a word and its context, the smaller the amplitude of the N400.
3. The amplitude of the N400 varies with word position. The first open-class word in a sentence produces a larger negativity than open-class words in later positions. This reduction most likely reflects the increase in semantic constraints throughout the sentence.
4. The N400 is elicited by spoken, signed, and written language.
5. The N400 is not directly elicited by grammatical processes, although it can follow from them (see further on for more details on this point).

The overriding finding that emerges from the literature is that the amplitude fluctuations of the N400 are a function of ongoing semantic processing, ranging from outright anomalies to subtle variations in the goodness-of-fit of words in context. We have argued elsewhere (cf. Brown & Hagoort, 1993; Chwilla, Brown, & Hagoort, 1995; Hagoort et al., 1993) that the functional interpretation of the N400 effect relates to lexical integration processes. That is, following access to the mental lexicon, the activated word meaning has to be integrated into a message-level representation of the context within which that word occurs. It is this meaning integration process that is reflected by the N400 effect. The easier the integration process is, the smaller the amplitude of the N400 (for a similar position see Holcomb, 1993; Osterhout & Holcomb, 1992; Rugg, 1990; see also Kutas & King, 1995).

9.3 Syntactic Processing and Electrophysiology

Until some five years ago, almost no ERP results had been published on syntactic processing during language comprehension. Early work by Kutas and Hillyard (1983) included grammatical agreement errors as one of the conditions. No clear syntactic effects emerged that were dissociable from the standard N400 component, other than an enhanced negativity in the 300 to 500 ms range. With the upsurge in ERP and language research in the early 1990s, several groups have begun to focus on ERP manifestations of syntactic processing. As a result, there are now two basic ERP effects that are thought to reflect aspects of the parsing process.

The first effect concerns a relatively early negative shift with a peak latency at about 250 ms following relevant stimulation, which has been reported to be primarily observed at electrode sites over left anterior regions of the scalp. Hence, this effect is referred to as the left-anterior negativity, or LAN (Kluender & Kutas, 1993). The LAN has been observed following phrase structure violations (Neville, Nicol, Barss, Forster, & Garrett, 1991; Friederici, Pfeifer, & Hahne, 1993), subject-object relative sentences (King & Kutas, 1995),[3] long-distance dependencies (Kluender & Kutas, 1993), and word category violations (Münte, Heinze, & Mangun, 1993). At present, the functional interpretation of the LAN remains unclear. Some authors see the LAN as a reflection of differential working memory load related to thematic integration processes (King & Kutas, 1995; Kluender & Kutas, 1993). Others interpret it as an index of initial syntactic assignment on the basis of word category information (Friederici, 1995; Friederici & Mecklinger, 1996). These disparate views reflect the current lack of understanding about the functional nature of the LAN. Clearly, further research is called for. One issue that will need to be addressed is the extent to which we are actually dealing with one and the same effect. Some caution is called for here in the light of the variability in both the peak latency of the LAN and its distribution over the scalp. The peak latencies vary between 200 and 400 ms, with the range of the entire enhanced negativity running from just over 100 ms to beyond 500 ms. This leaves considerable scope for multiple processes to be operative. Furthermore, although the maximal effect is indeed observed over left anterior regions of the scalp, in most studies it is not restricted to these regions. The enhanced negativity has been reported to extend over left temporal, central, and parieto-temporal electrode sites, and it has even been observed over right anterior regions of the scalp.

The present uncertainties about the specificity of the enhanced negativity should not be taken to imply that the reported ERP effects do not reflect on-line comprehension processes. The number of published reports in which enhanced negativities have been reported is by now large enough to suggest that something interesting is emerging here. However, given the variety of linguistic manipulations that give rise to the effect(s), and given the variability in latency

[3] But see Mecklinger, Schriefers, Steinhauer, and Friederici (1995), who report a positivity with a peak latency of 345 ms for object-relative sentences.

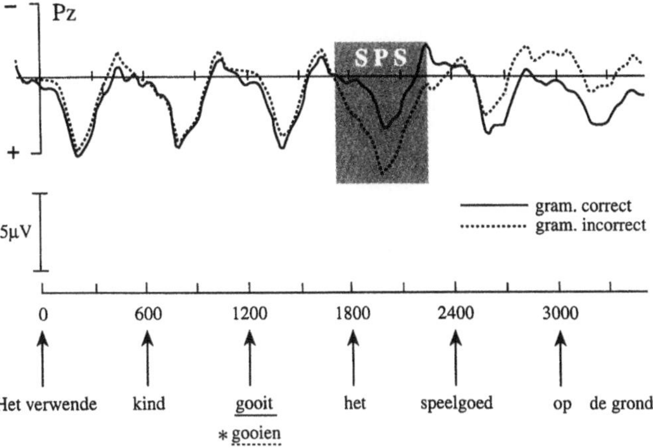

Figure 9.4. Grand average ERPs at electrode site Pz for visually presented grammatically incorrect (subject-verb number agreement, dotted line) and correct words (solid line) in mid-sentence position in normal prose. The critical words were presented at 1200 ms. The figure shows the critical words preceded by two and followed by three words. The translation of the example sentence is *The spoilt child throws/throw the toy on the ground.* The region within which the Syntactic Positive Shift developed is shaded, and labelled with SPS. Figure adapted from Hagoort and Brown, © 1994 Erlbaum.

and distribution, more detailed experimentation is required before the exact relationship with the comprehension process is elucidated.

The second effect that has been reported in the ERP literature on sentence processing is a late positivity. This effect starts at about 500 ms, extends for several hundred milliseconds, and has a broad distribution over the scalp, with a centro-parietal maximum. The effect was independently reported by two research groups, one working with American English (Osterhout & Holcomb, 1992), the other with Dutch (Hagoort, Brown, & Groothusen, 1993). Osterhout and Holcomb (1992) examined ERPs in response to violations of verb subcategorization and phrase structure constraints. Hagoort et al. (1993) additionally included agreement violations between a subject NP and the finite verb (e.g., **The spoilt child* throw *the toy on the ground*). An example from the latter work is shown in Figure 9.4, which depicts the ERP elicited by a number agreement, in comparison with its grammatically correct counterpart, using visual presentation.

The agreement error elicited a sustained positive shift, starting at 500 ms after the incorrect word (i.e., *throw*). This effect has been labelled the P600 (Osterhout & Holcomb, 1992), or the Syntactic Positive Shift (SPS; Hagoort et al., 1993). We will use the latter term in this chapter. As can be seen in Figure 9.4, the SPS is not the only processing effect that emerges in the ERP waveform. After the SPS in response to the grammatical violation, the waveform transforms into a negative shift for the next words in the incorrect condition, relative to the control condition. On the basis of its morphology and scalp topography, this negative shift can be classified as an N400 effect. We hypothesize that the origin of the N400 effect lies in the preceding syntactic violation. Due to the agreement error, the experimental subject is confronted with a problem in constructing a syntactic representation for the string of words. This structural problem has consequences for the ease with which further incoming words can be processed. In particular, an inadequate structural representation creates a problem for the integration of words into the overall message representation of the sentence. It is this integrational problem that emerges as an N400 effect.

In the Hagoort et al. (1993) experiment, the same pattern of positive and negative polarity effects was obtained for phrase structure violations.[4] Here, subjects read sentences in which the obligatory Dutch word order of adverb–adjective–noun was altered, such that the adjective preceded the adverb (e.g., **The man was startled by the emotional rather response of his partner*). An SPS was observed at the grammatical violation (i.e., *response*), in combination with an N400 effect on the words following the violation. An additional and important effect in terms of the functional characterization of the SPS was the occurrence of an SPS on the adverb preceding the noun (i.e. *rather*). At this point in the sentence, a grammatically correct continuation is still possible (e.g., *the emotional rather outspoken response*), but the syntactic structure of such a continuation is more complex than the more commonly occurring adverb–adjective–noun sequence. We propose that the SPS elicited by the adverb reflects a processing effect related to the fact that at this position a non-preferred syntactic structure (i.e., either a more complex, or a less frequent, or both) has to be assigned to the sentence (cf. Hagoort et al., 1993; Hagoort & Brown, 1994).

The sensitivity of the SPS to syntactic violations provides a potentially revealing finding on the nature of the syntax-semantic interface involved in sentence processing. However, before the significance of this finding can be fully assessed, more evidence is needed on the validity of the SPS. We will discuss two issues here. First, is the SPS specific to syntactic processing during on-line language comprehension? In particular, can we reliably isolate the SPS

[4] But not for subcategorization violations. See Hagoort et al. (1993) and Hagoort and Brown (1994) for discussion.

from the N400? Second, how sensitive is the SPS with respect to the on-line comprehension process? In particular, can the SPS also be observed during the processing of sentences that do not contain outright violations? Although this latter question has in part been answered by the SPS in response to the adverb in the ungrammatical phrase structure condition, further data on the SPS in non-violating contexts is required. We conclude this section on syntactic processing with a few remarks on the functional characterization of the SPS.

9.3.1 The Specificity of the SPS

Under normal stimulation conditions, it is notoriously difficult to factor out the contributions to understanding of possibly distinct sources of linguistic information. However, in the case of syntax, so-called syntactic prose offers a way to especially focus on syntactic processing. In standard syntactic prose experiments, subjects read or listen to sentences that are semantically uninterpretable, but accord with the grammatical rules of the language. For example, *The boiled watering can smokes the telephone in the cat.*[5] Despite the fact that this string of words does not convey any coherent meaning, subjects readily grasp the grammatical relations that hold between the words and are able to parse the sentence into its constituent parts. This demonstrates that in the absence of a message-level meaning representation, subjects do activate syntactic knowledge and use this knowledge to parse the sentence.

We used a syntactic prose manipulation to investigate the specificity of the SPS. The main issue was whether an SPS would be observed to grammatical violations in syntactic prose. For example, in the sentence *The boiled watering can* smoke *the telephone in the cat*, *smoke* creates an agreement error in combination with its preceding subject noun phrase. This grammatical error holds independently of the semantic uninterpretability of the sentence. The question then is, if we strip a sentence of meaning, and only vary its grammaticality, is an SPS still elicited by the word that instantiates the ungrammaticality, just as in normal prose?

A second and related question concerns the independence of SPS and N400 effects. In the normal prose experiment discussed previously, the SPS was followed by an N400 effect. We interpreted this effect as a reflection of problems with meaning integration, originating from the preceding grammatical

[5] Note that this kind of prose is different from so-called Jabberwocky, made famous by Lewis Carroll, which has been used by psycholinguists to investigate language comprehension. Jabberwocky contains a mixture of real words and pseudo-words. Syntactic prose contains only real words, so that the categorical and morphological lexical information is transparent.

Number agreement, syntactic prose

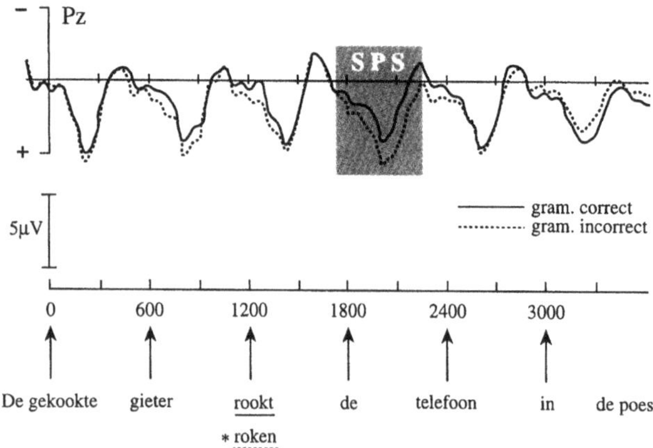

Figure 9.5. Grand average ERPs at electrode site Pz for visually presented grammatically incorrect (subject-verb number agreement, dotted line) and correct words (solid line) in mid-sentence position in syntactic prose. The critical words were presented at 1200 ms. The figure shows the critical words preceded by two and followed by three words. The translation of the example sentence is *The boiled watering can smokes/smoke the telephone in the cat*. The region within which the Syntactic Positive Shift developed is shaded, and labelled with SPS. Figure adapted from Hagoort and Brown, © 1994 Erlbaum.

violation. If this analysis is correct, and if the SPS and the N400 are related to different processing events, then we predict that no N400 effects should be observed in syntactic prose, since in this kind of context no higher-order meaning integration can occur.

Figure 9.5 shows the ERP waveform for the syntactic prose variant of the agreement errors that we investigated in the original normal prose experiment. The structure of the sentences in the syntactic prose experiment was identical to the normal prose sentences they were derived from, and the errors occurred in the same position.

Once again the agreement errors elicited an SPS. The onset of the effect and its morphology and topography are the same as for the normal prose experiment, though the size of the effect is slightly reduced in the syntactic prose experiment. Similar results were obtained for the syntactic prose variant of the phrase structure condition (e.g., *The heel tripped over the rather inhabited/inhabited rather cat on his pocket*). Here, an SPS was observed in response to both the adverb and the noun, replicating the findings of the normal prose experiment. These results provide a clear demonstration that the SPS is indeed a reflection of syntactic processing during language comprehension.

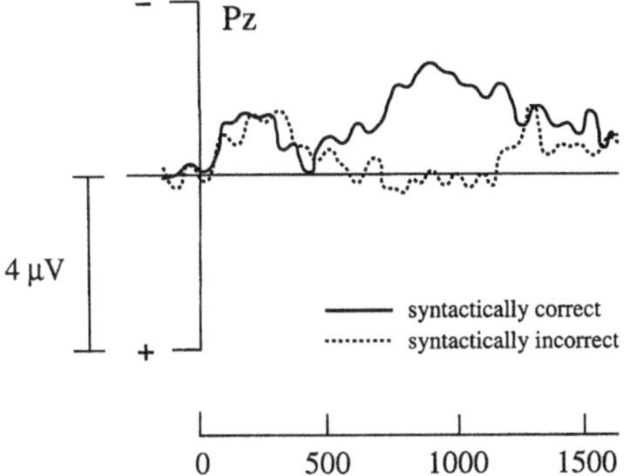

Figure 9.6. Grand average ERPs at electrode site Pz for grammatically incorrect (subject-verb number agreement, dotted line) and correct words (solid line) in mid-sentence position in normal prose with naturally produced connected speech. The onset of the critical words is at 0 ms in the figure.

In addition, the results provide evidence in favour of the independence of the SPS and N400 effects. As predicted, no N400 effects were observed in syntactic prose, neither for the agreement nor for the phrase structure condition.[6] Not only does this underscore the difference between the SPS and the N400, but it also provides supporting evidence for our functional interpretation of the N400 effects that we observed in the normal prose experiment.

All of the results that we have presented so far were obtained on the basis of visual stimulation. Just as with the N400, it is important to verify that the SPS is a modality-independent effect. If the SPS is indeed an electrophysiological signature of syntactic processing, then it should be obtained in both the visual and auditory modality. That this is indeed the case can be seen in Figure 9.6 (which shows data from Hagoort and Brown, 1997). These waveforms are for the correct and incorrect agreement conditions of the normal prose sentences, presented as naturally produced connected speech.

Just as with the connected speech data of the N400 congruity experiment that we presented earlier, here too the overall shape of the waveform does not show readily discernable stimulus components. However, a clear condition effect is observed for the agreement errors, showing a positivity with an onset latency of 500 ms, and a centro-parietal distribution. Although not shown in this figure,

[6] The difference following the agreement error did not begin to approach statistical significance, and was absent at other electrode sites. Note also that the N400 component as such is visible in the waveforms, with clear N400s in response to the individual words in both conditions. This is in accordance with the literature. The crucial point is the absence of an N400 effect (i.e., a difference within the N400 time domain between the two conditions).

just as with visual stimulation, an N400 effect emerges in the ungrammatical condition for words following the syntactic error. These findings are in accordance with the work of Osterhout and Holcomb (1993). We can conclude from these data that the SPS is a modality-independent effect.

9.3.2 The Sensitivity of the SPS

In the experiments discussed so far, most of the manipulations concerned grammatical violations. Although the SPS in response to the adverb in the phrase structure manipulation already indicated that the presence of violations is not a necessary condition for eliciting the SPS, this effect was observed in the context of materials containing a series of grammatical violations. Therefore, just as was the case for the N400 component, the question needs to be addressed whether the SPS is more than a violation detector. We tackled this issue by presenting subjects with structurally ambiguous sentences.

The ambiguity that we focussed on was one of the so-called attachment ambiguities. In our manipulation the sentence ultimately could be assigned only one structural analysis, but the initial part could be assigned two different analyses. For example: *The sheriff saw the cowboy and the Indian spotted the horse in the bushes*. Until the second verb (i.e., *spotted*) it is unclear whether the two nouns *cowboy* and *Indian* are part of one, conjoined noun phrase, or whether the second noun (i.e., *Indian*) is the subject of a second clause. Obviously, these two structural analyses are not trivially different, and they have consequences for the overall meaning of the sentence. In the example sentence, if readers opt for the conjoined NP analysis they will be confronted with a parsing problem on the verb *spotted*.

This kind of attachment ambiguity has been under investigation in the literature on the autonomous or interactive nature of the parser. It has been claimed that the conjoined NP analysis is a less complex syntactic structure than the conjoined S analysis (cf. Frazier, 1987). If the real-time operation of the parser is based in part on principles of economy and efficiency, such that less complex structures are preferred over more complex ones, then it follows that in the case of the example sentence, the conjoined NP structure will be considered the more viable analysis.[7] Therefore, at the moment that the parser is confronted with a word that refutes this preferred analysis (i.e., at the verb *spotted*), a parsing problem should occur. Note that we are not dealing with an overt grammatical

[7] In the example that we present here, we have not included an additional semantic manipulation, biasing for one of the two readings. In this chapter, we will not discuss ERP data on semantic effects during on-line parsing. For current purposes, we need to first discover whether the SPS is at all sensitive to structural ambiguities.

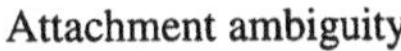

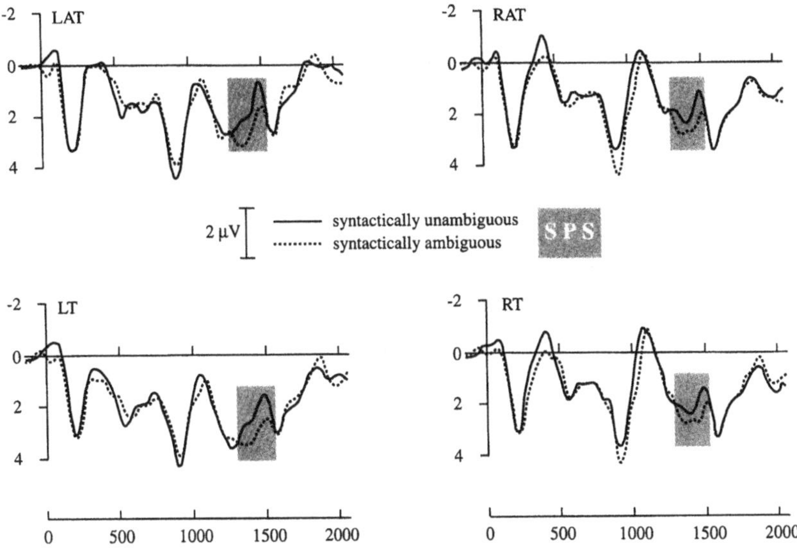

Figure 9.7. Grand average ERPs over left and right anterior temporal (LAT, RAT) and left and right temporal (LT, RT) electrode sites for visually presented sentences. In the ambiguous condition (dotted line) the sentences were initially syntactically ambiguous. At the point of disambiguation (at 686 ms in the figure), the sentence continued with a grammatically correct but non-preferred reading. In the control condition (solid line), unambiguous versions of the same non-preferred structures were presented. In the figure, the disambiguating words are preceded and followed by one word. The region within which the Syntactic Positive Shift (SPS) developed is shaded.

violation here. The sentence is entirely grammatical. The origin of the (putative) problem lies in the proposed operating characteristics of the parser.

Figure 9.7 shows the waveform for the syntactically ambiguous sentence and its control. The zero time point marks the presentation of the noun preceding the second verb. The verb was presented at 686 ms. The control sentence was identical to the ambiguous one, with the exception of the inclusion of a comma after the second noun (i.e., *The sheriff saw the cowboy, and the Indian spotted the horse in the bushes*). In Dutch, a comma in this position is a normal, though not obligatory part of written language. When included, the comma rules out the possibility of conjoining the nouns preceding and following it.

The waveforms for the ambiguous condition deviate from the control condition following the presentation of the second verb (i.e., *spotted*). In the ambiguous condition, this is the position at which the ambiguity is resolved in favour of the second clause reading, which is hypothesized to be the non-preferred structural analysis. Although the scalp topography of the effect is somewhat different from that observed for violations (in the present case the effect has a more anterior distribution), the effect is a positive shift, with an onset latency of 500 ms relative to the onset of the presentation of the critical verb. Given its similarity to the previously observed syntactic effects, we classify this effect as an SPS. Our conclusion, therefore, is that the SPS is not only elicited by syntactic violations, but is also sensitive to processing operations related to parsing preferences.

9.3.3 The Functional Characterization of the SPS

We have provided evidence that the SPS is elicited by a variety of syntactic phenomena. Although we have focussed on our own work, the sensitivity of the SPS (also known as the P600) to syntactic processes has by now been reported by several research groups, working with various aspects of word order, agreement, and subcategorization (cf. Neville et al., 1991; Osterhout & Holcomb, 1992; Osterhout & Mobley, 1995; Osterhout, Holcomb, & Swinney, 1994; see also Friederici & Mecklinger, 1996; Mecklinger et al., 1995). The SPS is obtained in both the visual and the auditory modality, with a remarkably invariant onset latency of 500 ms, and with a broad distribution over the scalp, showing slight topographical variations as a function of whether the SPS is elicited in violating or in ambiguous contexts.

Clearly, then, with the SPS we have an ERP effect in hand that can be used as a tool with which to probe on-line parsing. What remains to be elucidated, and what lies beyond the scope of the currently available data, is the functional nature of the SPS. Exactly which aspect of syntactic processing is reflected by the SPS? On the basis of the work that has been reported, we can confidently claim that the SPS is elicited by the word in a sentence that indicates that the current structural assignment is an incorrect or non-preferred syntactic analysis for the incoming string of words. What still has to be established is whether the elicitation of the SPS is a direct consequence of a failing first parse, or whether the SPS is related to a process of syntactic reanalysis, occurring after a first-pass structural assignment has resulted in a misanalysis. A further issue that needs to be addressed concerns the topographical differences that we have observed between outright syntactic violations and parsing preferences. It is possible that we are seeing a family resemblance among ERP effects related to different aspects of syntactic processing.

9.4 Conclusions

In this chapter, we have presented ERP data on different aspects of language comprehension, comparing electrophysiological manifestations of semantic and syntactic processes. What the data clearly show is that the brain response to semantic processing is distinct from the response to syntactic processing. In particular, the N400 component has proven to be an especially sensitive index of meaning integration processes, whereas within the domain of language processing the SPS is only observed in the context of specifically syntactic processes. It is important to note that we are not claiming that either the N400 or the SPS is unique to the language domain. What we do claim is that during language processing the N400 and SPS are separate components with separate sensitivities. The two effects are dissociable by experimental manipulation: a semantic cloze manipulation elicits only an N400, whereas a syntactic prose manipulation elicits only an SPS. At the same time, they can be observed during the processing of one and the same sentence (e.g., the succession of SPS and N400 effects in the agreement and phrase structure violation conditions), in a manner that makes sense in terms of the ongoing comprehension process. Moreover, the N400 and the SPS are qualitatively entirely different effects in terms of their electrophysiological characteristics: Semantic processing emerges as a negative-going shift in the ERP waveform, whereas syntactic processing emerges as a positive-going shift.

With this evidence in hand, we can return to the issue that we raised at the beginning of this chapter, namely the separation of linguistic knowledge sources during on-line comprehension. Based on the separate identity and sensitivity of the SPS and the N400, our claim is that separable, non-identical brain processes underlie syntactic and semantic processing. If this claim is correct, then it provides a boundary condition for models of language processing. At the very least, these models will have to allow for a qualitative distinction between syntactic and semantic processing effects. This boundary condition is not compatible with interactionist models that argue against the existence of intermediate products of syntactic computation (e.g., Bates et al., 1982; McClelland et al., 1989). If no distinction is made at the representational level, it becomes difficult to account for the different brain responses elicited by syntactic and semantic constraints. In this respect, garden-path models fit neatly with the ERP data that we have discussed in this chapter. Constraint-based lexicalist models, although denying an initial category-based parsing stage (cf. Tanenhaus & Trueswell, 1995), can also accommodate the ERP data, since these models incorporate elaborate lexical-syntactic representations.

In sum, the evidence on the differential sensitivity of the SPS and the N400 is more compatible with models that include a separate level of syntactic computation during the process of language understanding. This should not be taken to imply that we can now distinguish between autonomous or interactive processing accounts of the parser. The mere existence of the N400 and the SPS is insufficient evidence in this respect. However, given these two separate reflections of the brain's electrical activity during language comprehension, we have good tools in hand with which to attempt to obtain further insights into the architecture and mechanisms of the human language system.

References

Allison, T., Wood, C.C., & McCarthy, G.M. (1986). The central nervous system. In M.G.H. Coles, E. Donchin, & S.W. Porges (Eds.), *Psychophysiology: systems, processes, and applications*. (pp. 5–25) New York: Guilford.

Altmann, G., & Steedman, M. (1988). Interaction with context during human sentence processing. *Cognition* 30, 191–238.

Altmann, G.T.M., Garnham, A., & Dennis, Y. (1992). Avoiding the garden path: Eye movements in context. *Journal of Memory and Language* 31, 685–712.

Bates, E., McNew, S., MacWhinney, B., Devescovi, A., & Smith, S. (1982). Functional constraints on sentence processing: A cross-linguistic study. *Cognition*, 11 245–299.

Boland, J.E., Tanenhaus, M.K., & Garnsey, S.M. (1990). Evidence for the immediate use of verb control information in sentence processing. *Journal of Memory and Language* 29, 413–432.

Brown, C.M., & Hagoort, P. (1993). The processing nature of the N400: Evidence from masked priming. *Journal of Cognitive Neuroscience* 5, 34–44.

Chwilla, D. J., Brown, C. M., & Hagoort, P. (1995). The N400 as a function of the level of processing. *Psychophysiology* 32, 274–285.

Clifton, C., & Ferreira, F. (1989). Ambiguity in context. *Language and Cognitive Processes* 4, 77–104.

Coles, M.G.H., & Rugg, M.D. (1995). Event-related brain potentials: An introduction. In M.D. Rugg, & M.G.H. Coles (Eds.), *Electrophysiology of mind: Event-related brain potentials and cognition*. (pp. 1–26) New York: Oxford University Press.

Connolly, J.F., & Phillips, N.A. (1994). Event-related potential components reflect phonological and semantic processing of the terminal word of spoken sentences. *Journal of Cognitive Neuroscience* 6, 256–266.

Crain, S., & Steedman, M. (1985). On not being led up the garden-path: The use of context by the psychological parser. In D. Dowty, L. Karttunen, & H. Zwicky (Eds.), *Natural language parsing*.(pp. 320–358) Cambridge: Cambridge University Press.

Elman, J.L. (1990). Representation and structure in connectionist models. In G.T.M. Altmann (Ed.), *Cognitive models of speech processing: Psycholinguistic and computational perspectives*. (pp. 345–382) Cambridge, MA: MIT Press.

Ferreira, F., & Clifton, C. (1986). The independence of syntactic processing. *Journal of Memory and Language* 25, 348–368.

Fodor, J.A. (1983). *The modularity of mind*. Cambridge, MA: MIT Press.

Frazier, L. (1987). Sentence processing: A tutorial review. In M. Coltheart (Ed.) *Attention and performance XII. The psychology of reading*. (pp. 559–586) London: Erlbaum.

Frazier, L. (1990). Parsing modifiers: Special purpose routines in the HSPM? In G.B. Flores d'Arcais, K. Rayner, & D. Balota (Eds.), *Comprehension processes in reading*. Hillsdale, NJ: Erlbaum.

Frazier, L., & Clifton, C. (1996). *Construal*. Cambridge, MA: MIT Press.

Friederici, A.D. (1995). The time course of syntactic activation during language processing: A model based on neuropsychological and neurophysiological data. *Brain and Language* 50, 259–281.

Friederici, A.D., & Mecklinger, A. (1996). Syntactic parsing as revealed by brain responses: First-pass and second-pass parsing processes. *Journal of Psycholinguistic Research* 25, 157–176.

Friederici, A.D., Pfeifer, E., & Hahne, A. (1993). Event-related brain potentials during natural speech processing: Effects of semantic, morphological and syntactic violations. *Cognitive Brain Research* 1, 183–192.

Hagoort, P., & Brown, C.M. (1994). Brain responses to lexical-ambiguity resolution and parsing. In C. Clifton, L. Frazier, & K. Rayner (Eds.), *Perspectives on sentence processing*. (pp. 45–80) Hillsdale, NJ: Erlbaum.

Hagoort, P., & Brown, C.M. (1997). Semantic and syntactic ERP effects of listening to speech compared to reading. Submitted for publication.

Hagoort, P., Brown, C.M., & Groothusen, J. (1993) The Syntactic Positive Shift (SPS) as an ERP-measure of syntactic processing. *Language and Cognitive Processes* 8, 439–483.

Hagoort, P., Brown, C.M., & Swaab, T.S. (1996). Lexical-semantic event-related potential effects in patients with left hemisphere lesions and aphasia, and patients with right hemisphere lesions without aphasia. *Brain* 119, 627–649.

Holcomb, P.J. (1993). Semantic priming and stimulus degradation: Implications for the role of the N400 in language processing. *Psychophysiology* 30, 47–61.

Holcomb, P.J., & Neville, H.J. (1990). Semantic priming in visual and auditory lexical decision: A between modality comparison. *Language and Cognitive Processes* 5, 281–312.

Holmes, V.M. (1987). Syntactic parsing: In search of the garden path. In M. Coltheart (Ed.), *Attention and performance XII. The psychology of reading*. (pp. 587–599) London: Erlbaum.

King, J.W., & Kutas, M. (1995). Who did what and when? Using word- and clause-level ERPs to monitor working memory usage in reading. *Journal of Cognitive Neuroscience* 7, 376–395.

Kluender, R., & Kutas, M. (1993). The interaction of lexical and syntactic effects in the processing of unbounded dependencies. *Language and Cognitive Processes* 8, 573–633.

Kutas, M., & Hillyard, S.A. (1980). Reading senseless sentences: Brain potentials reflect semantic incongruity. *Science* 207, 203–205.

Kutas, M., & Hillyard, S.A. (1983). Event-related brain potentials to grammatical errors and semantic anomalies. *Memory & Cognition* 11, 539–550.

Kutas, M., & King, J.W. (1995). The potentials for basic sentence processing: Differentiating integrative processes. In T. Inui & J. McClelland (Eds.), *Attention and performance XVI: Information integration in perception and communication*. Cambridge, MA: MIT Press.

Kutas, M., & Van Petten, C. (1988). Event-related brain potential studies of language. In P.K. Ackles, J.R. Jennings, & M.G.H. Coles (Eds.), *Advances in Psychophysiology, Volume 3*. Greenwich, CT: JAI Press.

Kutas, M., & Van Petten, C. (1995). Psycholinguistics electrified: Event-related brain potential investigations. In M. Gernsbacher (Ed.), *Handbook of psycholinguistics*. New York: Academic Press.

Kutas, M., Lindamood, T., & Hillyard, S.A. (1984). Word expectancy and event-related brain potentials during sentence processing. In S. Kornblum & J. Requin (Eds.), *Preparatory states and processes*. (pp. 217–238) Hillsdale, NJ: Erlbaum.

Kutas, M., Neville, H.J., & Holcomb, P.J. (1987). A preliminary comparison of the N400 response to semantic anomalies during reading, listening and signing. In R.J. Ellingson, N.M.F. Murray, & A.M. Halliday (Eds.), *The London Symposium (EEG Suppl. 39)*. Amsterdam: Elsevier.

MacDonald, M.A., Pearlmutter, N.J., & Seidenberg, M.S. (1994). The lexical nature of syntactic ambiguity resolution. *Psychological Review* 101, 676–703.

McCallum, W.C., Farmer, S.F., & Pocock, P.K. (1984). The effects of physical and semantic incongruities on auditory event-related potentials. *Electroencephalography and Clinical Neurophysiology* 59, 447–488.

McClelland, J.L., St. John, M., & Taraban, R. (1989). Sentence comprehension: A parallel distributed processing approach. Language and Cognitive Processes, 4, 287–335.

Mecklinger, A., Schriefers, H., Steinhauer, K., & Friederici, A.D. (1995). Processing relative clauses varying on syntactic and semantic dimensions: An analysis with event-related potentials. *Memory & Cognition* 23, 477–494.

Münte, T.F., Heinze, H., & Mangun, G. (1993). Dissociation of brain activity related to syntactic and semantic aspects of language. *Journal of Cognitive Neuroscience* 5, 335–344.

Näätänen, R. (1992). *Attention and brain function*. Hillsdale, NJ: Erlbaum.

Neville, H.J., Coffey, S.A., Lawson, D.S., Fischer, A., Emmorey, K., & Bellugi, U. (1997). Neural systems mediating American Sign Language: Effects of sensory experience and age of acquisition. *Brain and Language* 57, 285–308.

Neville, H.J., Nicol, J.L., Barss, A., Forster, K.I., & Garrett, M.F. (1991). Syntactically based sentence processing classes: Evidence from event-related brain potentials. *Journal of Cognitive Neuroscience* 3, 151–165.

Nunez, P.L. (1981). *Electric fields of the brain*. New York: Oxford University Press.

Nunez, P.L. (1990). Physical principles and neurophysiological mechanisms underlying event-related potentials. In J.W. Rohrbaugh, R. Parasuramen, & R. Johnson (Eds.), *Event-related brain potentials*. (pp. 19–36) New York: Oxford University Press.

Osterhout, L., & Holcomb, P.J. (1992). Event-related brain potentials elicited by syntactic anomaly. *Journal of Memory and Language* 31, 785–806.

Osterhout, L., & Holcomb, P.J. (1993). Event-related potentials and syntactic anomaly: Evidence of anomaly detection during the perception of continuous speech. *Language and Cognitive Processes* 8, 413–437.

Osterhout, L., & Holcomb, P.J. (1995). Event-related potentials and language comprehension. In M.D. Rugg, & M.G.H. Coles (Eds.), *Electrophysiology of mind: Event-related brain potentials and cognition*. (pp. 171–215) New York: Oxford University Press.

Osterhout, L., & Mobley, L.A. (1995). Event-related brain potentials elicited by the failure to agree. *Journal of Memory and Language* 34, 739–773.

Osterhout, L., Holcomb, P.J., & Swinney, D.A. (1994). Brain potentials elicited by garden path sentences: Evidence of the application of verb information during parsing. *Journal of Experimental Psychology: Learning, Memory, and Cognition* 20, 786–803.

Picton, T.W., Lins, O.G., & Scherg, M. (1995). The recording and analysis of event-related potentials. In F. Boller & J. Grafman (Eds.), *The handbook of neuropsychology, Volume 10*. Amsterdam: Elsevier.

Rayner, K., Carlson, M., & Frazier, L. (1983). The interaction of syntax and semantics during sentence processing: Eye movements in the analysis of semantically biased sentences. *Journal of Verbal Learning and Verbal Behavior* 22, 358–374.

Rayner, K., Garrod, S., & Perfetti, C.A. (1992). Discourse influences during parsing are delayed. *Cognition*, 45, 109–139.

Rugg, M.D. (1990). Event-related brain potentials dissociate repetition effects of high- and low-frequency words. *Memory & Cognition*, 18, 367–379.

Rugg, M.D., & Coles, M.G.H. (Eds.). (1995). *Electrophysiology of mind: Event-related brain potentials and cognition*. New York: Oxford University Press.

Spivey-Knowlton, M.J., & Sedivy, J.C. (1995). Resolving attachment ambiguities with multiple constraints. *Cognition* 55, 227–267.

Tanenhaus, M.K., & Trueswell, J.C. (1995). Sentence comprehension. In J. Miller, & P. Eimas (Eds.), *Handbook of perception and cognition, Volume 11: Speech, language, and communication*. (pp. 217–262) New York: Academic Press.

Taraban, R., & McClelland, J.L. (1990). Parsing and comprehension: A multiple-constraint view. In D. Balota, G.B. Flores d'Arcais, & K. Rayner (Eds.), *Comprehension processes in reading*. (pp. 231–263) Hillsdale, NJ: Erlbaum.

Van Petten, C., & Kutas, M. (1991). Electrophysiological evidence for the flexibility of lexical processing. In G.B. Simpson (Ed.), *Understanding word and sentence*. (pp. 129–174). North-Holland: Elsevier Science.

Wood, C.C. (1987). Generators of event-related potentials. In A.M. Halliday, S.R. Butler, & R. Paul (Eds.), *A textbook of clinical neurophysiology*. (pp. 535–567) New York: Wiley.

10

Parsing and Incremental Understanding During Reading

MARTIN J. PICKERING AND
MATTHEW J. TRAXLER

This chapter discusses a range of findings from our eye-tracking research in relation to current theories of parsing. First, we discuss findings that implicate extremely rapid semantic processing and findings that suggest that the degree of semantic processing affects the ease of recovery from misanalysis. We then provide an analysis of theories of initial parsing decisions that emphasises two dimensions: whether they can draw upon all available information or not; and whether they attempt to select or foreground the analysis that is most likely to be correct at the point of ambiguity. We next discuss a range of evidence from our laboratory that provides support for theories that do not attempt to select the most likely analysis. The evidence may support an account where at least some parsing decisions are driven by syntactic information alone. Alternatively, it may support an account in which the parser draws upon all available information, but where its goal is to select the most informative analysis, not the most likely one.

10.1 Immediate Effects of Plausibility

One of the clearest conclusions of research into language comprehension is that a great deal of processing occurs incrementally. Thus, lexical access, syntactic analysis, and semantic interpretation are not delayed, but begin as soon as the relevant word is heard or read (e.g., Marslen-Wilson, 1973; Just & Carpenter, 1980). The strongest of these findings is that the processor does not delay in providing a semantic interpretation for a sentence fragment as a whole: such

The order of authorship is arbitrary. The research discussed in this chapter was supported by ESRC Grant No. R000234542 and a British Academy Postdoctoral Fellowship (both awarded to the first author).

semantic processing of course requires that lexical and syntactic processing have already occurred.

Even more strikingly, this interpretation is immediately integrated with relevant background knowledge and information provided by discourse context. In Traxler and Pickering (1996b), we found that such semantic integration sometimes can have taken place by the time that the eye finishes its first fixation on a word. This finding suggests that semantic processing can occur as soon as about 250 ms after fixating a word. However, we cannot be certain that integration can occur within 250 ms, because some semantic processing of a word may occur during the previous fixation if it occurred towards the end of the previous word (e.g., Rayner & Pollatsek, 1989).

For instance, in one experiment, participants read sentences like (1a–d):

(1) a. That's the pistol with which the heartless killer shot the hapless man yesterday afternoon.
b. That's the garage with which the heartless killer shot the hapless man yesterday afternoon.
c. That's the pistol in which the heartless killer shot the hapless man yesterday afternoon.
d. That's the garage in which the heartless killer shot the hapless man yesterday afternoon.

The fragments up to the verb *shot* in sentences (1b, c) are likely to form the beginnings of implausible sentences, because it is impossible to shoot with a garage, or to shoot in a pistol. This contrasts with (1a, d), which are plausible. We found that subjects spent longer reading *shot* in (1b, c) than (1a, d) from the first fixation onwards. Our results cannot be due to low-level lexical effects (e.g., priming from *pistol* to *shot*), because of the crossed design. So readers must have assessed the plausibility of shooting with a garage or pistol, or shooting in a garage or pistol, as soon as they encountered the verb *shot*.

Note that the semantic anomalies in (1b, c) are fairly gross, in that the sentences describe impossible or absurd situations. In many cases, the anomaly corresponds to a selection-restriction violation. Our intention was to determine the effects of strong plausibility manipulations, and so we selected materials for which subjects rated the plausible sentences as highly plausible (5 or more on a 0–7 scale) and the implausible sentences as highly implausible (2 or less on such a scale). However, the implausible sentences are clearly grammatical. We conclude that some semantic processing begins very rapidly (though more elaborate semantic processing may, of course, be delayed, or never occur at all).

The implausible sentence fragments are not complete sentences, nor do they normally constitute possible complete sentences. For example, when the verb *shot* is encountered, it lacks an NP-object argument. Chater, Pickering, and Milward (1995) pointed out that such fragments do not have propositional interpretations according to standard formal semantics. They suggested that the processor incrementally constructs two semantic representations at different representational levels. The representation at the input level corresponds to the standard formal semantic analysis for a sentence fragment. At *shot*, this representation does not correspond to a proposition, because the verb *shot* is a two-place predicate, and it has only been combined with one semantic argument. Assuming that only propositions can serve as premises in inference, and that semantic integration involves inferences using premises drawn from both the sentence fragment and background knowledge, the input level cannot form the basis of incremental understanding. Hence Chater et al. proposed that the processor also constructs a knowledge-level representation, which is propositional; it is this representation that is integrated with general knowledge and can, for instance, explain the immediate effects of plausibility in the processing of sentence fragments.

Other experiments show that locally ambiguous fragments are incrementally understood. In a second experiment, Traxler and Pickering (1996b) contrasted sentences like (2a, b), which were embedded in short contexts:

(2) a. We like the book that the author wrote unceasingly and with great dedication about while waiting for a contract.
b. We like the city that the author wrote unceasingly and with great dedication about while waiting for a contract.

Although both sentences are globally plausible (as measured by pre-tests), the plausibility of the sentences differ on a misanalysis where *the book* or *the city* serves as the NP object of *wrote*. At *wrote*, (2a) is plausible, because an author is likely to write a book, but (2b) is implausible, because an author is not likely to write a city. We found that subjects took longer to read (2b) than (2a) from the first fixation after encountering *wrote*. Again, we suggest that the source of the plausibility effect is the integration of the knowledge-level representation with background knowledge.

Interestingly, both experiments found first-fixation plausibility effects on a (finite) verb. In other studies, we have found rapid plausibility effects resulting from the processing of nouns, but never on first fixation. For instance, Pickering and Traxler (1998a) had subjects read subordinate clause ambiguities like (3) and complement clause ambiguities like (4), together with disambiguated control sentences:

(3) a. As the woman edited the magazine about fishing amused all the reporters.
    b. As the woman sailed the magazine about fishing amused all the reporters.

(4) a. The criminal confessed his sins which upset kids harmed too many people.
    b. The criminal confessed his gang which upset kids harmed too many people.

The misanalyses in (3a) and (4a) are plausible, and the misanalyses in (3b) and (4b) are implausible. Subjects made more regressive eye-movements from *the magazine* in (3b) than in (3a) before the eye went past this region. Subjects made more regressive eye-movements from *which upset kids* in (4b) than in (4a), though there were no differences between *his sins* in (4a) and *his gang* in (4b). These experiments again show rapid effects of plausibility in ambiguous sentences. No such differences occurred in the disambiguated control sentences, indicating that the initial (mis)analysis was the locus of the plausibility effect. We have shown similar effects in other experiments for which the misanalysis is unlikely to be correct (see below).

Pickering and Traxler (1998a) found comparable effects in sentences where the manipulation of plausibility would only have an effect if subjects integrated material from a previous sentence:

(5) a. The janitor polished bronze statues of the old maths professor that the principal hated and the dean of the art school. While the janitor was polishing the professor that the principal hated reviewed the spring term teaching schedule.
    b. The janitor polished bronze statues for the old maths professor that the principal hated and the dean of the art school. While the janitor was polishing the professor that the principal hated reviewed the spring term teaching schedule.

In (5a), the misanalysis of the target sentence is plausible, because *the professor that the principal hated* can refer to the statue. But in (5b), the misanalysis is implausible, because the same phrase can only refer to an actual professor. Participants spent longer reading this phrase during first pass (but not on first fixation) in (5b) than (5a). But in control sentences disambiguated by a comma after *polishing*, the manipulation of context had no effect. Hence, we found that participants made rapid use of plausibility information that involved integrating material across sentences.

All of these experiments provide clear evidence for incremental understanding. We have three explanations for why we have only found first-fixation plausibility effects on the verbs in Traxler and Pickering (1996b), besides chance. First, the processor may be more likely to perform rapid semantic processing on verbs than on other words, because they are the central elements of sentences. Second, there may be more alternative analyses available for nouns than for verbs. For example, *The woman sailed the magazine* might be the beginning of the plausible *The woman sailed the magazine owner's yacht*, where *magazine* is not the head noun of the object of *sailed*. The existence of this alternative might slow semantic processing of *magazine* slightly. However, it does not prevent rapid attachment of *magazine* as the head noun of the object of *sailed*, as the regressions effect demonstrates. Finally, both first-fixation effects occurred at points where the processor formed an unbounded dependency. Perhaps the processor is particularly alert when it performs this fairly unusual syntactic operation.

Our findings are, of course, compatible with the range of evidence for incremental understanding during the processing of both spoken and written language (e.g. Boland, Tanenhaus, Garnsey, & Carlson, 1995; Garnsey, Tanenhaus, & Chapman, 1989; Garrod, Freudenthal, & Boyle, 1994; Marslen-Wilson, 1973, 1975; Marslen-Wilson, Tyler, & Koster, 1994; Swinney, 1979). The main conclusion of interest is the extreme rapidity with which such effects can occur during normal reading.

10.2 Plausibility of Misanalysis Affects Reanalysis

At the point of disambiguation, a locally ambiguous sentence becomes unambiguous. If a reader has adopted the wrong analysis, then this analysis will have to be abandoned at this point at the latest. Recovery from some forms of misanalysis is harder than others (e.g. Ferreira & Henderson, 1991; Warner & Glass, 1987). In a number of studies, we have shown that semantic characteristics of the misanalysis affect recovery. In particular, recovery is harder if the misanalysis is plausible than if it is implausible.

Consider (3) again, from Pickering and Traxler (1998a):

(3) a. As the woman edited the magazine about fishing amused all the reporters.
b. As the woman sailed the magazine about fishing amused all the reporters.

We have already shown that subjects initially treated the NP *the magazine about fishing* as the object of *edited* or *sailed*, and that they incrementally understood the fragment under this analysis. Now consider what might happen next. In (3a), readers should strongly commit to this interpretation and should successfully integrate it with general knowledge. But in (3b), readers should commit less strongly to this interpretation. They might abandon the misanalysis even before reaching the point of disambiguation, and adopt the correct analysis. They might retain the implausible misanalysis, but commit themselves to this interpretation only weakly. Finally, their strategy might vary between these two alternatives.

Pickering and Traxler (1998a) argued that readers commit more strongly to an analysis if its interpretation is plausible than if it is implausible. Participants spent longer reading, and produced more regressions from, the disambiguating region from the verb *amused* onwards, in (3a) than in (3b), though first-pass effects on the verb itself were weak. Since they spent longer reading the ambiguous NP in (3b) than in (3a), we found a characteristic crossover pattern, with more disruption occurring in sentences with implausible misanalyses during the ambiguous region, but more disruption occurring in sentences with plausible misanalyses after disambiguation.

We found similar effects with sentences like (4), repeated here:

(4) a. The criminal confessed his sins which upset kids harmed too many people.
b. The criminal confessed his gang which upset kids harmed too many people.

Participants made more regressions after the disambiguating verb *harmed* in the initially plausible (4a) than in the initially implausible (4b), and they read the verb for longer in (4a) than (4b) in one experiment. We also found similar effects with (5a, b), discussed earlier. Here, the effects on the disambiguating verb were significant from the first fixation onwards.

These findings provide strong evidence that subjects commit more strongly to an analysis if that analysis is plausible than if it is implausible. It is less clear whether implausible sentences trigger immediate reanalysis or not. In sentences like (4), processing difficulty after disambiguation for sentences with implausible misanalyses (i.e., (4b)) was greater than processing difficulty for unambiguous control sentences. This provides some evidence that participants do not always abandon the misanalyses before the point of disambiguation. In any case, these experiments strongly suggest that the degree of semantic commitment to an analysis affects the process of reanalysis.

These effects of plausibility on analysis and reanalysis provide good evidence about how the parser selects an analysis. For instance, the finding of disruption on *the magazine* in (3b) compared with (3a) indicates that the parser selected the transitive analysis under which *the magazine* is the object of the subordinate verb during very early processing. This conclusion is reinforced by the finding of disruption in (3a) compared with (3b) after the point of disambiguation. Hence, we can conclude that readers adopted the transitive analysis on at least a high proportion of occasions whilst reading these sentences.

Since most or all verbs in this study were preferentially transitive, the result is not in itself particularly surprising, and would be predicted by current theories (e.g., Ford, Bresnan, & Kaplan, 1982; Frazier, 1979; Trueswell, Tanenhaus, & Kello, 1993). The interesting point is that the conclusion does not depend on the comparison of different construction types or different uses of punctuation between conditions. This removes a possible confound that occurs in many studies of this construction (e.g., Clifton, 1993; Ferreira & Henderson, 1991; Frazier & Rayner, 1982; Mitchell, 1987; Warner & Glass, 1987). Similar conclusions can be drawn about the complement clause ambiguities in (4).

Hence, we can employ the manipulation of plausibility to investigate the processing of sentences that may shed light on more controversial aspects of the parsing process. In particular, we can use it to determine how the parser makes an initial choice of analysis at a point of ambiguity. We next outline some relevant aspects of current controversies and then interpret a number of our experiments in relation to these controversies.

10.3 Models of Parsing

Current theories of language comprehension pay great attention to the process of syntactic ambiguity resolution. Let us briefly outline a taxonomy of possible models of this process, and remove those models that are not serious contenders. First, incremental models can be contrasted with delay models. In an incremental model, each new word is syntactically and semantically integrated with the context as it is encountered. The evidence for incremental understanding, as well as the mere existence of garden paths, demonstrates that the parser constructs analyses in an incremental manner. We cannot rule out the possibility that the parser employs some delay under some circumstances, but the most straightforward assumption is that it does not.

Incremental models can be serial, with only one analysis being constructed and interpreted, or parallel, with more than one analysis being constructed at once. We can rule out unranked parallel models, where the parser treats all different analyses as equally important, because such models would not predict garden-path effects. Hence, the only reasonable possibilities are serial models and ranked-parallel models. In both cases, the parser makes a single analysis most prominent, choosing it in a serial model, foregrounding it in a parallel model (see Pickering, in press, for further discussion).

We now focus on the question of how the parser selects this analysis. (We use 'selects' for both serial and ranked parallel models.) Rather than discuss the predictions of different parsing models in detail, we ask a general question: does the parser select the analysis that is most likely to be correct, given the information available at the point of ambiguity? Such an account would appear to make for a well-adapted parser, assuming that reanalysis involves some cost, because selecting the most likely analysis would minimise the need for reanalysis. Additionally, if the person immediately acted upon the interpretation of the most likely analysis in some way, then the chances of that person acting in an inappropriate manner would be minimised. We call this a likelihood account. Later, however, we shall suggest that likelihood may not be as adaptive as it initially appears.

But likelihood certainly has an intuitive merit, so it is perhaps surprising that no one has explicitly proposed it. This may, in part, be because most researchers in sentence processing have concentrated on algorithmic or mechanistic models rather than on models that emphasise the higher-level goals of the system (Anderson, 1991; Marr, 1982). However, some models make predictions closely related to likelihood. One class of account proposes that the parser selects the analysis that corresponds to the most frequent subcategorisation frame of the verb (Ford et al., 1982; see J.D. Fodor, 1978, with reference to unbounded dependencies). Subcategorisation frame preferences are not the only factor involved in the computation of likelihood, but they are clearly a very important component, at least for ambiguities involving the attachment of arguments. Hence, such models are roughly compatible with the goal of maximising the likelihood that the selected analysis will ultimately be correct.

In addition, parallel models that assume that parsing preferences are based on the simultaneous interaction of multiple constraints approximate to likelihood models (MacDonald, 1994; MacDonald, Pearlmutter, & Seidenberg, 1994; Trueswell, Tanenhaus, & Garnsey, 1994; Trueswell et al., 1993; cf. Taraban & McClelland, 1988; Tyler & Marslen-Wilson, 1977). These constraints relate to any properties of the encountered sentence that may influence its continuation, including subcategorisation preferences, other syntactic cues, the meaning of the fragment, the nature of the discourse context, and prosody or punctuation. Hence, such models are unrestricted, in that all potentially relevant sources of information can be employed during initial processing (Pickering, in press; Traxler & Pickering, 1996a). Data about these sources of information can be obtained from corpus counts or from production tasks where subjects complete sentences from the point of ambiguity onwards. For instance, a few subjects might complete *The man realised* using a noun phrase (e.g., *his goals*), but more using an embedded sentence (e.g., *his goals were unattainable*). From this, such models would assume that the parser would foreground the embedded-sentence analysis (e.g., Trueswell et al., 1993). This is as predicted by likelihood accounts. However, recent constraint-based models sometimes assume that the parser pays attention to broader classes in making decisions (e.g., Juliano & Tanenhaus, 1994; see Mitchell, Cuetos, Corley, & Brysbaert, 1995). It might note that more verbs are transitive than intransitive, say, and thus support a transitive analysis of a fairly rare intransitive-preference verb. Unless the verb were extremely rare (with the data about preferences being unreliable), such a heuristic would go against likelihood. Constraint-based models therefore approximate to likelihood, but may diverge from it, and are not directly motivated by it.

Other current models are restricted, in that only some sources of information may be employed during initial processing (e.g., Abney, 1989; Crocker, 1996; Ferreira & Henderson, 1990; Frazier, 1979, 1987; Gorrell, 1995; Mitchell, 1987, 1989; Pritchett, 1992). These models assume that initial parsing decisions are based on structural principles. They are in general serial. They do not approximate to likelihood, because a great deal of information that might be needed to determine likelihood is inaccessible. In many cases, the parsing assumptions support the construction of the structurally simplest analysis. For instance, Frazier's (1979) principle of minimal attachment supports the construction of the analysis with the fewest nodes in a phrase-structure tree. The models differ in some of their predictions, of course, but they overlap considerably.

In such models, the goal of initial processing is not to adopt the most likely analysis. As mentioned above, this is intuitively strange, in that it does not appear to approach optimality (Anderson, 1991). For instance, Frazier (1979) assumes that the parser adopts the minimal attachment analysis because it requires fewer computational steps than alternative analyses. The different analyses compete in a race, and the minimal attachment analysis wins. But since this analysis is not in general the most likely analysis, the system appears to be set up in a way that makes reanalysis more prevalent than necessary (with the average number of steps necessary to reach the correct analysis being higher than if the most likely analysis were adopted immediately). Why is it not designed to slow down a bit and obtain the most likely analysis first time? On the surface, restricted accounts such as Frazier's seem maladaptive in comparison to unrestricted accounts based on likelihood.

But there is experimental evidence against likelihood accounts, though it is highly controversial (e.g., Ferreira & Henderson, 1990; Mitchell, 1987). In the next two sections, we outline experimental results from our laboratory that provide strong evidence against likelihood accounts. It therefore appears that the parser operates in a fundamentally suboptimal way. In the final section, we address this paradox, by suggesting that adhering to likelihood is not in fact as adaptive as it appears.

10.4 Evidence Against Likelihood from Local Dependencies

We now consider experiments suggesting that the processor does not adopt the most likely analysis, using subordinate clause ambiguities and complement clause ambiguities. In both cases, the ambiguity concerns the question of whether a noun phrase should be treated as an argument of a verb or not. Most structural accounts predict that the parser should prefer to attach a noun phrase as an argument if possible. In our experiments, this analysis is less likely than the alternative analysis, so likelihood models make different predictions. The next section reports a comparable experiment using unbounded dependencies.

As before, we manipulated the plausibility of an analysis that is ultimately shown to be incorrect. In addition, we kept the plausibility of the ultimately correct analysis constant. Hence any plausibility effects must be due to the parser selecting the ultimately incorrect analysis. If this analysis is implausible, then we predict immediate difficulty, but if it is plausible, then we predict difficulty at the point of disambiguation. Either one of these effects would provide a clear index of misanalysis. If misanalysis occurs in our experiments, then the parser must be initially considering an analysis that is not the most likely analysis. Parallel likelihood models may also experience problems, as we discuss below.

One important factor in a likelihood account is subcategorisation frame preferences. Consider (6a, b) (Pickering, Traxler, & Crocker, 1998):

(6) a. The young athlete realised her potential one day might make her a world-class sprinter.
    b. The young athlete realised her exercises one day might make her a world-class sprinter.

The verb *realised* can take an NP object, as in *The young athlete realised her potential*, or a complement clause, as in (6a, b). It can also be used in other, irrelevant, ways, such as with a complementiser. Our pre-tests indicated participants more often write sentences using *realised* with a *that*-less complement clause than with an NP object. Another pre-test showed a similar preference when participants completed sentences beginning *The young athlete realised*. When (6a, b) are presented in isolation, these are the only cues available to participants. Hence, the serial likelihood model predicts that the processor should adopt the complement clause analysis initially if the sentence is presented in isolation. The same prediction is made by Ford et al. (1982), where ambiguity resolution is determined by subcategorisation preferences alone.

Further pre-tests showed that the plausibility of the object analyses of (6a) and (6b) differed, since it is plausible to realise potential, but implausible to realise exercises, but that the plausibility of the complement clause analyses did not differ. However, eye-tracking data showed that readers found (6b) more difficult than (6a) before reaching the disambiguating word *would*, and that they found (6a) more difficult than (6b) after disambiguation. Hence subjects displayed the crossover pattern demonstrated in Pickering and Traxler (1998a). The only explanation of these results is that readers considered the object analysis of (6a) and (6b), even though this analysis was not the most likely analysis. Hence, serial likelihood is incorrect.

Pickering et al. (1998) present two other experiments that reinforce this conclusion. In one, (6a, b) were placed in short discourse contexts consisting of a title, an initial sentence, the target sentence, and a final sentence. The initial sentence mentioned the two nouns that were manipulated between conditions (here, *potential* and *exercises*). The results were similar, which indicated that the results did not reflect any special strategies that might be employed when a series of unrelated sentences are encountered in isolation. In the other experiment, subordinate clause ambiguities were employed, using the same design as (6a, b):

(7) a. While the pilot was flying the plane that had arrived stood over by the fence.
b. While the pilot was flying the horse that had arrived stood over by the fence.

Pre-tests showed that *flying* is preferentially intransitive, and also that participants preferentially complete *The pilot was flying* intransitively. According to serial likelihood, the following noun phrase should not be attached as its object. However, eye-tracking data suggested that it was attached: readers had more difficulty with (7b) before disambiguation, but more difficulty with (7a) after disambiguation.

Our results therefore present serious problems for serial likelihood accounts. Do parallel likelihood accounts fare any better? Consider (6) again:

(6) a. The young athlete realised her potential one day might make her a world-class sprinter.
b. The young athlete realised her exercises one day might make her a world-class sprinter.

After *realised*, the parser could consider both the object and complement analyses, but would foreground the more likely complement analysis. It might then integrate only the foregrounded analysis with background knowledge. If so, no plausibility effect is predicted at any point, because plausibility is only manipulated on the initially backgrounded and eventually abandoned analysis.

Alternatively, it might integrate both analyses with background knowledge. This is only possible if readers can think about two things at once (contra J.A. Fodor, 1983). Readers might experience processing difficulty when the parser reordered its preferences. This might happen in (6a) during the ambiguous region. After *The young athlete realised*, readers know that the probability of the complement analysis is higher than the probability of the object analysis. But after *The young athlete realised her potential*, the probability of an object analysis might be higher than the probability of a complement analysis, thus leading to reordering. But readers would not reorder preferences in (6b), because the object analysis becomes even more unlikely after *her exercises* (as *The young athlete realised her exercises* is very implausible on the object analysis).

Thus, the parallel likelihood account has two possible predictions about processing during the ambiguous region: either (6a) will be harder to process than (6b), or (6a) and (6b) will not differ. In fact, we found that (6b) causes difficulty in comparison to (6a). Hence parallel likelihood is very difficult to reconcile with our findings.

10.5 Processing Unbounded Dependencies: Evidence for Immediacy and Against Likelihood

The processing of unbounded dependencies has traditionally been treated rather separately from other work on syntactic ambiguity resolution (e.g., J.D. Fodor, 1978). In contrast, we suggest that they can be integrated into a unified theory (e.g., Pickering, 1994). One purpose of this section is to show how this can be done. Additionally, we provide evidence that unbounded dependencies are formed immediately, at the verb, even when this is not the most likely analysis. We have addressed two issues in the processing of unbounded dependencies. First, Traxler and Pickering (1996b) found that the processor formed and interpreted unbounded dependencies at the verb. Consider (1b) again, repeated here:

(1) b. That's the garage with which the heartless killer shot the hapless man yesterday afternoon.

Readers experienced difficulty with this sentence as soon as they encountered *shot*. However, the purported gap location is after *man*, as the canonical form of the relative clause is something like *The heartless killer shot the hapless man with the garage yesterday afternoon.* Hence, readers do not wait until the purported gap location before forming the unbounded dependency, in accord with Pickering and Barry (1991) and Pickering (1993).

Some of our other work attempts to explicate the mechanisms of initial choice at a point of ambiguity and makes the same assumptions. Sentences containing unbounded dependencies are often locally ambiguous (J.D. Fodor, 1978). For instance, the fragment *We like the book that the author wrote* can continue as in (8a) or (8b):

(8) a. We like the book that the author wrote during the winter.
 b. We like the book that the author wrote unceasingly about.

In (8a), *the book* forms the unbounded dependency with *wrote*; in (8b), it forms the unbounded dependency with *about*. Hence, the sentences are locally ambiguous after *wrote*. Fodor discussed various possible (serial) strategies that the parser might use, balancing the advantages of incremental processing against the disadvantages of excessive reanalysis. Current evidence indicates that the parser sometimes forms unbounded dependencies immediately. This rules out many cautious models in which the parser waits for fairly certain evidence before forming the unbounded dependency.

There is little doubt that readers form the unbounded dependency immediately if the verb (e.g., *wrote*) preferentially takes an argument of the same category as the filler. Traxler and Pickering (1996b) demonstrated that this occurred during normal reading, using (2a, b), repeated here:

(2) a. We like the book that the author wrote unceasingly and with great dedication about while waiting for a contract.
 b. We like the city that the author wrote unceasingly and with great dedication about while waiting for a contract.

As discussed earlier, readers experienced more difficulty with (2b) than with (2a) from the first fixation on *wrote* onwards. Because the plausibility only differed on the misanalysis, readers must have formed the unbounded dependency at *wrote* and treated the filler as the object of *wrote*. Many other experiments suggest the same conclusion, using plausibility (e.g., Boland et al., 1995; Garnsey et al., 1989; Stowe, Tanenhaus, & Carlson, 1991), the "filled-gap" technique (e.g., Boland et al., 1995; Crain & Fodor, 1985; Stowe, 1986), or cross-modal priming (Nicol & Swinney, 1989). We also found a suggestion of the crossover effect, as (2a) may have been harder than (2b) after the disambiguating word *about*.

But the parser does not appear to form an unbounded dependency, even with transitive-preference verbs, if the dependency is rendered ungrammatical by island-constraint information (Ross, 1967). In the same experiment, readers also encountered sentences like:

(9) a. We like the book that the author who wrote unceasingly and with great dedication saw while waiting for a contract.
  b. We like the city that the author who wrote unceasingly and with great dedication saw while waiting for a contract.

In (9), there is a potential unbounded dependency between the filler and *wrote*. However, it is ungrammatical, as the contrast between (10a) and (10b) shows:

(10) a. The author who wrote that book died.
  b. *That book, the author who wrote died.

We found no evidence that readers formed the ungrammatical potential unbounded dependency in (9), in contrast to (2). This suggests that parsing is closely bound by the constraints of linguistic knowledge (see also Stowe, 1986; but cf. Clifton & Frazier, 1989).

What happens when the verb does not preferentially take an argument of the same category as the filler? According to serial likelihood, the processor does not form the unbounded dependency at the verb; according to parallel likelihood, this analysis may be constructed but is backgrounded. Pickering and Traxler (1998b) conducted two self-paced reading experiments to investigate this, using sentences like (11):

(11) a. That's the plane that the pilot landed (carefully) behind in the fog at the airport.
  b. That's the truck that the pilot landed (carefully) behind in the fog at the airport.
  c. Those are the lines that the actor spoke (briefly) about to the acting coach after the rehearsal.
  d. Those are the props that the actor spoke (briefly) about to the acting coach after the rehearsal.

The adverb in brackets was included in one experiment and excluded in the other; the results from both experiments were similar. Sentences (11a, b) contained the verb *landed*, which preferentially takes an NP argument; they were essentially similar to (9a, b). Sentences (11c, d) contained the verb *spoke*, which preferentially does not take an NP argument. We concentrate on (11c, d) here.

The experiments provided strong evidence that the processor ignores lexical preferences in forming unbounded dependencies. We found the familiar crossover pattern for sentences (11c, d): participants spent longer before disambiguation in (11d) than in (11c), but longer after disambiguation (i.e., from *about* onwards) in (11d) than in (11c). As with the findings of Pickering et al. (1998), these results are incompatible with serial likelihood and very hard to reconcile with parallel likelihood. They are, however, compatible with first-resort strategies, in which the processor forms any potential unbounded dependency as soon as possible. One possibility is the Active Filler Strategy (Clifton & Frazier, 1989; Frazier & Clifton, 1989; Frazier & Flores D'Arcais, 1989). Pickering (1994) proposed a gap-free alternative, which is more compatible with the findings of Pickering and Barry (1991) and Traxler and Pickering (1996b).

Pickering and Traxler (1998b) also considered unbounded dependencies where the subcategorisation frame of the verb was not in doubt, but where the filler could associate with two different arguments of the verb:

(12) a. That's the diver that the coach persuaded a few pupils to watch before the tournament.
  b. That's the event that the coach persuaded a few pupils to watch before the tournament.

The filler, *the diver* or *the event*, serves as the object of the infinitival complement *to watch*. However, the sentences are locally ambiguous: at the verb *persuaded*, it is possible that the filler will serve as the object of the verb. This analysis becomes impossible as soon as the parser encounters *a few pupils*. Again, we manipulated plausibility to see if the parser adopted the object analysis: the object analysis in (12a) was more plausible than the object analysis in (12b), but the plausibility of the infinitival complement analysis did not differ. We conducted closely related experiments using self-paced reading and eye tracking.

Participants had greater difficulty with (12a) than with (12b) after disambiguation (i.e., from *a few pupils* onwards). This is half of the crossover pattern and indicates that the processor must have adopted the object analysis in (12a) by the time it encountered *a few pupils*. However, participants did not experience significant difficulty with (12b) at the verb *persuaded*. These results closely reflect the findings of Boland et al. (1995), who used a much less natural task in which readers had to indicate when a sentence appears to stop making sense.

According to first-resort strategies, the processor should form the object analysis at *persuaded*. If this is correct, we have to explain the absence of a plausibility effect at this point. Experimentally, the conditions of the self-paced reading experiment were very similar to one of the experiments using sentences like (11) (e.g., there was no adverb after the verb, and the presentation region ended at the verb).

The crucial theoretical difference between (11) and (12) is that (11) involves a subcategorisation ambiguity, whereas (12) does not. According to the first-resort strategy, participants adopt the object analysis in both (11) and (12). In (11b), the implausibility of the object analysis causes difficulty, because readers have to abandon one subcategorisation and adopt another. In some cases, the different subcategorisations will also reflect rather different verb meanings as well, so semantic reanalysis will also be necessary. But in (12b), readers can abandon the implausible analysis and adopt the alternative analysis without having to access a different subcategorisation for the verb.

However, the results are also compatible with a parallel account, in which the processor considers both the object and infinitival complement analyses at once. This may be possible because the ambiguity is not one of subcategorisation. For this to be correct, one implausible analysis cannot be enough to cause processing difficulty if there is a plausible analysis available as well. If this account is right, then readers initially consider the analyses in parallel. But by the time they leave the verb *persuaded*, they have adopted the object analysis in (12a) and the complement analysis in (12b). The complement analysis is adopted in (12b) because the object analysis is implausible. However, this account has to explain why the object analysis is adopted in (12a), since both analyses are plausible. Hence, we currently favour the first-resort account of these results.

10.6 Explaining the Data Using Unrestricted Informativity

We have now reached a kind of paradox. Our experimental evidence shows fairly conclusively that the parser does not obey likelihood. In many different types of sentence, it appears to adopt an analysis that is not the most likely analysis, given all the information that it has available. Why might the parser do this?

One possibility is simply that the parser is not adaptively designed. We suggest that traditional restricted accounts of parsing (e.g., the garden-path model) do not attempt to approximate to adaptiveness. Such accounts may of course be correct. However, there is an alternative: it may in fact not be adaptive to initially adopt the most likely analysis. The parser may well ultimately seek the most likely analysis; but it does not follow that initially adopting the most likely analysis is the right way to achieve this goal.

Crocker, Pickering, and Chater (1998) propose a rational analysis of parsing that suggests that the parser should not initially adopt the most likely analysis (see also Chater, Crocker, & Pickering, 1998). Instead, the goal of ultimately obtaining the most likely analysis is best served by adopting what they term an informative analysis. An interesting aspect of this account is that it is unrestricted: all potentially relevant information is employed during initial processing. However, this information is not used to initially select or foreground the most likely analysis. Pickering et al. (1998) employ this account in explaining some of the experimental results discussed earlier. We now sketch essential aspects of the account.

An informative analysis means an analysis for which it is likely to be clear quickly whether it is likely to be correct or not. Consider (6) again:

(6) a. The young athlete realised her potential one day might make her a world-class sprinter.
b. The young athlete realised her exercises one day might make her a world-class sprinter.

If the parser adopts the object analysis after *The young athlete realised*, it may encounter a word that provides good evidence about whether it was correct or not. In (6a), it becomes clear that the object analysis is likely to be correct for *The young athlete realised her potential*, because potential can be realised. In fact, the probability of the object analysis being correct is high, because most times that readers have encountered *realised her potential* (say), it will be as part of an object analysis. In (6b), it becomes clear that the object analysis is very unlikely to be correct for *The young athlete realised her exercises* (as it will never have occurred, or because it has no sensible interpretation). In this case, then, the complement analysis must be correct.

Of course, the parser will normally not encounter either *potential* or *exercises* after *realised*. But if the object analysis is adopted, and if some word is encountered, the parser will normally be able to determine whether the object analysis is quite likely, or whether it is almost impossible: *realise her potential*, *realise her ambitions*, or *realise her aspirations* are quite likely to form part of object analyses: whereas *realise her foot*, *realise her house*, or *realise her dinner* are almost impossible on this analysis. Hence, the parser can decide whether to continue with the object analysis or whether to abandon it, and its chances of having taken the right course of action are fairly high.

But if the parser adopts the complement analysis, it may not have chosen an informative analysis. The reason is that almost any NP is possible after *realised* on the complement analysis. So, for instance, it would not abandon the complement analysis after *The young athlete realised her potential* any more than it would abandon it after *The young athlete realised her exercises.* The fact that *The young athlete realised her potential* is likely on the object analysis would be irrelevant, because the complement analysis would have been chosen. Because almost any NP is possible on the complement analysis, but not on the object analysis, we say that the complement analysis is less testable than the object analysis.

Thus, it may make sense for the parser to pay some attention to testability, and not to base its initial decision, or choice of preferred analysis, on likelihood alone. One assumption is that most reanalysis must be fairly straightforward, with severe garden paths being very much the exception. Given this assumption, the parser may employ both testability and likelihood in making its decision, because it might not be optimal to adopt an extremely unlikely analysis just because it is the more testable analysis. We therefore suggest that the informative analysis involves some input from likelihood and some from testability. All our experimental results that provide evidence against likelihood show that the parser prefers to attach an NP as an argument to an verb over alternatives. We suggest that attaching as an argument will almost invariably lead to the more testable analysis. For such an account to predict our results, the influence of testability must outweigh likelihood on these occasions.

In conclusion, we argue that our experimental data can be explained by the informativity account proposed by Crocker et al. (1998). In this account, the parser pays attention to both the likelihood and testability of different analyses so that it can initially obtain the most informative analysis. This account predicts that the processor will initially adopt the less likely analysis in many locally ambiguous sentences, even though it draws upon all available information in making its choice. Our experimental evidence provides good support for this proposal.

References

Abney, S.P. (1989). A computational model of human parsing. *Journal of Psycholinguistic Research* 18, 129–144.

Anderson, J.R. (1991). Is human cognition adaptive? *Behavioral and Brain Sciences* 14, 471–517.

Boland, J.E., Tanenhaus, M.K., Garnsey, S.M., & Carlson, G.N. (1995). Verb argument structure in parsing and interpretation: Evidence from wh-questions. *Journal of Memory and Language* 34, 413–432.

Chater, N., Crocker, M.W., & Pickering, M.J. (1998). The rational analysis of inquiry: The case of parsing. In M. Oaksford & N. Chater (Eds.), *Rational models of cognition* (pp. 441–469). Oxford: Oxford University Press.

Chater, N.J., Pickering, M.J., & Milward, D. (1995). What is incremental interpretation? In D. Milward & P. Sturt (Eds.), *Edinburgh Working Papers in*

Cognitive Science 11: Incremental interpretation (pp. 1–22). Centre for Cognitive Science, University of Edinburgh.

Clifton, C., Jr., (1993). Thematic roles in sentence parsing. *Canadian Journal of Experimental Psychology* 47, 222–246.

Clifton, C., Jr., & Frazier, L. (1989). Comprehending sentences with long distance dependencies. In G. Carlson & M. Tanenhaus (Eds.), *Linguistic structure in language processing* (pp. 273–317). Dordrecht: Kluwer.

Crain, S., & Fodor, J.D. (1985). How can grammars help parsers? In D.R. Dowty, L. Karttunen & A. Zwicky, A. (Eds.), *Natural language parsing* (pp. 94–128). Cambridge: Cambridge University Press.

Crocker, M.W. (1996). *Computational psycholinguistics: An interdisciplinary approach to the study of language*. Dordrecht: Kluwer.

Crocker, M.W., Pickering, M.J., & Chater, N.J. (1998). *A rational analysis of parsing and interpretation*. Unpublished manuscript.

Ferreira, F., & Henderson, J. (1990). Use of verb information in syntactic parsing: Evidence from eye movements and word-by-word self-paced reading. *Journal of Experimental Psychology: Learning, Memory, and Cognition* 16, 555–568.

Ferreira, F., & Henderson, J. (1991). Recovery from misanalyses of garden-path sentences. *Journal of Memory and Language* 30, 725–745.

Fodor, J.A. (1983). *The modularity of mind*. Cambridge, MA: MIT Press.

Fodor, J.D. (1978). Parsing strategies and constraints on transformations. *Linguistic Inquiry* 9, 427–473.

Ford, M., Bresnan, J.W., & Kaplan, R.M. (1982). A competence based theory of syntactic closure. In J.W. Bresnan (Ed.), *The mental representation of grammatical relations* (pp. 727–796). Cambridge, MA: MIT Press.

Frazier, L. (1979). *On comprehending sentences: Syntactic parsing strategies*. Ph.D. thesis, University of Connecticut. West Bend, IN: Indiana University Linguistics Club.

Frazier, L. (1987). Sentence processing: A tutorial review. In M. Coltheart (Ed.), *Attention and performance XII* (pp. 559–586). Hillsdale, NJ: Erlbaum.

Frazier, L., & Clifton, C. Jr. (1989). Successive cyclicity in the grammar and parser. *Language and Cognitive Processes* 4, 93–126.

Frazier, L., & Flores D'Arcais, G.B. (1989). Filler driven parsing: A study of gap filling in Dutch. *Journal of Memory and Language* 28, 331–344.

Frazier, L., & Rayner, K. (1982). Making and correcting errors during sentence comprehension: Eye movements in the analysis of structurally ambiguous sentences. *Cognitive Psychology* 14, 178–210.

Garnsey, S.M., Tanenhaus, M.K., & Chapman, R. (1989). Evoked potentials and the study of sentence comprehension. *Journal of Psycholinguistic Research* 18, 51–60.

Garrod, S.C., Freudenthal, D., & Boyle, E. (1994). The role of different types of anaphor in the on-line resolution of sentences in a discourse. *Journal of Memory and Language* 33, 39–68.

Gorrell, P. (1995). *Syntax and perception*. Cambridge: Cambridge University Press.

Juliano, C., & Tanenhaus, M.K. (1994). A constraint based lexicalist account of the subject-object attachment preference. *Journal of Psycholinguistic Research* 23, 459–471.

Just, M.A., & Carpenter, P.A. (1980). A theory of reading: From eye fixations to comprehension. *Psychological Review* 87, 329–354.

MacDonald, M.C. (1994). Probabilistic constraints and syntactic ambiguity resolution. *Language and Cognitive Processes* 9, 157–201.

MacDonald, M.C., Pearlmutter, N.J., & Seidenberg, M.S. (1994). Lexical nature of syntactic ambiguity resolution. *Psychological Review* 101, 676–703.

Marr. D. (1982). *Vision*. San Francisco, CA: Freeman.

Marslen-Wilson, W.D. (1973). Linguistic structure and speech shadowing at very short latencies. *Nature* 244, 522–523.

Marslen-Wilson, W.D. (1975). Sentence perception as an interactive parallel process. *Science* 189, 226–228.

Marslen-Wilson, W.D., Tyler, L.K., & Koster, C. (1993). Integrative processes in utterance resolution. *Journal of Memory and Language* 32, 647–666.

Mitchell, D.C. (1987). Lexical guidance in human parsing: Locus and processing characteristics. In M. Coltheart (Ed.), *Attention and performance XII* (pp. 601–618). Hillsdale, NJ: Erlbaum.

Mitchell, D.C. (1989). Verb guidance and lexical effects in ambiguity resolution. *Language and Cognitive Processes* 4, 123–154.

Mitchell, D.C., Cuetos, F., Corley, M.M.B., & Brysbaert, M. (1995). Exposure-based models of human parsing: Evidence for the use of coarse-grained (non-lexical) statistical records. *Journal of Psycholinguistic Research* 24, 469–488.

Nicol, J., & Swinney, D. (1989). The role of structure in coreference assignment during sentence comprehension. *Journal of Psycholinguistic Research* 18, 5–19.

Pickering, M.J. (1993). Direct association and sentence processing: A reply to Gorrell and to Gibson and Hickok. *Language and Cognitive Processes* 8, 163–196.

Pickering, M.J. (1994). Processing local and unbounded dependencies: A unified account. *Journal of Psycholinguistic Research* 23, 323–352.

Pickering, M.J. (in press). Sentence comprehension as an adaptive process. In S.C. Garrod & M.J. Pickering (Eds.), *Language processing*. London: UCL Press.

Pickering, M.J., & Barry, G. (1991). Sentence processing without empty categories. *Language and Cognitive Processes* 6, 229–259.

Pickering, M.J., Traxler, M.J., & Crocker, M. (1998). *Ambiguity resolution in sentence processing: Simplicity or likelihood?* Unpublished manuscript.

Pickering, M.J., & Traxler, M.J. (1998a). Plausibility and recovery from garden paths: An eye-tracking study. *Journal of Experimental Psychology: Learning, Memory, and Cognition* 24, 940–961.

Pickering, M.J., & Traxler, M.J. (1998b). *Strategies for processing unbounded dependencies: First resort versus lexical guidance*. Unpublished manuscript.

Pritchett, B. (1992). *Grammatical competence and parsing performance*. Chicago: University of Chicago Press.

Rayner, K., & Pollatsek, A. (1989). *The psychology of reading*. Englewood Cliffs, NJ: Prentice-Hall.

Ross, J.R. (1967). *Constraints on variables in syntax*. Ph.D. thesis, MIT. Bloomington, IN: Indiana University Linguistics Club.

Stowe, L.A. (1986). Parsing WH-constructions: Evidence for on-line gap location. *Language and Cognitive Processes* 1, 227–245.

Stowe, L.A., Tanenhaus, M.K., & Carlson, G.M. (1991). Filling gaps on-line: Use of lexical and semantic information in sentence processing. *Language and Speech* 34, 319–340.

Swinney, D.A. (1979). Lexical access during sentence comprehension: (Re)consideration of context effects. *Journal of Verbal Learning and Verbal Behavior* 15, 681–689.

Taraban, R., & McClelland, J.R. (1988). Constituent attachment and thematic role assignment in sentence processing: Influence of content-based expectations. *Journal of Memory and Language* 27, 597–632.

Traxler, M.J., & Pickering, M.J. (1996a). Case-marking in the parsing of complement sentences: Evidence from eye movements. *Quarterly Journal of Experimental Psychology* 49A, 991–1004.

Traxler, M.J., & Pickering, M.J. (1996b). Plausibility and the processing of unbounded dependencies: An eye-tracking study. *Journal of Memory and Language* 35, 454–475.

Trueswell, J., Tanenhaus, M.K., & Garnsey, S. (1994). Semantic influences on parsing: Use of thematic role information in syntactic disambiguation. *Journal of Memory and Language* 33, 285–318.

Trueswell, J., Tanenhaus, M.K., & Kello, C. (1993). Verb-specific constraints in sentence processing: Separating effects of lexical preference from garden-paths. *Journal of Experimental Psychology: Learning, Memory, and Cognition* 19, 528–553.

Tyler, L.K., & Marslen-Wilson, W.D. (1977). The on-line effects of semantic context on syntactic processing. *Journal of Verbal Learning and Verbal Behavior* 16, 683–692.

Warner, J. & Glass, A.L. (1987). Context and distance-to-disambiguation effects in ambiguity resolution: Evidence from grammaticality judgments of garden path sentences. *Journal of Memory and Language* 26, 714–738.

11

Syntactic Attachment and Anaphor Resolution: The Two Sides of Relative Clause Attachment

BARBARA HEMFORTH, LARS KONIECZNY, AND CHRISTOPH SCHEEPERS

11.1 Introduction

In psycholinguistic research, models of sentence processing prevail which explain human parsing preferences with a set of universal principles derived either from general features of the architecture of the human language processor (e.g., Frazier & Fodor, 1978; Konieczny, 1996), or universal features of grammar (e.g., Pritchett, 1992; Gorrell, 1995), or combinations of both (Gibson, 1991). These accounts usually see the human language processor as a modular subsystem (or a set of subsystems, e.g., Frazier, 1990a) of the cognitive machinery (Fodor, 1983). As Pickering, Crocker, & Clifton (this volume) point out, psycholinguists try to uncover the basic architectures and mechanisms of this module, or more pointedly, the natural laws of the human language processor. These laws, i.e., the basic principles of language processing, should be valid across individuals as well as across languages. The simplest interpretation of this approach to sentence processing implies that similar constructions should be parsed in similar ways irrespective of interindividual or interlingual differences.

This approach has been challenged by a series of experiments on relative-clause attachment in sentences like (1), whose results were first published by Cuetos and Mitchell (1988). Cuetos and Mitchell provided evidence for a marked preference to attach the relative clause to the first of the two potential

This research was supported by the German National Research Foundation (Deutsche Forschungsgemeinschaft, DFG, Str 301/4-3). We would like to thank Gerhard Strube, Don Mitchell, and Lyn Frazier for many helpful discussions, Martin Pickering for his detailed comments on an ealier version of this chapter, Thomas Mulack, Christoph Hölscher, and Thilo Weigel for running the experiments, and Nick Ketley and Harold Paredes-Frigolett for proofreading an earlier version of this chapter.

hosts in Spanish, whereas in English, relative clauses were preferentially attached low.

(1) Someone visited the daughter of the teacher who came from Germany.

Since then, this particular structure has been investigated in many languages: in most languages (such as Spanish, e.g., Cuetos & Mitchell, 1988, Carreiras & Clifton, 1993; French, e.g., Zagar, Pynte, & Rativeau, S., 1997; German, e.g., Hemforth, Konieczny, & Scheepers, 1994; Italian, de Vincenzi & Job, 1995, and Dutch, e.g., Brysbeart & Mitchell, 1996b; among many others) a final preference for attaching the relative clause to the first NP was established. In English, on the other hand, either no preference at all or a preference to attach the relative clause to the second NP was found. For universal approaches of the kind just described, these results were worrying in two ways: firstly, the high attachment preference found in most languages contradicted any kind of recency preference as postulated for most models of human sentence processing (e.g., late closure,[1] Frazier & Rayner, 1982; most recent head attachment, Konieczny, Hemforth, Scheepers, & Strube, 1994). A preference for more local as opposed to more distant attachment, however, is plausible from a general cognitive perspective as it may serve to reduce working memory load. In fact, many modifiers exhibit a tendency to attach to more recent heads (e.g., *Tom said Bill will die yesterday*, where *yesterday* preferentially attaches to the pragmatically implausible *will die*).

Secondly, if parsing preferences are the result of universal constraints of the human language processor, there should be no crosslinguistic variation.[2] Several approaches were taken to account for the data:

1. Denying the validity of the data as evidence for initial parsing preferences (refined garden-path theory, Frazier, 1990b; de Vincenzi & Job, 1995).
2. Introducing universal principles specialized for modifier attachment parametrized for different languages (e.g., modifier straddling, Mitchell & Cuetos, 1991).
3. Distinguishing between modifier attachment and argument attachment for which different parsing options hold (e.g., Construal Theory, Frazier & Clifton, 1996).

[1] "If grammatically permissible, attach new items into the clause or phrase currently being processed; i.e., the phrase or clause postulated most recently" (Frazier, 1987, p. 562).

[2] For the moment, we ignore the possibility of an interaction of parsing principles and particular properties of the grammar of the respective languages.

4. Resolving attachment ambiguities by competing principles whose relative strength varies across languages (e.g., recency and predicate proximity, Gibson, Pearlmutter, Canseco-Gonzales, & Hickok, 1996).
5. Attributing the crosslinguistic variation of attachment preferences to the statistical distribution of attachments in the respective language to which the human language processor is tuned, thus giving up the idea of universal parsing principles (tuning, Mitchell, Cuetos, Corley, & Brysbaert, 1995; Brysbaert & Mitchell, 1996a,b).

The rest of this chapter will be devoted to the argument that there is no need for any specialized parsing account for modifiers per se, and that there is surely no need to give up universal parsing principles in favor of purely statistical approaches. We will argue that relative-clause attachment is special because it includes the syntactic attachment of a modifier to the current partial phrase marker as well as the anaphoric binding of the relative pronoun to a discourse referent. In the following sections, we will compare relative-clause attachment preferences to "purely syntactic" preferences in PP attachment in constructions like (2), as well as to "purely anaphoric" binding preferences as they show up for pronouns in constructions like (3).

(2) Someone visited the daughter of the teacher from Germany.

(3) Someone visited the daughter of the teacher when she came from Germany.

But why do relative-clause attachment preferences vary across languages? We will argue that different partial processes for ambiguity resolution may be tuned according to the usefulness and consistency of the information available from the input. The inconsistent use of relative pronouns in English, where they may be replaced by the generalized complementizer *that* or even omitted, would then be responsible for a decreased sensitivity to anaphoric processes in these constructions. Thus, binding preferences do not show up to the same degree as in other languages.

11.2 Some Explanations of Crosslinguistic Variations of Relative-Clause Attachment

Before going into more detail on the empirical evidence on modifier attachment in German, we give a brief overview of explanations that have been given for the preference to attach relative clauses high in Spanish, and, in particular, for the crosslinguistic variation of preferences. For a much more detailed overview, we refer the reader to Cuetos, Mitchell, & Corley (1996).

11.2.1 The Refined Garden-Path Theory

The earliest studies on relative-clause attachment (Cuetos & Mitchell, 1988) suffered from two problems: Cuetos and Mitchell investigated attachment preferences for Spanish and English with questionnaires and with a self-paced reading experiment where they disambiguated the structures rather late (for example on the PP *with her husband* in (4)).

(4) Someone shot the (male) servant of the actress who was on the balcony with her husband.

Preferences found so long after the beginning of the ambiguous region (i.e., on the relative pronoun *who*) need not reflect the first analysis pursued, but may be the result of more elaborate pragmatic processing. This idea was proposed by Frazier (1990b) and de Vincenzi and Job (1995). According to what has been called the refined garden-path theory (Mitchell, 1994), relative clauses are first attached low following universal principles. Later on, a pragmatic re-evaluation based on the principle of relativized relevance in (5) may result in a final preference for high attachment.

(5) *Principle of relativized relevance*
Other things being equal (e.g., all interpretations are grammatical, informative, and appropriate to discourse), preferentially construe a phrase as being relevant to the main assertion of the current sentence. (Frazier, 1990b, p. 321)

A number of self-paced reading studies in Spanish, however, failed to reveal any early low attachment preference (e.g., Carreiras & Clifton, 1993). A study on Italian relative clauses, on the other hand, seemed to provide evidence for early low attachment changing to a late high attachment preference in the final interpretation (de Vincenzi & Job, 1995). Since there are still only very few studies measuring attachment preferences at a very early stage (e.g., Brysbaert & Mitchell, 1996a,b; Hemforth, Konieczny, & Scheepers, 1997), and since the data are not fully unequivocal, recency may still hold for the initial attachment of relative clauses but is overridden by pragmatic principles.

11.2.2 The Modifier Straddling Hypothesis

One explanation for the crosslinguistic variation that has been offered by Cuetos and Mitchell (1988) is the modifier straddling hypothesis. They assume that in some cases, frequency-based preferences may override universal principles. In Spanish, it might be the case that NP–NP–RC sequences fall into one category with other NP–modifier–RC sequences. In this category, the most frequent structure would be NP–adjective–RC, for which only RC attachment to the head noun is allowed. Since high attachment is necessarily the most frequent attachment in the category, a universal preference for low attachment may be overridden in this particular case, though still being applicable to other structures.

The predictions which can be derived from the modifier straddling hypothesis are clearcut: high attachment preferences should be found for languages with postnominal adjectives, but low attachment preferences for those with prenominal adjectives. From the range of languages investigated since 1988, it can be shown that this hypothesis is clearly inadequate. In German (Hemforth, Konieczny, & Scheepers, 1994) as well as Dutch (Brysbaert & Mitchell, 1996a,b), both prenominal adjective languages, a clear preference for high attachment of relative clauses could be established. Thus, the difference between the languages cannot be attributed to a parametrization due to the position of adjectives in the respective language.

11.2.3 Construal Theory

According to Construal Theory (Gilboy et al., 1995, Frazier & Clifton, 1996), different attachment processes have to be assumed for so-called primary relations (roughly, arguments) and non-primary relations (roughly, modifiers). Architecture-based principles like late closure only apply to primary relations. Phrases which have to be modifiers, like relative clauses, are not directly attached to the phrase marker of the sentence straight away, but only construed as part of the current thematic processing domain. Attachment preferences then follow from a complex set of pragmatic, thematic, and syntactic constraints. Contrary to the refined garden-path theory, Frazier and Clifton (1996) do not assume an initial late closure–based attachment for relative-clause modifiers.

Crosslinguistic differences are explained by the interaction of pragmatic principles. The Gricean principle of clarity is assumed to lead to a low attachment preference for modifiers in English because there is an unambiguous alternative to the constructions discussed so far, as shown in (6).

(6) Someone shot the actress's servant who was on the balcony.

In sentences like (6) the relative clause can only be attached to the head noun *servant*. Since this alternative exists, readers should presuppose that the writer would have chosen the unambiguous form if head noun attachment had been intended. Thus, a preference for low attachment in structures like (1) overrides the principle of relativized relevance in English. In Spanish, no alternative form could have been chosen, so no preference follows from the principle of clarity. Only the principle of relativized relevance applies, leading to a preference for high attachment.[3]

11.2.4 Recency and Predicate Proximity

An alternative account based on a parametrization of principles was proposed by Gibson et al. (1996a). In this account, the cost of attaching the relative clause to one of the potential sites is calculated on the basis of two competing principles, recency (7) and predicate proximity (8).

(7) *Recency*
Preferentially attach structures for incoming lexical items to structures built more recently. (Gibson et al., 1996a, p. 26)

(8) *Predicate proximity*
Attach as close as possible to the head of a predicate phrase. (Gibson et al., 1996a, p. 41)

Whereas recency is assumed to be based on the architecture of the human language processor and is therefore not subject to crosslinguistic variation, the relative strength of the tendency to attach a phrase close to the predicate may vary from language to language. The strength of predicate proximity may, for example, depend on the average distance between a verb and its arguments in a language: if this average distance is rather large, the predicate must be activated more strongly to get the attachment of its arguments right. The stronger the activation of the predicate, the more costly a violation of predicate proximity will be. Languages with larger average distances between predicates and their arguments are thus assumed to give more strength to predicate proximity, resulting in a high attachment preference for relative clauses in the case of two-site NPs.

English, in contrast to most of the other languages investigated, has a rather rigid Subject-Verb-Object order, where subject and object are both close to the predicate. Therefore, recency wins over predicate proximity. Spanish, however, also allows a Verb-Object-Subject order, where the subject is further from the predicate (as do German and Dutch, among others). Hence, predicate proximity is predicted to be stronger in Spanish. Apparently the crosslinguistic data can be

[3] It seems to be difficult to think of a parser applying the principle of clarity, because this would mean that alternative constructions to the one that is currently processed would have to be generated on-line.

accounted for by this approach. As we will see below, however, the explanation only extends to the case of relative clauses.

11.2.5 Only a Question of Statistics?

An alternative conception to universal approaches was proposed in the past few years: the tuning hypothesis in (10) (Mitchell & Cuetos, 1991). According to Mitchell and Cuetos, the only universal principle is that parsing preferences are exposure-based.

(9) *Linguistic Tuning Hypothesis*
Parsing strategies result from the frequency of structural analyses during the history of exposure to linguistic structures.

To predict parsing preferences from the tuning hypothesis, careful corpus analyses must be carried out. For those cases where corpus statistics are available, structures which can be shown to be preferred in on-line parsing usually are more frequent, which appears to support an exposure-based account on parsing. However, it could very well be the case that less preferred structures are less frequent in corpus analyses because they are more difficult to parse. But there are notable exceptions to this rule: for three-site relative clause attachment ambiguities (Gibson et al., 1996a) as well as for three-site coordination ambiguities (Gibson et al., 1996b) corpus data and parsing preferences clearly do not match. Aditionally, Brysbaert and Mitchell (1996b) provided evidence that data from several Dutch corpora stand in striking contrast to the high attachment preference for relative clauses: in all the corpora examined, low attachment of the relative clause was more frequent.

11.2.6 Relative-Clause Attachment: An Intermediate Conclusion

Although relative-clause attachment preferences and their crosslinguistic variation have been discussed for more than eight years now, there is still a considerable debate about what they really tell us. At least three of the accounts presented in this section are fairly compatible with most of the data currently available: refined garden-path theory, which only includes minor extensions to the classic garden-path theory; construal theory, which is a much more significant deviation because of the division of primary and secondary relations; and competitive application of recency and predicate proximity. Only modifier straddling is clearly incompatible with the evidence, and tuning, at least in its strongest form, does not seem to work very well either.

11.3 Relative Clauses and PPs

If preferences in relative clause attachment are attributed to parsing principles that are only valid for modifiers (as for example in Construal Theory) or to the relative strengths of parsing principles valid for a particular language (as in the recency/predicate proximity approach), the predictions generalize far beyond the constructions discussed so far. At least all sorts of modifying relations should be handled by the same set of principles. To find out whether this prediction holds, we conducted a series of experiments to compare relative clauses and prepositional phrases in sentences like (10a,b). Note that in German, PPs headed by a thematically empty *of* translate to genitive-marked NPs. Finite verbs in relative clauses always appear in the clause-final position.

(10) a. Die Tochter der Lehrerin, die aus Deutschland kam, traf John.
The daughter the teacher$_{gen}$ who from Germany came met, John
The daughter of the teacher who came from Germany met John.
b. Die Tochter der Lehrerin aus Deutschland traf John.
The daughter the teacher$_{gen}$ from Germany met John.
The daughter of the teacher from Germany met John.

German is a generalized verb-second language, i.e., only one constituent may be fronted to the position before the finite verb in main clauses. Therefore, the PP *aus Deutschland* in (10b) cannot be analyzed as a verb argument, but must be a modifier of one of the preceding NPs. So, according to construal theory as well as recency/predicate proximity, it should behave similarly to relative clauses in comparable constructions (10a).[4]

11.3.1 Questionnaire I

In this questionnaire study, we asked our subjects to mark one of two partial paraphrases of each item to indicate which one matched their first interpretation of the respective sentence, e.g., (10) as either (11a) or (11b). Twenty-four sentences were constructed, each in a version with a PP modifier and a version with a relative clause modifier. We prepared two lists such that each list

[4] Traxler, Pickering, and Clifton (1996) pointed out the possibility that PPs may be "generalized primary relations" because they can be primary relations in other constructions. Then late closure would apply and a low attachment preference would be predicted. It is not very clear to us what the consequences of such a move would be. Even relative clauses can be argued to have an argumentlike status in some kinds of quantified constructions. The question is whether any clear cases of non-primary relations will remain if the concept of a generalized primary relation is brought in.

contained an equal number of relative clauses and PPs, but only one version of each sentence. From these two lists, sixteen lists were derived using eight different randomizations for each list. Each of these sixteen lists was presented to two subjects. The experimental items were embedded in a list of twenty-four fillers of various syntactic structures. Thirty-two undergraduates at the University of Freiburg were paid 5 DM each for completing the questionnaire.

(11) a. Die Tochter kam aus Deutschland.
The daughter came from Germany.
b. Die Lehrerin kam aus Deutschland.
The teacher came from Germany.

Results

Figure 11.1 shows the number of high and low attachments for relative clauses and PPs. There was an interaction between modifier type (PP vs. RC) and attachment preference (F1[1, 31] = .35.68, p < .001, F2[1, 23] = 30.79, p < .001). Whereas high attachment is preferred for RCs (F1[1, 31] = 4.89, p < .05, F2[1, 31] = 9.39, p < .01), PPs are preferentially attached low (F1 [1, 31] = 10.10, p < .01, F2 [1, 26] = 6.55, p < .02).

11.3.2 Questionnaires II and III

This finding is supported by two further questionnaire studies. Two new versions of the twenty-four sentences of Questionnaire I were constructed by replacing the second NP with a proper noun, as in (12a,b).

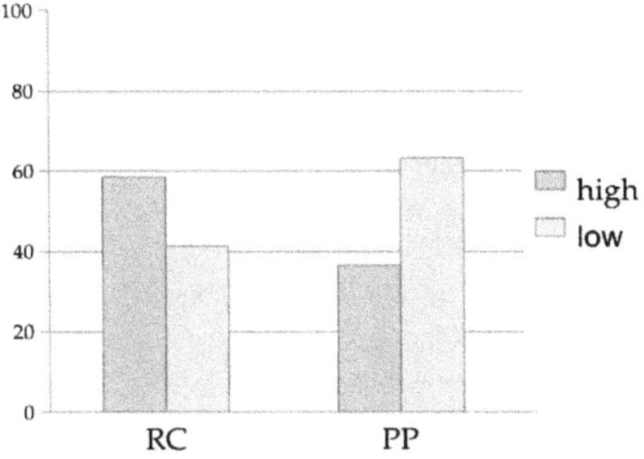

Figure 11.1. Attachment decisions for relative clauses and PPs, written questionnaire.

(12) a. Die Tochter von Mary, die aus Deutschland kam, traf John.
The daughter of Mary, who came from Germany, met John.
b. Die Tochter von Mary aus Deutschland traf John.
The daughter of Mary from Germany met John.

Since proper nouns do not like to take (restrictive) modifiers, low attachment should be avoided in these cases. Some sentences had to be slightly adjusted because four raters agreed that the modifiers used in Questionnaire I were not fully ambiguous with the new versions of the materials. Four lists of experimental items were prepared, including the new versions as well as the old ones, so that each version of each item appeared on one list and each list contained an equal number of sentences per condition. Four differently randomized versions of each list were then constructed, resulting in sixteen different lists. The experimental items were embedded in a list of twenty-four filler items.

In Questionnaire II, subjects had to mark their attachment preferences in the same way as in the earlier experiment. In Questionnaire III, the acceptability of the sentences (from 1 "not acceptable" to 4 "fully acceptable") had to be rated. Twenty-six subjects, all undergraduates at the University of Freiburg, were paid to complete the first questionnaire, and thirty-four different students from the same population completed the second one. None of them had participated in the earlier experiment.

Results

As in our earlier experiment, RCs were attached high more often than PPs. Figure 11.2 shows the percentage of N1-attachments for the different conditions, N1- and N2-attachments always total 100 percent; $F1[1, 25] = 12.56, p < .01$; $F2[1, 23] = 7.05, p < .02$), but we did not find a low attachment preference for PPs in this experiment. For PPs, the number of high-attachment decisions increased slightly if the second NP was a proper noun ($F1[1, 25] = 2.07, p < .17$; $F2[1, 23] = 4.79, p < .04$). Somewhat unexpectedly, in 41 percent of these cases subjects chose the syntactically preferred but pragmatically implausible low-attachment reading. The interaction of modifier type and type of second NP was not reliable ($F1[1, 25] = .98$, ns, $F2[1, 23] = 3.55, p < .08$).

In sentences where high attachment was induced for pragmatic reasons by introducing proper nouns as the second host, the acceptability of the sentences was reduced if the modifier was realized as a PP ($F1[1, 33] = 40.52, p < .001$; $F2[1, 23] = 22.17, p < .001$). Figure 11.3 shows the mean acceptability of the different constructions irrespective of final attachments. Since no such reduction of acceptability was observed for relative clauses, there was an

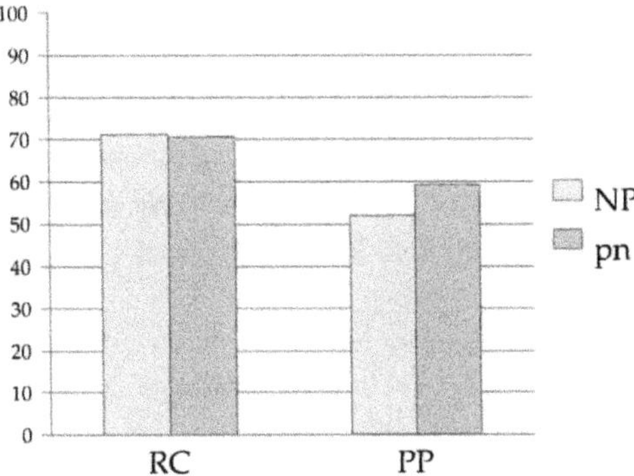

Figure 11.2. Percentage of high attachment decisions for RCs and PPs attached to full NPs or proper nouns.

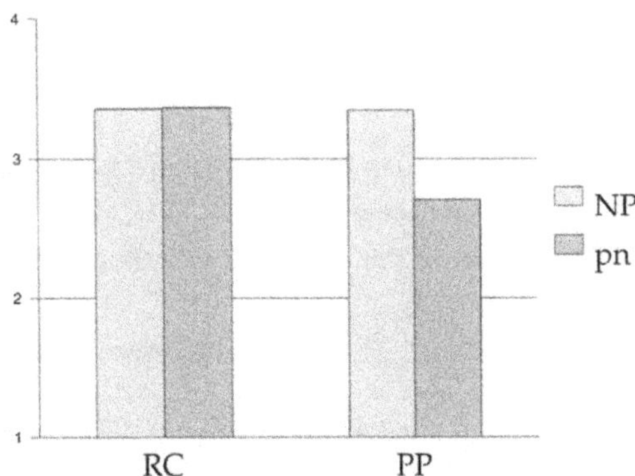

Figure 11.3. Acceptability ratings (1 not acceptable, 4 fully acceptable) for RCs and PPs attached to full NPs or proper nouns.

interaction between modifier type and type of second NP (F1[1, 33] = 30.54, $p < .001$; F2[1, 23] = 11.15, $p < .01$). The difference in acceptability found for PP modifiers can easily be accounted for by conflicting syntactic and pragmatic constraints: PPs are initially attached low to the most recent site. This attachment conflicts with the pragmatic interpretation of the proper noun, which tends to avoid taking modifiers. Wherever the PP is finally attached, one of the constraints is violated. Since relative clauses are preferentially attached high anyway, no conflict arises and, thus, no reduction of acceptability occurs for relative-clause constructions.

To sum up the results presented so far: there are considerable differences between relative-clause attachment and PP attachment in comparable constructions at least in German – and there is some evidence that this is also true for some other languages like English (Traxler, Pickering, & Clifton, 1996) or Spanish (Igoa, pers. communication). A psycholinguistic theory that does not differentiate between these different kinds of modifiers obviously cannot account for the data. It may be the case that relative-clause attachment does not follow a recency preference in German (as in many other languages), but PP attachment in comparable constructions obviously does.

11.3.3 On-line Evidence

The preferences discussed so far were fully validated in on-line experiments (Hemforth, Konieczny, & Scheepers, 1997). In two eye-tracking experiments we found a clear high attachment preference for relative clauses irrespective of whether they were disambiguated by number marking (13a,b), gender marking (13c,d), or by their pragmatic/encyclopedic content (14a,b). On the other hand, we found a low attachment preference for PPs (14c,d) that were closely matched to the relative clauses in (14a,b).

(13) a. Klaus traf die Lehrerin der Töchter, die in Deutschland lebten, und freute sich, sie wiederzusehen.
Klaus met the teacher of the daughters who lived (plural) in Gemany, and was glad to see her again.

b. Klaus traf die Lehrerin der Töchter, die in Deutschland lebte, und freute sich, sie wiederzusehen.
Klaus met the teacher of the daughters who lived (sing) in Gemany, and was glad to see her again.

c. Klaus traf den Lehrer der Töchter, die in Deutschland lebte, und freute sich, ihn wiederzusehen.
Klaus met the teacher (masc) of the daughter (fem) who (fem) lived in Gemany, and was glad to see him again.

d. Klaus traf den Lehrer der Töchter, der in Deutschland lebte, und freute sich, ihn wiederzusehen.
Klaus met the teacher (masc) of the daughter (fem) who (masc) lived in Gemany, and was glad to see him again.

(14) a. Der Autor des Bestsellers, der eine klangvolle Stimme hatte, war beim Publikum besonders beliebt.
The author of the bestseller who had a sonorous voice enjoyed great popularity.

b. Der Bestseller des Autors, der eine klangvolle Stimme hatte, war beim Publikum besonders beliebt.

The bestseller of the author who had a sonorous voice enjoyed great popularity.

c. Der Autor des Bestsellers mit der klangvollen Stimme war beim Publikum besonders beliebt.
The author of the bestseller with the sonorous voice enjoyed great popularity.

d. Der Bestseller des Autors mit der klangvollen Stimme war beim Publikum besonders beliebt.
The bestseller of the author with the sonorous voice enjoyed great popularity.

11.4 What Makes Relative Clauses and PPs Different?

11.4.1 Punctuation and Prosodic Effects

There are several options one can follow in order to find out why attachment preferences for relative clauses and PPs are different. One rather obvious reason may be that there is a rather superficial dissimilarity between these constructions in German: German relative clauses, but not PPs, must be separated from the main clause by commas. The comma may reflect a stronger prosodic break for relative clauses than for PPs, i.e., an intonational phrase boundary as opposed to a phonological phrase boundary. As Schafer and Speer (1997) point out, intonational phrase boundaries may define an interpretational domain. Therefore, an increased amount of semantic/pragmatic compacting may occur before relative-clause modifiers than before PP modifiers, resulting in an increased accessibility of main discourse referents.

In contrast to other languages like English or Dutch, the comma for German relative clauses is not optional but obligatory. There is thus no straightforward way to control for a possible effect of the comma in any kind of reading experiment. Consequently, we developed a questionnaire with auditory stimulus presentation.

11.4.2 Questionnaire IV

For this questionnaire, each sentence from Questionnaire I (twenty-four experimental items and twenty-four fillers) was recorded in sixteen-bit quality with a relative-clause modifier as well as a PP modifier. To control for prosodic effects, the parts of the sentences preceding the modifiers were cross-spliced. We prepared four lists such that an original as well as a cross-spliced version of each relative clause and PP modifier sentence appeared across lists and the number of sentences per condition was identical per list. Each list started with at least two filler items. The order of presentation was individually randomized. Each subject heard the sentences through headphones, half of the materials in its original version and half of it in a cross-spliced version. Prosody was kept as neutral as possible. Thirty subjects were paid for participating in the experiment.

To work through the questionnaire, subjects first had to click on a "play" button with the mouse. The respective sentence was then played to them via headphones only once. Then, two partial paraphrases appeared on the computer screen which were identical to those used in the written questionnaire (cf. (11)). Subjects had to mark their preferred interpretation by selecting it with the mouse.

Results

Figure 11.4 shows the number of high and low attachment decisions for relative clauses and PPs in the auditory questionnaire. Again, we found a high attachment preference for relative clauses (though only marginal across subjects: $F1[1, 29] = 3.88$, $p < .06$; $F2[1, 23]$, $p < .05$), but no low attachment preference for PPs (all $Fs < 1$). The interaction between modifier type and attachment preference was statistically reliable across subjects ($F1[1, 29] = 11.39$, $p < .01$) and across items ($F2[1, 23] = 4.90$, $p < .05$). The number of high attachments was reliably higher for relative clauses than for PPs ($F1[1, 29] = 12.35$, $p < .01$; $F2[1, 23] = 5.07$, $p < .05$).

Most probably, the lack of a low attachment preference for PPs is due to purely technical reasons. To allow cross-splicing, we had to pronounce the last word

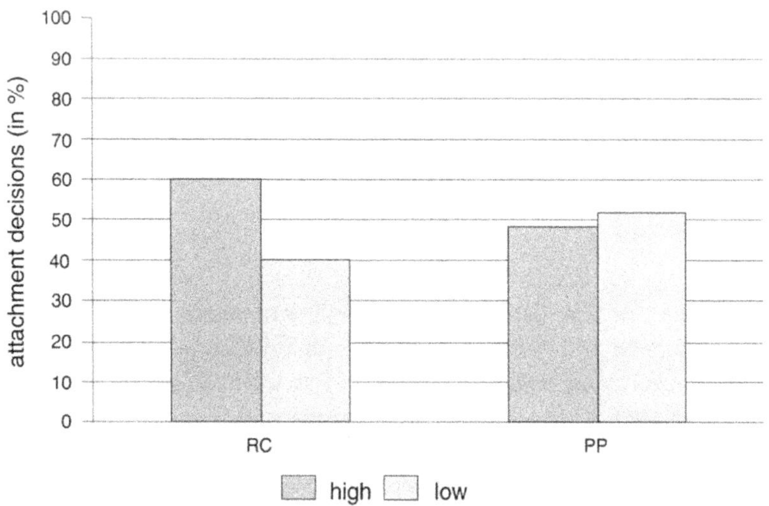

Figure 11.4. Attachment decisions in percent, auditory questionnaire.

of the complex NP and the first word of the modifier as clearly separate entities, thereby inserting a brief prosodic break. The length of this break was controlled over conditions by the cross-splicing procedure. Such prosodic breaks show effects on attachment preferences, as has been shown by Pynte & Prieur (1996) for PP attachment in sentences like (15a,b), with # marking prosodic breaks.

(15) a. The police accused # the ambassador of Indonesia.
b. The police accused # the ambassador # of Indonesia.

Such prosodic breaks appear to block the attachment of a phrase to a preceding constituent, at least temporarily. In our auditory questionnaire, this kind of prosodic effect may have masked the preference to attach the PP low. Most importantly, however, the difference in attachment preferences between relative clauses and PPs is still present. Despite the prosodic break, we did not find a high attachment preference for the PPs whereas we did for relative clauses. Most probably, the difference between these two kinds of modifiers is neither due to the obligatory comma we need for relative clauses nor to prosodic effects alone.

11.4.3 Anaphoric Binding

There is at least one more obvious difference between relative clauses and PPs. Resolving the correct interpretation of a relative clause not only involves syntactic attachment to the partial phrase marker constructed so far, but also the resolution of a relative pronoun that might plausibly have to be properly bound to a discourse entitity. Therefore, for relative clauses, anaphoric binding processes are involved for the resolution of the relative pronoun, whereas no such resolution is required for PPs.

But why does the relative pronoun want to be bound to the higher antecedent? Here we would assume that a pragmatic factor comes in, addressed, for example, by the relativized relevance principle in (5) proposed by Frazier (1990b), de Vincenzi and Job (1995), and Frazier and Clifton (1996). Entities which are part of the main assertion of the sentence make better discourse referents. Similarly, this appears to underlie a preference to attach a relative clause to an item close to the predicate, as expressed in (8).

Questionnaire data from Gilboy et al. (1995) show that referentiality clearly plays a role for relative-clause attachment. If the second (low) noun phrase in the complex NP is not referential (for example, if there is a substance (a pullover of wool) or a quantity relation (a glass of water) involved), subjects preferred attaching a succeeding relative clause high to the referential NP, in Spanish as well as in English. In a German questionnaire matched as closely as possible to the Gilboy et al. materials, we found highly comparable results for German (see Hemforth et al., 1997).

Gilboy et al. (1995) attribute this preference to a referentiality principle, stated in (16), which is assumed to hold for all kinds of modifiers.

(16) *Referentiality principle*
The heads of some maximal projections are referential in the sense that they introduce discourse entities (e.g., participants in events described in the discourse) into a discourse model (at least temporarily), or correspond to already existing discourse entities. Restrictive modifiers (e.g., restrictive relative clauses) preferentially seek hosts which are referential in this sense. (Gilboy et al., 1995; p. 136)

We agree that this is a particularly viable principle for relative-clause attachment, though for slightly different reasons. We do not believe that it applies to modifier attachment per se, but that it is relevant for relative-clause attachment, because of the anaphoric processes specifically involved in their interpretation.

11.4.4 Questionnaire V: Attachment and Binding

If the attachment preferences found for relative clauses were at least partly due to the anaphoric nature of the process of binding the pronoun to a discourse referent, we should find comparable high attachment effects for simple pronouns as they are realized in sentences like (17a,b). We ran another questionnaire experiment in which binding preferences of a pronoun in an adverbial clause which was either adjacent to the complex NP (17a) or nonadjacent to it (17b)[5] were compared to relative-clause attachment (18) and PP attachment(19).

(17) Adverbial clauses
a. Die Ergebnisse las der Student des Professors, als er in dem neuen Labor war.
The results$_{acc\text{-}object}$ read the student$_{nom\text{-}subject}$ of the professor, when he in the new lab was.
The student of the professor read the results when he was in the new lab.
b. Der Student des Professors las die Ergebnisse, als er in dem neuen Labor war.

[5] Note that the marked Object-Verb-Subject order may change the focus structure of the sentences.

The student$_{\text{nom-subject}}$ of the professor read the results$_{\text{acc-object}}$, when he in the new lab was.

The student of the professor read the results when he was in the new lab.

(18) Relative clause

Der Student des Professors, der in dem neuen Labor war, las die Ergebnisse.

The student of the professor who was in the new lab read the results.

(19) Prepositional phrase

Der Student des Professors in dem neuen Labor las die Ergebnisse.

The student of the professor in the new lab read the results.

We constructed twenty-four sentences, each in the four versions described earlier. The procedure was identical to the first questionnaire described in this chapter. Twenty-four students from the same population as in the earlier experiments participated in this one. Since it was to be expected that there would be a high attachment/binding preference for three-quarters of the materials (17a,b, 18), we also included twelve sentences with three-site relative-clause attachment ambiguities like (20) and three-site binding ambiguities like (21) as fillers in this questionnaire.

(20) Jemand strich den Zaun neben *der Tränke mit der Pumpe, die repariert werden mußte.*

Someone painted the fence (masc) near the watering place (fem) with the pump (fem) that (fem) had to be repaired.

(21) Jemand strich den Zaun neben *der Tränke mit der Pumpe, als sie repariert werden mußte.*

Someone painted the fence (masc) near the watering place (fem) with the pump (fem) when it (fem) had to be repaired.

For three-site attachment ambiguities like (20), Gibson et al. (1996a) found a strong low attachment preference in English. Furthermore, the possibility of N1 attachment/binding in these constructions was excluded by gender marking. The four two-site attachment/binding variants (17–19) and the two variants of the three-site ambiguities were distributed across four lists so that each variant appeared on one list and an equal number of sentences per condition appeared on each list. We randomized the items on each list twice so that one of eight different lists was presented to each subject. Fourteen fillers of various syntactic forms were also included, two of which served as training items.

Results

We first present the results for the two-site attachment/binding preferences. Figure 11.5 shows the percentage of N1-attachments. N1-attachments and N2-attachments always total 100 percent. Binding of the simple pronouns to N1 occurs reliably more often than attachment of PPs to N1 (NP-adjacent adverbial clause: $F1[1, 23] = 17.49$, $p < .001$; $F2[1, 23] = 10.83$, $p < .01$; non-adjacent adverbial clause: $F1[1, 23] = 99.91$, $p < .001$; $F2[1, 23] = 61.96$; $p < .001$). Relative clauses are also attached high more often than PPs ($F1[1, 23] = 17.33$, $p < .001$; $F2[1, 23] = 26.86$, $p < .001$). Binding preferences in sentences where the adverbial clause immediately followed the complex NP did not differ from relative clause attachment/binding preferences ($F1[1,23] = .01$; $F2[1,23] = .01$). Pronouns in non-adjacent adverbial clauses, on the other hand, were reliably more often bound to N1 than relative pronouns ($F1[1,23] = 10.69$, $p < .01$; $F2[1, 23] = 17.50$, $p < .001$).

We do not want to go into too much detail with respect to the question of why the preference for binding the pronoun to N1 increases in the case of non-adjacent adverbial clauses. Several factors probably contribute to this phenomenon. The mere distance between the complex NP and the pronoun may let the less relevant discourse referent fade away, it may be the parallelism in grammatical function or syntactic position that enhances N1 preferences (Beardley and Caramazza, 1978), or a backward-looking center in the adverbial clause may be searching for the most highly ranked element of the set of

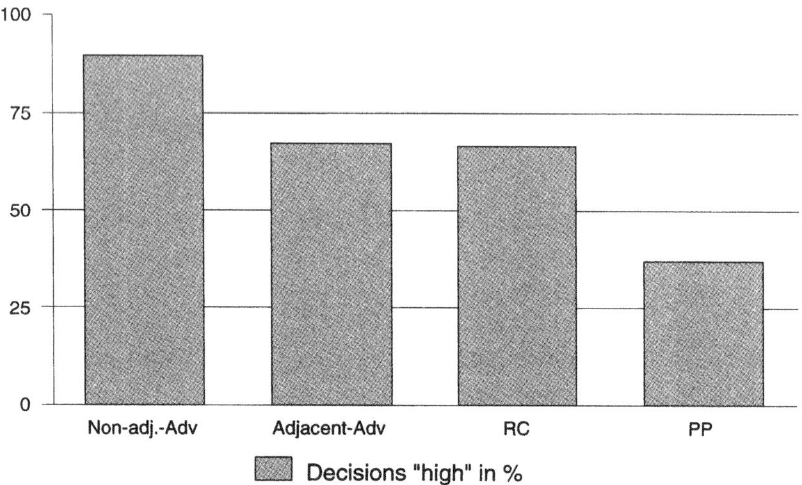

Figure 11.5. Attachment and binding preferences, N1 decisions in percent.

forward-looking centers as described in centering theory (Gordon, Grosz, & Gilliom, 1993; Grosz, Joshi, & Weinstein, 1983).

In any case, there is a strong preference for binding a pronoun to the head of the complex NP that is highly similar to the attachment preferences established for German relative clauses. Plausibly, common principles underlie these preferences, which may be based on the anaphoric processes for pronoun resolution.

From the similarity of binding preferences of pronouns in adverbial clauses that are adjacent to the complex NP and attachment preferences of relative clauses, it could also be argued that the preferences we find for relative-clause attachment are not syntactic attachment preferences at all. It might be the case that the so-called attachment preferences discussed so far are nothing but binding preferences. If this were the case, relative pronouns should behave similarly to simple pronouns in all sorts of comparable constructions.

The preferences for three-site attachment/binding ambiguities, however, show that this is not the case. Whereas there is a clear low attachment preference for the relative clauses (31.11% N2 attachments), the low binding preference of pronouns in adverbial clauses is much less clear (45.28% N2 attachments; N2 attachments/bindings in relative clauses vs. N2 attachments/bindings in adverbial clauses: $F1[1, 23] = 4.55$, $p < .05$; $F2[1, 11] = 5.21$, $p < .05$). This evidence is somewhat clouded, however, since many of our subjects told us that they chose N2 binding of pronouns in the adverbial clauses because N1 binding, which they would have strongly preferred, was excluded by gender marking. Experiments with different versions of fully ambiguous three-site attachment/binding ambiguities show that a very strong N1 binding preference for pronouns in constructions like (21), whereas the clear low attachment preference of relative clauses still holds (see Hemforth et al., 1997).

In any case, it is obvious that relative-clause attachment preferences are not only based on binding preferences resulting from the anaphoric processes involved in resolving the relative pronoun. Some kind of syntactic attachment principle (presumably recency-based) seems to be at work here. On the other hand, the attachment preferences do not seem to be based on syntactic attachment principles alone, as the contrast to attachment preferences of PPs in comparable constructions suggests.

11.5 Discussion

The following picture is suggested by the experiments in this chapter: relative-clause attachment differs from other kinds of attachment because it involves at least two kinds of processes, the attachment of the relative clause to the current partial phrase marker and the resolution of the relative pronoun.

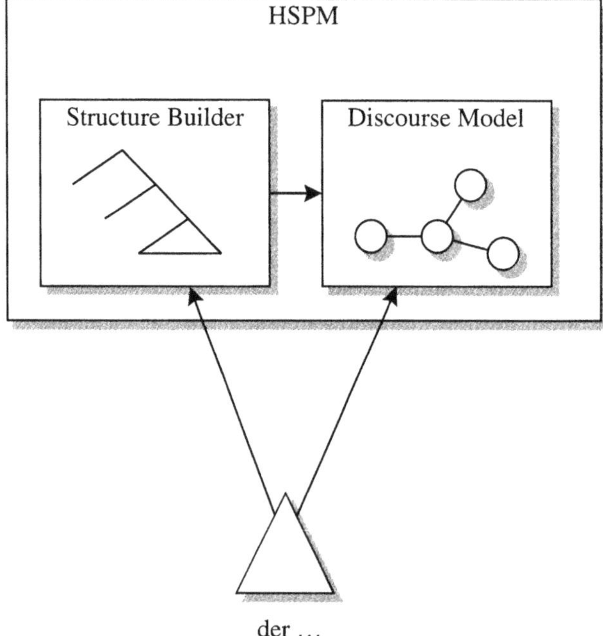

Figure 11.6. The process of relative clause attachment.

How can we assume then that a relative clause is processed? It could be the case that as soon as the relative pronoun is read, syntactic as well as anaphoric processes are triggered in parallel (see Figure 11.6). The different modules involved in syntactic structure building and binding[6] are working independently, each based on its own principles (see also Frazier, 1990a).[7] The module that settles on an analysis first determines the initial interpretation.

[6] For a detailed discussion of parser internal modularity, see Frazier (1990a).

[7] There is a problem with this fully parallel account, however: the relative pronoun can only trigger pronoun specific anaphoric processes if it is recognized as a pronoun. Since relative pronouns in German as in many languages are lexically ambiguous, allowing a relative pronoun reading as well as a determiner reading, it is somewhat unclear how the language processor knows what to do with the input without some parsing, i.e., some kind of syntactic analysis (we thank Angela Friederici for her helpful comments on this issue). There are several solutions to this problem that are still very speculative. First, all kinds of referentially relevant parts of speech could trigger anaphoric processes. Thus, the binding module would be set to work by a definite determiner as well as a relative pronoun. Only later would the structure builder tell the binding module which analysis was to be cancelled. A second possibility is that, as assumed by the refined garden-path theory, there is an initial preference for low attachment. The relative clause would then be reanalyzed in a later stage if there is a strong conflicting preference coming from the binding module. Since the exact time course of relative-clause attachment preferences is still somewhat debated, this version is still a viable option.

But why do we find high attachment for two-site relative clause ambiguities and low over middle attachment for three-site ambiguities? We assume that discourse entities are represented in a structured discourse model whose local part is the current content of the working memory section that is relevant for language processing (beyond the phonological loop) (Baddeley, 1986). Prominent discourse entities are more highly activated than less prominent ones and, consequently, easier to access. As soon as the local environment contains more than one discourse entity, however, these entities interfere and their activation decreases. This interference does not do too much harm in the case of two-site ambiguities. In the case of three-site ambiguities, however, the reduced activation of the discourse entities handicaps the anaphoric processes such that syntactic (recency-based) attachment processes win the race.

Why then does English differ from most other languages? One of the reasons could be that English makes only very inconsistent use of relative pronouns. In many cases, a generalized complementizer is used instead of a proper pronoun (22a), and the relative pronoun may even be omitted (22b).

(22) a. The daughter of the teacher that Peter visited ...
b. The daughter of the teacher Peter visited ...

Thus, for attaching relative clauses in English, anaphoric processes cannot be relied on very strongly. Still, anaphoric processes may be at work in English as well, as data from Traxler, Pickering, and Clifton (1996) indicate. Numerically, though not statistically reliably, they also found a slightly more pronounced low attachment preference for PPs than for relative clauses in English. Anaphoric processes only seem to be handicapped because of their reduced reliability, so that they cannot win the race against syntactic attachment processes as clearly as in many other languages.

To see whether the consistency of use of relative pronouns is a relevant parameter for relative clause attachment processes, we will have to look at other languages which omit relative pronouns.[8] Thus, a central line of research will have to have a strong crosslinguistic perspective: we will have to find languages differing in the amount of anaphoric processes involved in relative-clause attachment.

[8] Japanese is an example of such a language. Kamide and Mitchell (1997) present evidence in favor of an initial low attachment preference for Japanese relative clauses that is quite consistent with our approach. Unfortunately, though, in more recent experiments this preference has turned out to be very likely due to segmentation artifacts (Kamide, personal communication). Japanese data on relative-clause attachment must be interpreted with care in any event. Since relative clauses in Japanese precede their attachment sites, preferences may be due to different processes than in languages where relative clauses follow their attachments sites.

References

Baddeley, A.D. (1986). *Working memory*. Oxford: Oxford University Press.

Brysbaert, M., & Mitchell, D. (1996a). Modifier attachment in sentence parsing: evidence from Dutch. *Quarterly Journal of Experimental Psychology* 49A, 664–695.

Brysbaert, M., & Mitchell, D. (1996b). *Modifier attachment in Dutch: deciding between garden-path, construal, and statistical tuning accounts of parsing*. Paper presented at the Workshop on Computational Psycholinguistics, Wassenaar, NL.

Carreiras, M., & Clifton, C. (1993). Relative clause interpretation preferences in Spanish and English. *Language and Speech* 36, 353–372.

Cuetos, F., & Mitchell, D. (1988). Cross linguistic differences in parsing: restrictions on the issue of the Late Closure strategy in Spanish. *Cognition* 30, 73–105.

Cuetos, F., Mitchell, D.C., & Corley, M. (1996). Parsing in different languages. In M. Carreiras, J. Garcia-Albea, & N. Sebastian-Galles (Eds.), *Language Processing in Spanish* (pp. 145–187). Hillsdale, NJ: Erlbaum.

De Vincenzi, M., & Job, R. (1995). An investigation of late closure: the role of syntax, thematic structure and pragmatics in initial and final interpretation. *Journal of Experimental Psychology: Learning, Memory, & Cognition* 21(5) 1303–1321.

Fodor, J. (1983). *The modularity of mind*. Cambridge, MA: MIT Press.

Frazier, L. (1990a). Exploring the architecture of the language-processing system. In G. Altmann (Ed.), *Cognitive models of speech processing* (pp. 409–433). Cambridge, MA: MIT Press.

Frazier, L. (1990b). Parsing modifiers: Special purpose routines in the human sentence processing mechanism. In D.A. Balota, G.B.F. D'Arcais, & K. Rayner (Eds.), *Comprehension process in reading* (pp. 303–331). Hillsdale, NJ: Erlbaum.

Frazier, L., & Clifton, C. Jr. (1996). *Construal*. Cambridge, MA: MIT Press.

Frazier, L., & Fodor, J.D. (1978). The sausage machine: a two stage parsing model. *Cognition* 6, 291–325.

Frazier, L., & Rayner, K. (1982). Making and correcting errors during sentence comprehension: eye movements in the analysis of structurally ambiguous sentences. *Cognitive Psychology* 14, 178–210.

Gibson, E. (1991). *A computational theory of human linguistic processing: memory limitations and processing breakdown*. Unpublished doctoral dissertation, Carnegie-Mellon University.

Gibson, E., Pearlmutter, N., Canseco-Gonzalez, E., & Hickok, G. (1996a). Recency preference in the human sentence processing mechanism. *Cognition* 59, 23–59.

Gibson, E., Schütze, C.T., & Salomon, A. (1996b). The relationship between the frequency and the processing complexity of linguistic structure. *Journal of Psycholinguistic Research* 25, 59–92.

Gilboy, E., Sopena, J., Frazier, L., & Clifton, C. (1995). Argument structure and association preferences in Spanish and English complex NPs. *Cognition* 54, 131–167.

Gordon, P.C., Grosz, B.J., & Gilliom, L.A. (1993). Pronouns, names, and the centering of attention in discourse. *Cognitive Science* 17, 311–348.

Gorrell, P. (1995). *Syntax and parsing*. Cambridge: Cambridge University Press.

Grosz, B.J, Joshi, A.K., & Weinstein, S. (1983). Providing a unified account of definite noun phrases in discourse. *Proceedings of the 21st International Meeting of the Association for Computational Linguistic*. Cambridge, MA.

Hemforth, B., Konieczny, L., & Scheepers, C. (1994). Probabilistic or universal approaches to sentence processing: how universal is the human language processor? In H. Trost (Ed.), *KONVENS94* (pp. 161–170). Berlin: Springer.

Hemforth, B., Konieczny, L., & Scheepers, C. (1997). *Modifier attachment in German: evidence from eyetracking experiments*. Manuscript in preparation, University of Freiburg, Germany.

Kamide, Y., & Mitchell, D.C. (1997). Relative clause attachment: non-determinism in Japanese parsing. *Journal of Psycholinguistic Research* 26, 247–254.

Konieczny, L. (1996). Human sentence processing: a semantics-oriented parsing approach. *IIG-Berichte* 3/96.

Konieczny, L., Scheepers, C., Hemforth, B., & Strube, G. (1994). Semantikorientierte Syntaxverarbeitung. In S. Felix, C. Habel, & G. Rickheit (Eds.), *Kognitive Linguistik: Repräsentationen und Prozesse*. Opladen: Westdeutscher Verlag.

Mitchell, D.C. (1994). Sentence Parsing. In M. A. Gernsbacher (Ed.), *Handbook of psycholinguistics* (pp. 375–410). San Diego: Academic.

Mitchell, D.C., & Cuetos, F. (1991). The origins of parsing strategies. In C. Smith (Ed.), *Current issues in natural language processing*. Austin, TX: Center for Cognitive Science, University of Texas.

Mitchell, D.C., Cuetos, F., Corley, M.M.B., & Brysbaert, M. (1995). Exposure-based models of human parsing: evidence for the use of coarse-grained (non-lexical) statistical records. *Journal of Psycholinguistic Research* 24, 469–488.

Pritchett, B. (1992). *Grammatical competence and parsing performance*. Chicago: University of Chicago Press.

Pynte, J., & Prieur, B. (1996). Prosodic breaks and attachment decisions in sentence parsing. *Language and Cognitive Processes* 11, 165–191.

Traxler, M. J., Pickering, M.J., & Clifton, C. (1996). *Architectures and mechanisms that process prepositional phrases and relative clauses*. Paper presented at the AMLaP-96 Conference, Torino, Italy.

Schafer, A., & Speer, S. (1997). *The effect of intonational phrasing on lexical interpretation*. Paper presented at the 10th Annual CUNY Conference on Human Sentence Processing.

Zagar, D., Pynte, J., & Rativeau, S. (1997). Evidence for early closure attachment on first-pass reading times in French. *Quarterly Journal of Experimental Psychology* 50A, 421–438.

12
Cross-Linguistic Psycholinguistics

MARICA DE VINCENZI

12.1 Introduction

Historically, most, if not all, of the research on sentence processing has been based on English. In recent years, however, several systematic studies of languages other than English have started. A natural question to ask is what are the reasons to study the processing aspects of languages other than English. The simple answer is to find out what the processing strategies are that the speakers of a specific language adopt. However, there can be two quite different views of psycholinguistics behind such an answer. One reason to do cross-linguistic studies might be the expectation that different languages show different processing strategies, under the assumption that processing strategies are a byproduct of the exposure to a given language. This view of cross-linguistic psycholinguistics implies that processing strategies are not universal, but rather language specific, and that therefore there is no need, at least in principle, to test the same strategy in different languages.

An alternative view of cross-linguistic psycholinguistics stems from the hypothesis that there are universal processing strategies that apply to all languages, because the processing strategies are independent of specific languages and are based on cognitive universals. Several processing strategies are based on such assumptions: Minimal Attachment and Late Closure (Frazier and Fodor, 1978), Right Association (Kimball, 1973), Superstrategy (Fodor, 1979), and the Active Filler Hypothesis (Frazier, 1987). In particular, the two cognitive needs on which the assumed universal parsing strategies are based are economy of derivation and economy of representation. These principles of economy in parsing are based on the limitation of human short term memory and the consequent need to structure the incoming material quickly and to use the fewest rules and simplest representation possible.

However, when we extend the application of a processing strategy to a new language, the need may arise to further specify the strategy to include the parsing of structures that were not present in a previously studied language. This was the case with Italian. Italian, like many other languages, allows phonetically null subjects (as in (1)) and the correlated possibility of postverbal, or inverted, subjects (as in (2b)).

(1) pro Telefonerà
pro will telephone.
(She/he will telephone)

(2) a. Gianni telefonerà.
Gianni will telephone.
b. pro_i Telefonerà $Gianni_i$.
pro_i will telephone $Gianni_i$
(Gianni will telephone)

This means that Italian exhibits linguistic dependencies not present in English and that therefore the parsing principles referring to movement dependencies and empty elements must be revised to include the types of structures in (1) and (2b).

The Minimal Chain Principle (De Vincenzi, 1991), developed for precisely this reason, abstracts away from the type of elements involved (wh-element, overt NP, or null *pro*) and instead focuses attention on the type of relation between an empty element and a lexical element. In this way, the principle unifies the processing of declarative and interrogative sentences.

In so doing, the principle also offers a new perspective on the processing of linguistic dependencies long studied in English. As I will try to show, it permits an account of some psycholinguistic findings that are otherwise irreconcilable with previously formulated processing strategies.

12.2 The Minimal Chain Principle

The hypothesis is that the parser is sensitive to syntactic complexity, in particular to the complexity of chains, which are linguistic objects that define relations among positions in sentences (Chomsky, 1981).

> Minimal Chain Principle (MCP): Avoid postulating unnecessary chain members at surface structure, but do not delay required chain members (De Vincenzi, 1991).

A chain is a syntactic object defined as a set of elements non-distinct in indices (if they have indices), feature content, or category, sharing a single thematic role and a single case, and with each element of the chain in the syntactically defined relation of antecedent government with the next one. The

MCP embodies the idea that chains are costly structures to maintain in short term memory and that therefore the parser tries to complete them as soon as possible, because only in this way is a semantic interpretation of the noun phrase possible. Although the MCP was originally formulated and tested in the processing of Italian, it is based on two processing principles already proposed for English. One is the Active Filler Hypothesis (Frazier, 1987), which says that once an element of category XP is identified as moved from its argument position, the parser posits a corresponding empty XP category as soon as the grammar of the language allows it. The second principle is Fodor's (1979) Superstrategy, which says that a string is analyzed as a well formed deep structure, postulating movement as a last resort. In the MCP, the two principles are subsumed in the following way: Preferentially analyze an element in a singleton chain (i.e., in its deep structure position, as predicted by Superstrategy), but if a chain is required, then complete it as soon as possible (as predicted by Active Filler).

Being based on the notion of chain, the MCP is cast in terms independent of a specific language (there is no reference to language specific structures, elements, or word order). It is therefore applicable to different languages as well as to different structures, such as declaratives and interrogatives, as illustrated in the following sections.

12.2.1 The MCP and the Processing of Declarative Sentences

The shortest chains are singleton chains, with only one linguistic element, such as *pro* in (1) or *Gianni* in (2a). A structure with a postverbal subject as in (2b) contains a two-member chain. There can be an ambiguity between a subject or an object interpretation of a postverbal noun. In this case, the MCP predicts a preference for analyzing a postverbal noun as direct object (occupying its deep structure position) rather than as inverted subject (a two-member chain). There is confirming evidence for this prediction from both Italian and Russian:

In Italian, De Vincenzi (1991) tested sentences like (3), which are structurally ambiguous between the interpretation (3a), where *the seller* is the direct object, and (3b), where *the seller* is the inverted subject. (3c) was the control condition: the verb is intransitive, so the postverbal NP can only be an inverted subject. The prediction was that if the parser follows the MCP, then *the seller* should be initially taken as object in (3a, b). Then, when later information disambiguates it as an inverted subject (as in (3b)), there should be longer reading times due to a reanalysis process. The results confirmed the predictions, showing that the reading times on the dependent clause (*to ask for/offer a discount*), which disambiguates the object or subject analysis of the postverbal noun, are significantly longer in (3b) (the inverted subject condition) than in (a) or (c).

(3) a. Ha richiamato il venditore per chiedere uno sconto.
called the seller to ask for a discount.
(He/she called the seller to ask for a discount)
b. Ha richiamato il venditore per offrire uno sconto.
called the seller to offer a discount.
(The seller called to offer a discount)
c. Ha insistito il venditore per offrire uno sconto.
insisted the seller to offer a discount.
(The seller insisted to offer a discount)

In Russian, Sekerina (1995) has shown the same preferences in processing declaratives with a subject/object ambiguity: namely, reading times were faster for the interpretation in (4a), where the preverbal noun is the subject, than for the one in (4b), where the preverbal noun must be analyzed as an inverted subject.

(4) Trolleybus obonal avtobus
Trolleybus-NOM/ACC passed bus-NOM/ACC
a. The trolleybus passed the bus.
b. The bus passed the trolleybus.

12.2.2 The MCP and the Processing of Wh-Questions

Wh-questions are situations in which the parser unambiguously knows that a non-singleton chain has to be postulated. In this case, the MCP predicts that the missing and obligatory chain member(s) will be postulated as soon as possible. This prediction is similar to the Active Filler Hypothesis, except that while the Active Filler Hypothesis applies to all moved categories, the MCP applies only to those movements that involve an antecedent-government chain. Regarding wh-questions in particular, Cinque (1991) and Rizzi (1990) propose that non-referential wh-phrases (such as WHO, WHAT) enter into antecedent-government chains, while referential wh-phrases (such as WHICH N) enter binding relations. If the parser adopts the MCP and is sensitive to this linguistic distinction, then only non-referential wh-phrases should obey the MCP and show strong active filler behavior.

The reason that the MCP does not apply to WHICH N elements (or to binding chains more generally) is that WHICH N elements can start receiving an interpretation through their D(iscourse)-linking properties[1] (they refer to a group of objects pre-existing in the discourse representation; Enc, 1991), whereas WHO elements can start being interpreted only when linked to the argument structure of a verb.[2]

To illustrate the predictions of the MCP in parsing wh-questions, I will take an Italian example. In Italian, a string of the form WH–transitive verb–NP, as illustrated in (5), is ambiguous between a subject and an object extraction of the wh-phrase, and consequently an object or a subject analysis of the postverbal noun phrase.

(5)

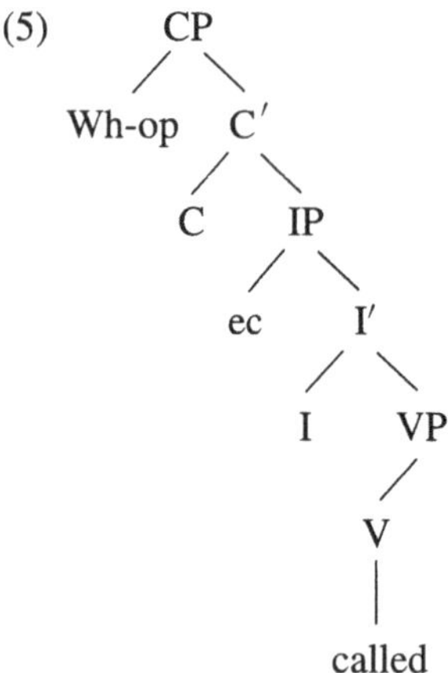

At the verb *called* (i.e., a simple transitive verb) only the required syntactic structure, the IP and VP structures, will be projected. There is an obligatory argument (subject) position, which is lexically empty. If the wh-phrase is of the

[1] See De Vincenzi (1991), chapter VII, for a detailed description of this type of interpretation.

[2] Frazier (this volume) proposes a similar approach. In particular, she proposes that "by allowing a modular interpretation of a DP, its 'referential' interpretation may begin immediately without waiting until a thematic assigner is available to support thematic interpretation of the phrase." My proposal is fully compatible with Frazier's processor: when an element can be referentially interpreted, such as the WHICH N, the processor is relieved by holding it unstructured in short-term memory. However, I crucially propose that this partial semantic interpretation is enough for the parser to suspend an active filler–gap search. This course of action is not possible for WHO-type questions, given that they don't have any specific referential information. In these cases, the processor will start an active gap search to reach a semantic interpretation in terms of thematic role.

WHO type, given the MCP, and given that WHO falls under the MCP, the WHO will immediately enter into an antecedent-government chain with the subject position.

If the wh-phrase is of the WHICH N type, the quantifier can start receiving a partial interpretation through its D-linking properties. When the verb is read, the same syntactic structure can be projected as in (5). However, WHICH N does not fall under the MCP, and the parser is under no pressure to complete an antecedent-government chain. The parser will instead evaluate the possible options for interpreting the available structure. I assume that the decision about the coindexation of the WHICH N and an argument position is made by the coreference processor (cf. Nicol, 1988, 1993), given that the WHICH N dependency is a binding relation, i.e., a relation of coreference similar to the one holding between a pronoun and an antecedent. I assume, following Nicol (1988), that the coreference processor "constitutes an intermediate stage between purely structural processes and interpretative processes".[3] The parser has a lexically empty subject position and a WHICH N dependency, this latter being already partially interpreted. To be fully interpreted, the WHICH N requires an argument position (either empty or lexically filled by a resumptive pronoun) to be coindexed with. Given that the subject position is a possible variable position available for coindexing with the WHICH N, the coreference processor will do so, resulting in a full interpretation for the WHICH N.

Although both WHO and WHICH N end up preferentially coindexed with the first argument (subject) position, the two coindexations are carried out in different manners and for different reasons. In particular, the coindexation of the WHICH N does not occur as a result of a syntactic parsing principle, but rather as a result of a principle of interpretation. One prediction is that WHICH N relationships should be more sensitive to lexical properties of the verb, on the grounds that the coindexing decision is taken on an already built syntactic representation.

When the postverbal NP is reached, it should be immediately attached as direct object (see (6)), the position requiring the least addition of syntactic structure.

[3] In particular, Nicol (1988) proposes that "the parser provides input to the coreference device. Thus, presented with a parse tree and applying information concerning valid coreference relations, the coreference device determines which referents are potential antecedents of a referentially dependent item, and accesses only those referents. This candidate set of referents may then be examined by higher level processes, and the most appropriate referent selected as the antecedent" (Nicol, 1988, p. 124).

(6)

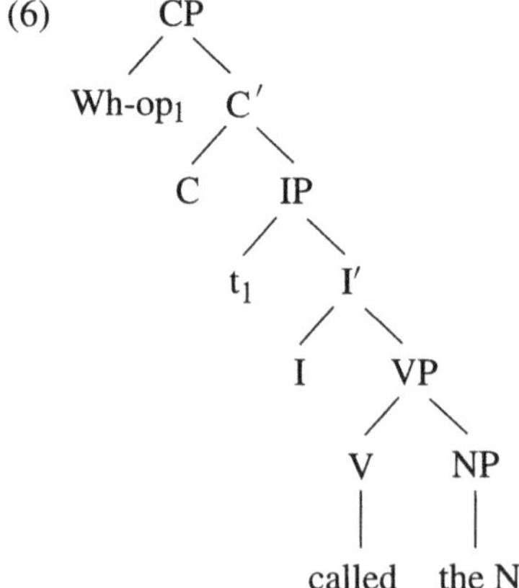

If this attachment has to be revised, there must be a reanalysis process for both types of wh-questions: the postverbal NP should be reanalyzed as the postverbal subject, in a chain with a preverbal position, and the variable in direct object position should be coindexed with the wh-phrase (see (7)).

(7)

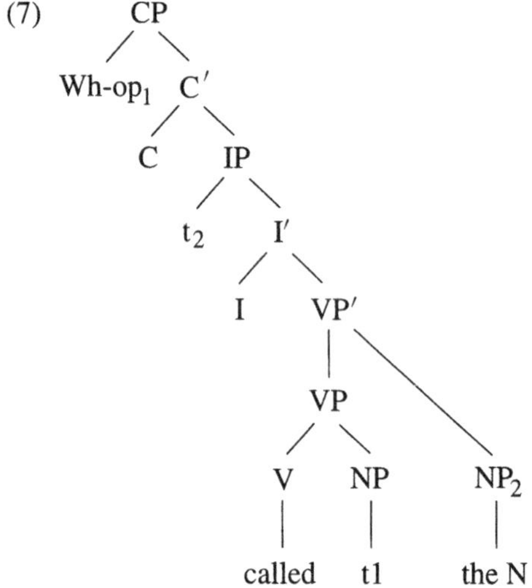

However, we predict a difference in reanalysis between WHO and WHICH N, due to the different types of linguistic relations they enter into. In particular, we predict that the reanalysis of an antecedent-government chain should be more costly than the reanalysis of a binding chain. An antecedent-government relation is a chain relation in which case and thematic role are transmitted from the variable to the operator. This means that for WHO types, changing the analysis from subject to object extraction means changing the case and thematic role features not only on the trace, but also on the wh-element. However, in the case of WHICH N, changing a binding leaves intact its referential index (see De Vincenzi, 1998). What needs to occur is simply the movement of that referential index from a variable in subject position to a variable in object position (cf. Carlson and Tanenhaus, 1988, for a similar interpretation of WHICH N dependencies). It is at some higher, discourse-level interpretation that the WHICH N and its variable are interpreted, in much the same way as a pronoun and its antecedent are interpreted.

These predictions regarding wh-dependencies have been tested in Italian (De Vincenzi, 1996). In the following, I will summarize the Italian data and then discuss their implications for processing theories of wh-movement in general.

12.3 Processing Data from Italian Wh-Questions

12.3.1 On-line Experiments

The Italian experiments (De Vincenzi, 1996) used sentences of the underlying structure WH–Verb–Noun, which presents a subject/object structural ambiguity, given the possibility that the subject appears either pre- or postverbally. We used this structure and a WHO/WHICH N manipulation to test the predictions of the MCP. For both types of wh-phrases, we should find a subject extraction preference, because in this structure the postverbal NP is in a base generated position, as was shown in (6).

However, there should be a further advantage for the subject extraction of the WHO, because the parser, following the MCP, tries to complete a chain immediately.

The experimental sentences had a pragmatic disambiguation on the postverbal noun.[4] The sentences were presented in segments and the task was self-paced reading (see (8)). At the end of each sentence there was a comprehension task, which consisted in the verification of an assertion about the wh-question (two examples are given as Q′ and Q″ in (8)). Therefore, there were three measurements: the reading time on each segment, the time to answer the comprehension question, and the accuracy in the comprehension task.

[4] The material was selected after a rating study to ensure that the plausibility of the subject/object extractions was similar for the two types of wh-phrase. See De Vincenzi, 1994 for a detailed description of the rating study and the material.

(8) a. Chi/ha licenziato//il metalmeccanico//senza dare/il preavviso?
a. Who/ fired// the steelworker// without giving/ notice?
a′. Chi/ha licenziato//il proprietario//senza dare/il preavviso?
a′. Who/ fired// the owner// without giving/ notice?
b. Quale ingegnere/ha licenziato//il metalmeccanico//senza dare/il preavviso?
b. Which engineer/fired//the steelworker//without giving/notice?
b′. Quale ingegnere/ha licenziato//il proprietario//senza dare/il preavviso?
b′. Which engineer/fired//the owner//without giving/notice?
Q′. Il metalmeccanico è stato licenziato da qualcuno, SI o NO?
Q′. The steelworker was fired by someone, YES or NO?
Q″. L'impiegato è stato licenziato da qualcuno, SI o NO?
Q″. The white collar was fired by someone, YES or NO?

The results showed faster reading times and higher accuracy for subject extraction for both types of wh-phrases. However, there was a processing asymmetry between WHO and WHICH N at two points. First, on the disambiguating segment, reading was faster for the subject extraction only for WHO. Second, in the comprehension task, questions about subject extraction were answered significantly faster than questions about object extraction only for WHO.

The same effects were obtained for wh-extraction across a clause boundary in a second experiment. The sentences were modified introducing main verbs that take sentential complements, such as *think* or *believe*. Consider the example in (9):

(9) Chi pensi abbia licenziato il metalmeccanico senza preavviso?
Who do you think fired the steelworker without notice?

The results of this second experiment are important in establishing that the parsing routines are the same across clause boundaries (as found in English by Frazier and Clifton, 1989), as long as the relevant syntactic structures remain the same. Once this baseline was established, a third experiment tested the same ambiguity and extraction across a clause boundary, but this time manipulating the structure of the embedded sentence, in such a way that antecedent-government chains, and only antecedent-government chains, were affected. In Italian, wh-subject extraction from an embedded sentence with a lexically filled complementizer is associated with a three-member chain (cf. Rizzi, 1982), in order to fulfill the syntactic requirement of proper government of the empty category in embedded subject position:

(10) Chi$_i$ credi che pro$_i$ telefonerà t$_i$?
Who$_i$ do you think that pro$_i$ will telephone t$_i$?

Thus the subject extraction of a wh-element that enters in a antecedent-government chain (such as WHO/WHAT) should be penalized because it is more complex than a wh-object one. By contrast, wh-dependencies that do not entail an antecedent-government chain, such as WHICH N, should not be affected by this manipulation.

The sentences of the previous experiment were thus modified introducing the complementizer *che* 'that' after the upstairs verb, as in (11).

(11) Chi pensi che abbia licenziato il metalmeccanico senza preavviso?
Who do you think that fired the steelworker without notice?

The results showed that subject extraction cases were still facilitated in terms of reading times and higher accuracy. However, contrary to the preceding experiments, the facilitation in the reading time on the disambiguation segment and in the comprehension time for the WHO subject extraction was lost. This selective effect on the WHO subject extraction therefore confirms the hypothesis that only WHO enters antecedent government chains, the only chains affected by the Empty Category condition.[5]

12.3.2 Questionnaire Data

As suggested in the preceding discussion, a consequence of the fact that the WHICH N coindexation does not fall under the MCP, but rather is performed by the coreference processor, is that WHICH N dependencies should be more open to nonstructural manipulations; they should be more likely to be influenced by those aspects of sentence interpretation that are not purely structural. If this is true, an interesting prediction is that the manipulation of definiteness of the postverbal noun phrase should have a significant effect on WHICH N dependencies, but not on WHO dependencies. This hypothesis was tested in a questionnaire study (De Vincenzi, 1990) that used subject/object ambiguities of wh-extraction in Italian, manipulating the type of wh-phrase (WHO vs. WHICH N) and the definiteness of the postverbal noun phrase, as illustrated in (12):

(12) a. Who called the boy?
b. Who called a boy?

[5] This result supports the psychological reality of empty categories, contra Pickering and Barry (1991) and Sag and Fodor (1995).

a′. Which girl called the boy?
b′. Which girl called a boy?

The questionnaire was administered to thirty-two native speakers of Italian. Each subject saw twelve experimental sentences, plus other sentences with different constructions, like declaratives and embedded wh-questions, for a total of forty sentences. Subjects received a booklet with one sentence on each page. The task was to indicate with a mark one of two alternative interpretations. The results in (13) confirmed our hypothesis:

(13) Percentage of wh-subject interpretation

Who – definite NP	89%
Who – indefinite NP	97%
Which N – definite NP	65%
Which N – indefinite NP	89%

In particular, the results showed that the effect of definiteness, that is, the preference to take a definite NP as signalling a discourse topic and therefore subject (cf. Firbas, 1966; Halliday, 1979), shows up only with WHICH N cases (a decrement to 65% of WHICH N subject interpretation), which do not enter strictly syntactic antecedent-government chains and therefore are more open to nonstructural manipulations.

12.3.3 Some Conclusions from the Italian Data

The first conclusion that we can draw is that the parser is sensitive to syntactic chain complexity (cf. Experiments 1 & 2) and that the relevant notion of minimal chain is not merely the shortest distance between filler and gap, but rather the complexity of the chain (in number of elements) between filler and gap (cf. Experiment 3).

The second conclusion is that there are asymmetries in the processing of WHO and WHICH N. The first asymmetry is in the type of movements that the two types of wh-phrases entail. In particular, as shown by Experiment 3, WHO must move successive-cyclically, that is, it has to obey syntactic locality conditions, and therefore it shows the ECP effects in subject extraction across a lexical complementizer. WHICH N, on the other hand, can move long-distance, presumably coindexing with an empty pronominal subject and thereby avoiding the ECP effect.

This finding supports Rizzi's and Cinque's theory of movement. Further, it is important to underline that this analysis of the difference between WHO and WHICH N is not restricted to Italian, neither linguistically (cf. Pesetsky, 1987, for English; Engdahl, 1985, for Swedish; Comorovsky, 1985, for Romanian;

Chung, 1994, for Chamorro) nor empirically. It is corroborated by similar findings with English aphasics (see Hickok and Avrutin, 1995, for a processing dissociation of WHO and WHICH N types of dependencies) and with children. Thornton (1995) has found evidence that in embedded-subject extraction, children treat WHICH N questions differently from WHO questions: In WHO questions (14) they produce a medial wh-phrase, as if doing successive-cyclic movement. In WHICH N questions (15) children leave a resumptive pronoun, as if doing long movement.

(14) Who do you think who's under there?
What do you think what's in the box?

(15) Which bug do you think it jumped onto Superman's hand?
Which bear do you think it ate a piece of chocolate?
Which boy do you think it fell down?

A second asymmetry between WHO/WHICH concerns reanalysis: at comprehension time we found reanalysis costs for WHO, but not for WHICH N. We predicted this effect on the basis of the hypothesis that WHICH N entails binding relations, similar to the ones holding between a pronominal element and its antecedent.

Finally, a third difference between the wh-phrases is that WHICH N dependencies are more open to nonstructural manipulations. This difference is again a consequence of the fact that WHICH N enters binding relations, which are established at a stage after structure building operations.

12.4 Extending the Observations from Italian to Other Languages

We have seen that the two types of wh-dependencies described by linguistic theory are treated differently by the parser. This parsing difference is important because, given that the distinction between types of wh-dependencies has been found in linguistic data, acquisition, and aphasic performance, it would have been very peculiar if that the human language processor ignored such a distinction (cf. De Vincenzi, 1998, for discussion). Further, the fact that this distinction has been found in so many areas of language processing allows us to hypothesize that a processing difference should be present not only in Italian, but also in other languages that have the two types of dependencies. In the following, I will therefore briefly review some psycholinguistic literature that seems to support this processing distinction in other languages. I will show that apparent inconsistencies in the literature can be understood under the assumption that only WHO-type dependencies, which enter antecedent-government chains, count for the MCP and elicit an active filler search.

12.4.1 Back to English

The first prediction that we can draw is that the experiments that use bare quantifiers will be the ones most likely to show syntactic effects on filler-gap dependencies, given that bare wh-phrases enter a stricter grammatical relation, subject to all the constraints on proper government. This has been shown in Italian in extraction from an embedded clause with a lexical complementizer (Experiment 3). Interestingly, if we look at experiments conducted in English, we find that those experiments showing syntactic effects on wh-movement did in fact use quantifiers of the WHO/WHAT type: Stowe (1986) and Traxler and Pickering (1996) showed subject-island violation effects with WHO-type quantifiers, and Frazier and Clifton (1989) showed evidence for successive-cyclic movement across a clause boundary with WHICH-types of quantifiers.

Another prediction that we can make on the basis of the Italian data is that WHICH N dependencies should be more sensitive to lexical properties. Given that a binding relation is a structure coindexing operation, as opposed to a structure building operation (see Berwick and Weinberg, 1984, for a similar distinction), it may take place after the building of the syntactic structure, when other types of linguistic information are available and may be used by the parser.

It seems that there is supporting evidence for this hypothesis from English. Boland, Tanenhaus, Garnsey, and Carlson (1995) have shown an effect of verb-argument structure in processing WHICH N questions. The experiments tested wh-questions containing either simple transitive verbs (16) or verbs (17) that provide more than one potential gap site due to their subcategorization properties.

(16) Which client/contract did the secretary call before going to lunch?

(17) Which film/audience did the salesman show at the medical convention?

The experimental task was to press a button as soon as the sentence stopped making sense; the WHICH N were either plausible or implausible with respect to the first gap position. The results show that in the case of simple transitive verbs there was a plausibility effect at the verb. The effect was absent when the verb provided multiple gap positions and the second gap was plausible for the filler. The result is consistent with the model proposed here. In the Boland et al. experiment, the MCP should not apply, because the WHICH N cases are not antecedent-government chains. Rather, they involve binding relations, where we assume that it is the coreference processor which evaluates the possible argument positions for a coindexation of the WHICH N phrase. If the verb has more than one obligatory argument position, then if the direct object (theme) position is not a plausible position for coindexation, coindexation will not be performed.[6] Notice that the Boland et al. result (as also pointed out by Gorrell, 1996) is inconsistent with a parsing model which predicts a preference to fill the first available gap position, such as a pure Active Filler hypothesis, regardless of the type of wh-dependency.

The distinction between types of wh-elements seems necessary to explain some conflicting evidence on the use of lexical information in processing wh-questions in English. Tanenhaus, Stowe, and Carlson (1985) and Stowe, Tanenhaus, and Carlson (1991), using a grammaticality judgment task and self-paced, word-by-word reading, provide evidence in favor of lexical effects, specifically verb transitivity, in parsing wh-questions. The experimental sentences contained an embedded wh-question in which the wh-phrase was either the object of the verb (Early Gap condition) or the object of a preposition that followed the verb (Late Gap condition). The wh-phrases were either plausible or implausible as the object of the verb for the Early Gap sentences. Both plausible and implausible wh-phrases were equally plausible for the Late Gap sentences. So, plausibility effects with Late Gap sentences are taken to mean that subjects initially filled the false Early Gap.

(18) Transitive preference verbs
  a. The district attorney found out which (witness/church) the reporter ASKED ( ) about the meeting. (Early Gap)
  b. The district attorney found out which (witness/church) the reporter ASKED anxiously about ( ). (Late Gap)

(19) Intransitive verbs
  a. The sheriff wasn't sure which (horse, rock) the cowboy RACED ( ) down the hill. (Early Gap)
  b. The sheriff wasn't sure which (horse, rock) the cowboy RACED ( ) desperately past ( ). (Late Gap)

While for the preferred transitive verbs there was an effect of plausibility with both Early and Late Gap (18a, b), with the preferred intransitive verbs there was an effect of plausibility only with Early Gap sentences (19a), suggesting that the parser does not preferentially posit a gap after an intransitive verb. This indicates that gaps are initially posited only following preferred transitive verbs, therefore supporting a lexical expectation model of filler-gap assignment. Furthermore,

[6] A prediction of the MCP is that if the wh-elements had been of the WHO/WHAT type, a plausibility effect would have shown up also with dative verbs, at least when compared to WHICH N sentences.

for transitive preference verbs, Late Gap sentences were not more difficult to comprehend than Early Gap sentences, suggesting that there was little cost in reassigning a wh-filler from an Early to a Late Gap. Carlson and Tanenhaus (1988) suggest that wh-filler–gap assignment is not a syntactically driven process, but rather "a process of thematic assignment, where thematic assignment is an indexing and reindexing operation of the same general sort as reference assignment operations." However, Frazier and Clifton (1989) found the opposite result, that is, an effect of wh-assignment to a gap following intransitive verbs:

(20) Intransitive verbs
   a. What did the silly young man whisper ( ) to his fiancee during the movie? (Early Gap)
   b. What did the silly young man whisper ( ) to his fiancee about ( ) during the movie? (Late Gap)

The reading time on the critical words in (20b, *to his fiancee about*) were longer than in (20a, *to his fiancee*), as if subjects had initially posited a gap after the verb in (20b) as well. Frazier and Clifton concluded that gaps are posited after transitive and intransitive expectation verbs, and therefore that wh-assignment is a filler-driven process, as predicted by the Active Filler Hypothesis.

The conclusions from these two sets of experiments are mutually exclusive: either you have a view of the parser that treats wh-dependencies as active fillers, positing gaps in a top-down manner, or you have a parser that treats wh-dependencies as thematic relations, positing gaps in a bottom-up manner. However, the type of wh-elements used in the two sets of experiments were different. In particular, Tanenhaus, Stowe, and Carlson (1985) and Stowe, Tanenhaus, and Carlson (1991) used WHICH N, while Frazier and Clifton (1989) used WHAT/WHO. The WHICH N cases showed lexical effects, while the WHO/WHAT cases showed a filler-gap effect regardless of lexical effects. This distinct behavior is predicted by the MCP: there is a unique parser, which operates in a modular fashion, and consequently it treats wh-dependencies differently depending on the type of linguistic dependencies they entail and on the different levels of linguistic representation at which these dependencies are relevant.

A third observation made in the Italian data was that there were no reanalysis costs for WHICH N quantifiers. This is directly confirmed by Tanenhaus et al.'s finding of no cost for Late Gaps with transitive sentences, given that they used only WHICH N types of quantifiers, where only a re-coindexing operation is needed.

12.4.2 Extending the Observations to Other Languages

A prediction made on the basis of the WHO/WHICH N type distinction is that in general and cross-linguistically, bare wh-phrases will show stronger "active filler" behavior, given that they are the only ones that fall under the MCP, and that they will elicit a top-down, active filler-gap search. It seems to me that there is some support for this claim from Dutch and German. Although I won't review or discuss all the experiments on wh-questions, I would like to point to some experiments that show a variable active filler behavior for WHICH N and a stronger one for WHO. In Dutch and German, a string such as WH–Verb–NP has the same subject/object extraction ambiguity as in Italian (although based on a different underlying structure). Several experiments have shown conflicting evidence for the WHICH N subject preferences in Dutch and German.

In Dutch, Frazier and Flores D'Arcais (1989) studied subject/object ambiguities in wh-questions. The sentences had number agreement disambiguation for the subject or object extraction; the task was speeded grammaticality judgment.

(21) a. Welke arbeiders prijzen de voorman?
Which workers praise-pl. the foreman?
b. Welke arbeiders prijst de voorman?
Which workers praise-sg. the foreman?
Which workers did the foreman praise?

The results showed that the wh-subject extractions (as in (21a)) had significantly fewer errors than wh-object extractions (as in (21b)). However, Kaan (1997) in two experiments with self-paced reading and in one with continuous grammaticality judgment, failed to observe a WHICH N subject-extraction preference. In particular, the (22b) versions, with a wh-object extraction, were not slower to read than the (22a) versions.

(22) a. Accusative Grammatical/Ungrammatical (SOV)
Ik vroeg welke vrienden hem in het dorp aan de kust hadden/*had opgezocht.
I asked which friends him in the village at the seaside had-pl/*had-sg visited
b. Nominative Grammatical/Ungrammatical (OSV)
Ik vroeg welke vrienden hij in het dorp aan de kust had/*hadden opgezocht.
I asked which friends he in the village at the seaside had-sg/*had-pl visited

While these conflicting results are problematic for a simple active filler treatment of wh-dependencies, they are compatible with the MCP. In particular, the failure to observe an immediate filler-gap effect in sentences with WHICH N dependencies suggests that the WHICH N is coindexed by a coreference processor. This processor presumably operates on the independently created syntactic structures and results in easily revised coindexing assignments. In particular, in Kaan's experiment, it is possible that the parser does not commit itself to a subject extraction, unless unambiguously required by the grammar. In this case, the appearance of subject pronoun (as in the (b) versions) does not provoke any reanalysis.

In German, using sentence with a case-marking disambiguation on the postverbal noun phrase, Farke and Felix (1994) found WHICH N object extraction preference, and Schlesewsky, Fanselow, Kliegl, and Krems (in press) found no subject- or object-extraction preference.

(23) Welche Frau liebt der/den Mann?
Which woman loves the nom/acc man?

These results are problematic for the assumption of simple active filler effects in processing wh-questions, but are predicted by the MCP. Further, the MCP predicts that in sentences containing a WHO type of wh-phrase, there should be a subject-extraction preference. This prediction seems confirmed by some preliminary results obtained by Schlesewsky et al. (in press), who found a subject-extraction preference for the bare quantifier WHAT, using the same type of postverbal disambiguation:

(24) a. Was erforderte den Einbruch in die Nationalbank?
What required the-acc break into the national bank?
b. Was erforderte der Einbruch in die Nationalbank?
What required the-nom break into the national bank?

Notice that the different results in (23) and (24) cannot be explained in terms of types of disambiguation, because the disambiguation was the same in both cases, namely case marking on the postverbal noun phrase.[7]

[7] Interestingly, with number disambiguation on the verb, both Schlesewsky et al. and Meng (1995) found a WHICH N subject-extraction preference. The WHICH N was always singular, and the verb could be either singular or plural. The results showed that the plural verb was read slower than the singular verb, as if the parser had to reanalyze the WHICH N from subject to object. However, an alternative interpretation is possible: namely, that the slower reading times in the case of WHICH N object extraction at the plural verb are due to the fact that more structure must be built than in the singular verb case.

12.5 Conclusions

The aim of this presentation was to show how cross-linguistic testing of universal parsing strategy can be a useful enterprise for several reasons. One reason is to study language processing routines in several different languages. The second is that processing facts that are more easily observable in one language can feed back new insights in analyzing some conflicting evidence in other languages. Further, extending parsing strategies to new languages, with different types of linguistic elements and different constructions, can help us to clarify what are the really general parameters of parsing, such as the concept of chain, that unify the processing of declarative and interrogative sentences.

References

Berwick, R. and Weinberg, A. (1984) *The grammatical basis of linguistic performance.* Cambridge, MA: MIT Press.

Boland, J., Tanenhaus, M., Garnsey, S., and Carlson, G. (1995) Verb argument structure in parsing and interpretation: Evidence from wh-questions. *Journal of Memory and Language* 34, 774–806.

Chomsky, N. (1981) *Lectures on Government and Binding.* Dordrecht: Foris.

Chung, S. (1994) Wh-agreement and "referentiality" in Chamorro. *Linguistic Inquiry* 25, 1–44.

Cinque, G. (1992) *Types of A′ dependencies*, Cambridge, MA: MIT Press.

Carlson, G. and Tanenhaus, M. (1988) Thematic Roles and Language Comprehension. In W. Wilkins (ed.), *Thematic Relations*, 263–288. New York: Academic Press.

Comorovsky, I. (1985) Discourse-linked wh-phrases. Paper read at the Annual Meeting of the LSA, Seattle, WA.

De Vincenzi, M. (1990) Processing of wh-dependencies in a null-subject language: Referential and non-referential whs. In B. Plunkett (ed.) *UMOP 15, Psycholinguistics*, 91–118.

De Vincenzi, M. (1991) *Syntactic parsing strategies in Italian.* Dordrecht: Kluwer.

De Vincenzi, M. (1994) The use of syntax in the comprehension process: evidence from Italian. *Folia Linguistica: Acta Societatis Linguisticae Europeae* 28, 139–173.

De Vincenzi, M. (1996) Syntactic analysis in sentence comprehension: Effects of dependency types and grammatical constraints. *Journal of Psycholinguistic Research* 25, 117–133.

De Vincenzi, M. (1998) Reanalysis aspects of movement. In J. Fodor and F. Ferreira (eds.), *Reanalysis in sentence processing*. Dordrecht: Kluwer.

Enç, M. (1991) The semantics of specificity. *Linguistic Inquiry* 22, 1–25.

Engdahl, E. (1980) Wh-constructions in Swedish and the relevance of subjacency. *Proceedings of NELS 10*, 89–108.

Farke, H. and Felix, S. W. (1994) Subject-Objektasymmetrien in der Sprachverarbeitung. In S. W. Felix, C. Habel, and G. Rickheit (eds.), *Kognitive Linguistik*, 75–106. Opladen: Westdeutscher Verlag.

Firbas, J. (1966) On defining the theme in functional sentence analysis. *Travaux Linguistiques de Prague* 1, 267–280.

Fodor, J. D. (1979) Superstrategy. In W. E. Cooper and E. C. T. Walker (eds.), *Sentence processing*, Hillsdale, NJ: Erlbaum.

Frazier, L. (1987) Processing syntactic structures: Evidence from Dutch. *Natural Language and Linguistic Theory* 5, 519–559.

Frazier, L. and Fodor, J. D. (1978) The sausage machine: A new two-stage parsing model. *Cognition* 6, 291–326.

Frazier, L. and Flores D'Arcais, G. B. (1989) Filler-driven parsing: A study of gap-filling in Dutch. *Journal of Memory and Language* 28, 331–344.

Frazier, L., and Clifton, C. (1989) Successive cyclicity in the grammar and the parser. *Language and Cognitive Processes* 4, 93–126.

Gorrell, P. (1996) *The Subject-before-object preference in German clauses.* Unpublished manuscript, Max Planck Institute for Cognitive Neuroscience.

Halliday, M. A. K. (1970) Language structure and language function. In J. Lyons (ed.), *New horizons in linguistics*, 140–165. Baltimore: Penguin.

Hickok, G. and Avrutin, S. (in press) Comprehension of wh-questions in two Broca's aphasics. *Brain and Language.*

Kaan, E. (1997) *Processing subject-object ambiguities in Dutch.* Doctoral dissertation, Universiteit Groningen.

Kimball, J. (1973) Seven principles of surface structure parsing in natural language. *Cognition* 2, 15–47.

Meng, M. (1995) Processing wh-questions in German and Dutch: Differential effects of disambiguation and their interpretation. Poster presented at AMLaP95, Edinburgh.

Nicol, J. L. (1988) *Coreference processing during sentence comprehension.* Doctoral dissertation, MIT.

Nicol, J. L. (1993) Reconsidering reactivation. In G. Altmann and P. Shillcock (eds.), *Cognitive models of speech processing.* Hillsdale, NJ: Erlbaum.

Pesetsky, D. (1987) Wh-in-situ: Movement and unselective binding. In A. Ter Meulen and E. Reuland (eds.), *Representation of (in)definiteness*, Cambridge, MA: MIT Press.

Pickering, M. and Barry, G. (1991) Sentence processing without empty categories. *Language and Cogntive Processes* 6, 229–259.

Rizzi, L. (1982) *Issues in Italian syntax.* Dordrecht: Foris.

Rizzi, L. (1990) *Relativized Minimality.* Cambridge, MA: MIT Press.

Sag, I. and Fodor, J. D. (1995) Extraction without traces. In R. Aranovich, W. Byrne, S. Preuss, and M. Senturia (eds.) *Proceedings of the 13th West Coast Conference on Formal Linguistics*, 365–384. Stanford, CA: Stanford Linguistics Association.

Schlesewsky, M., Fanselow, G., Kliegl, R., and Krems, J. (in press) Locally ambiguous wh-questions in German. To appear in B. Hemforth and L. Konieczny (eds.), *Cognitive Parsing in German.*

Sekerina, I. (1995) Ambiguity and scrambling in Russian syntactic processing. Paper presented at the 8th CUNY Conference on Human Sentence Processing.

Stowe, L. (1986) Parsing wh-constructions. *Language and Cognitive Processes* 2, 227–246.

Stowe, L., Tanenhaus, M., and Carlson, G. (1991) Filling gaps on-line: use of lexical and semantic information in sentence processing. *Language and Speech* 34, 319–340.

Tanenhaus, M., Stowe, L., and Carlson, G. (1985) The interaction of lexical expectation and pragmatics in parsing filler-gap constructions. *Proceedings of the Seventh Annual Cognitive Science Society Meeting*, 361–365. Hillsdale, NJ: Erlbaum.

Thornton, R. (1995) Referentiality and Wh-movement in child English: Juvenile D-linkuency. *Language Acquisition* 4, 139–175.

Traxler, M. J. and Pickering, M. J. (1996) Plausibility and the processing of unbounded dependencies: An eye-tracking study. *Journal of Memory and Language* 35, 454–475.

Part IV

Interpretation

13
On Interpretation: Minimal 'Lowering'

LYN FRAZIER

13.1 Introduction

In psycholinguistics, the investigation of grammatical aspects of interpretation has lagged behind the study of parsing. Ambiguity in the interpretation of a phrase has not generally been studied except in the case of lexical ambiguity. The present chapter will explore the preferences perceivers exhibit when a phrase might be interpreted in more than one way, focusing on the interpretation of Determiner Phrases (DPs). This will allow us to address the issue of whether the referential interpretation of a DP and its thematic interpretation must go hand in hand, occurring simultaneously, or whether these interpretation processes are initially (potentially) distinct. What is meant by "early" interpretation of a phrase (see the introductory chapter of this volume) is completely unclear until this issue of interpretive separability, or non-separability, has been resolved.

Two recent developments in linguistic theory open up a promising avenue to pursue in the investigation of semantic interpretation. The first development, critical to the arguments presented here, is Diesing's (1992) Mapping Hypothesis, which establishes a constraint between syntax and interpretation. DPs outside VP (at L(ogical) F(orm), in English) are presupposed or quantificational; the VP is identified as the "nuclear scope," where asserted and thus focal information typically appears. Hence, only DPs within VP get an existential interpretation – essentially an interpretation where a new entity (one not presupposed in context or by shared background assumptions of the speaker and hearer) is introduced into discourse.[1] Compare (1a) and (1b).

I am grateful to Chuck Clifton, Janina Radó, and two anonymous reviewers for comments on the manuscript. This work was supported by NIH Grant HD-18708 to Clifton and Frazier and NSF Grant DBS-9121375 to Rayner and Frazier.

[1] The specific version of Diesing's Mapping Hypothesis that I will adopt is summarized in (i).

(i) VP-external at LF: presuppositional interpretation, quantificational interpretations | VP-internal at LF: existential interpretations

I will assume that the VP is the nuclear scope, where asserted information is expected to appear. Perceivers seem to expect non-contrastively focused information to appear in the VP. However, I will not assume that only asserted information can appear in the VP.

(1) a. There's a dog in the garden.
b. A (certain) dog is in the garden.

A dog is in VP in (1a) and therefore receives an existential interpretation.[2] In (1b) *a dog* may get an existential interpretation if the subject 'lowers' into its VP-internal subject position at LF. However, it need not lower. If it doesn't lower, it may be presupposed. (Consider *A certain someone is in the garden*, which naturally receives a presupposed interpretation.)

The predictions of the Mapping Hypothesis concerning the possible interpretation of a DP depend on the position that a DP occupies at LF. Following Runner (1995), I will assume that all subject and object DPs sit outside VP at surface structure in English. In this theory, the subject and object(s) move from VP-internal positions to Agreement nodes to receive case in the specifier of Agreement, as indicated in (2). The verb raises above the object to the Tense node. (Runner actually views movement as a copy and deletion process.)[3] I make the standard assumption that a moved phrase and its corresponding trace(s) are coindexed and thus form a chain.

[2] In the theory presented by Runner (1995), there is no expletive replacement at LF. (All forms of A-movement are prohibited at LF.) Therefore, *A dog* in (1a) must remain in VP at LF.

[3] In Runner's theory, case is systematically checked in specifier position of subject agreement phrases (Agr_SP) and object agreement phrases (Agr_OP). Case checking occurs at s-structure, before the split to Logical Form (LF). Runner develops this idea in a theory where movement of a phrase is treated as copy and deletion, yielding structures like (1) before the Phonetic Form (PF)/LF split (essentially before s-structure). Deletion of a particular copy of a phrase at a particular level of representation is then governed by grammatical conditions. In (i), the lower copies must delete by s-structure (before the PF/LF split) because only the higher phrases in Spec Agr_SP, Tense Phrase (TP) and Spec Agr_OP are in the appropriate positions for checking case and tense features.

Runner's theory is adopted here because it is explicit and offers an independently motivated theory of representations which places DPs in positions at s-structure (specifier positions) where they could be interpreted with respect to their referential (i.e., nonthematic) properties. Given Runner's representations, a subject or object DP could be interpreted as an operator at s-structure because it is not in an argument position – a position where an operator generally cannot appear since there would be no variable for it to bind. (Here and throughout, I set aside the strictly local prefixing required to get restricted quantification where only entities of the type of the N are quantified over.) Runner's representations are also motivated by a wide range of basic empirical observations showing (a) that the direct object in English is external to VP, as indicated by coordination, right node raising, stylistic inversions, adverb placement, etc., (b) that the second object in double-object structures is VP-external, as indicated by binding properties, quantifier scope, coordination, and adverb placement, and (c) that the accusative NP in Exceptional Case Marking constructions (*I believe* him *to have convinced Ben*) is raised to Spec Agr_OP, as indicated by binding properties, the distribution and interpretation of adverbs, the behavior of floated quantifiers, and the behavior of particle verbs (where the particle may follow the accusative phrase, as in *I made him out to be a liar.*) In short, the representations are quite well motivated, especially with respect to the property that is crucial here, namely, VP-external placement of both subject and DP objects at s-structure.

(i) $[_{SpecAgr_SP} \text{John}_i\ [_{TP} \text{kissed}_j\ [_{SpecAgr_OP} \text{Mary}_k\ [_{VP} \text{John}_i\ [_{V'} \text{kissed}_j\ [_{DP} \text{Mary}_k]]]]]]$

(2)

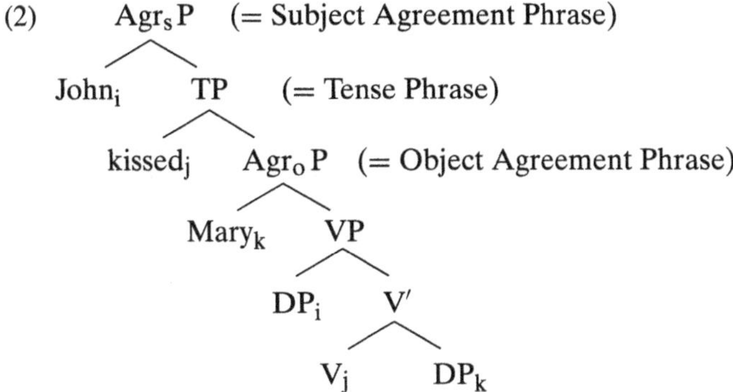

Given Runner's surface structures, the subject and object already occupy potential operator positions (nonargument positions) at surface structure. Therefore, I will assume that Quantifier Raising of a subject or object is not obligatory for quantificational subjects or objects. In other words, in a sentence like *Everyone kissed someone*, the s-structure (one just like in (2)) already corresponds to a potential LF representation, namely the wide-scope universal representation, where the subject (*everyone*) takes scope over the object.

The assumption that the subject of an English sentence occupies a VP-external position at s-structure is completely uncontroversial. The assumption that objects of the verb also occupy a VP-external position at s-structure is controversial (see Note 3 for arguments supporting the assumption). However, only one of the arguments in this chapter (Section 2.5) crucially depends on this assumption. The other arguments would stand even if the assumption about the surface position of objects should prove incorrect.

Turning now to psycholinguistic issues, the question is how the processor interprets ambiguous DPs. With others, I assume that the parser initially constructs a s-structure representation of a sentence, as part of the overall comprehension process. In this chapter, I will argue that the position of (the overt copy of) a phrase, not the position of its trace, determines its interpretation with respect to referential (nonthematic) properties. Specifically, I will argue that the processor follows the Minimal 'Lowering' principle in (3). To forestall any terminological confusion, it should be emphasized at the outset that 'lowering' is not a grammatical operation – this term is adopted only for expositional convenience to indicate where in a structure the referential content of a phrase is interpreted.

(3) 'Lower' only when necessary, e.g., interpret a DP in its surface position if possible.

The principle in (3) may be viewed as an instruction to the language processor to assume, in the absence of evidence to the contrary, that the lexical phrase (overt copy) is in the highest position in its chain and interpret the phrase in that position. The principle in (3) instructs the processor to lower the phrase (e.g., to a VP-internal position) only when presented with evidence requiring lowering. The referential interpretation of a phrase, as opposed to its thematic interpretation (what thematic role it receives), will be assigned to the overt phrase, not to its trace. Thus a phrase will, if possible, be referentially interpreted in the highest position it could occupy in the surface syntactic representation.

The Minimal Lowering (ML) principle makes numerous specific predictions. It is to these that we now turn.

13.2 Predictions and Evidence

13.2.1 Interpretation of Indefinite DPs

The ML principle predicts that lowering a lexical phrase into the VP will be dispreferred. Schematically, this is shown in (4), where lowering of the subject into the VP is not required.

(4) A dog was in the garden.

a. $[_{\text{SpecAgr}_s\text{P}}$ A dog_i $[_{\text{TP}}$ was $[_{\text{VP}}$ $t_i t_v$ $[_{\text{PP}}$ in the garden]]]]

b. [DP_i [was $[_{\text{VP}}$ a dog_i t_v [in the garden]]]]

(lowering from DP_i to a dog_i marked X)

This predicts that a presupposed interpretation of the subject is preferred. Intuitions in this case are subtle and complicated: the indefinite determiner *a* resists a presuppositional interpretation, which may constitute evidence that lowering of the DP is necessary.

In order to test the ML principle, it is necessary to find genuinely ambiguous examples where either a lowered or an unlowered interpretation is possible. Consider (5), for example. In (5b) *three ships* may be presupposed (included in the set of five ships introduced in (5a)), or *three ships* may be interpreted existentially, as introducing the existence of three new ships into the discourse context.

(5) a. Five ships appeared on the horizon.

b. Three ships sank.

Given the context provided by (5a), there is a clear intuitive preference to give a specific (presupposed) interpretation to (5b), where *three ships* are taken as a subset of the five ships introduced in (5a). In a written questionnaire study conducted with Chuck Clifton (Frazier and Clifton, in progress), twenty subjects were given sixteen examples like (5) and asked a question about the interpretation of the subject of the second sentence. For example, following (5b), the question was: Were the three ships that sank among the five ships that appeared on the horizon? 80% of the responses indicated that perceivers assigned the presuppositional interpretation. Thus, the unlowered interpretation was preferred, as predicted by the ML principle.

Intuitions about scope provide further evidence that indefinites are preferentially interpreted in their surface position. Consider (6).

(6) a. A man seems/doesn't seem to be sick.
 b. It seems/doesn't seem a man is sick.

Despite the presence of the indefinite determiner *a* in (6),[4] *a man* preferentially receives a presupposed interpretation in (6a), with scope over the entire sentence. This is clearest with the negative sentence form. *A man doesn't seem to be sick* can clearly be used in a context where there are many sick men, providing that some man isn't sick. Not so in (6b). *It doesn't seem a man is sick* only receives the interpretation where *a man* is under the scope of the negative, meaning, roughly, that *it seems no man is sick.* Intuitions suggest that the initial or preferred interpretation of (6a) differs from the interpretation of (6b), indicating that perceivers have not taken the option of lowering the subject in (6a).

13.2.2 Quantifier Scope in Sentences with Multiple Quantifiers

The details of perceivers' preferred interpretation of scopally ambiguous sentences are complicated and have never been fully explained. However, the gross pattern of preferences is clear. In cases of ambiguity involving more than one plausible interpretation, the subject tends to take scope over the indirect object (of a double object verb), which itself takes scope over the direct object, which in turn tends to take scope over a prepositional object (see Kurtzman and MacDonald, 1993, Ioup, 1975, Van Lehn, 1978, Pritchett and Whitman, 1995, Tunstall, in progress). For example, Ioup (1975) reports that perceivers of the seven languages she checked preferred the indirect object to take scope over

[4] It is unclear whether resistance to lowering the subject in (6a) is a result of the need to lower over a clause boundary, or a result of the availability of an alternative form (6b), where the subject already appears in the lower position at s-structure.

the direct object in sentences like *Martha told every child a story,* resulting in the reading where the particular story told may differ for each child. Van Lehn (1978) argues for an embeddedness hierarchy which itself correlates with c-command. Kurtzman and MacDonald (1993) argue for, among other things, a linear-order principle based on data from reading sentences like *Every/a kid climbed every/a tree.* Tunstall (1996, in progress) argues for a surface scope principle (where quantifier scope is determined by surface c-command relations) using reading time data for sentences like *Kelly showed a/every photo to every/a critic.* In short, though investigators agree about the gross preferences in scope assignment, they have disagreed about whether these preferences follow from linear order, a grammatical function hierarchy, or some other principle.

On any account of scope preferences in scopally ambiguous sentences, the grammar must delimit the grammatically permissible readings of the sentence. I assume that a quantifier phrase may grammatically take scope over another phrase only if it c-commands that phrase at s-structure or LF. Some further principle, presumably a processing principle, must characterize the preferred scope assignment when the grammar allows various possibilities. The basic preferences just noted would follow automatically from the ML principle. At s-structure, the subject c-commands the indirect object, which (in Runner's theory) c-commands the direct object, which c-commands in turn all material in the VP. Hence, ML can explain the basic preference for, e.g., a wide-scope universal interpretation of (7), where the choice of three men may differ for each woman.

(7) Every woman loves three men.

The ML principle is not required just for the treatment of scope. Hence, an independently motivated principle (ML) suffices to explain the gross scope preferences just noted. The ML account makes a further prediction which is of interest here. It leads us to expect that distinct quantifier phrases may have distinct intrinsic scope preferences related to their preference to be interpreted VP-internally versus VP-externally. It is well known that quantifier preferences do depend on the particular quantifiers in a sentence. Ioup (1975) and Van Lehn (1978) argue for a hierarchy where, for example, *each* is more likely to take wide scope than *every*, and *some* is more likely to take wide scope than *a*. For example, Ioup (1975) found that *each* took wide scope in sentences like *John made each girl a cake* in all of the thirteen languages she checked. She argued that *each* is highest on the scope hierarchy, above *every*, which in turn is above *some* and *a*. The preference of each quantifier to take wide scope seems to mirror its preference to be interpreted as presupposed or interpreted as d(iscourse)-linked. Indeed the paradigm in (8) and (9) may be related to this preference. Within each pair of quantifiers, the universals (*each*, *every*) and the 'existentials' (*some*, *a*), the quantifier with a stronger preference for wide scope may grammatically occur with the presupposed set overtly expressed, as indicated.

(8) a. each of the men
b. *every of the men

(9) a. some of the men
b. *a of the men

An indication that the wide-scope preferences of individual quantifiers may reflect presupposition differences comes from intuitions about the preferred antecedents for pronouns. In a study with Radó and Clifton, we explored the processing of d-linked phrases like *which man*. A d-linked phrase is assumed to be presupposed in discourse in the sense that it selects a subset from an already familiar context set of entities (e.g., *men*). In the experiment, a d-linked phrase was chosen as the antecedent of a pronoun more often than a non-d-linked interrogative (*who*) in ambiguous sentences like those in (10a, b). The second segment of unambiguous d-linked examples (10c) was also processed faster than the second segment of unambiguous *who* examples (10d) in a self-paced reading study using sentences that were disambiguated by eliminating all but the wh-constituent as a permissible antecedent of the pronoun, as in (10c, d). (In (10), the "/" indicates presentation segments.)

(10) a. Which guy did Bradley send a rifle to when he was threatened?
(60% he = which guy)
b. Who did Bradley send a rifle to when he was threatened?
(44% he = who)
c. Which little boy did Polly tell a story to / before he had an operation?
(76 ms/character)
d. Who did Polly tell a story to / before he had an operation?
(84 ms/character)

As noted above, if *each* and *some* are intrinsically d-linked, like *which person*, then they intrinsically provide evidence that a presuppositional interpretation is appropriate whereas *every* and *a* do not. The d-linked property of *each* and *some* could explain the position of these quantifiers on the scope hierarchy. This approach predicts that position on the scope hierarchy (with which we can now dispense except as a descriptive convenience) should correlate with the goodness of a phrase as an antecedent for the pronoun: higher position on the hierarchy (*each* > *every*; *some* > *a*) should be reflected in goodness as an antecedent. My intuitions suggest that *each* (*man*) is indeed more likely to be chosen as antecedent than *every* (*man*) in (11a, b), and that *some* (*man*) is more likely than *a* (*man*) (11c, d).

(11) a. John hinted to every man that he needed to rectify the problem personally.
b. John hinted to each man that he needed to rectify the problem personally.
c. John hinted to a man that he needed to rectify the problem personally.
d. John hinted to some man that he needed to rectify the problem personally.

If these intuitions are confirmed by systematic testing, they would further support the idea that quantifiers are interpreted in their surface position if possible, but may need to move due to inherent specification of the quantifier as d-linked (to a presupposed context set) or not d-linked.

13.2.3 Reconstruction

The ML principle states that DPs are lowered only when necessary. In reconstruction sentences where an anaphor is contained in a moved constituent, it predicts a preference for the anaphor to be interpreted with a matrix antecedent, on the basis of a representation where the wh-phrase lowers only to the complementizer position. To obtain an interpretation where the anaphor has an embedded antecedent, further lowering is necessary. In a self-paced reading study, Frazier, Plunkett, and Clifton (1996) investigated the processing of sentences like those in (12).

(12) a. Which rumor about herself did the matron claim the actress made up? (ambiguous, 68% matrix antecedent)
b. Which rumor about herself did the actress claim the newspaper made up? (matrix antecedent, 85 ms/character)
c. Which rumor about herself did the newspaper claim the actress made up? (embedded antecedent, 89 ms/character)

In ambiguous questions like (12a), perceivers typically (68% of the time) assigned the matrix antecedent (*matron*) to the reflexive, as indicated by answers to questions following the target sentence. Further, in unambiguous questions like (12b) and (12c), reading times were significantly faster when the antecedent for the reflexive was in the matrix clause (12b) rather than the embedded clause

(12c). This suggests that perceivers lowered the wh-phrase only as low as necessary to bind the reflexive.[5]

13.2.4 Focus

The expression of focus in natural languages is complex and differs considerably from one language to the next. In English, focus is largely conveyed by pitch accents. I will assume the grammar of focus proposed by Selkirk (1995). In this system, a pitch accent introduces a focus feature (F-marking) into the syntactic representation. In the syntactic representation, this feature may project from an internal argument to its head and from a head to its maximal projection (see especially, Selkirk, 1984, 1995 and, for experimental support, Birch and Clifton, 1995, Schafer, 1996). Focused material typically appears within the nuclear scope (= VP), where asserted information is expected to occur.

Given these assumptions, the focus structure of a sentence is often ambiguous. Intuitions suggest that perceivers prefer narrow focus. Consider (13), for example.

(13) a. The caterer only delivered some POTATOES.
b. He didn't deliver any ONIONS.
b′. He didn't SELECT the potatoes personally.
b″. He didn't PREPARE the meal.

The grammar permits F-marking to optionally project from the direct object to the VP in (13a). But intuitions suggest that preferentially it does not project, and that therefore perceivers expect a continuation like (13b), not (13b′) or (13b″) where (either the verb or) the entire VP is in focus.[6]

[5] Reconstruction examples are interesting precisely because they allow distinct aspects of interpretation to be teased apart. The examples in (12) indicate that each aspect of interpretation is preferentially accomplished as high in the already computed structure as is grammatically permissible. The scope of the wh-phrase is determined in the highest (s-structure) position. Binding of the reflexive requires lowering at least to a position where a c-commanding antecedent is available, i.e., the specifier of the embedded CP. Thematic interpretation requires further lowering to a theta-position within the lower clause. If the grammar permitted the reflexive to be bound in the highest (scope-determining) position of the wh-phrase, then ML would predict that the reflexive would preferentially be bound in that position. In short, on the theory advocated here, a syntactic chain is not interpreted all at once. Different aspects of interpretation may be separated, each occurring as high in the already computed surface structure as the grammar permits.

[6] Sentence (13a) contains the focus particle *only*. The role of *only* in such examples is not entirely clear (Rooth, 1985, 1992). It seems to magnify and clarify perceivers' intuitions about focus. If *only* is deleted, the same narrow-focus preference seems to be present, though the contrast between different continuations (e.g., (13b) vs. (13b′)) is less sharp.

There is also some experimental evidence supporting a preference for narrow focus of just the phrase bearing the pitch accent, without projection of F-marking to a higher phrase. Crain, Philip, Drozd, Roeper, and Matsuoka (1992), reported in Crain, Ni, and Conway (1994), examined adult preferences in interpreting sentences like (14).

(14) The dinosaur is only painting a house,
  a. not doing anything else (VP focus)
  b. not painting anything else (DP focus)

Adults systematically preferred (14b), indicating that sentence (14) was assigned narrow focus on just the direct object. Though Crain et al. (1994) do not attribute this preference to a preference for narrow focus, the results are exactly what are expected given a general preference not to project focus out of an F-marked phrase. (Crain et al., 1994, attribute the effect to a preference for the reading with a smaller contrast set. See Frazier, 1999, for problems with such an account.)

The preference for narrow focus can be derived from the ML principle. Assuming that (noncontrastively) focused material appears in the nuclear scope (= VP), then narrow focus on the direct object requires only the object to lower into VP, as indicated in (15).

(15) $[_{\text{Spec, Agr}_s\text{P}}$ The caterer$_i$ $[_{\text{TP}}$ delivered $[_{\text{Spec, Agr}_o\text{P}}$ some POTATOES$_j$ $[_{\text{VP}}\ t_i\, t_v\, t_j]]]]$

X

Projecting focus beyond the object would presumably entail also lowering the verb into VP. The verb and the object cannot lower together. The only constituent containing both of them (TP) could not lower since the VP contains no trace corresponding to this constituent.[7]

13.2.5 Conflicting Evidence About Whether DP Must Lower

If the ML principle is correct, perceivers should have difficulty interpreting a DP when evidence about whether it should be interpreted as VP-internal is mixed. To this point, the evidence discussed includes evidence about whether the DP may receive a VP-external interpretation (i.e., a presuppositional, quantificational, or generic interpretation), intrinsic properties of determiners (e.g., *some* easily receives a specific interpretation, *a* does not), as well as evidence about the scope of the DP, binding of an anaphor in the DP, and

[7] This account entails that projection of F-marking is defined at deep structure or more likely at LF.

(noncontrastive) focus. The various bits of evidence available to the perceiver need not all point in the same direction – a fact exploited in the account of scope preference in Section 13.2.3. For example, in (16a) the presence of *every* and *some* allows the universal quantifier in subject position to take narrow scope: *every* does not clearly demand an already familiar context set, and *some* easily receives a specific or presuppositional interpretation. Thus, intuitions about scope do not necessarily strongly converge on a particular reading.

(16) a. Every girl kissed some boy.
 b. Each girl kissed a boy.

By contrast, in (16b), *each* does seem to imply a familiar context set of girls, and *a* does not easily receive a specific interpretation. Thus, in (16b) all evidence converges on the wide-scope universal interpretation of the subject.

In general, other things being equal, the ML principle predicts a preference for a specific/presuppositional interpretation of a subject. However, when the subject contains the determiner *a*, as in (17), a specific or presuppositional interpretation does not seem to be readily available.

(17) A tall man appears.

In a null context, given the determiner *a*, the present (nonpast) tense and a predicate which resists a generic interpretation as in (17), the perceiver has little choice but to assign the subject an existential (VP-internal) interpretation. Along with the existential (VP-internal) interpretation of the subject, it is well known that a pitch accent in (17) will fall on the subject (on *man*), thereby ending up with focus in the nuclear scope (in VP), as expected. Hence, despite the fact that the subject needs to be lowered in (17), the sentence should be easy to process because all evidence converges: the subject must be lowered.

Beckman (1996) investigates a case where the evidence about whether lowering is required does not converge. She studied double object sentences. In Runner's (1995) theory, double objects are analyzed as clausal DPs, as illustrated in (18).

(18)

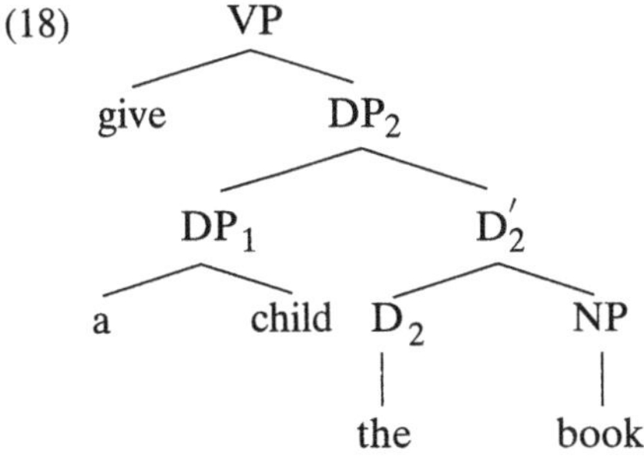

Each DP raises to its own Agr_oP, as illustrated in (19): the whole clausal DP raises to $Agr_{o2}P$, then DP_1 raises out of the clausal DP to $Agr_{o1}P$.

(19)

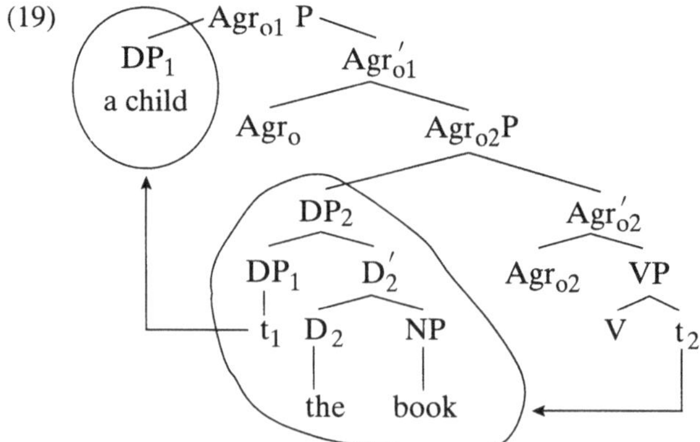

Now consider sentences like those in (20), which Beckman investigated in her self-paced reading study. She showed that a sentence like (20b) with an indefinite first object (Goal) takes longer to comprehend than a sentence like (20a) with an indefinite second object (Theme).

(20) a. John gave the man a book.
b. John gave a man the book.

In (20a), there are no problematic constraints on the focal structure of the sentence. *John* and *the man* may both be presupposed; *a book* may be lowered into VP and presumably be assigned focus. By contrast, in (20b), there is a problem. DP_1 (*a man*) provides the likely focus of the sentence. It is not marked as being already familiar and, as new material, it would likely receive focus. Hence, it is a likely candidate for lowering into the nuclear scope (= VP). But in order for DP_1 to lower into VP, DP_2 must lower into VP: until DP_2 lowers, the VP does not contain a trace of DP_1. This is illustrated in (21a), where no trace of DP_1 is in VP before lowering DP_2. (21b) illustrates that a trace of DP_1 is contained in VP once DP_2 has lowered.

(21) a. [subject [verb [$_{\text{SpecAgr}_{o1}\text{P}}$ a child$_1$ [$_{\text{SpecAgr}_{o2}\text{P}}$ t_1 the book$_2$ [$_{\text{VP}}$ $t_{subject}$ t_{verb} t_2]]]]]
b. [subject [verb [$_{\text{SpecAgr}_{o1}\text{P}}$ a child$_1$ [t_2 [$_{\text{VP}}$ $t_{subject}$ t_{verb} [$_{\text{DP}_2}$ t_1 the book]]]]]]

The fact that DP_2 must lower in order for DP_1 to be interpreted VP-internally is the source of the difficulty in (21b), where DP_1 is indefinite and DP_2 is definite. The processor receives conflicting evidence about whether to lower DP_2. In order to interpret DP_1 as focused and nonpresupposed, DP_1 should lower (hence, DP_2 needs to lower). But, the definite DP_2 is marked as familiar and likely presupposed. Thus DP_2 looks as if it needn't lower.

This account can explain why (20b) took longer to read than (20a) in Beckman's study. It also explains why it is (20b) which seems awkward intuitively. The contrast in (20) may be considered in the fuller paradigm in (22).

(22) a. John gave the man the book.
b. John gave a man a book.
c. John gave the man a book.
d. John gave a man the book.

A problem or a conflict arises only in (20b), repeated as (22d). In (22d), there is a pressure for DP_1 to lower without also lowering DP_2. But in the other sentences (22a–c), there is no conflict. In (22a), nothing might lower. In (22b), DP_1 and DP_2 may lower: both phrases naturally receive an existential interpretation. Alternatively, DP_2 alone might lower, as in (22c). It is only in (22d) that conflicting evidence is present. The fact that (22b) is not awkward or complex intuitively suggests that in (22d) it is not the complexity of the structure or the lowering per se that is at issue (since the same structure/lowering is needed in (22b)), but that instead it is the conflicting interpretive requirements of DP_1, which wants to lower, and DP_2 which wants not to lower but needs to in order for DP_1 to lower.

13.3 Fitting ML into the Human Language Processor

Why does the human language processor behave in accord with the ML principle? Though in general the human language processor does seem to build the minimal structure consistent with its evidence, notice that minimizing representational complexity at any given level does not really explain why the processor adopts the ML principle. A DP's entire chain must be constructed, whether the DP lowers or not, in order for the phrase to receive a theta-role. Further, there's no particular reason to believe that a representation with a high copy (23a) is any easier or less complex than a representation with a low copy (23b).

(23) a. $[_{\text{SpecAgr}_s\text{P}}$ A man_i $[_{\text{TP}}$ arrived $[_{\text{VP}} t_i\ t_v]]]$ PF
b. $[_{\text{SpecAgr}_s\text{P}}\ t_i\ [_{\text{TP}}\ t_v\ [_{\text{VP}}$ a man arrived$]]]$ LF

One possibility is that Minimal Lowering is favored because it allows a correspondence between levels of representation, i.e., given a P(honetic) F(orm) or s-structure of a given form, perceivers assume an identical LF when possible.

To evaluate this Correspondence Hypothesis, a summary of the basic generalizations in Section 13.2 may be helpful. Those generalizations are summarized schematically in (24).

(24) a. subject [$_{TP}$ [$_{VP}$]] (specific interpretation of subject)

b. [$_{SpecAgr_sP}$ QP_1 [[$_{SpecAgr_oP}$ QP_2 [$_{VP}$ $t_1 t_2$]]]] (QP_1 takes scope over QP_2)

c. [which picture of self$_i$ [. . . [$_{VP}$ [$_{CP}$ t_i . . . [$_{VP}$ t_i (matrix antecedent)

d. . . . [$_{TP}$ verb [[$_{SpecAgr_oP}$ object$_i$ [$_{VP}$ . . . $t_v t_i$]]] (narrow focus)

e. . . . [$_{Agr_{o1}P}$ [$_{Agr_{o2}P}$ [$_{VP}$ . . . $t_v t_2$]]] (definiteness constraint)

It is readily apparent in (24) that (a), (b), and (d) would follow from a preference for correspondence between s-structure and LF, because the higher copy of a phrase (the overt phrase in the input) need not lower at LF to receive its referential interpretation. Arguably, the double object facts summarized in (24e) also could be seen to follow from the Correspondence Hypothesis, though explaining why two indefinite objects seem more natural than an indefinite DP_1 followed by a definite DP_2 will still require an account based on conflicting evidence about where DP_2 should be interpreted. What will not follow is the preference for matrix antecedents in reconstruction sentences (24c). Perhaps one could argue that (25b) corresponds more closely to the s-structure representation (25a) than (25c) does.

(25) a. [$_{CP}$ which picture of: self$_i$ [$_{SpecAgr_sP}$ . . . [$_{VP}$[$_{CP}$ t_i . . . [$_{VP}$ t_i
b. [$_{CP}$ t_i [$_{SpecAgr_sP}$[$_{VP}$[$_{CP}$ which picture of: self$_i$ . . . [$_{VP}$ t_i
c. [$_{CP}$ t_i [$_{SpecAgr_sP}$[$_{VP}$[$_{CP}$ t_i . . . [$_{VP}$ which picture of self$_i$

In Runner's (1995) copy and deletion theory, in effect each member of the chain is a copy at each level (see Note 3). 'Free' deletion deletes all but one copy. Which copy remains is determined by the particular well-formedness conditions at that level of representation. In this framework, it would be necessary to assume that at LF copy deletion is harder if it deletes a copy nearer to the s-structure copy, as in (25c), than if it deletes a copy farther away, as in (25b). It is not obvious why this should be the case.

A second possibility is that the ML principle follows from 'laziness' on the part of the processor. The processor doesn't execute a task unless confronted with evidence that it is necessary to do so. Though this sort of explanation is appealing in general, it does not really apply to the circumstances discussed in Section 13.2. Constructing the lower position of a DP is necessary regardless of whether the (referential) interpretation of the DP is determined in the higher (surface) or lower (e.g., deep structure) position. In all cases, the lower position will be required, e.g., for thematic role assignment. Thus not lowering a DP for referential interpretation does not result in a savings of effort, because the lower position must be constructed in any event.

A third possibility is that perceivers expect both given and new information to appear in a sentence, and that they expect given information to precede new information, at least in English. It is not clear how this could explain the quantifier scope generalizations, however. Nor is it obvious how it would explain the preference for narrow focus (24d). In fact, even data supporting Beckman's definiteness constraint (24e) is not readily explained by this account, since a given–new preference seems to apply only to DPs in a double object structure, not to the DPs in a DP–PP structure. For example, *John gave a book to the girl* is not intuitively odd, even though the indefinite object *a book* precedes the definite goal (*to*) *the girl*. Thus even for characterizing the fully acceptable or felicitous order of internal arguments, a given–new constraint is not satisfactory.

Another possibility is that perceivers prefer early interpretation, and that ML is just a consequence of this preference. In general, one may not simply claim that all linguistic interpretation takes place as soon as possible without further specifying a grammatical framework and a processing framework. To take a simple example, immediate interpretation of a prenominal adjective implies that the adjective in a phrase like *an old friend* is interpreted before the noun is processed, there is an x and old(x). This incorrectly predicts a preference for the intersective interpretation, where the friend is old, not the subsective interpretation, where the friendship is old. To correctly account for interpretive preferences, one needs to assume the existence of some form of head primacy principle (see Kamp and Partee, 1995). (See Frazier, 1999, for discussion and for a range of counterexamples to a strong immediate interpretation principle.) However, given particular explicit assumptions about the grammar and the processor's tasks, something along the lines of early interpretation seems correct or at least defensible.

Imagine that interpreting some phrase necessarily involves both assignment of a thematic role to the phrase and assignment of a referential value and, further, that the processor treats this task as a single step in its analysis of a sentence, with thematic processing and referential processing inextricably bound to each other. This approach to interpreting a phrase implies the existence of a unified process that could be carried out only when both thematic and referential information about the phrase is available to the processor. However, if instead we distinguish the referential interpretation of a DP from its thematic interpretation, then two distinct interpretive steps may be postulated, by dissociating referential and thematic interpretation, allowing each interpretive task to be accomplished on its own. By allowing this type of modular interpretation of a DP, referential interpretation of the phrase may begin immediately without waiting until a theta-assigner is available to support thematic interpretation of the phrase.

We might look at Minimal Lowering in terms of a language processing system which is task-driven, such as the system sketched in Frazier (1990) (also Frazier, 1995), where linguistic representations define the tasks the processor must accomplish. Dealing only with postlexical modules, Frazier (1990) suggests that (26) characterizes the architecture of the human language processing system.

(26)

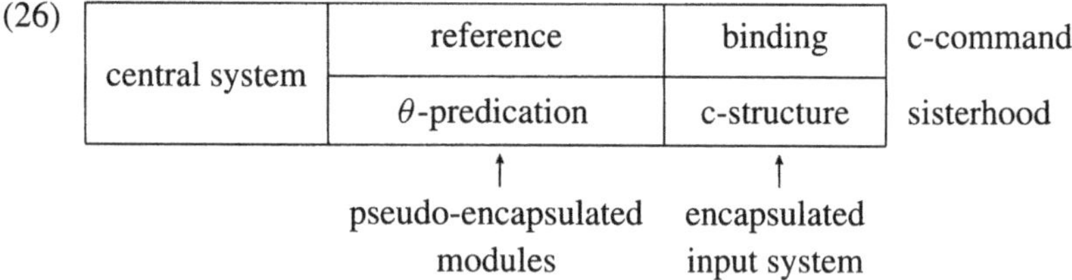

The task of the syntactic modules is to build a well-formed syntactic representation using only the output of the phonological and lexical modules and relevant syntactic information: information about sisterhood relations and constituent structure for the c-structure module, and information from c-structure and c-command relations for the binding module. An input sentence together with the grammar defines the tasks implicit in identifying a well-formed representation for the sentence. For instance, a connected phrase marker must be identified with all positions licensed and all non-head members of a chain appropriately bound. The grammatical form of a phrase may also define a processing task. For example, reflexives must be bound to be grammatical; hence, they intrinsically define a task for the processor.

Two interpretive modules were also postulated: a theta- or predication module that takes the c-structure as input and identifies the appropriate thematic representation (see discussion of the thematic processor in Frazier, 1987); and a reference module concerned with c-command and the interpretation of DPs and scope. The interpretive modules are 'pseudo-encapsulated': they may import nonlinguistic world knowledge into the module in order to accomplish a particular task. For example, the theta- (or thematic) processor may consult world knowledge (and the discourse representation) to determine whether *binoculars* would make a good instrument for seeing or for shooting in the analysis of sentences like those in (27).

(27) a. John saw the cop with binoculars. ⟨Exper, Theme, Instr⟩
b. John shot the cops with binoculars. ⟨Agent, Theme, Instr⟩

The reference processor might also import world knowledge (and discourse) to accomplish a task. For example, to determine whether a generic interpretation may be assigned in (28) the processor may need to find out something about the properties of genies and Jesuits (as well as the basic meaning of *appears*).

(28) a. A genie (just) appears.
b. A Jesuit (just) appears.

Intuitions suggest that a (non-lowered) generic interpretation is all right in (28a) due to the properties of genies, whereas an existential (lowered) interpretation is required in (28b) since, under normal conditions, *appear* cannot easily be generic and hence cannot support a non-lowered generic interpretation of *a Jesuit.*

Where in this system does Minimal Lowering apply? Assuming that LF is the interface between syntax and (nonthematic aspects of) interpretation, it belongs in the reference module – the subsystem which takes the output of the binding module and determines the (nonthematic) interpretation of DPs and their scope.

The view just sketched perhaps elucidates the division of labor in interpreting a chain. The overt copy of a DP needs to be interpreted as quantificational, generic, existential, and so on. The position where an overt copy is interpreted (its LF position) need not be its underlying position, where it receives a theta-role. The reference module is thus a specialist bringing to bear on its task information relevant to the interpretation of overt copies at s-structure or LF. By contrast, the theta- (or thematic) processor is concerned with the tail of a chain (where the overt copy sits at d-structure).

Now imagine that each task is accomplished as soon as possible. The Minimal Lowering generalizations would immediately follow without any need to assume that deletion of one copy is easier than deletion of some other copy (see discussion of (24)).

Why would the human language processor accomplish each of its tasks as soon as possible? After all, early decisions are also risky decisions since they may be incompatible with subsequent information. Further, it is clear that a complete chain must be established regardless of when a referential interpretation is assigned to an overt DP. So early interpretation does not reduce the complexity of the DP's chain.

Early interpretation of a DP does nevertheless seem to have two advantages. Once a DP has been securely, or confidently, interpreted, presumably the overt lexical copy of the phrase need not be held in immediate memory, which has a highly restricted capacity. For whatever reason, humans are simply better at holding semantically interpreted material in memory than semantically uninterpreted material. Thus, holding the interpretation of a DP in immediate memory may impose a lesser burden than holding an overt copy of its surface form in memory (if it is assumed that the theta-module only requires an indexed trace to assign a theta-role, no overt copy of the DP is needed once referential interpretation occurs). An obvious further advantage of early referential interpretation is that it will aid the theta-processor. Determining the most plausible assignment of thematic roles is dependent not on the overt phrase of, say, the external argument, but on the interpretation of that phrase, including, for example, the particular discourse entity to which it is used to refer. For example, though binoculars might make a plausible instrument for seeing in general and thus favor VP attachment of *with binoculars* in (27), the effect of the bias may be contravened if the external argument of *see* has a referent known not to be in possession of binoculars whereas the internal argument is a phrase used to refer to an individual in possession of binoculars.[8]

The division of labor in (26) allows early interpretation of a DP by separating referential interpretation of the DP from theta-role assignment to the DP (though obviously the ultimately most plausible interpretation will depend on both types of information). The proposed division of labor also offers an explanation for an empirical puzzle concerning unexpressed theta-roles.

Carlson and Tanenhaus (1988) argued that unexpressed theta-roles are immediately entered into the discourse representation as an index. This allows a subsequent phrase to be more readily integrated into the discourse if it (or its referent) may be taken to satisfy the implicit theta-role. For example, in (29a) *unloaded* introduces an implicit theme into discourse. When (29b) is processed, *the suitcases* may be taken to instantiate this role.

[8] I assume, as in earlier work (Frazier, 1987), that *with binoculars* is first (minimally) attached to the VP during initial syntactic processing, and that this initial syntactic hypothesis is thematically evaluated. During the later evaluation stage, referential information might contravene a 'positive' thematic evaluation of the initially computed syntactic structure.

(29) a. John unloaded his car.
a′. John was hurrying to catch his plane.
b. The suitcases were very heavy.

By contrast, in (29a′) *hurrying* does not introduce an implicit theme. As predicted, comprehension times for (29b) were faster following (29a) than following (29a′).

Let's assume that Carlson and Tanenhaus are correct. This would seem to suggest that any time after a verb's complement has been processed, implicit theta-roles should be available to guide subsequent processing. However, some recent results of Frazier and Clifton (1998) indicate otherwise. In a series of self-paced reading studies of sluicing (constructions where only the wh-phrase of an embedded question remains overt), we tested sentences like those in (30) with argument (30a, b) or adjunct (30c, d) antecedents for the wh-phrase. The antecedent for the wh-phrase was either overt (30a, c) or covert (30b, d).

(30) a. The secretary typed something but I don't know what. (overt argument)
b. The secretary typed but I don't know what. (covert argument)
c. The secretary typed somewhere but I don't know where. (overt argument)
d. The secretary typed but I don't know where. (covert adjunct)

Given the findings of Carlson and Tanenhaus, we expected an interaction: the expected penalty for a covert (as opposed to overt) antecedent should be greater for adjuncts than for arguments. After all, the covert argument should already be represented in the verb's theta-grid and in discourse representation according to their proposal. But this is not what was found. Instead, the penalty for covert antecedents was just as large for arguments as for adjuncts.

The discrepancy between these findings and those of Carlson and Tanenhaus makes sense given the architecture sketched in (26). In constructing an LF, the reference module is operating on the output of the binding module. An unexpressed theta-role will presumably not be present in this representation, assuming that it is the theta-module that operates with a verb's theta-grid.[9] The discourse representation of the unexpected theta-role will appear irrelevant to the reference module. Only phrases at LF will appear to be relevant, because the

[9] In order to "sprout" an antecedent for a wh-phrase with an implicit argument antecedent (see Chung, Ladusaw, and McCloskey (1995), presumably the processor must check that the 'antecedent' verb (*typed* in (30)) may take an argument of the syntactic category of the wh-phrase. But assigning the most plausible thematic role to the wh-phrase will presumably be accomplished by the thematic module as usual.

antecedent for the wh-phrase in a sluicing construction must be checked at LF to insure that it is a free indefinite (see Chung, Ladusaw, and McCloskey, 1995).

13.4 Conclusions

Various generalizations (some old, some novel) have been used to argue that phrases are interpreted in a position no lower than necessary, in their surface position if possible. The ML principle has been developed in a task-driven processing system where tasks are defined implicitly by grammatical representations and organized into subsystems based on basic relations of the grammar (sisterhood for constituent structure, theta-relations, and predication; c-command for binding and reference). Given this division of labor, a chain is interpreted in possibly distinct stages: interpretation of a DP is accomplished in the reference module, and interpretation of its theta-role in the theta-module. This division of labor permits the ML principle to be derived from a pressure for each processing task to be accomplished early. It also explains why unexpressed theta-roles sometimes act as if they are present, and sometimes not.

References

Beckman, J. (1996) Double objects, definiteness and extractions: A processing perspective. In M. Dickey and S. Tunstall (eds.), *University of Massachusetts Occasional Papers* 19, 27–70.

Birch, S. and Clifton, C. (1995) Focus, accent and argument structure. *Language and speech* 33, 365–391.

Carlson, G. and Tanenhaus, M. (1988) Thematic roles and language comprehension. In W. Wilkins (ed.), *Syntax and semantics, vol. 21*, (pp. 263–289). London: Academic Press.

Chung, S. Ladusaw, W. and McCloskey, J. (1995) Sluicing and logical form. *Natural Language Semantics* 3, 239–282.

Crain, S., Philip, W., Drozd, K., Roeper, T., and Matsuoka, K. (1992) Only in Child Language. Unpublished manuscript. University of Connecticut, Storrs, CT.

Crain, S., Ni, W., and Conway, L. (1994) Learning, parsing and modularity. In C. Clifton, L. Frazier, and K. Rayner (eds.), *Perspectives on sentence processing* (pp. 443–467). Hillsdale, NJ: Erlbaum.

Diesing, M. (1992) *Indefinites*. Cambridge, MA: MIT Press.

Frazier, L. (1987) Sentence processing: a tutorial review. In M. Coltheart (ed.), *Attention and performance XII* (pp. 559–586). Hillsdale, NJ: Erlbaum .

Frazier, L. (1990) Exploring the architecture of the language system. In G. Altmann (ed.), *Cognitive models of speech processing: Psycholinguistic and computational perspectives* (pp. 409–433). Cambridge, MA: MIT Press.

Frazier, L. (1995) Issues of representation in psycholinguistics. In J. L. Miller and P. D. Eimas (eds.), *Handbook of perception and cognition, vol. 11: Speech, language and communication*. San Diego, CA: Academic Press.

Frazier, L. (1999) *On sentence interpretation*. Dordrecht: Kluwer.

Frazier, L. and Clifton, C. (1998) Comprehension of sluiced sentences. *Language and Cognitive Processes* 13, 499–520.
Frazier, L. and Clifton, C. (in progress) Context and sentence processing: Presuppositional interpretations and restrictor clauses.
Frazier, L., Plunkett, B., and Clifton, C. (1996) Reconstruction and scope. In M. Dickey and S. Tunstall (eds.), *University of Massachusetts Occasional Papers in Linguistics* 19, 239–260.
Ioup, G. (1975) Some universals for quantifier scope. In J. Kimball (ed.), *Syntax and semantics, vol. 4*, (pp. 37–58). New York: Academic Press.
Kamp, H. and Partee, B. H. (1995) Prototype theory and compositionality. *Cognition* 57, 129–191.
Kurtzman, H. and MacDonald, M. E. (1993) Resolution of quantifier scope and ambiguities. *Cognition* 48, 243–279.
Pritchett, B. L. and Whitman, J. B. (1995) Syntactic representation and interpretive preference. In R. Mazuka and N. Nagai (eds.), *Japanese sentence processing* (65–76). Hillsdale, NJ: Erlbaum .
Rooth, M. (1985) *Association with Focus*. University of Massachusetts doctoral dissertation.
Rooth, M. (1992) A theory of focus interpretation. *Natural Language Semantics* 1, 75–116.
Runner, J. (1995) *Noun phrase licensing and interpretation*. University of Massachusetts doctoral dissertation.
Schafer, A. (1996) Bounded projection: Constraints on focus interpretation. In E. Benedicto, M. Romero, and S. Tomioka (eds.), *Proceedings of the Workshop on Focus* (277–241). Amherst, MA: GLSA.
Selkirk, E. (1984) *Phonology and syntax: The relation between sound and structure*. Cambridge, MA: MIT Press.
Selkirk, E. (1995) Sentence prosody: Intonation, stress and phrasing. In J. Goldsmith (ed.), *Handbook of phonological theory* (550–569). London: Blackwell.
Tunstall, S. (1996) Processing quantifier scope in dative sentences. Presented at the 1996 Annual Meeting of the Linguistics Society of America, San Diego, CA.
Tunstall, S. (in progress) *The interpretation of quantifiers and indefinites: Semantics and processing*. University of Massachusetts doctoral dissertation.
Van Lehn, K. A. (1978) Determining the scope of English quantifiers. MIT M. A. thesis.

14
Focus Effects Associated with Negative Quantifiers

LINDA M. MOXEY AND ANTHONY J. SANFORD

14.1 Introduction

Much of this book has explored the timing and effects of various processes which are initiated as a result of reading particular sentences or types of sentence. To understand the meaning of a sentence, we make use of information from sentence structure and content, but we also make use of information which the reader already has about the situation described. However, the role of such background knowledge in theories of natural language semantics varies between approaches to the problem. In this chapter, we will argue that semantic processing is at least partially driven by the inferences which the interpreter makes, and that the knowledge state of language users is therefore of paramount importance in the process of understanding discourse.

One possible approach to modelling the semantic processes involved in sentence comprehension is exemplified by the Discourse Representation Theory (DRT) account, which is based on a set-theoretic approach to reference (Kamp and Reyle, 1993). Solving reference and scope problems is central to DRT, because inadequate reference resolution leads to incoherence in the representation of a discourse. Thus, in DRT, reference resolution is the process which occurs earliest. There is little if any emphasis on inference and the utilisation of world knowledge in comprehension within such a framework, because the spirit of the approach is to try to capture the facts of language, independent of world knowledge.

An alternative view is that human language comprehension is driven by more general coherence-establishment mechanisms, of which reference resolution is merely a part and not necessarily the first or most fundamental thing to be established. This has been recognised by a number of researchers (see especially Hobbs, 1979). In the psychological literature there are many demonstrations of how reference resolution frequently depends upon more general aspects of coherence establishment, frequently requiring the use of general (world) knowledge (Garrod and Sanford, 1994).

The inadequacies of a set-theoretic approach seem to us to be nicely illustrated by the distinction between (1) and (1′):

(1) The bottle is half full.
(1′) The bottle is half empty.

In terms of the volume of the bottle occupied by water, there is no difference between these two statements. What is different is how they are interpreted: what inferences they license. It would be a curious theory of discourse which did not capture the difference between these two cases. We view the difference as similar to that between the use of the two natural language quantifiers *a few* and *few*. In purely set-theoretic terms there is no real difference between these two. However, we propose that there is a difference in the inference patterns they lead to and in the sets which become focussed as a result.

14.2 The Phenomenon

Consider the following sentences:

(2) A few of the football fans were at the match.
(2′) They hissed at the referee when he held up the yellow card.

(3) Few of the football fans were at the match.
(3′) They were boycotting the game because the club has increased ticket prices twice in one season.

Notice that while (2′) follows (2) with ease, it seems a little odd following (3). Also note that while (3′) follows (3), it does not make sense after (2), since people who attend a match cannot be boycotting it. The problem is that for (2′) to make sense *they* must refer to the fans who were at the match (we have called this subset the reference subset or refset; see Moxey and Sanford, 1987). For (3′) to make sense we argue that *they* must refer to those fans who were not at the match (we have called this subset the complement subset or compset, since it only contains members of the overall set of fans who are not members of the refset). Moxey and Sanford (1987) have shown that plural pronouns following certain quantifiers, such as *few* and *not many*, tend to put focus on the compset while others, such as *many* and *a few* always seem to put focus on the refset. Our argument assumes that the referent of a plural pronoun can be taken as diagnostic of which set is in focus for those involved in the communication.

Empirical support for the focus differential first came from a study in which subjects were asked to read a quantified statement and complete a sentence beginning with the plural pronoun which followed it, for example:

(4) Few of the MPs were at the meeting.
They ...

Any one subject completed only one sentence so that subjects would be unaware of the purpose of the experiment. Having completed their sentence, the subjects were asked to check one statement about the referent of the plural pronoun in the sentence they had just produced. Options included the refset, the compset, the set generally, the whole set, or something other than those just listed. Compset focus occurs with negative quantifiers (including those in the lefthand group below). In contrast, refset focus occurs with positive quantifiers (including those in the righthand column).

not quite all	nearly all
not all	almost all
less than 80%	more than 80%
less than 50%	more than 50%
less than 30%	more than 30%
not many	many
few	a few
hardly any	

Note that some of the negative expressions refer to small amounts or proportions (e.g., *few*) so that the compset is large, while others (e.g., *not quite all*) refer to large amounts so that the compset is small, even approaching zero. The importance of this last point will become apparent in Section 14.3. A second general observation is that although the refset pattern seems to occur almost inevitably with positive quantifiers, compset reference occurs a little over half of the time after negative quantifiers across all of the experiments.

A number of studies have also been carried out on the time course of the processes involved in understanding refset versus compset references (Paterson, Moxey and Sanford, 1996; Sanford, Moxey and Paterson, 1996). Self-paced reading time measurements have shown that target sentences which refer to the set which is not in focus take longer to read than targets which are in focus. Thus compset following positives is slow, as is refset following negatives. Similar results occur using eye-tracking techniques, where total time effects reflect the findings of the self-paced reading studies. The compset focus phenomenon thus occurs in reading as well as in production.

14.3 Compset, Generalisations and Maxset

Corblin (1996) puts forward the main argument which has been made against the idea that compset reference is a genuine phenomenon. Certainly within theories such as DRT, which is Corblin's starting position, it is argued that "apparently subtracting one set from another is not a permissible operation for the formation of plural antecedents" (Kamp and Reyle, 1993, p. 307; quoted by Corblin, 1996). The evidence provided is the so-called marbles example:

(5) Eight of ten marbles are in the bag. They are under the sofa.

In order for a pronoun to refer to the compset, the refset (in this case the eight marbles) must be subtracted from the whole set (the ten marbles), and the marbles example is intended to illustrate the impossibility of such a manoeuvre. Of course, the point that Moxey and Sanford made is that one would not expect a non-negative quantifier such as *eight of the ten* to license a complement set reference, in line with the empirical data. If the quantified noun phrase in (5) was *Few of the marbles*, then *they* would easily refer to the compset.

Clearly the position taken by Corblin is not consistent with our interpretation of the data discussed earlier. That is, if it is not permissible to form a plural antecedent by subtracting one set from another, then reference to the compset (the whole set minus the refset) is not possible. What is apparently compset reference in our data must be explained in some other way. Corblin therefore attempts to explain our data in terms of generalization rather than "set subtraction."

Kamp and Reyle (1993) define a process of abstraction which can occur given a quantified sentence. So, given (6), three levels of abstraction are deemed possible:

(6) Few women from this village came to the feminist rally.

1. Total Abstraction: Set of women from this village coming to the rally
2. Intermediate abstraction: Women from this village
3. Minimal Abstraction: Women in general (generic)

The essence of Corblin's idea is that cases of compset reference can be understood in terms of anaphora to one of the more general (minimally abstracted) sets. For instance, consider (7):

(7) Few of the fans went to the match.
(7′) They didn't want to watch the team lose again.

It is possible that none of the fans wanted to watch the team lose, so *they* refers to the set of fans (of that team) in general, many of whom didn't go to the match for that reason. Thus, there is no need for set subtraction. According to this argument, compset reference is apparent, not real, and the existing theory is preserved. So-called compset reference is really reference to what Corblin calls the maxset (the set generally). But at this stage, let us simply point out that *they* could just as easily refer to the compset, if we suspend all theoretical prejudices.

We believe that a quantified statement like (6) will lead people to make inferences either about the women from this village, or some subset of them, or about the feminist rally. Since there is a negative quantifier linking these, focus will be on not being at the feminist rally, e.g. possible reasons for not being there, including things about such rallies and things that are perhaps weird about the women in this village. Not liking rallies would be a typical reason for not attending them:

(8) Few women from this village came to the feminist rally. They don't like political rallies very much.

The plural pronoun will be taken to refer to a set of whom the continuation (in this case the typical reason for not attending) might be true. We would argue that this may turn out to be various sets, including *all women*, *all women of the village*, *all women of the village who are not at the rally* – possibly even in this case *all people of the village*. What dictates what subjects see as the referent of *they* (and what we can define as such) is the content of the continuation, which is in turn determined by the inferences which people tend to want to make given a quantified statement. Typically, the inference is likely to be relevant only to the compset, or to the set generally (as opposed to the whole set), or to the refset, but this changes not only with quantifier but also with context. Note also that the first sentence in (6) could be followed with (9):

(9) They are going to talk about differences between male and female wages and most of the people in this village are unemployed.

They in (9) clearly refers to people at the rally, some of whom are unlikely to be women from this village. This is an unlikely referent for *they* even in the context of the first sentence in (6), but it is a possible referent which becomes very likely in the light of this particular reason for not going to the rally, i.e., in terms of what's going on at the rally and inconsistencies with properties of the people of this village.

Corblin argues that all instances of so-called compset can be analysed as maxsets (the set generally). He proposes that "if the plural pronoun is a reference to compset, the substitution of an explicit reference to compset should preserve any property of the pronoun sentence (grammaticality, inferences, implicatures)" (Corblin 1996 : 59). The example he uses is as follows:

(10) a. Few French voters voted for the candidate of the communist party.
b. They voted for the right wing at about 40%.
c. Those who didn't voted for the right wing at about 40%.

First, our guess is that in an experiment, native speakers of English would never produce sentences like (10b) or (c). The quantity information would normally be at the start of the sentence – *About 40% voted for the right wing*. Note that *about 40%* is an abbreviation for *about 40% of them*, and that the *them* in *about 40% of them* does indeed refer to the maxset. Also note that if *a few* replaces *few* in (10), *them* still refers to the maxset, and not to the refset as would normally be the case with a simple pronoun. It is true that in the corrected (10c), *about 40% of those who didn't* is a different set from that denoted by *about 40% of them*, but this is for reasons other than those put forward by Corblin.

Another of Corblin's examples is based on the idea that certain sentence pairs create a tautology. If a quantified statement followed by an explicit reference to the compset leads to a tautology, and if a plural pronoun replacing the explicit reference in the second statement really refers to the compset, then the quantified statement followed by the *they* statement would also lead to a tautology. Thus he argues that after (11a), (11b) is not a tautology while (11c) is – therefore (11b) and (c) cannot mean the same thing and *they* cannot refer to the compset:

(11) a. Few French people are going on holiday this year.
b. They are staying at home instead.
c. Those who aren't going on holiday are staying at home instead.

In fact it is not clear to us that either of (11b) and (c) are tautologies following (11a). But examples like (11) can never show that *they* cannot ever really be refering to the compset. We need to turn the argument round: if (11a) + (b) does lead to a tautology then the *they* in (b) must refer only to the compset, i.e. it cannot include any of the refset, and hence cannot refer to the maxset which includes the refset (or at least a large part of it).[1] Consider the following:

(12) a. Few of the doctors were male.
b. They were female.
c. Those who were not were female.

[1] If the maxset can still be a referent even when it excludes the refset, then, by definition, in such instances, it is the compset.

Clearly both (12b) and (c) are tautologies (if taken literally) given (12a).[2] Since (b) is a tautology, the plural pronoun in (b) must refer to the compset.

Thus we do not dispute the fact that many instances where subjects have said they were using *they* to refer to the compset might sensibly also be seen as referring to the maxset. We would resist the view that such instances necessarily refer to the maxset, however. The example which Corblin has chosen is unfortunate in that although reference to the compset is difficult, so is reference to the refset. Furthermore, we believe that the reasoning behind Corblin's tautology argument is flawed. Such an argument cannot prove that compset reference never happens.

Our own data also suggests that compset reference is not the same as maxset reference. There are many cases where it is impossible for *they* to refer to the set generally, and where the only possibility is compset reference. Let us enumerate these points. First, in our continuation experiments subjects were presented with a quantified statement and asked to complete the second sentence. They were then given the option to select which set or subset the *they* in their continuations referred to. Although on some occasions they chose the refset after negative quantifiers, they predominantly chose the compset, and only on rare occasions ticked the "in general" or "all" categories (the first of which is equivalent to the maxset). Corblin argues that subjects who report that their *they* refers to a compset do so because *they* really refers to something like *MPs in their majority*, which is arguably nearer the compset than *MPs in general*. It is unclear to us what Corblin means by *MPs in their majority*, and particularly by his view that it might be nearer in meaning to the compset than to *MPs in general*. Corblin suggests that the task we presented to our subjects was difficult because we asked them to choose between the compset and the set generally, and that this was essentially the same thing. In fact, the task was for subjects to write a sentence and then consider what their *they* referred to in the sentence they had completed. No one took longer than about a minute, and no one said it was a difficult task, even in pilot studies where such feedback was greatly encouraged.

Our second argument for the reality of compset reference is based on the forms of expression which are notable by their absence (Sanford et al., 1996). There are almost no cases like:

> Few of the MPs were at the meeting.
> They mostly/generally/typically preferred to be with their secretaries or to prop up the bar.

[2] If not taken literally, (19b) and (c) are at least equivalent in the extent to which they may be seen as leading to a tautology.

or even simply

> They preferred to be doing other things on the whole.

If subjects intended the reference to be to a set in general, one might expect them to say so, using expressions such as those just shown.

A third argument is based on the expressions which are included in subjects' continuations, such as *instead* or *couldn't* in the following:

> Few of the MPs were at the meeting.
> They were campaigning in their constituencies instead.

or

> Not many football fans were at the match.
> They couldn't get to the park because of the train strike.

The continuations above rule out reference to the refset since an MP cannot be both at the meeting and in his constituency (at least no more than one of them can be), and a fan cannot both be at the match and unable to get there.

Moxey and Sanford (1993a) noted the presence of compset references in cases where the compset is very small (as in *Not quite all of the fans went to the match*). It is logically possible that compset reference is a generalisation even in these cases:

(13) Not quite all of the MPs were at the meeting.
They had no interest in the topic in question.

For instance, it may be the case that none of the MPs had any interest, but that most of them felt obliged to go. However, a detailed analysis of the continuations resulting from cases where the compset is very small showed a high proportion of continuations of the following type (Sanford et al., 1996):

(14) Not quite all of the MPs were at the meeting.
They were back in their consituencies trying to muster support.

The predicate of the second sentence here eliminates any possibility of this sentence being a generalisation. Logically, it must be a reference to the compset, or at least to some subset of elements within the compset. Corblin made no comment about the issue of compset reference to quantifiers where compset is much smaller than the refset.

We find the conclusion that compset reference is occurring inescapable, though we are happy to admit that there are also instances which are logically undecidable between generalisations and compset references. We shall further propose that in many ways this is a side issue, and that what really matters is that the pattern of inference is generated by a particular quantifier.

14.4 A Process Model for Quantifier Focus Effects

Our model is based on the relatively uncontentious idea that negations (and other forms of markedness) generate specific patterns of inference-making in the listener, and that these patterns of inference support the focus observations in both production and comprehension situations (Sanford et al., 1996).

The continuations produced to the various quantifier types were classified by independent judges in the experiments of Moxey and Sanford (1987, 1993a; Sanford et al., 1996), following a schema developed in pilot studies. The main distinctions were between the following classes of continuation:

(A) Reasons for the predicate of the quantified sentence being the case (RT):
A few of the fans went to the match.
They wanted to offer the team strong support.

(B) Reasons for the predicate not being the case (RNT):
Few of the fans went to the match.
They did not want to see the team lose.

(C) Consequence of the quantified statement:
Only a few of the fans went to the match.
They had a problem cheering loud enough.

(D) Simple (noncausal involvement):
A few of the fans went to match.
They enjoyed it very much.

The principal observation for the present purpose was that negative quantifiers tended to induce continuations of type (B). Positive quantifiers tend to produce those of type (D). The facts about negative expressions fit well with the idea that a negative is used to deny a supposition: for instance *not many* will be used when there is reason to believe that *many* may have been the case (see, e.g., Clark, 1976). Moxey and Sanford (1993b) carried out a direct test of this idea and confirmed that the negatives *few* and *not many* appeared to induce in the listener a belief that the speaker did indeed expect more to have been the case than was induced by a positive quantifier, such as *a few*.

In the case of continuations generated to negative-quantified expressions, we suggest that the types of continuations reflect the need for an explanation of the denied supposition. Thus, in *few MPs went to the meeting*, the supposition that more might have gone is denied, and so there is a need for (and hence in comprehension, an expectation of) an explanation. In the continuation procedure, such explanations are provided following a search of general knowledge.

The focus pattern is generated by the pattern of inferential activity set up by the supposition denial inherent in negative usage. The simplest way to describe a reason for, say, MPs not being at a meeting is to describe the actions or properties of those who do not attend, i.e., to produce a description anchored on the compset. Of course, an inference-driven scheme of this sort could lead to other (related) patterns of inference, such as the discovery of consequences of the number of MPs being smaller than was expected. In this case, descriptions would tend to be anchored on the refset. The inference-driven mechanism is thus an account which explains the rather more diffuse pattern of reference types which occurs with negatives. In fact, we should say that the exact distribution of reference types and of underlying patterns of inference will be determined by the content of the situation to which the quantified statement is referring.

Thus, if the situational knowledge which a subject accesses upon reading a quantified statement contains lots of inferences concerning the compset relative to those inferences concerning the refset, or any other set, then there will be a high probability that the subject will produce a compset reference if asked for a continuation of the statement. Likewise in a comprehension task, the subject will be expecting a compset reference to the extent that inferences relating to that set are in focus. However, if it turns out that the text continues with a pronoun which refers to the refset (or some other set), this will not cause problems as long as the continuation makes sense and was easily accessible. Thus, (15) can be followed by (a), (b) or (c), though overall we might argue that a compset reference is most likely. Elsewhere we have argued that the content of a mental model (what is determined as distinct from what is left undecided) is governed by what is important about the situation to which the utterance generating the model refers (Sanford and Moxey, in press).

(15) Few of the football fans were at the match.

a. They were determined to support their team regardless of the weather. (Refset reference, giving a reason for attending in spite of presupposed norm of nonattendance)
b. They were boycotting the match because of the club's decision to increase ticket prices. (Compset reference, giving a reason for not attending)
c. They had been playing really badly recently. (Reference to the football team, by focusing on reasons for nonattendance and relying on the

reader knowing the link between team performance and the satisfaction of fans, and therefore their attendance at matches)

Consistent with the idea that inferential activity drives compset focus, Moxey and Sanford (1987) showed that the presence of *because* joining the quantified statement and the pronoun (as in (16)) increased the tendency to use a compset reference.

(16) Few of the football fans went to the match because they ...

The pattern of continuations with the expression *only a few* is especially interesting when considered in the light of the inference model. Moxey and Sanford (1987) found that continuations following *only a few* were mainly of the refset type, with a predominance of continuations about the consequences of a small number (type C). This is quite unlike other negative expressions, which gave rise to a predominance of reasons-not (type B). When the connective *because* was used, a shift took place in which a preponderance of compset references (and type B continuations) was produced after *only a few* (this shift has also been found with *only x%*). One might speculate at this point that *only* not only underlines the smallness of the number relative to prior expectations, but leads us to focus on the consequences of this number more often than on the cause of it. The presence of *because* forces the cause to be in focus, and this increases the likelihood of focus on the compset rather than on the refset.

This account explains the results of reading-time tasks, where the ease of integrating successive sentences is being measured. Target sentences which fit the pattern of inference triggered by the quantified sentence will be processed easily, whereas mismatches with the inference patterns will be processed with more difficulty. However, the account predicts that mismatches are only noticed when the interpreter attempts to integrate the target sentence with a pattern of inference generated by the quantified sentence. This implies that the predicate of the target sentence (or of the main clause at least) has to be processed before integration is possible (and hence before a mismatch can be detected). In eye-tracking experiments, initial data showed a total time effect consistent with the global observations obtained with the reading time experiments of Sanford et al. (1996) (Paterson et al., 1996).

14.5 Compset Focus, Negation and Monotonicity

It is easy to justify the need for expressions like *few* and *not many*, which refer to one subset yet place focus on another in terms of human communication. Often it may be difficult to refer to the compset directly, or the indirect introduction of the compset may underline its importance by making new information appear as if it is presupposed. What such expressions do is assert a weak positive relationship between a set and a predicate while paving the way for inferences which relate to the stronger negative relationship between set and predicate. In normal usage, readers are more influenced by the effects of the negative inferences than by the positive assertion. This claim is based on experiments on memory for text containing positive and negative quantified statements (Moxey and Sanford, 1993a). The results of such studies suggest that inferences made after negative quantified statements overlap considerably with those made after an absolute negative statement, and certainly overlap more with these than with inferences made after a positive quantified statement. For instance, *Few of the teachers were happy* will be more often misremembered as *None of the teachers were happy* than as *A few of the teachers were happy*, although both *few* and *a few* denote a small proportion of the teachers. This suggests that the inferences made after *few* and *none* are very similar relative to those made after *a few*. Now let us consider how this relates to monotonicity.

We have established that the compset-focusing property is related to the polarity of quantifiers (Moxey and Sanford, 1987; 1993a; Sanford et al., 1996). In carrying out experiments with various types of expressions it became apparent that those having the compset focusing property also appear to be monotone decreasing (see definition further on), with the possible exception of *only a few*. This led us to investigate this linguistic property and to consider theories which might explain both the property and the quantifiers. Monotonicity is a well-defined concept in mathematics, but its application to natural language expressions is problematic, and there are differences in opinion as to which quantifiers can be analysed this way as well as to whether the property may be attached to various quantifiers (compare, for example, Keenan and Stavi, 1986, with Barwise and Cooper, 1981). Tests for monotonicity involve inferring the truth of a predicate following one set from its truth following a related set. In other words, monotonicity judgements are dependent on inference patterns. Since natural language quantifiers have been shown to influence inference patterns, any correlation between groups of quantifiers, their preferred focus patterns, and their monotonicity is clearly of interest. (17) is a test of monotonicity:

(17) a. If not many of the children came to the party, then not many of the children came to the party early.
b. If a few of the children came to the party early, then a few of the children came to the party.

The children who came to the party early is a proper subset of the superset *the children who came to the party*. For a quantifier to be monotone decreasing, a statement containing it which is true of a superset must also be true of a proper subset of that set, as in (17a); for a quantifier to be monotone increasing, a statement containing it which is true of a proper subset must also be true for the whole set, as in (17b).

The property monotone decreasing is one which is held by all negative expressions, and for that reason it has been described as a weak form of negation (Zwarts 1994),[3] with stronger negatives having extra properties.

For an expression to be 'monotone decreasing' it requires that a statement containing it can be followed by a second statement containing the same expression such that the second mention now means anything between the amount denoted by the first mention and zero; for monotone increasing the second mention now means anything between the amount denoted by the first mention and the whole set. In this way expressions like *more than X* are logically predestined to be monotone increasing, while *less than X* must be monotone decreasing. What of expressions like *few* or *not many*? Tests like (18) and (19) suggest that these are not as straightforward as the logically determined *less than X*:

(18) A: Less than five people complained about my lectures.
B: Tony said no one did.
A: Like I said, less than five did.

(19) A: Few people complained about my lectures.
B: Tony said no one did.
A: Like I said, few did.

In (18), A seems to be saying that *less than five* is another description of zero, while in (19) he or she is implying that Tony was stretching the truth. *Few* does not normally include zero in its denotation. However, it is much more acceptable than a positive quantifier (*a few* in (19), for example). When we asked subjects to rate quantifiers such as *few* in tests of monotonicity, they said that it was monotone decreasing (though their confidence in such ratings was lower than with the "logical" *less than* variety). Likewise, it is possible to make *few* refer to zero with the use of a small hedge – *Few complained, if any* – while it is not possible to do this with *a few*.

Our explanation for these facts is simple. A quantified statement containing *few* (or any other compset focusing quantifier) is designed to lead the interpreter

[3] The strongest forms of negativity in Zwarts's analysis arise when the expressions are not only monotone decreasing, but anti-additive and anti-multiplicative as well.

to make a set of inferences about the compset. In most cases such inferences will be true when the quantifier denotes any quantity between its "normal" value and zero. Thus, if it turns out that the quantity in question is zero, the use of the quantifier has not been misleading as far as the interpreter is concerned, and the mismatch between the normal denotation of the quantifier and the one required to maintain coherence is not relevant. Thus, the same inference pattern which tends to make people focus on the compset is consistent with the pattern when the refset is empty.

Corblin (1996) discusses our idea that there is a relationship between decreasing monotonicity and the zero interpretation possibility just described. He argues that in real life there are examples where *few* cannot be interpreted as zero, and so in those cases compset references should not be possible, yet the compset effect occurs. We wish to clarify our position. Our argument has not been that compset is only possible if *few* can mean zero, but that focus on compset often leads to the same inference pattern in the interpreter as that which would be in evidence if zero was the case. It doesn't matter whether the set actually is empty – what matters is that the inferences actually made are consistent with those that would have been made if the set was empty.

What we have argued is that for a natural language quantifier to be judged monotone decreasing, it must be logically possible for its meaning to include zero, i.e., few might mean "a small number at most." This is because a statement of the form *Few of the X are Y* often (but not necessarily always) will lead interpreters to focus on the X which are not Y and on inferences which are likely to hold if X are not Y, and so on. Normally these inferences will largely overlap with the inferences which would have been made if the speaker had said *None of the X are Y*. What we believe is that when subjects (even professional linguists) are asked to make judgements about the meaning of an expression, they consider the effects which that expression has on the inferences which they would normally make after a statement containing that expression. If two separate expressions, say *Q1 X are Y* and *Q2 X are Y* lead people to make identical inferences then they will be judged to mean the same thing. To the extent that inferences made after two expressions are similar, their meanings will be judged to be similar. Now what we are saying is that often *few* and *none* are judged to mean the same thing in the sense that they lead to the same inferences because *few* leads people to focus on the compset, as does *none*. It is this phenomenon which means that inferences about the superset will hold for proper subsets of that superset. Logically, if the superset is empty, so must all of its proper subsets. To the extent that a quantifier means the same as the logical quantifier *none*, it will be judged (intuitively) to have empty subsets, if the superset is declared empty.

Corblin produces the following example for which he argues that the empty set is ruled out:

(22) Less than 20% of Paris citizens take their car to go to work. They use the tube.

Although *less than 20%* is unlikely to be interpreted as zero, it does not logically rule out zero. Also note that using the tube and inferences about the citizens are consistent with none of them taking the car. *Less than 20%* is likely to lead readers to focus on other forms of transport and if it turned out that no one in Paris used a car, the inference pattern would be consistent.

To summarize, regardless of whether the refset actually turns out to be empty in any one case, it is the possibility of this zero interpretation which makes the quantifier appear monotone decreasing in tests of monotonicity. After all, tests of monotonicity involve the logical limits of the meaning of a word rather than its meaning in normal use.

Many expressions are placed in linguistic categories on the basis of intuitive tests like those just described. This begs the question of whether or not similar focus effects might explain the results of such tests. In fact, we have argued that to turn linguistic theories into psychological ones, we need to explain the basis of such intuitive judgements in terms of psychological mechanisms.

14.6 Conclusion: Compset in Perspective

We have argued that compset reference cannot be explained in terms of reference to general sets, or Corblin's idea of maxset. We would argue (see also Moxey and Sanford, 1993a) that quantifiers are best seen as controlling the kinds of inferences that people make. Indeed, the kinds of inferential patterns described above find parallels in frequency adverbs (Moxey, Sanford, and Barton, 1990) and in terms of probability and subjective confidence (Teigen and Brun, 1995). The latter findings replace the idea that confidence terms express points on a scale with the idea that they manipulate the kinds of evidence people think about, paralleling our own earlier work on quantifiers.

Unlike DRT, our account is founded on observations regarding the nature of quantifiers rather than on a formal account of reference. Rather than preceding further interpretation, in our scheme reference resolution follows from interpretation involving inference. Such an account allows the occurrence of a wide variety of patterns of reference, including generalisations and reference to the compset. In the present chapter, we have seen instances where negative quantifiers give rise to clear references to the compset, to the reference set, (possibly) to subsets of the general set, and to sets clearly only available through inference, such as to entities not explicitly mentioned but only recoverable from a model of the situation. For positive quantifiers, there is no evidence of references being made to the compset, but there is evidence of reference being made to subsets of the general set other than the refset. These patterns follow from the kinds of inference patterns underlying the general process of coherence establishment, which inevitably recruits information beyond that directly available from the text itself. Elsewhere, we have argued that constraints on plural reference can only be properly explained with respect to the utilisation of world knowledge in the service of general comprehension (Sanford and Moxey, 1995). Also, others have demonstrated a dependence of reference resolution on polarity (Jarvella & Lundquist, 1994). Their demonstration is completely compatible with the argument which we have made here, although they have associated it with a different (but related) theoretical framework (Ducroit, 1988; Anscombre, 1985).

The question of whether true compset reference really occurs in data seems to us answered. But the real issue, we believe, is whether patterns of reference resolution can be properly explained without recourse to models of discourse processing which do not give the use of world knowledge a central, and indeed prior, role. We believe that it cannot be properly explained without such recourse.

References

Anscombre, J.-C. (1985) Théorie de l'argumentation, topoi et structuration argumentative. *Revue de Linguistique Québecoise* 18, 13–65.

Barwise, J., & Cooper, R. (1981) Generalized quantifiers and natural language. *Linguistics and Philosophy* 4, 159–219.

Clark, H. H. (1976) *Semantics and comprehension*. The Hague: Mouton.

Corblin, F. (1997) Quantification et anaphore discursive: la reference aux complementaires. *Languages* 123, 51–74.

Ducroit, O. (1988) Topoi et formes topiques. *Bulletin d'Etudes de Linguistique Française* 22, Tokyo.

Garrod, S. C., & Sanford, A. J. (1994) Resolving sentences in a discourse context. In M. A. Gernsbacher (Ed.), *Handbook of psycholinguistics*, 675–698. New York: Academic Press.

Hobbs, J. R. (1979) Coherence and coreference. *Cognitive Science* 3, 67–90.

Jarvella, R. J., & Lundquist, L. (1994) Scales in the interpretation of words, sentences and texts. *Journal of Semantics* 11, 171–198.

Kamp, H., & Reyle, U. (1993) *From discourse to logic*. Dordrecht: Kluwer.

Keenan, E. L., & Stavi, J. (1986) A semantic characterization of natural language determiners. *Linguistics and Philosophy* 9, 253–326.

Moxey, L. M., & Sanford, A. J. (1987) Quantifiers and focus. *Journal of Semantics* 5, 189–206.

Moxey, L. M., & Sanford, A. J. (1993a) *Communicating quantities: A psychological perspective*. Hillsdale, NJ: Erlbaum.

Moxey, L. M., & Sanford, A. J. (1993b) Prior expectation and the interpretation of natural language quantifiers. *European Journal of Cognitive Psychology* 5, 73–91.

Moxey, L. M., Sanford, A. J., & Barton, S. B. (1990) The control of attentional focus by quantifiers. In K. J. Gilhooly, M. T. Keane, R. H. Logie, & G. Erdos (Eds.), *Lines of thinking*, Vol. 1, pp. 109–124. Chichester: Wiley.

Paterson, K. B., Moxey, L. M., & Sanford, A. J. (1996) Pronominal reference to a quantified noun phrase. *Proceedings of DAARC Conference*, Technical Papers; volume 8, University Centre for Computer Corpus Research on Language.

Sanford. A. J., & Moxey, L. M. (1995) Notes on plural reference and the scenario-mapping principle in comprehension. In G. Rickheit & C. Habel (Eds.), *Focus and coherence in discourse processing*, 18–34. New York: de Gruyter.

Sanford, A. J. & Moxey, L. M. (in press). What are mental models made of? To appear in C. Habel and G. Rickheit, *Mental models of discourse comprehension*, Dordrecht: Kluwer.

Sanford, A. J., Moxey, L. M., & Paterson, K. B. (1996) Attentional focusing with quantifiers in production and comprehension. *Memory and Cognition* 24, 144–155.

Teigen, K. H., & Brun, W. (1995) Yes, but it is uncertain: Direction and communicative intention of verbal probabilistic terms. *Acta Psychologica* 88, 233–258.

Zwarts, F. (1994) Polarity items. In R. E. Asher & J. M. Y. Simpson (Eds.), *The encyclopedia of language and linguistics*. Oxford: Pergamon.

15
Constraints and Mechanisms in Theories of Anaphor Processing

AMIT ALMOR

15.1 Background

One of the most intriguing questions about the use of reference in language has to do with the multiplicity of possible forms that can be used to successfully identify a referent in a given situation. For example, a certain dog can be referred to by the definite descriptions *the dog* or *the animal*, by the proper name *Fido*, or by the pronoun *he*. Clearly, referential forms are not used randomly, and furthermore, their distribution exhibits some consistent patterns within and also across languages (Ariel, 1990; Givón, 1976). The question is then, what constraints underlie the distribution of referential forms and more specifically, what psychological mechanisms are involved in the production and resolution of referential expressions? The study of this question spans several disciplines which emphasize different aspects of the relevant issues.

Research in cognitive psychology on conceptual representation and categorization focuses on the question of what makes a certain expression more likely to be used for naming a certain object or event in the world (e.g., Rips, 1989; Rosch, 1978; Rosch & Mervis, 1975). The emphasis in this research is on how people's mental representation of world knowledge underlies naming and categorization. In contrast, much research in linguistics and psycholinguistics focuses on the study of anaphoric[1] expressions that are linked to referents by being coreferential with another linguistic expression, the antecedent. As in the case of referring expressions in general, there is more than one anaphoric form that can be used to successfully identify the antecedent. A central question for linguists and psycholinguists is, what factors affect the choice of a particular

[1] The term "anaphora" is used in this chapter to describe any expression that is coreferential with an antecedent, including definite descriptions (e.g., *the dog*), reflexive pronouns (e.g., *himself*), and non-reflexive pronouns (e.g., *he*). This use of the term differs from its use in the syntax literature, where it is used to describe a subset of pronominal expressions, primarily reflexives.

form in any given circumstance? In certain cases of anaphors that appear within the same clause as their antecedent, there seem to be strong syntactic constraints on the range of possible anaphoric forms (Chomsky, 1981). These syntactic constraints apply on the basis of the relative positions of the antecedent and anaphor in the structural representation of the embedding clause (Chomsky, 1981; although see Gordon & Hendrick, 1997, for behavioral evidence questioning the grammaticality intuitions underlying some of these structural principles). However, in most cases, anaphors appear in the same discourse as their antecedent but not within the local domain in which syntactic rules apply. These discourse anaphors are not bound by syntactic rules that render some forms grammatical and others not, but instead seem to be bound by a set of constraints that make certain forms "better" than others in a given situation (Ariel, 1990; Gundel, Hedberg, & Zacharski, 1993). Thus, the difference between the acceptability of most anaphoric forms is not categorical, unlike the difference between a grammatical utterance and a clearly ungrammatical utterance, but is rather a continuous measure, as in the case of object names.

Despite the obvious overlap between issues of anaphoric reference and issues of conceptual representation, theories of conceptual representation seem to have made little, if any, impact on theories of anaphor distribution and anaphor processing. Instead of appealing to notions of conceptual representation, many of these theories have stipulated strictly linguistic principles on the basis of distributional analysis. For example, a common claim (e.g., Gordon, Grosz, & Gilliom, 1993) is that pronouns are preferred by speakers and expected by listeners when referring to the subject of the previous utterance. This claim is based on the distributional fact that pronouns are the most frequently used referential form when referring to the subject of the previous utterance. However, merely identifying a certain distributional pattern does not explain why this pattern exists in the first place.

The central claim of the present chapter is that an appropriate explanation of the distribution of anaphoric forms must be based both on linguistic principles that can be derived from distributional analysis of anaphoric expressions and on psychological principles of conceptual representation. In other words, the claim is that any explanation based exclusively on distributional generalizations is insufficient. The chapter contrasts two theories of anaphor processing. On the one hand, the Informational Load Hypothesis (ILH; Almor, in press) is a theory of NP anaphor processing that is based on both conceptual and linguistic-pragmatic principles. On the other hand, Centering Theory (Grosz, Joshi, & Weinstein, 1983, 1995) represents an attempt to explain anaphor distribution and processing (Gordon et al., 1993) solely on the basis of distribution-derived generalizations.

It should be stated that the discussion in this chapter focuses primarily on two types of anaphors that are most commonly discussed in the literature – full noun phrases (proper names, like *Fido*, or definite descriptions, like *the dog*) and non-reflexive unstressed pronouns (like *him*). However, many of the principles and mechanisms described could be easily extended to explain the use of other kinds of discourse anaphors, and possibly referential expressions in general.

15.2 Anaphor Processing and the Informational Load Hypothesis (ILH)

Perhaps the most commonly made observation about the distribution of referring expressions is that there seems to be an inverse relation between the relative salience of the referent in the context of the discourse and the amount of information conveyed by the expression used to refer to it – the more salient the referent is, the less likely it is to be referred to by a highly explicit referring expression, such as a definite NP (e.g., Almor, in press; Ariel, 1990; Chafe, 1976; Gundel et al., 1993; Prince, 1981; Vallduví, 1992). Indeed, less explicit referring expressions like pronouns and null anaphors are almost exclusively used when the referent is very salient (Ariel, 1990; Gundel et al., 1993). For example, in the absence of preceding discourse context, a certain dog is likely to be referred to by the relatively explicit expression *the dog*, or even by the more explicit expression *the small dog* if there are other dogs that are relevant in that context that are bigger than that dog. However, if the particular dog happens to be salient by virtue of being the most recently mentioned referent, or even by virtue of having suddenly entered the room with a loud bark, the non-explicit pronoun *it* is the most likely referential form to be used (anaphorically in the first case, and deictically in the second).

This basic observation leads to several important questions that any theory of reference needs to address. First, what factors affect the salience of referents in the discourse? Second, what factors render an expression more or less explicit? And third, why are explicitness and salience inversely related? Although all three questions are important, it is the second and third questions that are of primary interest in the present chapter. The literature on the first question is extensive and will not be reviewed here, except to mention some of the factors that have been shown to affect salience. These factors include discourse topic (Givón, 1976), informational status (new information vs. given information; Chafe, 1976; Deemter, 1994), grammatical function (Gordon et al., 1993), syntactic construction (Almor, in press; Carpenter & Just, 1977; Cutler & Fodor, 1979), order of mention (Gordon et al., 1993), the amount of intervening text since the most recent mention (Sanford & Garrod, 1981), and relevant world knowledge (Sanford & Garrod, 1981).

Although the relation between referent salience and anaphor explicitness is acknowledged by many theories of reference, most theories focus on systematically describing this relation and not on explaining the reasons for its existence in the first place (e.g., Gundel et al., 1993). A common view (e.g., Gordon et al., 1993; Gundel et al., 1993; Vonk, Hustinx, & Simons, 1992) is that the form of referring expressions serves a communicative function – speakers and writers use specific anaphoric forms as cues to aid listeners' and readers' understanding of the following discourse. For example, Gordon et al. argue that the use of a pronoun to refer to the most salient referent serves as a cue for topic continuity, and Vonk et al. argue that the use of an NP anaphor to refer to the most salient referent signals a topic shift. Unfortunately, this communicative function of referential form, even if true, does not explain why there is an inverse relation between referent salience and anaphor explicitness, nor does it provide any insight into what anaphor explicitness is. In fact, any theory that ascribes the processing of pronouns and NP anaphors to different mechanisms (e.g., Garrod, Freudenthal, & Boyle, 1994) or different levels of representation (e.g., Cloitre & Bever, 1988) cannot provide a satisfactory answer to these questions.

There are several theories, however, which attempt to address the question of the relation between referent salience and anaphor explicitness. For example, Ariel's (1990) accessibility theory is based on the observation that, in general, the more salient (or accessible, in Ariel's terms) the referent is, the less information is contained in the anaphoric expression. To explain the inverse relation between anaphor informativeness and referent accessibility, Ariel, in accordance with Relevance Theory (Sperber & Wilson, 1986, 1995), associates different processing costs with the different forms of reference – definite NP anaphors have a high processing cost because they evoke a more detailed representation, whereas pronouns have a smaller processing cost because they evoke a very general representation containing only number and gender features. Ariel argues that establishing reference to a highly accessible referent only requires a low cost referring expression, whereas establishing reference to a referent that is not highly accessible requires a sufficiently informative referring expression that may have a higher cost.

In associating the explicitness of a referential expression with a notion of processing cost, Ariel's (1990) accessibility theory represents a significant insight into the nature of the inverse relation between referent salience and reference explicitness. Expanding on Ariel's work, Almor (in press) outlines the Informational Load Hypothesis (ILH), which states more generally that additional processing cost must serve some additional discourse function, where cost is defined in terms of conceptual representation (based on the semantic distance between the representation of the anaphor and the representation of the antecedent) and not just in terms of anaphoric form. Discourse function includes identifying the referent but also adding new information. The intuition behind the notion of processing cost is that the less specific the representation of the anaphor with respect to the representation of the antecedent, the less costly the anaphor is to process. For example, given the antecedent *a dog*, the anaphor *the little poodle* would be more costly than the repetitive anaphor *the dog*, which in turn would be more costly than the anaphor *the animal*, which in turn would be more costly than the pronominal anaphor *it*. Also, because cost is defined on the basis of the relation between the semantic representations of the anaphor and the antecedent, the anaphor *the animal* would be more costly when coreferring with the antecedent *the dog* than when coreferring with the antecedent *the little poodle*.

An important implication of the ILH is that anaphors are distinguished not only on the basis of their formal category (e.g., pronouns vs. NP anaphors) but also on the basis of their cost, which is defined in terms of conceptual representation, and on the basis of the discourse function they serve. Therefore, according to the ILH, there should be differences in the distribution and processing within the class of NP anaphors just as there are differences in distribution and processing between pronouns and certain NP anaphors. Clearly, anaphoric expressions from different classes tend to differ in their processing cost and functionality – pronouns bear a small computational cost by virtue of their impoverished conceptual representation, while definite NP anaphors accrue a higher computational cost but may have additional functionality in identifying the referent and in adding new information. However, according to the ILH, this difference is not an inherent property of the formal class of these anaphors but rather an outcome of the underlying conceptual representation and principles of pragmatics. According to the ILH, the processing of two distinct NP anaphors can be as different as processing an NP anaphor and a pronoun.

In a series of self-paced reading experiments, Almor (in press) tested the predictions of the ILH by measuring the reading time of NP anaphors under different conditions of discourse function and computational cost. The discourse function of anaphors was manipulated by syntactically changing the focal status of the antecedent – a syntactically unfocused antecedent should, according to the ILH, justify an anaphor with a higher cost. Syntactic focus was manipulated through the use of it- and wh-clefts. This manipulation allowed a control of the salience (i.e., focal status) of an antecedent without confounding it with the effects of word order and recency of mention. Computational cost was manipulated by changing the semantic distance between the conceptual representation of the anaphor and the conceptual representation of the referent. This was done by using an anaphor that is a category term (e.g., *the bird*) with antecedents that differ in their degree of typicality in that category (e.g., *the robin*, which is a typical instance, and *the ostrich*, which is atypical). The assumption underlying this manipulation is that the less detailed the representation of the anaphor is with respect to the representation of the antecedent, the less costly is the anaphor to process. Thus, the anaphor *the bird* would be less costly when the antecedent is *the ostrich* than when the antecedent is *the robin*. It should be noted that according to the ILH, reading times do not reflect merely the cost of referring expressions, but rather the relation between their cost and their discourse function.

Several main findings of these experiments support the claims of the ILH. First is the finding that repeated NP anaphors are read slower when their antecedent is focused than when it is not focused. The ILH attributes this repeated NP penalty to the use of an anaphor which has a high cost with no functional justification. Repetitive anaphors do not add new information and thus their high cost (due to evoking a representation that is as detailed as the representation of the antecedent) is only justified when they help identify the antecedent. Because the focused referent is the *default* antecedent, the high cost of a repetitive anaphor is better justified when its antecedent is unfocused.

The second finding is that non-repetitive NP anaphors are read faster when their antecedent is focused than when it is not focused. Indeed, the ILH states that anaphors with low cost, or high cost but that add new information, are easier to process when their antecedent is focused. Thus, while non-repetitive anaphors are read faster when their antecedent is focused (Finding 1), repetitive anaphors are read slower when their antecedent is focused (Finding 2).

The third finding is the inverse typicality effect – category NP anaphors with a focused antecedent are read faster if they are more semantically distant from their antecedent. The ILH states that for anaphors with focused antecedents, the less costly they are with respect to that antecedent, the easier they are to process. Cost is related to the difference between the conceptual representation evoked by the anaphor and the conceptual representation of the referent, such that the more general (i.e., less detailed) the representation of the anaphor with respect to the representation of the antecedent, the less costly the anaphor is. Therefore, a category anaphor is less costly when its antecedent is an atypical member of the category than when it is a typical member. Intuitively, using a category anaphor with an atypical antecedent is analogous to using a pronoun, whereas using a category anaphor with a typical antecedent is analogous to using a repeated NP anaphor. This analogy is further supported by the additional (fourth) finding that with category anaphors with unfocused antecedents, a regular typicality effect is observed – the category anaphor is read faster when its antecedent is a typical member of the category than when it is an atypical member. In summary, these findings show that the processing of NP anaphors presents heterogeneity compatible with their cost and function as argued by the ILH.

15.3 The ILH and Pronouns

The evidence reviewed in Section 15.2 shows the ILH to be an adequate account of the processing of NP anaphors. Crucially, some NP anaphors are processed more similarly to pronouns than to other NP anaphors. This leads to the question of whether the ILH can account for the processing of pronouns as well. Previous accounts have attributed the processing of pronouns and NP anaphors to different mechanisms. Cloitre and Bever (1988) have argued that pronouns access the conceptual representation of discourse referents, whereas definite NP anaphors access their phonological representation. Sanford and Garrod (1981) have argued that pronouns typically access discourse representations that are stored in a special memory type which they called "explicit focus," whereas definite NP anaphors typically access discourse representations in a different type of memory which they called "implicit focus." Greene, McKoon, and Ratcliff (1992) have argued that definite NP anaphors are processed online as they are encountered in text or speech, whereas the interpretation of pronouns may be delayed until the end of the utterance. Gordon et al. (1993) have argued that pronouns mark the coherent continuation of the discourse topic, whereas Vonk et al. (1992) have argued that NP anaphors mark a topic shift.

Most of the evidence for separate mechanisms for processing pronouns and definite NP anaphors is easy to explain by the ILH. Crucially, many of these studies (e.g., Cloitre & Bever, 1988; Gordon et al., 1993; Vonk et al., 1992) relied on evidence obtained with repetitive NP anaphors as the sole basis for their claims. As discussed earlier, the ILH claims that repetitive NP anaphors are in fact processed quite differently than many other kinds of NP anaphors. Thus, it is likely that many of these previous results represent only a difference between the processing of pronouns and the processing of repetitive NP anaphors and not between the processing of pronouns and the processing of NP anaphors in general.

Other evidence is also compatible with the ILH. As pronouns carry only little semantic information, they would be the preferred mode of reference according to the ILH when the referent is the most salient in the discourse. When a particular referent is not the most salient one in the discourse, additional cost is licensed, leading to an increased likelihood of nonpronominal reference. Thus, the principles of the ILH can be readily applied to account for the processing and distribution of pronouns as well as NP anaphors.

However, although the ILH can explain why pronouns are preferred when referring to the most salient referent, most other theories of reference processing can also account for this basic fact. To make the ILH an attractive general theory of reference, and not only of NP anaphors, it is important to see whether it can explain findings about pronouns that other theories of reference cannot. The next section addresses this issue by reviewing some recent findings about anaphor processing in Alzheimer's Disease. These findings are hard to account for without relying on notions of processing cost and discourse function, exactly the notions that distinguish the ILH from all other theories of reference.

15.4 Reference in Alzheimer's disease

The speech of patients with Alzheimer's disease (AD) is often described as "empty," as it contains a high proportion of high frequency words that convey little or no information (Kempler, 1995). One particular aspect of the empty speech in AD is the excessive use of pronouns. Interestingly, this overuse of pronouns in production is accompanied by a serious pronoun comprehension impairment. In particular, a recent study (Almor, Kempler, MacDonald, Andersen, & Tyler, in press), utilizing a cross-modal naming methodology, found that:

1. AD patients are less sensitive than age-matched healthy control subjects to violations of number and gender agreement between pronouns and their antecedents, as in (mismatching pronoun is capitalized): *The children loved the silly clown at the party. During the performance, the clown threw candy to HIM.*
2. AD patients are faster to name an adjective that is part of the representation of the antecedent when reference has been maintained through NP anaphors rather than through pronouns (e.g., the capitalized target is read faster in *The* housewife *watched the clumsy* plumber *working under the sink. The* housewife *showed the* plumber *where the leak was. The* housewife *could not believe that the* plumber *was so CLUMSY* than in *The* housewife *watched the clumsy* plumber *working under the sink.* She *showed* him *where the leak was.* She *could not believe that* he *was so CLUMSY*). In contrast, age-matched normal controls show exactly the opposite pattern – they are faster to name the adjective when reference is maintained through pronouns than through NP anaphors.

Thus, although the production of AD patients is characterized by an abnormally frequent use of pronouns, their ability to comprehend pronouns is significantly compromised, and they are better able to access information about the referent when an NP anaphor is used. This dissociation between comprehension and production requires an explanation. The global and patchy nature of the brain atrophy associated with AD (Terry et al., 1991), as well as the global cognitive impairment in AD, preclude an explanation based on selective and independent deficits to the comprehension and production systems. Rather, the nature of the brain and cognitive impairment in AD suggests that some general factor underlies both the reference production and the reference comprehension impairments. One likely factor is the reduction in activation differences between memory representations in AD. This general memory impairment has two important effects on reference processing in AD. First, it likely compromises the semantic representation of referents. Indeed, AD patients are notorious for making many semantic errors such as superordinate substitution (e.g., saying *animal* instead of *dog*) and coordinate-term substitution (e.g., saying *cat* instead of *dog*; Hodges, Salmon, & Butters, 1991). Second, the general memory impairment likely reduces the relative differences in activation (i.e., salience) between different referents. Again, there is indeed abundant evidence that AD impairs working memory (Waters, Caplan, & Rochon, 1995).

On the basis of this general memory impairment in AD, the ILH provides the following explanation for the pattern of referential impairment in AD. The task of language production requires the selection of an appropriate referring expression. The ILH characterizes this selection process as a choice of the best combination of cost and function. The AD memory impairment leads to a compromised semantic representation, which in general makes for less specific representation. For example, the representation of *dog* might become more similar to the representation of *animal*. According to the ILH, this loss of specific information about the referent causes an increase in the cost of all anaphors to this referent. Therefore, a more general and less costly term like a pronoun is likely to be used. For example, although the anaphor *the animal* has only little cost with respect to the antecedent *the dog*, it has a higher cost with respect to the antecedent *the animal* and is thus more likely to be replaced with the pronoun *it*. Thus, according to the ILH, the overall degraded semantic representation of referents in AD leads to an overall increase in the processing cost of all referring expressions, thus rendering the more general expressions more likely to be produced.

The task of language comprehension, on the other hand, requires the successful identification of the antecedent. Again, the ILH claims that the ease of processing a referring expression is determined by the relation between its cost and discourse function. Although NP anaphors are normally more costly and indeed may hinder the performance of healthy subjects, they may nevertheless serve a special function for AD comprehenders. For AD comprehenders, repetitive NP anaphors provide significant facilitation in identifying and reactivating the representation of the referent in working memory. Thus, the overall degraded working memory representation in AD leads to an overall decrease in discourse salience, thus enabling costly referring expressions to attain more functionality in AD comprehension by aiding the identification of the antecedent.

The evidence from the Alzheimer's research complements the evidence from young readers, suggesting that the processing of pronominal and NP anaphors complies with principles of cost and function as argued by the ILH. When cost or function changes, as in the case of AD patients, the processing of referential expressions changes accordingly.

15.5 Centering Theory

The appeal to processing cost and discourse function is not common to all theories of anaphor processing. In fact, one prominent theory of reference, Centering Theory (Gordon et al., 1993; Grosz et al., 1983, 1995), rests on the assumption that NP anaphor processing cannot be explained on the basis of general principles, like cost and function, but rather obeys a set of idiosyncratic coreference rules.

On the basis of the distribution of anaphoric references in short dialogues, Grosz et al. (1983, 1995) construe a set of abstract constraints that apply to referents ordered by salience. Although salience is assumed to have an independent status, it is operationally detected through the use of the first rule of Centering: A pronoun should be used when referring to the most salient referent if any pronoun is to be used at all. Clearly, in contrast to the ILH, Centering is a theory of reference that (a) differentiates between anaphors on the basis of their formal class (i.e., NP anaphors vs. pronouns), and (b) derives its mechanisms and principles from generalized distributional patterns and not from pragmatics or psychological notions.

Although originally devised to capture generalizations about the distribution of pronouns, Centering has been claimed to provide an adequate model of the actual psychological processing of anaphoric expressions. In particular, Gordon and his collaborators (Gordon, 1993; Gordon & Chan, 1995; Gordon et al., 1993; Gordon & Scearce, 1995) have established a paradigm based on a comparison between pronouns and repeated NP anaphors to support the psychological validity of the first Centering rule. Underlying the work of Gordon and his collaborators is a stricter interpretation of the first rule of Centering, which states that references to the most salient discourse entity should be realized by a pronoun. Although this interpretation was in fact part of the original Centering proposal (Grosz et al., 1983), the latest version of the theory (Grosz et al., 1995) used the less stringent version mentioned earlier, namely, that if any referent is referred to via a pronoun, then the most salient discourse entity must also be referred to via a pronoun. The psychological prediction Gordon et al. (1993) derived from the stricter interpretation of the first Centering rule is that its violation should accrue some processing cost. Indeed, in a series of self-paced reading experiments designed to test this prediction, Gordon et al. found that in each sentence there exists only one referent that, when realized as a repeated NP, leads to a slower sentence reading time than when realized as a pronoun. Because in all their experiments Gordon et al. compared pronouns to repetitive NP anaphors, they dubbed the additional processing time of those anaphors the repeated name penalty. Gordon et al. interpret this penalty as supporting the claim that a pronoun is better than an NP anaphor as a form of reference to the most salient referent.

Although the repeated name penalty observed by Gordon et al. (1993) is very similar to the NP anaphor penalty observed in Almor (in press), the two studies arrive at strikingly different conclusions. In contrast to the claims of Gordon et al., Almor claims that what makes a certain anaphor more or less acceptable in any given context is not its formal class but rather the relation between its processing cost and discourse function. If violating the first Centering rule is the explanation of the repeated name penalty, as Gordon and his collaborators argue, then there should be a more general "definite NP penalty" associated with referring to the most salient entity with a definite NP. In other words, the penalty should not be restricted to repetitive anaphors, but should also accrue for definite NP anaphors in general. However, the findings of Almor (in press) clearly show that only repetitive NP anaphors are read slower when their antecedent is focused than when it is not. This suggests that the repeated name penalty observed by Gordon et al. is a consequence of the repetitive nature of the anaphors they used, which renders them unnecessarily costly, and not a consequence of depriving readers of the pronoun cue, as Gordon et al. argue.

15.6 Concluding Comments

Centering Theory (Grosz et al., 1983, 1995) is established on the premise that anaphor distribution is determined by a set of idiosyncratic constraints, and that these constraints can be described on the basis of distributional analysis alone. Most significantly, these constraints do not relate directly to any psychological mechanisms. Instead, Centering establishes its own terminology that resembles, but is not systematically related to, psychological notions such as activation, attention, and working memory. The motivation for this comes from Grosz et al.'s (1983) observation that there are certain regularities in people's choices of referring expressions that are impossible to describe by pragmatic considerations alone, by syntactic considerations alone, or even by psychological considerations alone (e.g., working memory size and structure). On the basis of this observation, Grosz et al. (1983) argue that there must be a different set of principles, ones that are unique to representing and processing reference, that underlie people's choice of referring expressions. However, this argument holds only if there must be one module that underlies anaphor distribution. Alternatively, one can, in line with the ILH, view anaphor distribution as the outcome of underlying constraints from multiple domains.

The argument of Grosz et al. (1983, 1995) for construing a distinct and autonomous reference resolution module bears striking resemblance to the claims and assumptions within the field of generative linguistics. Indeed, the principled exclusion of general psychological factors from the theory of language is the trademark of generative linguistics. According to Chomsky (1964), one has to distinguish between the representation of linguistic knowledge – linguistic competence – and the factors which affect the use and application of that knowledge in actual behavior – linguistic performance. By this view, the role of linguistics is to use its theoretical tools to characterize the representation and organization of linguistic competence, while the role of psycholinguistics is to expose the ways in which these representations are actually used by the human mind (Frazier, 1995). The representations derived by linguistic analysis are based entirely on the distribution of word strings in the language and do not incorporate any constraints imposed by perceptual and cognitive processes that are not directly evident in the distribution. In this view, factors such as the amount of available memory, the cost of computation, and the degree of activation of mental representations do not affect the core representation of language but only the processing of these representations in actual language use.

Although the assumption that mental representations should be defined on the basis of the distribution of linguistic forms prevails in much of the work on the representation and the processing of syntactic structure, it is clearly problematic for theories of anaphor processing. Counting how many occurrences of each referential form occur in different contexts and stipulating principles to describe this distribution misses many important facts. As is demonstrated in Almor (in press), psychological factors do play an important role in anaphor processing. As these psychological factors change, as in Alzheimer's disease, the processing of referential expressions changes accordingly. Distributional analysis that is sensitive merely to the form of anaphoric expressions is not likely to provide all the necessary facts. Moreover, gross distributional patterns do not constitute mental representations but rather are the product of mechanisms operating on the basis of these representations by principles of cost and function.

References

Almor, A. (in press). NP anaphora and focus: The informational load hypothesis. *Psychological Review*.

Almor, A., Kempler, D., MacDonald, M., Andersen, E., & Tyler, L. (in press). Pronouns, full noun-phrases, and empty speech in Alzheimer's disease. *Brain and Language*.

Ariel, M. (1990). *Accessing noun-phrase antecedents*. London, New York: Routledge.

Carpenter, P. A., & Just, M. A. (1977). Eye fixations and comprehension. In M. A. Just & P. A. Carpenter (Eds.), *Cognitive processes in comprehension* (pp. 109–139). Hillsdale, NJ: Erlbaum.

Chafe, W. L. (1976). Givenness, contrastiveness, definiteness, subjects, topics, and point of view. In C. N. Li (Ed.), *Subject and topic* (pp. 25–55). New York: Academic Press.

Chomsky, N. (1964). *Syntactic structures*. The Hague: Mouton.

Chomsky, N. (1981). *Lectures on government and binding*. Dordrecht: Foris.

Cloitre, M., & Bever, T. G. (1988). Linguistic anaphors, levels of representation, and discourse. *Language and Cognitive Processes* 3, 293–322.

Cutler, A., & Fodor, J. A. (1979). Semantic focus and sentence comprehension. *Cognition* 7, 49–59.

Deemter, K. V. (1994). What's new? A semantic perspective on sentence accent. *Journal of Semantics* 11, 1–31.

Frazier, L. (1995). Issues of representation in psycholinguistics. In P. D. Eimas & J. L. Miller (Eds.), *Handbook of perception and cognition. Volume 11: Speech, language, and communication* (pp. 1–27). San Diego: Academic Press.

Garrod, S., Freudenthal, D., & Boyle, E.-A. (1994). The role of different types of anaphor in the on-line resolution of sentences in a discourse. *Journal of Memory and Language* 33, 39–68.

Givón, T. (1976). Topic, pronoun and grammatical agreement. In C. N. Li (Ed.), *Subject and topic* (pp. 149–188). New York: Academic Press.

Gordon, P. C. (1993). Computational and psychological models of discourse. In H. Brownell & Y. Joanette (Eds.), *Narrative discourse in normal aging adults and neurologically impaired adults* (pp. 23–46). San Diego, CA: Singular Publication Group.

Gordon, P. C., & Chan, D. (1995). Pronouns, passives and discourse coherence. *Journal of Memory and Language* 34, 216–231.

Gordon, P. C., Grosz, B. J., & Gilliom, L. (1993). Pronouns, names, and the centering of attention in discourse. *Cognitive Science* 17, 311–348.

Gordon, P. C., & Hendrick, R. (1997). Intuitive knowledge of linguistic coreference. *Cognition* 62, 325–370.

Gordon, P. C., & Scearce, K. A. (1995). Pronominalization and discourse coherence, discourse structure and pronoun interpretation. *Memory and Cognition* 23, 313–323.

Greene, S.-B., McKoon, G., & Ratcliff, R. (1992). Pronoun resolution and discourse models. *Journal of Experimental Psychology: Learning, Memory, and Cognition* 18, 266–283.

Grosz, B. J., Joshi, A. K., & Weinstein, S. (1983). *Providing a unified account of definite noun phrases in discourse*. Paper presented at the Proceedings of the 21st Annual Meeting of the Association for Computational Linguistics.

Grosz, B. J., Joshi, A. K., & Weinstein, S. (1995). Centering: A framework for modeling the local coherence of discourse. *Computational Linguistics* 21, 203–226.

Gundel, J. K., Hedberg, N., & Zacharski, R. (1993). Cognitive status and the form of referring expressions in discourse. *Language* 69, 274–307.

Hodges, J., Salmon, D., & Butters, N. (1991). The nature of naming deficit in Alzheimer's and Huntington's disease. *Brain* 114, 1547–1558.

Kempler, D. (1995). Language changes in dementia of the Alzheimer type. In R. Lubinski (Ed.) *Dementia and communication: Research and clinical implications* (pp. 98–114). San Diego, CA: Singular Publishing Group.

Prince, E. F. (1981). Towards a taxonomy of given-new information. In P. Cole (Ed.), *Radical pragmatics* (pp. 223–255). New York: Academic Press.

Rips, L. J. (1989). Similarity, typicality, and categorization. In S. Vosniadou & A. Ortony (Eds.), *Similarity and analogical reasoning* (pp. 21–59). Cambridge: Cambridge University Press.

Rosch, E. (1978). Principles of categorization. In E. Rosch & B. B. Lloyd (Eds.), *Cognition and categorization* (pp. 27–48). Hillsdale, NJ: Erlbaum.

Rosch, E., & Mervis, C. B. (1975). Family resemblances: Studies in the internal structure of categories. *Cognition* 3, 382–439.

Sanford, A. J., & Garrod, S. C. (1981). *Understanding written language*. Chichester: Wiley.

Sperber, D., & Wilson, D. (1986). *Relevance: Communication and cognition.* Cambridge, MA: Harvard University Press.

Sperber, D., & Wilson, D. (1995). *Relevance: Communication and cognition.* (2nd ed.). Oxford: Blackwell.

Terry, R., Masliah, E., Salmon, D., Butters, N., DeTeressa, R., Hill, R., Hansen, L., & Katzman, R. (1991). Physical basis of cognitive alternations in Alzheimer's disease: Synaptic loss is the major correlate of cognitive impairment. *Annals of Neurology* 30, 572–580.

Vallduví, E. (1992). *The Informational Component*. New York: Garland.

Vonk, W., Hustinx, L. G. M. M., & Simons, W. H. G. (1992). The use of referential expressions in structuring discourse. *Language and Cognitive Processes* 7, 301–333.

Waters, G.-S., Caplan, D., & Rochon, E. (1995). Processing capacity and sentence comprehension in patients with Alzheimer's disease. *Cognitive Neuropsychology* 12, 1–30.

Author Index

Subject Index

www.ingramcontent.com/pod-product-compliance
Ingram Content Group UK Ltd.
Pitfield, Milton Keynes, MK11 3LW, UK
UKHW040811180125
453697UK00004B/36

9 780521 631211